797,885 Books
are available to read at

Forgotten Books

www.ForgottenBooks.com

Forgotten Books' App
Available for mobile, tablet & eReader

ISBN 978-1-5276-8810-0
PIBN 10100481

This book is a reproduction of an important historical work. Forgotten Books uses state-of-the-art technology to digitally reconstruct the work, preserving the original format whilst repairing imperfections present in the aged copy. In rare cases, an imperfection in the original, such as a blemish or missing page, may be replicated in our edition. We do, however, repair the vast majority of imperfections successfully; any imperfections that remain are intentionally left to preserve the state of such historical works.

Forgotten Books is a registered trademark of FB &c Ltd.
Copyright © 2017 FB &c Ltd.
FB &c Ltd, Dalton House, 60 Windsor Avenue, London, SW19 2RR.
Company number 08720141. Registered in England and Wales.

For support please visit www.forgottenbooks.com

1 MONTH OF FREE READING

at

www.ForgottenBooks.com

By purchasing this book you are eligible for one month membership to ForgottenBooks.com, giving you unlimited access to our entire collection of over 700,000 titles via our web site and mobile apps.

To claim your free month visit:

www.forgottenbooks.com/free100481

* Offer is valid for 45 days from date of purchase. Terms and conditions apply.

English
Français
Deutsche
Italiano
Español
Português

www.forgottenbooks.com

Mythology Photography **Fiction**
Fishing Christianity **Art** Cooking
Essays Buddhism Freemasonry
Medicine **Biology** Music **Ancient Egypt** Evolution Carpentry Physics
Dance Geology **Mathematics** Fitness
Shakespeare **Folklore** Yoga Marketing
Confidence Immortality Biographies
Poetry **Psychology** Witchcraft
Electronics Chemistry History **Law**
Accounting **Philosophy** Anthropology
Alchemy Drama Quantum Mechanics
Atheism Sexual Health **Ancient History**
Entrepreneurship Languages Sport
Paleontology Needlework Islam
Metaphysics Investment Archaeology
Parenting Statistics Criminology
Motivational

Pitt Press Series

HERODOTOS
VIII
URANIA

London: C. J. CLAY AND SONS,
CAMBRIDGE UNIVERSITY PRESS WAREHOUSE,
AVE MARIA LANE.
Glasgow: 50, WELLINGTON STREET.

Leipzig: F. A. BROCKHAUS.
New York: THE MACMILLAN COMPANY.
Bombay and Calcutta: MACMILLAN AND CO., LTD.

[*All Rights reserved*]

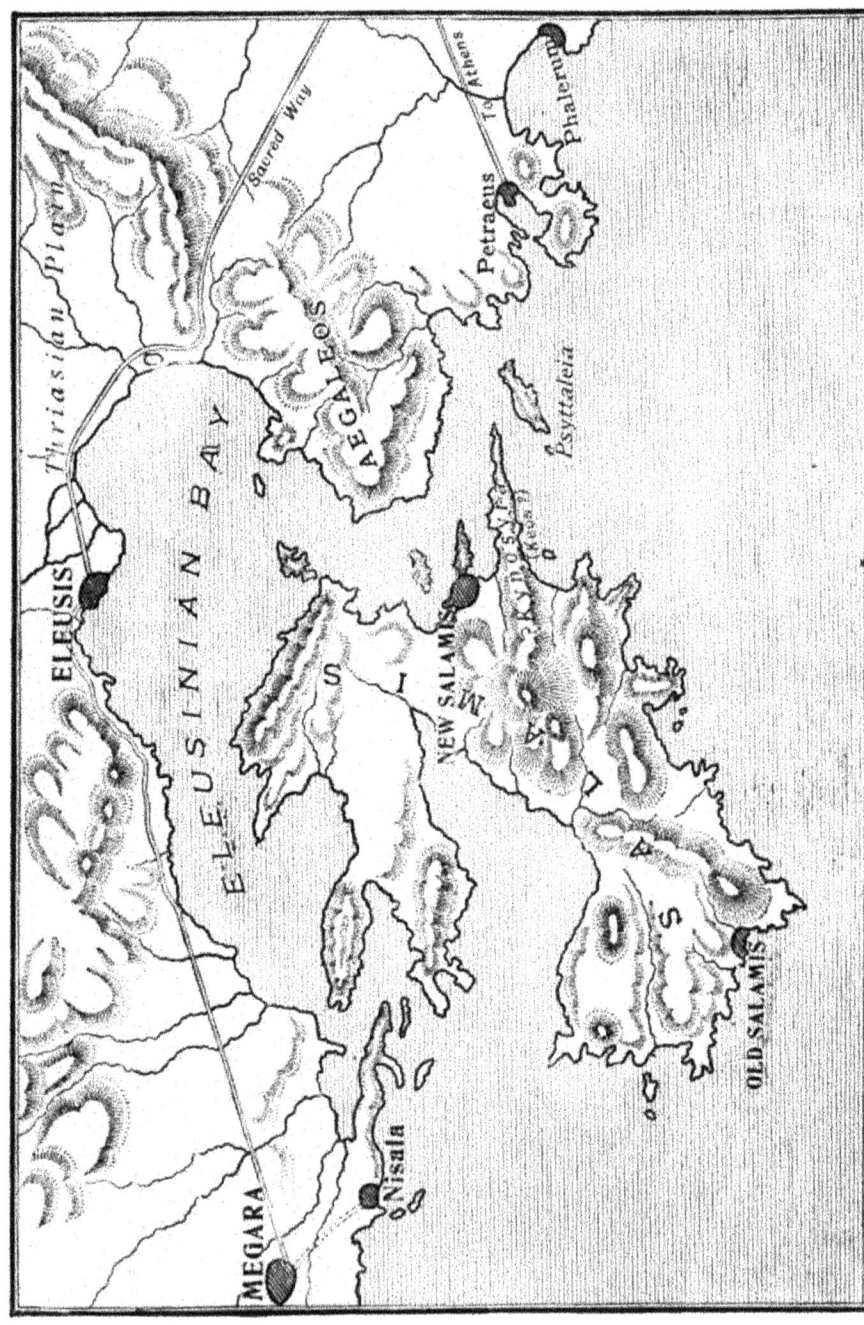

HERODOTOS
VIII
URANIA

EDITED BY

E. S. SHUCKBURGH, Litt.D.
LATE FELLOW OF EMMANUEL COLLEGE CAMBRIDGE
FORMERLY MASTER AT ETON

CAMBRIDGE
AT THE UNIVERSITY PRESS
1903

Educ T 21240.775.903

HARVARD COLLEGE LIBRARY
GIFT OF
CHARLES HALL GRANDGENT
JANUARY 14, 1933

First Edition 1893
Reprinted 1894, 1903

TABLE OF CONTENTS.

	PAGE
PREFACE	vii
INTRODUCTION	ix
NOTES ON THE TEXT	xxxvi
TEXT	1
NOTES	83
HISTORICAL AND GEOGRAPHICAL INDEX . .	199
APPENDIX. IONIC DIALECT	255
INDEX	271

MAP.

BATTLE OF SALAMIS . . . . *To face Title*

PREFACE.

THIS edition of the eighth book of Herodotos, expanded from a previous edition of the first ninety chapters, is designed to help students in all difficulties connected with the Greek language which it contains, and also to supply them with full information as to the historical facts which it includes, or to which it refers. I have hoped by the Historical and Geographical Index to help students to take a somewhat wider interest in Hellenic history, which is too apt to mean with most of us merely the history of Athens and Sparta. My chief obligations, acknowledged frequently in the notes, are, among others, to the editions of *Dr K. Abicht*, Leipzig, 1882; and *Dr H. Stein*, Berlin, 1882. Much illustrative matter, however, which I have found for myself, or which has long been the common property of scholars, I have not thought it necessary to put down to the credit of those editors, although it may be often found in their works.

CAMBRIDGE, 1890.

INTRODUCTION.

WHEN Darius died (B.C. 485) he left two tasks unfinished,—the subjugation of Greece for which he had made vast preparations, and on which his heart had been firmly set, and the reduction of a great revolt in Egypt.

The latter of these tasks engaged the attention of his successor first. It was thoroughly accomplished by B.C. 483; Egypt was brought to a state of still greater dependence than before, placed under the charge of Achaemenes one of the king's brothers, and forced to assist in the expedition against Greece [Her. 7, 1—7].

Xerxes now determined to carry out the other task, the subjugation of Greece. For this purpose preparations on a vast scale were made. All parts of the great empire were ordered to furnish men, provisions, money, and ships [7, 23—5]. Two expeditions had been attempted before; the first, under Mardonius, was conveyed by a fleet coasting down from the Thracian shore towards the south, but had been ruined by shipwreck while rounding the promontory of Athos [B.C. 492]: a second had crossed the Aegean by way of the islands and had been defeated at Marathon [B.C. 490]. But the present plan embraced a double method of attack. A fleet was to start from

B.C. 483—1.

INTRODUCTION.

the Hellespont and coast along the shore of Greece to the Peloponnese; while, keeping as nearly parallel with the fleet as possible, a grand army was to cross the Hellespont and march through Makedonia, Thessaly, and Boeotia into Attica, and thence to the Peloponnese. To secure the passage of these two armaments, a bridge of ships had, after one failure, been constructed across the Hellespont, while a canal had been dug across the neck of the peninsula of Athos.

These two works, constructed principally by the skilful engineers of Phoenikia, were well conceived and proved of the utmost service to the expedition. The shipment of so vast an army across the Hellespont would have occupied an inconveniently long time; while the canal enabled the fleet to avoid a headland which had already proved fatal to one Persian fleet, and was an object of terror to the sailors of the Levant.

By the Autumn of B.C. 481 both fleet and army were ready for starting in the following spring. The fleet consisted of 1207 ships of war, with innumerable other ships laden with provisions and material of war; the army, when numbered after crossing the Hellespont, amounted according to Herodotos to 517,610 men, without counting servants and camp-followers [7, 184][1]. Nor was the greatness of his army all that Xerxes could reckon upon in calculating his chances of success against Greece. A large part of the European country he was about to traverse already owned his authority. The parts of Thrace and Makedonia which bordered on the sea had submitted to Darius; and the suppression of the Ionian revolt had

[1] Herodotos reckons the whole number of land and sea forces at 2,317,610, without counting servants, or the crews of provision-ships.

placed the Islands of the Aegean north of Krete in the power of Persia, even including the Cyclades with the exception of some few south of Delos. While in Greece itself nearly all states north of Attica from policy or fear medized. The powerful family of the Aleuadae of Larissa had even invited the invasion, and though their action was not universally approved in Thessaly, the loyal party of Thessalians were too feeble to resist [7, 130, 172; 9, 1]. The Phokians were divided, but only a section of them ventured to offer a fitful resistance from their hiding-places on Parnassos [8, 32; 9, 17—8]; in Boeotia an overwhelming majority of states medized, only Plataea standing fast to its loyalty to Athens, while the Thespians abandoned their town and sought refuge in the Peloponnese. It was clear therefore that it was from Attica, and the states south of Attica, that resistance must come if it came at all. But even in the Peloponnese itself the important district of Argolis, with the insignificant exceptions of Mycenae and Tiryns, was ready, in its hatred of Sparta, to welcome the Barbarian [7, 150—2]. Still the greater part of the Peloponnese was loyal, and preparations were being made in Southern Greece to meet the storm.

The first news of the impending invasion is said to have been conveyed to Sparta by the exiled Demaratus, who was living at the Persian court [7, 239]. The great army was in winter quarters at Sardis and its neighbourhood when the first step was taken by a Congress of representatives from various loyal States meeting on the Isthmos of Corinth [7, 145]. This Congress seems to have met late in the year 481, and, while sending spies to Sardis to learn the truth about the vast preparations which the king was re-

B.C. 481.

ported to be making, sent at the same time envoys to various distant states calling upon them to aid the cause of Hellenic liberty.

The spies sent to Sardis were captured, but by the king's order were shown all the preparations of his camp, and allowed to return home in hopes that their report might deter the Greeks from venturing upon further resistance [7, 146].

Nor did the envoys sent to Greek states meet with success. The Argives absolutely refused all help, on the ground that the envoys did not bring authority to conclude a 30 years' peace between them and the Lacedaemonians, nor were able to admit their claim to a joint command: though the real reason seems to have been that they had already made terms with Persia [7, 148—152]. The tyrant Gelo of Syracuse also refused aid on the pretext of the rejection of his claim to command by sea or land; really perhaps because he was himself threatened with an invasion from Carthage [7, 157—165]. The Kretans referred the matter to Delphi. But the Oracle was temporizing[1] and gave an unfavourable reply, and they therefore declined to join in resistance [7, 169]. The Korkyreans indeed promised help and actually manned 60 triremes. But this squadron had secret orders to linger round the west and south of the Peloponnese, and wait to see which side would win; conduct which they afterwards tried to cover by alleging contrary winds as the cause of their absence from Salamis [7, 169][2].

---

[1] See note on p. 21, l. 19.
[2] The selfish policy of the Korkyreans seems to have been characteristic. See Thucyd. 1, 31, 2 οὐδενὸς Ἑλλήνων ἔνσπονδοι cp. c. 32 ibid.

The envoys therefore had met with nothing but coldness and rebuffs. The best report was brought by those sent to Thessaly. They brought word that the Thessalians had promised to help in guarding the defile of Tempe, between Olympus and Ossa [7, 175]. A certain number of ships were accordingly sent to Halos, where 10,000 soldiers were B.C. 480. landed and proceeded on foot to Tempe; the Athenian contingent being under the command of Themistokles[1]. But they remained there only a few days. Alexander of Makedonia warned them that the pass was too wide to be defended against the superior numbers of the enemy. This warning, backed by the knowledge that the pass of Tempe was not the only one into Thessaly, induced this force to withdraw to its ships and return home [7, 172—4]. This abortive expedition took place early in the spring of 480 B.C. just when the royal army was in the act of crossing the Hellespont.

The upshot of these transactions was that, Thessaly being definitely abandoned, the Thessalians were compelled to submit unconditionally to the Persians as well as much of the country south of Thessaly: and that it became necessary for the Congress of the Isthmos to reconsider their plan of campaign.

The Congress now decided on sending troops to guard the pass of Thermopylae, between Mount Oeta and the sea, both as being narrow enough to be defended, and as being a single one, for they knew nothing of the path which was afterwards treacherously pointed out to the Persians. At the same time messages were sent to the various states that could provide ships to muster them at Pōgōn the harbour of Troezen [8, 42], for

---
[1] Plutarch, *Them.* 7.

the purpose of proceeding to Artemisium, that the invaders might be met by sea and land at places nearly opposite each other.

But these arrangements seem to have taken a considerable time. For it was not until news came that *June—July. B.C. 480.* Xerxes was in Pieria, the southern district of Makedonia, that the leaders assembled in the Isthmos hurried off to their respective posts at Thermopylae and Artemisium [7, 177].

The Spartans had taken the initiative in sending to Thermopylae a small force of 300 citizens with their helots under the king Leonidas, that the allies might be encouraged to do the same; and eventually there were mustered under his command 2700 men from various cities in the Peloponnese, with 400 from Thebes, 700 from Thespiae, and about 1500 Phokians and Opuntian Lokrians. The Spartans looked upon this force as a mere advanced guard. They were kept at home by the approach of the festival of the Karneia, which hardly any extremity of danger would induce them to neglect. They expected that Leonidas would be able to hold the pass long enough to enable the main army to come to his support [7, 206].

The Athenians were not represented in this army. Their whole energies and all their available men were devoted to strengthening the fleet, to which they contributed almost as many vessels as all other states put together.

Meanwhile the two arms of the Persian host were steadily approaching. Starting from Therma (Thessalonika), eleven days in advance of the navy, the land forces made their way unopposed through Thessaly and Phthiotis (Achaia). They kept the road by the sea coast in order to pass most easily the range of Orthrys, and descended into Malis. There the chain of Oeta runs close down to the sea, leaving what was then an extremely narrow passage, but which now presents quite a different appearance. The sea has receded, and the Spercheios has brought down so much alluvial deposit that its course is changed, and a broad piece of marshy land covered with rice fields stretches between the mountains and the sea.

The pass at that time began after crossing from the north the mountain stream Asopos; and its narrowest point was a little further south still, where a small tributary of the Asopos, the Phoenix, flowed down from the hills. Behind this pass, 'where there is only a narrow causeway wide enough for a single carriage', there was a plain $1\frac{3}{4}$ miles long ending in the hot springs and the village round them, and containing another village called Anthela. At either end of this the two armies were stationed [7, 200—1], while between them was the wall built by the Phokians as a protection against their Thessalian enemies [7, 176].

Xerxes could not believe that such a puny force would venture to withstand his 'grand army'. But finding that there were no signs of giving in on the part of the Greeks, after waiting four days, on the fifth he sent some Medes and Kissians to clear the way. They were beaten back *1st day's fighting at Thermopylae.* with considerable loss, and even the Persian 'Immortals' fared no better.

Similar attempts next day met with no better success. The narrowness of the ground made large numbers a disadvantage rather than an aid, *2nd day.* and the Greeks were armed with longer spears than their enemies, and with heavy serviceable shields, which here, as afterwards at Plataea, gave them a vast superiority in a charge and at close quarters [7, 212].

But in the evening of that day a Malian named Ephialtes demanded an audience of the king; and being admitted offered to discover a pathway over the height called Kallidromos, which would conduct troops to the rear of the Greeks. Xerxes, who had watched the failure of his troops with every sign of violent emotion and anxiety, gladly accepted the proposal. At nightfall, just as the watchfires were being lit, 10,000 of the Immortals led by Hydarnes started under the guidance of Ephialtes to cross this height. By day break they were approaching the summit. Just below the crest 1000 Phokians had been stationed to guard against the possibility of this danger[1]. The hill was thickly covered with oak forest, and no sight of the coming enemy was possible even in the moonlight. But through the clear morning air the sound of their trampling through the brushwood was carried to the ears of the Phokian thousand. Yet their warning was brief: the Persians seemed to start suddenly into view, surprised no less than themselves to see a body of men hastily getting under arms where they had expected a bare mountain top. They fancied that they were the dreaded Spartans who had beaten them the day before: but reassured by Ephialtes, who told them the truth, they began pouring in volleys of arrows. The Phokians did not hold their ground, but fled hastily to the crest of the hill and there drew up. The Persians did not continue

3rd day.

---

[1] Her. 7, 217. For the existence of this path was well known in the Greek camp, although it had been unknown to the Congress, see 7, 175.

the attack, but following the path that wound round the slope avoided the hill top, and descended with all speed on the other side.

News had come early to the Greeks below at Thermopylae that they were betrayed. The sacrifices were unfavourable, and deserters came in bringing the intelligence; and these were soon followed by their own scouts, running down the hill with the fatal news. The allies immediately decided to depart, or, as some said, were dismissed by Leonidas that no more Hellenic lives should be lost. For him and his 300 the idea of retreat was intolerable. It was the duty of a Spartan to die at his post if necessary; it was an undying disgrace to quit it. With him the Thebans and Thespians alone remained; but with very different sentiments. The Thespians like the Spartans preferred death to deserting the post of danger: the Thebans, whose state was known to be medising, were retained by Leonidas as hostages, and took the first opportunity offered them in the battle of consummating the treason of their government.

At sunrise Xerxes poured libations to his god; and about 10 in the morning started once more for the pass. The Spartans, knowing themselves to be surrounded, were now grown desperate. They quitted the shelter of the Phokian wall and advanced into the wider part of the pass. A determined hand to hand fight followed: two of the king's half-brothers fell, many of the Persians were thrust into the sea, while many more were trodden to death by the feet of their own men. Presently Leonidas fell, and an obstinate battle raged round his corpse. But while engaged in this fierce struggle the Spartans found that the 'Immortals' who had been led over the hill were on their rear. They made one more desperate charge;

forced their way back to the Phokian wall, and thence to a piece of elevated ground; and there for some time maintained a gallant defence, with swords and hands and even teeth; till, completely surrounded, they were overwhelmed with missiles and perished to a man[1] [7, 223—5].

Such was the famous battle of Thermopylae. Its result was to leave the way clear to Xerxes to advance on Attica, the chief object of his expedition. The whole army therefore moved forward to Panopeis on the frontier of Boeotia, and there divided into two columns; the one with the king continuing its advance steadily towards Athens,—the other taking guides marched towards Delphi wasting the country as they went. The fortunes of the first column are recounted in cc. 51—55 of the text as far as their seizure of Athens, and capture of the Acropolis; while the proceedings of the column which was sent against Delphi are described in cc. 34—39.

The battle of Thermopylae was almost simultaneous with the three days' sea-fighting at Artemisium; and the proceedings of the Navy occupy the rest of the chapters of this book of Herodotos.

About the same time as Leonidas had started for Thermopylae, such of the ships as were ready proceeded to Artemisium, the rest being told to come to Pōgōn as soon as possible, and thence to join the main fleet wherever it might be [c. 42]. In the earlier chapters the doings of this fleet are detailed; their retreat to Chalkis; their return to Artemisium; their three days' skirmishing fight with the Persian fleet; and their back-

---

[1] Only one man—Aristodemus—survived, who was not actually engaged. But his life was made such a burden to him that he courted and found death next year at Plataea, 9, 71.

ward movement on hearing of the disaster at Thermopylae [cc. 4—20]. Then comes the history of the bay of Salamis, and the divisions in the counsels of the fleet as to whether it were better to fight there or nearer the Isthmos where the army was mustering; the trick of Themistokles; and the final struggle and victory [cc. 40—90].

Though the combined fleet was commanded by the Spartan Eurybiades, yet it cannot be too clearly understood that Athens was the life and soul of this patriotic effort. Of the 268 ships which were serving at Artemisium Athens supplied and manned 127, and lent 20 to the Chalkidians; and when the fleet was subsequently reinforced in the bay of Salamis by ships from other states, this proportion was still maintained; Athens supplying 180 triremes out of a total of 378[1]. And besides this superiority in numbers, it was the Athenian Themistokles who more than any other commander held the allies together, and by every means, persuasion, bribery, and threats, induced them to present a united front to the enemy.

The story of the decisive battle of Salamis is tolerably clear in Herodotos; but we have the good fortune to possess also the statement of an eye-witness, one actually engaged in the battle. And though this narrative is thrown into a poetical form, there seems every reason to suppose that it is meant to be a true and accurate account. The poet Aeschylos has put into the mouth of a messenger to Queen Atossa a detailed description of the battle, and though that description tallies generally with the account of Herodotos there are two points in which there is some difficulty in reconciling the two.

1. The first as might be expected is a question of

---

[1] Or 366. See notes on c. 48.

numbers. Herodotos (8, 48) reckons the numbers of the Greek triremes at 378: Aeschylos (*Pers.* 340—2) at 310. The difference may be accounted for I think by supposing Aeschylos to be speaking of the number of the ships actually engaged, while Herodotos takes the tale of ships originally supplied, which each state would afterwards take care to have set down as their contribution. It seems probable however that some managed to get away when the alarm caused by the capture of Athens first fell upon the fleet (8, 56); and we are told that the 40 Corinthian ships did in point of fact avoid engaging (8, 94). Thucydides represents the Athenian envoy in B.C. 432 as reckoning the number of the united fleet to be 400 [1, 74, 1]: but the orator is evidently speaking in round numbers, and is more intent on emphasizing the proportion which the Athenian ships bore to the whole than on accuracy of totals. Still wider differences are to be found in later writers. Ktesias, a contemporary of Xenophon, stated the number as 700 [Photios 72]; but his whole account of the campaign is so confused that not much weight is to be attached to his authority. Demosthenes [*de Coron.* 306] states the number as 300, in which he is nearly in agreement with Aeschylos. But the same criticism applies to him as to the speech in Thucydides. He is speaking in round numbers, and intent chiefly on showing that the Athenians contributed about two-thirds of the whole. I believe, then, that Herodotos gives the official list of ships supplied, Aeschylos the actual numbers engaged.

2. The second point in which there is some difficulty is connected with the movements of the Persian fleet the night before the battle. In c. 76 Herodotos says

that when the king had received as in good faith the message sent him by Themistokles three steps were taken in consequence. *First*, Psyttaleia was occupied; *secondly*, at midnight the right (or westernmost) wing was moved forward 'close to Salamis by way of surrounding [the enemy]'; *thirdly*, the left wing which lay off Keos and Kynosura[1] filled all the strait between Salamis and Munychia. It is the second of these movements that seems inadequately described by Herodotos. Aeschylos says distinctly that the Persian fleet was divided into three, and that one of these divisions was sent round Salamis[2]; and Diodoros (11, 17) says that it was the Egyptians who were sent 'to barricade the strait between Salamis and the Megarid'. Rawlinson suggests that the second movement was not *round*

---

[1] As to the position of these places see Historical and Geogr. Index. The three views regarding them are (1) *Blakesley's*, who regards them as indicating the Kynosura near Marathon and the Island of Keos. The objection is that this extension of the Persian line is much too great, and the time assigned for such a movement (in that case) much too short. (2) *Stein's*, who thinks these two names refer to the same tongue of land on the S. of Salamis, one of them being the ordinary, the other the less known name. See note on the passage. The objection to this is that the geography is entirely conjectural: while on the other hand its advantage is that it suits the words of Herod. better than any other, 'the ships round K. and K. put to sea and occupied all the strait up to Munychia' seems to imply that Herod. is conceiving them as starting from Salamis. (3) *Grote's*, who looks upon these names as belonging to two unknown spots on the coast of Attica. This involves geography equally conjectural as the last, and does not explain the movement so satisfactorily.

[2] *Pers.* 370 ἄλλας δὲ κύκλῳ νῆσον Αἴαντος πέριξ. Hence some would read in c. 76 κυκλούμενοι πέριξ τὴν Σαλαμῖνα instead of πρός.

Salamis, but close along its northern shore so as to pass the Greek fleet. The object of blocking up the strait between Salamis and Megara would thus be equally secured. But I think the account of Aeschylos, as an eye-witness of the particular manner in which this object was secured, deserves the greater credence; and moreover, if the movement was as Rawlinson supposed, and as certainly seems deducible from Herodotos, on the *inside* between Salamis and Attica, the men of the Greek fleet would have seen it for themselves, and would not have required the information of the Tenian trierarch (c. 82), nor would Aristeides have been an 'eye-witness' of the movement on his voyage from Aegina (c. 78—79).

In order to enable the student to compare the two accounts, as well as to appreciate the feelings with which this great achievement was regarded, the following nearly literal translation of the speech of the Persian Messenger in the play of Aeschylos is appended[1]:

> Madam, the fountain-head of all our woe
> was, sure, some vengeful sprite or baleful god.
> Thus 'twas: to Xerxes from the Attic host
> a man of Hellas came with words like these:
> 'Soon as the shade of black-browed night shall fall
> 'the Greeks will stay no more: the rowers' bench
> 'will they spring on, departing for dear life,
> 'one this way and one that, in secret flight'.
> So spake he: and my Lord knew not his guile,
> his true Greek guile, nor all the hate of heaven;
> but bade his captains straight obey this word:
> 'Soon as the sun has ceased with rays t' illume
> 'the earth, and darkness holds the court of heaven,
> 'range ye my ships in triple line, and guard
> 'the straits and outlets of the running tides:
> 'others send circling round the isle of Ajax.
> 'Nay! if the Hellenes 'scape the woe of death
> 'your heads shall answer it: this is my doom'.
> Thus spake he with a heart bemused, and blind

[1] *Persae*, 355—434.

to all the ill that fate and God had willed.
  So they, in no disorder, but with minds
attuned to discipline, begat them straight
to their poor meal; and every sailor looped
his oar upon the thole, and made all well.
But when the light o' the sun had paled and gone
and night was drawing on, each man of them
that plied an oar betook him to his ship,
and every captain of the armèd host:
warship to warship passed a word of cheer:
and on they float each keeping order due.
So all night long the masters of the ships
held all their folk to labour at the oar,
thridding the narrow seas: and night waned fast,
yet never did the Hellenes strive to make
a secret way of flight, or raise a sail.
But when the white car of the risen day
held all the earth with the sweet rays of dawn,
first rang there forth from the Hellenic host
a loud clear note, like to some joyous hymn;
and sharp and clear from rock and island came
an answering echo. Cold on Persian hearts
struck sudden fear: far other than we deemed
the tale that pæan told! Not as for flight
this solemn strain issued from Grecian lips,
but as of men with hearts of high resolve
eager for battle. Then rang shrill and clear
a clarion, filling all the bay with sound:
and straight with even stroke of dashing oars,
that fell responsive to the master's voice,
they smote the yielding bosom of the deep;
and in brief space stood out before our eyes
full plain to see. The right wing led the way
in order fair; and following hard astern
the whole long fleet streamed on, not silently,
but with shouts manifold and plain to hear:
'Sons of the Greeks arise! your country free!
'free home, and wife, and child, and grandsires' tombs,
'and all the seats loved of your fathers' gods!'
Nor were we silent: Persian lips gave back
challenge for challenge. And now the hour was come:
and straightway ship on ship did dash
its brazen beak: and first to strike a blow
a Grecian ship brake all the forward gear
of a Phœnician bark: then in wild war
ship fell on ship, or charging drave its prow
right on a foe. At first the Persian line
held out and brake not: but whenas the host
of myriad ships, cramped in the narrow bay,

H·VIII

>   crashed each on each, entangled in a maze,
>   nor could yield mutual succour,—friend on friend
>   struck with their brazen beaks, and oars
>   were splintered in the rowers' hands; and all
>   the Grecian ships not letting slip the chance
>   rowed round them, and charged: and many a hull
>   keel uppermost went drifting: the wide sea
>   was hidden with the wreckage and men's limbs,
>   and all the jutting headlands and the strands.
>   Then every ship of ours as chance gave way
>   sped off in flight disordered; and our foes
>   like tunny-fishers speared the swimmers' backs
>   with splintered spars and oars: a dolorous cry
>   filled all the reaches of the open sea;
>   until the closing eye of black-browed night
>   stayed that fell work. But the full tale of woes,
>   if I should count them through ten livelong days,
>   I could not reckon; for be sure of this,
>   one day has never seen such hosts of slain.

Though the Greeks had won a victory greater than they had dared to hope, they had no reason to think that its effect would be so decisive as turned out to be the case. A large number of the enemy's ships had been sunk or disabled, and the shores of Salamis as well as Attica bore witness by the corpses that were washed up that the slaughter had been great. Still an immense fleet remained, and a vast army was in occupation of Attica. Their experience at Artemisium had taught the Greeks that one day's fighting at sea with such great numbers was not necessarily decisive; and they were prepared to find that they still had some hard work to do. The Persian fleet had retired to Phalerum, harassed as they went by the ships of the Aeginetans and Athenians, and were well out of sight of the Greeks. But they might reappear the next morning; and at daybreak the Greeks began their preparations for renewing the fight [c. 108]. To their surprise no ship of the enemy hove in sight; and

Sept. B.C. 480.

they presently learned that the whole fleet had started in the night and was making for the Hellespont. This, then, was indeed a victory. They determined that the beaten foe should not thus escape them, and with all speed they set out in pursuit.

What had happened is told in cc. 97—107. Xerxes was thoroughly frightened; and, so far from thinking of renewing the engagement, was set upon returning to Asia with as little delay as possible. But even the master of the Persian Empire was obliged to have some regard for appearances; and a hasty retreat from an army that as yet had met with nothing but success, and from a fleet, which after all had scarcely lost a sixth of its whole tale of ships, was too barefaced a confession of selfish cowardice.

The battle had begun early in the morning, and must have been finished some hours before night; for Xerxes had time, not only to punish some of those who had shewn cowardice in the fight[1], but also to take some measures for the completion of the mole across to Salamis, which had apparently been determined upon, and probably begun before the battle[2]. Some Phoenikian transports (γαυλοί) were lashed together to form a temporary bridge across the strait, apparently with a view of aiding the formation of a more permanent causeway. He then summoned a council of war, as though he were desirous of their advice as to the measures for continuing the struggle. Mardonios however was fully aware of what was passing in his master's mind. He knew too that his own life depended on being able to redeem the disaster; and that his only chance of being allowed to attempt to

---

[1] C. 90, Diodor. Sic. 11, 19 τῶν μὲν Φοινίκων τῶν ἀρξάντων τῆς φυγῆς τοὺς αἰτιωτάτους ἀπέκτεινε.

[2] Ktesias, *Pers.* 26; Strabo, 9, 1, 13.

do so was to get Xerxes out of the reach of personal danger. He therefore gave just the advice that he knew was desired. Xerxes must return to Asia, and he himself be left to renew the war in the next year. The proposal was supported by queen Artemisia, whose advice Xerxes had previously found to be good[1], and who had shewn great personal gallantry in the battle. This plan was accordingly adopted. Xerxes himself was to retire under the escort of his whole army as far as Boeotia, and thence with a body of sixty thousand men under Artabazos to the Hellespont. Mardonios was to select the flower of the army to winter with him in Thessaly, with which to attack Peloponnesos in the spring. But Xerxes chiefly feared that the victorious Greeks would shut him out from Asia by proceeding at once to the Hellespont, and breaking the bridge of ships which had been made with such labour for the passage of the army in the spring. This bridge had in fact already been broken up by a storm, or was so broken before Xerxes reached it; but even if the bridge were not intact, he would have no difficulty in being conveyed across, provided that his fleet commanded the channel. The first thing therefore was to secure that. Immediate orders were accordingly given, and the fleet started under cover of night for the Hellespont, though the Phoenikian contingent appears for the most part to have deserted, and made the best of its way home[2].

Having committed the care of some of his children who were with him to Artemisia, to be conveyed to Ephesos, whence they could easily reach Sardis[3], Xerxes,

---

[1] c. 68. [2] Diodor. Sic. 11, 19.
[3] Plutarch's sneer (*de Malign.* 38)—ἐπελέλησto γὰρ ἐκ Σούσων, ὡς ἔοικεν, ἄγειν γυναῖκας, εἰ γυναικείας ἐδέοντο παραπομπῆς οἱ παῖδες

after a few days' delay, set out on his march northward. Of this retreat and of the sufferings of the Persian army in the course of it, many tales were current among the Greeks; and naturally enough exaggerated stories were passed from mouth to mouth. One of these is related by Herodotos (c. 118), which he gives good reason for disbelieving. And others were embodied by Aeschylos in his tragedy of the *Persae*, first represented, it appears, seven years after the battle of Salamis, in B.C. 473. There the fleet is said to flee before the wind in great disorder (κατ' οὖρον οὐκ εὔκοσμον αἴρονται φυγήν), while part of the army remained in Boeotia suffering from want of water and disease, and the rest marched painfully through Doris, and along the Malian gulf to Thessaly, where many died of want of food and drink, and thence to Magnesia and Makedonia. By this time it was late in the season, and their sufferings were increased by severe weather. The Strymon was frozen[1], though it

—is quite misplaced. It was not because she was a woman, but because she had proved her fidelity and courage, that Artemisia was selected for this service; and Herodotos would have good means of learning such a fact.

[1] Aeschyl. *Pers.* 484—516. Grote (IV. 489) objects 'that a large river such as the Strymon near its mouth (180 yards broad and in a latitude about N. 40° 50'), at a period which could not have been later than the beginning of November, should have been frozen *over in one night* so hardly and firmly as to admit of a portion of the army marching over it at daybreak—before the sun became warm—is a statement which surely requires a more responsible witness than Aeschylus to avouch it'. But to assert that the frost was only of *one night* is, I think, pressing the poet's words too closely. The frost was unusual at the time of year (θεὸς χειμῶν' ἄωρον ὦρσε); and Aeschylos' words imply that there was one specially severe night, which was regarded as portentous, and the result of which induced the army to attempt to cross. Still the river may have been frozen

was at an unusually early time of the year for that (November), and the army attempting to cross lost a large number of men owing to a sudden thaw. Thence the remainder painfully struggled on to the Hellespont.

But whether the incident of the Strymon has or has not any foundation of fact, the account given by Herodotos of the retreat (c. 115) sufficiently indicates that it was accompanied by severe suffering to all concerned. The end of it was that Xerxes got safe to Sardis, and one act of the great drama which Herodotos undertakes to present is brought to a conclusion. Xerxes,—the type of Eastern pride, arrogance, and unrestricted power,—has been brought into conflict with Greek civilisation and Greek divinities, and has retired beaten and in disgrace. He does not appear again on the scene, except in that revolting tale of lust and cruelty (9, 108—113), with which Herodotos seems of set purpose to have concluded his History as far as the Persian monarchy was concerned.

Thus it was that the Greeks found no ships to fight on the day after the battle of Salamis. The Persian camp was still visible on the Attic shore, but no ships were in sight. Presently they learnt the truth, that the fleet had departed in the night; and they at once set off in pursuit. But when they had got as far as the island of Andros without sighting the enemy, they stopped to

before. More serious perhaps was the objection that a bridge of boats had been thrown across the Strymon (7, 114), over which the army had marched in the spring, and which there is no reason to suppose had been broken up. It may perhaps have been temporarily open to allow passage for vessels up and down the stream, and the hard frost may have prevented it being joined again soon enough for the impatience of the suffering and demoralised army.

INTRODUCTION.   xxix

consider what to do. Two courses appeared open to them. First, to make at once for the Hellespont, break the bridge of ships, and so guard the strait as to shut off the Persian army from Asia. The second was to give every facility for the enemy's army to quit Greece as soon and as readily as possible. Themistokles was for the former course: Eurybiades, the commander in chief, for the latter, which was also supported by the other Peloponnesian commanders [c. 108]. Finding his energetic counsel rejected Themistokles took up the other line, and advised an immediate return home; a disbandment of the fleet until the spring; and that all should go to their own states, and employ themselves in restoring all that had been destroyed by the Persians, and in making preparations for the coming year. With characteristic cunning he took care that this advice should be reported to Xerxes, and should be represented to him as having been given in order to allow him time to secure his safety [109—110][1].

There were still some weeks left of the time during which Greek sailors ventured to stay out at sea; and instead of returning home, some at least of the fleet remained at Andros, apparently at the instigation of Themistokles, for another purpose: that namely, of exacting punishment on those of the Andrians or inhabitants of other islands, who had medized; and of levying contributions for the support of a fleet to keep the Aegean free of the Persians in the future[2]. These proceedings perhaps

---

[1] Plutarch *Them.* c. 16.

[2] It seems probable that it was only the Athenian fleet which was engaged in this business: for Themistokles is spoken of exclusively as managing and directing it; whereas Eurybiades was the commander in chief, and would have been responsible if he had

were so far damaging to Themistokles' reputation at home as to prevent his being elected Strategus for the following year[1]; but we do not hear that the Athenians refused to avail themselves of the money thus collected or extorted; and in fact the measures of Themistokles seem to have been the forerunners of that confederacy of Delos, afterwards cemented by the vigour of Kimon and the integrity of Aristeides [B.C. 477]; the foundation of which was the idea that, as the islanders and other states were chiefly interested in the security of the Aegean, they were bound to contribute to the maintenance of a fleet whereby that security was to be guarded. The banishment of individuals also for Medism, though apparently accompanied by corrupt practices on the part of Themistokles, was the expression of the idea, also involved in the constitution of the Confederacy of Delos, that there was a Panhellenic authority capable of taking cognizance of offences against Hellenic safety. This principle was again, and with greater show of legality, exemplified in the following year by the fine of a tenth levied on Thebes for medizing, as well as the execution of the most guilty of her citizens[2].

Before quitting the events of this year it may be well to consider another passage, which called for severe animadversion from our author's critic Plutarch. This is his

remained. Thus we find that it is Themistokles who is attacked afterwards for the proceedings of this autumn. Plut. *Them.* 21.

[1] Jealousy was also roused by the honours he received at Sparta, see c. 124. Cp. Diodor. Sic. 11, c. 27 δεξαμένου δὲ τοῦ Θεμιστοκλέους τὰς δωρεάς, ὁ δῆμος τῶν Ἀθηναίων ἀπέστησεν αὐτὸν ἀπὸ τῆς στρατηγίας, καὶ παρέδωκε τὴν ἀρχὴν Ξανθίππῳ τῷ Ἀρίφρονος. But he was afterwards Strategus, apparently with the special command at sea (ναύαρχος), Plut. *Them.* c. 18.

[2] Herod. 9, 86—88. Polyb. 9, 39.

statement as to the cowardice shewed by the Korinthian admiral Adeimantos at the battle of Salamis. It is true that he ends his chapter (c. 94) by acknowledging that the Korinthians deny the allegation, and are supported in their denial by the other Greeks. Still he tells the story first, without prefacing or concluding it with an expression of his own personal doubt, as he does when he is incredulous (cp. c. 119): and there does seem some unfairness in telling a story, confessedly grounded on the report of what was, at the time when he must have narrated it, a hostile state. And here Plutarch is more successful in his refutation than on most other points. He argued rather absurdly that it could not be true that the Greeks had determined to retreat from Artemisium before they heard of the death of Leonidas, *because* Pindar, a citizen of medizing Thebes, spoke of Artemisium as a place 'Where sons of Athenians laid a brilliant foundation-stone of Liberty'[1]. But in regard to the conduct of the Korinthians, he was able to point to the fact that Korinthians who fell in the battle were buried in Salamis with a complimentary inscription:

ὦ ξένε, εὔυδρόν ποτ' ἐναίομεν ἄστυ Κορίνθου,
νῦν δ' ἄμμ' Αἴαντος νᾶσος ἔχει Σαλαμίς·
ἐνθάδε Φοινίσσας νῆας καὶ Πέρσας ἑλόντες
καὶ Μήδους ἱερὰν Ἑλλάδα ῥυόμεθα.

Beside the Cenotaph on the Isthmus with the lines:

Ταῦτ' ἀπὸ δυσμενέων Μήδων ναῦται Διοδώρου
ὅπλ' ἀνέθεντο Λατοῖ, μνάματα ναυμαχίης.

The proverb 'as lying as an epitaph' is not wholly

---

[1] *de Malign.* 34,
ὅθι παῖδες Ἀθηναίων ἐβάλοντο
φαεννὰν κρηπῖδ' ἐλευθερίας.

inapplicable to Greek inscriptions; and the Cenotaph on the Isthmus may perhaps be held to be of no greater worth as evidence than the epigram on Adeimantos' tomb:

Οὗτος Ἀδειμάντου κείνου τάφος, ὃν δία πᾶσα
Ἑλλὰς ἐλευθερίας ἀμφέθετο στέφανον.

But the fact of the tomb with its inscription having been set up at Salamis, without remonstrance from Athens, is a strong if not conclusive proof that at the time, at any rate, the Athenians did not hold the Korinthians guilty of desertion or cowardice. On the contrary, as Plutarch points out, they are always admitted to the place of honour next the Spartans and Athenians, as on the bronze serpents which supported the tripod offered after Plataea, which are still extant[1].

From c. 130 to the end of the book Herodotos relates the first movements of the following spring, which prepared the way for the final contests at Plataea and Mykalè. The Persian fleet, which had wintered at Kymè, now mustered at Samos, being intent on preventing any movement from Ionia, while Mardonios was engaged in crushing the Greeks on the mainland [c. 130]. The Greek fleet on the other hand met at Aegina under the command of Leotychides, king of Sparta. There they were visited by envoys from Ionia begging for help: but though they proceeded with some reluctance as far as Delos, nothing could induce them to go any further [cc. 131—2]. There then we leave the two combatants for the present, —at Samos and Delos,—watching each other's movements, and neither being willing to strike the first blow.

Spring of B.C. 479.

---

[1] Plutarch, *de Malign.* 39. See also the bronze serpents engraved in the introduction to the 9th book.

INTRODUCTION.

Meanwhile Mardonios on land, having reassured himself by consultation of oracles [cc. 133—5], determined to utilise the feeling of jealousy, which he was assured existed between Athens and the Peloponnesians, by an attempt to detach the Athenians from alliance with the other Greeks[1]. He chose as his envoy that Alexander of Macedon, who on a former occasion had shewn that he was not prepared to submit to every indignity from his conquerors[2]; and who was connected by special ties with Athens. This man seems to have been only serving with Mardonios under compulsion, and though he gave his message, and added formal words of his own in support of it, there is an air of coldness on his part which betrays that his wishes were not with his tongue,—a fact more conclusively proved, later in the year, by his volunteering to warn the Greeks before the battle of Plataea[3]. Naturally enough news of this negociation excited alarm among the Spartans: for though they meant once more to abandon Attica to the enemy, while they sheltered themselves behind the wall, which was being rapidly built across the Isthmus; yet they had learnt from the events of the past year that the only way to prevent an attack by sea, which would render the defence of the wall nugatory, was the maintenance of an effective fleet; and that to this end the Athenians were of

---

[1] διαβοηθείσης δὲ τῆς τῶν Ἀθηναίων πρὸς τοὺς Ἕλληνας ἀλλοτριότητος ἧκον εἰς τὰς Ἀθήνας πρέσβεις παρὰ Περσῶν καὶ παρὰ τῶν Ἑλλήνων. Diodor. Sic. 11, 28. Though Herodotos does not distinctly say anything of the alienation of feeling between the Athenians and the rest of the Greeks, yet substituting 'Peloponnesians' for 'Greeks' his narrative implies it; and the offer which Alexander was instructed to make was an appeal to a separatist feeling, which it was presumed would be actuating them.

[2] 5, 19. [3] 9, 44—6.

supreme importance. They therefore hurriedly sent off envoys to counteract the offers of Mardonios. The Athenians had felt sure that they would do so, and therefore waited for the arrival of these envoys from Sparta before giving their final answer to Alexander. The scene and the speeches which follow are of course partly dramatic, but there is no reason to doubt that they represent substantially what occurred. They bring into prominence, as they were meant to do, the contrast between the truly Hellenic spirit at that time animating the Athenians, who had dared and suffered so much in defence of Greece, and the selfish caution which chilled and retarded the efforts of the Spartans in the cause of Hellenic liberty.

The mention of a king of Makedonia leads Herodotos to a digression on the origin of the Makedonian dynasty. He could, of course, have no prescience of the great part which the Temenid kings were destined to play in Greek history; and preeminently in the final destruction of that vast empire, whose unwilling agent Alexander then was: but he may have felt even then the importance to Hellenism of a power which was ever struggling with the barbarian and piratic tribes of the West; and which formed a breakwater against attacks on that side, whilst it was fighting for its life on the East. It is the reward of a diligent observer, who lets nothing escape him as uninteresting, that what seemed his least important record should be fruitful in interest and importance to posterity.

The great drama is now approaching its final denouement. The two opposing forces, Barbarism and Hellenism, have been depicted by the aid of every kind of research which was open to a man of the time. Nothing that could throw the least light on any of the incidents of the great contest, or on the characters of the parties to the struggle, has been omitted. They have met at sea and the fortune of the contest has been settled there: it remains only to see whether the god of battles will decide in the same sense on land; and, that having been put beyond question at Plataea, Mykalè will prove to be the beginning of a system of retaliation by the Greeks upon their enemy; which, after many vicissitudes, will reach its final consummation a century and a half later in the victories of Alexander.

NOTES ON THE TEXT.

[A, Medicean MS. in Laurentian Library, 10th Century.
B, Angelicanus, 11th Century.
R, Vatican, 14th Century.
V, Vindobonensis (Vienna), 10th Century.
S, Sandcroft, 14th Century.
C, Florentine, 11th Century.]

p. 2, l. 23. ἐβούλευον. One group of MSS. has ἐβουλεύοντο. But this use of βουλεύεσθαι with an accusative seems unexampled. Cp. cc. 18, 97, 100; 5, 124.

p. 10, l. 19. ἑκάστους πῦρ. Cobet ἕκαστον πυρά.

p. 12, l. 17. Ξέρξην. Here and at p. 36, l. 19, one group of MSS. has Ξέρξεα. See App. C. 1. (4) n.

p. 13, l. 22. πάντες δὲ ἠπιστέατο τοὺς κειμένους εἶναι πάντας. Cobet πάντας δὲ ἠπιστέατο τοὺς κειμένους εἶναι.

p. 16, l. 16. δοκέειν. Cobet δοκέει, but cp. p. 12, l. 14.

p. 19, l. 18. ἱρά. Naber ἀρήια.

p. 19, l. 21. Προνηίης. Two MSS. (S and V) have Προνοίης. Cp. Pausan. 10, 8, 6 Ἀθηνῆς Προνοίας.

p. 21, l. 19. ὑπεκθέσθαι. Gomperz would omit, Holder brackets. But it seems naturally implied by the ὑπεξεκέετο of p. 22, l. 2.

p. 21, l. 24. ἐστί, Kallenberg omits, and Holder brackets. The MSS. vary the order, some giving ἐστὶ μελιτόεσσα, others μελιτόεσσά ἐστι. This however, a very common occurrence, is not a sufficient reason for omitting a word which it is not the general manner of Herodotos to leave out.

p. 23, l. 22. ἄλλαι. Cobet proposes δέκα, for which the symbol was ι΄.

p. 30, l. 3. τὸ ἥκιστα. I have omitted the ἐς of the MSS.

NOTES ON THE TEXT. xxxvii

p. 35, l. 8. δέ. Valcknaer would omit this word; but it is much in Herodotos' manner to begin a speech with it. See cc. 137, 142 and 5, 33.

p. 36, l. 17. τῇ κρίσι. This is the reading of the Vatican MS. (R), and of the Vienna and Emmanuel MSS. (V, S). Stein reads ἀνακρίσι with the Medicean and Augustinian (A and B) MSS. He quotes two passages of Plato [176 C, 277 E] to prove the interpretation which he gives the word, 'remonstrance', 'contradiction' (*Einrede*, *Widerspruch*). But in both these passages the sense seems rather to be that of 'questioning' than of 'contradiction'; and so probably in Her. 3, 53, though there is there a variant ὑπόκρισις. On the other hand Herodotos elsewhere uses κρίσις as equivalent to 'quarrel', 'contention', not as here 'expression of opinion' [5, 5; 7, 26]. Stein supports his interpretation of ἀνάκρισις by referring to ἀνακρίνεσθαι in 9, 56. The two words were sometimes confounded. See Lysias 22, § 3.

p. 52, l. 11. κατά περ Ἕλλησι. Stein proposes παρά.

p. 53, l. 26. ἐν τοῖσι Πέρσῃσι. One group of MSS. has ἐν Πέρσῃσι τοῖσι. Stein omits τοῖσι. Valcknaer proposes τοί τι, which Holder adopts.

p. 55, l. 8. περὶ οἶκον τὸν σόν. Abicht brackets: Stein connects the words with συμφορή, Baehr (as I do) with πρηγμάτων. Wesseling conjectures εὖ κειμένων for ἐκείνων.

p. 55, l. 24 to p. 56, l. 4. οἱ δὲ Πεδασέες—Ἑρμότιμος ἦν. Valcknaer with one MS. omits this passage. See 1, 175. Such a repetition however is not unexampled in Herodotos; and it is difficult to see why a copyist should have introduced it here.

p. 58, l. 19. διαφθαρέεται. Stein διαφθερέεται. ἐπιχειρέοντι. The MS. R has ἐπιχωρέοντι.

p. 59, l. 8. βαλλόμενοι. Some MSS. have βαλόμενοι. But I think the present is the right tense in such conventional phrases.

p. 59, l. 11. νενικημένους. Cobet omits. Holder brackets. But it is not a mere explanation of ἐς ἀναγκαίην ἀπειληθέντας,—'I have known many when brought to bay, *though conquered*, yet renew the fight etc.'

p. 67, l. 16. διενέμοντο. Two MSS. [R and S] have ἔφερον. Cp. the parallel passage from the *de Corona*, § 229, quoted in the note, p. 177. The MSS. A and B have διενέμον, which Stein adopts. The middle is explained by Abicht by saying that each general divided the voting pebbles among the soldiers of his own division. I think the middle is rather to be explained by the fact that the generals did not make the distribution with their own hands:—they caused it to be done. Nor can we imagine that all the soldiers voted; it must have been only the officers of the several divisions.

p. 67, l. 17. κρίνοντες. Valcknaer κρινέοντες, I think unnecessarily.

p. 68, l. 6. ἴδοσαν. Cobet would supply ἀνδραγαθίης or ἀνδρηίης from Plutarch *Them.* 17. But ἀριστήϊα may be considered to include this idea.

p. 69, l. 28. παρὰ τάς. Valcknaer, from Aeneas Tac. 31, would read περί.

p. 70, l. 11. καταπλῆξαι. Some MSS. have καταπλέξαι. In favour of the latter is the fact that Herodotos does not elsewhere use καταπλήσσω, nor is it true that καταπλέξαι is only given by the *schlectere Handschriften*, as Abicht says; for one of them is the excellent R.

p. 73, l. 21. χρησόμενον R. Other MSS. have χρησάμενον.

p. 76, l. 14. φέροι ἐς. Stein with MSS., other than R and S, omits ἐς.

p. 80, l. 5. πιεζομένοισι BCZ. Stein with other MSS. πιεζευμένοισι. Cp. 3, 146; 6, 108. See Veitch.

p. 82, l. 11. προβωθῆσαι. So MSS. R and S. The other MSS. have προβοηθῆσαι, which Stein adopts.

ΗΡΟΔΟΤΟΥ ΟΥΡΑΝΙΑ.

BOOK VIII.

The States which contributed ships to the Greek fleet, under the command of the Spartan 'Eurybiades.

I. Οἱ δὲ Ἑλλήνων ἐς τὸν ναυτικὸν στρατὸν ταχθέντες ἦσαν οἵδε· Ἀθηναῖοι μὲν νέας παρεχόμενοι ἑκατὸν καὶ εἴκοσι καὶ ἑπτά· ὑπὸ δὲ ἀρετῆς τε καὶ προθυμίης Πλαταιέες, ἄπειροι τῆς ναυτικῆς ἐόντες, συνεπλήρουν τοῖσι Ἀθηναίοισι τὰς νέας· Κο- 5
ρίνθιοι δὲ τεσσεράκοντα νέας παρείχοντο, Μεγαρέες δὲ εἴκοσι. καὶ Χαλκιδέες ἐπλήρουν εἴκοσι Ἀθηναίων σφι παρεχόντων τὰς νέας, Αἰγινῆται δὲ ὀκτωκαίδεκα, Σικυώνιοι δὲ δυώδεκα, Λακεδαιμόνιοι δὲ δέκα, Ἐπιδαύριοι δὲ ὀκτώ, Ἐρετριέες δὲ ἑπτά, Τροι- 10
ζήνιοι δὲ πέντε, Στυρέες δὲ δύο καὶ Κεῖοι δύο τε νέας καὶ πεντηκοντέρους δύο. Λοκροὶ δέ σφι οἱ Ὀπούντιοι ἐπεβοήθεον πεντηκοντέρους ἔχοντες ἑπτά.
II. Ἦσαν μὲν ὦν οὗτοι οἱ στρατευόμενοι ἐπ' Ἀρτεμίσιον, εἴρηται δέ μοι καὶ ὡς τὸ πλῆθος ἕκαστοι τῶν 15
νεῶν παρείχοντο. ἀριθμὸς δὲ τῶν συλλεχθεισέων νεῶν ἐπ' Ἀρτεμίσιον ἦν, πάρεξ τῶν πεντηκοντέρων, διηκόσιαι καὶ ἑβδομήκοντα καὶ μία. τὸν δὲ στρατηγὸν τὸν τὸ μέγιστον κράτος ἔχοντα παρείχοντο Σπαρτιῆται Εὐρυβιάδην τὸν Εὐρυκλείδεω. οἱ γὰρ 20

σύμμαχοι οὐκ ἔφασαν, ἢν μὴ ὁ Λάκων ἡγεμονεύῃ, Ἀθηναίοισι ἕψεσθαι ἡγεομένοισι, ἀλλὰ λύσειν τὸ μέλλον ἔσεσθαι στράτευμα.

The unselfish patriotism of the Athenians.

III. Ἐγένετο γὰρ κατ' ἀρχὰς λόγος, πρὶν ἢ καὶ ἐς Σικελίην πέμπειν ἐπὶ συμμαχίην, ὡς τὸ ναυτικὸν Ἀθηναίοισι χρεὸν εἴη ἐπιτράπειν. ἀντιβάντων δὲ τῶν συμμάχων εἶκον οἱ Ἀθηναῖοι, μέγα πεποιημένοι περιεῖναι τὴν Ἑλλάδα, καὶ γνόντες, εἰ στασιάσουσι περὶ τῆς ἡγεμονίης, ὡς ἀπολέεται ἡ Ἑλλάς, ὀρθὰ νοεῦντες· στάσις γὰρ ἔμφυλος πολέμου ὁμοφρονέοντος τοσούτῳ κάκιόν ἐστι, ὅσῳ πόλεμος εἰρήνης. ἐπιστάμενοι ὦν αὐτὸ τοῦτο οὐκ ἀντέτεινον, ἀλλ' εἶκον, μέχρι ὅσου κάρτα ἐδέοντο αὐτῶν, ὡς διέδεξαν. ὡς γὰρ διωσάμενοι τὸν Πέρσην περὶ τῆς ἐκείνου ἤδη τὸν ἀγῶνα ἐποιεῦντο, πρόφασιν τὴν Παυσανίεω ὕβριν προϊσχόμενοι ἀπείλοντο τὴν ἡγεμονίην τοὺς Λακεδαιμονίους. ἀλλὰ ταῦτα μὲν ὕστερον ἐγένετο·

The fleet arrives at **Artemisium**. *Seeing the Persian armament at Aphetae the Greeks are minded to retreat southwards, but the people of Euboea induce Themistocles by a bribe to use his influence to keep them there.*

IV. Τότε δὲ οὗτοι οἱ καὶ ἐπ' Ἀρτεμίσιον Ἑλλήνων ἀπικόμενοι ὡς εἶδον νέας τε πολλὰς καταχθείσας ἐς τὰς Ἀφετὰς καὶ στρατιῆς ἅπαντα πλέα, ἐπεὶ αὐτοῖσι παρὰ δόξαν τὰ πρήγματα τῶν βαρβάρων ἀπέβαινε ἢ ὡς αὐτοὶ κατεδόκεον, καταρρωδήσαντες δρησμὸν ἐβούλευον ἀπὸ τοῦ Ἀρτεμισίου ἔσω ἐς τὴν Ἑλλάδα. γνόντες δέ σφεας οἱ Εὐβοέες ταῦτα βουλευομένους ἐδέοντο Εὐρυβιάδεω προσμεῖναι χρόνον ὀλίγον, ἔστ' ἂν αὐτοὶ τέκνα τε καὶ τοὺς οἰκέτας ὑπεκθέωνται. ὡς δὲ οὐκ ἔπειθον, μεταβάντες τὸν Ἀθηναίων στρατηγὸν πείθουσι Θεμιστοκλέα ἐπὶ μισθῷ τριήκοντα ταλάντοισι, ἐπ' ᾧ τε καταμείναντες 5 πρὸ τῆς Εὐβοίης ποιήσονται τὴν ναυμαχίην. V. Ὁ δὲ Θεμιστοκλέης τοὺς Ἕλληνας ἐπισχεῖν ὧδε ποιέει· Εὐρυβιάδῃ τούτων τῶν χρημάτων μεταδιδοῖ πέντε τάλαντα ὡς παρ' ἑωυτοῦ δῆθεν διδούς. ὡς δέ οἱ οὗτος ἀνεπέπειστο, Ἀδείμαντος γὰρ ὁ Ὠκύτου Κο- 10 ρινθίων στρατηγὸς τῶν λοιπῶν ἤσπαιρε μοῦνος, φάμενος ἀποπλώσεσθαί τε ἀπὸ τοῦ Ἀρτεμισίου καὶ οὐ παραμενέειν, πρὸς δὴ τοῦτον εἶπε ὁ Θεμιστοκλέης ἐπομόσας· "Οὐ σύ γε ἡμέας ἀπολείψεις, ἐπεί τοι ἐγὼ "μέζω δῶρα δώσω, ἢ βασιλεὺς ἄν τοι ὁ Μήδων πέμ- 15 "ψειε ἀπολιπόντι τοὺς συμμάχους." Ταῦτά τε ἅμα ἠγόρευε καὶ πέμπει ἐπὶ τὴν νέα τὴν Ἀδειμάντου τάλαντα ἀργυρίου τρία. οὗτοί τε δὴ πάντες δώροισι ἀναπεπεισμένοι ἦσαν, καὶ τοῖσι Εὐβοεῦσι ἐκεχάριστο, αὐτός τε ὁ Θεμιστοκλέης ἐκέρδηνε, ἐλάνθανε δὲ τὰ 20 λοιπὰ ἔχων, ἀλλ' ἠπιστέατο οἱ μεταλαβόντες τούτων τῶν χρημάτων, ἐκ τῶν Ἀθηνέων ἐλθεῖν ἐπὶ τῷ λόγῳ τούτῳ τὰ χρήματα.

The Persians send 200 ships round Euboea to entrap the Greek fleet.

VI. Οὕτω δὴ κατέμεινάν τε ἐν τῇ Εὐβοίῃ καὶ ἐναυμάχησαν. ἐγένετο δὲ ὧδε· ἐπεί τε δὴ ἐς τὰς 25 Ἀφετὰς περὶ δείλην πρωίην γινομένην ἀπίκατο οἱ βάρβαροι, πυθόμενοι μὲν ἔτι καὶ πρότερον περὶ τὸ Ἀρτεμίσιον ναυλοχέειν νέας Ἑλληνίδας ὀλίγας, τότε

δὲ αὐτοὶ ἰδόντες, πρόθυμοι ἦσαν ἐπιχειρέειν, εἴ κως ἔλοιεν αὐτάς. ἐκ μὲν δὴ τῆς ἀντίης προσπλώειν οὔ κώ σφι ἐδόκεε τῶνδε εἴνεκεν, μή κως ἰδόντες οἱ Ἕλληνες προσπλώοντας ἐς φυγὴν ὁρμήσειαν, φεύ-
5 γοντάς τε εὐφρόνη καταλαμβάνῃ· καὶ ἔμελλον δῆθεν ἐκφεύξεσθαι, ἔδεε δὲ μηδὲ πυρφόρον τῷ ἐκείνων λόγῳ ἐκφυγόντα περιγενέσθαι. VII. Πρὸς ταῦτα ὦν τάδε ἐμηχανέοντο· τῶν νεῶν ἀπασέων ἀποκρίναντες διηκοσίας περιέπεμπον ἔξωθεν Σκιάθου, ὡς
10 ἂν μὴ ὀφθέωσι ὑπὸ τῶν πολεμίων περιπλώουσαι Εὔβοιαν κατά τε Καφηρέα καὶ Γεραιστὸν ἐς τὸν Εὔριπον, ἵνα δὴ περιλάβοιεν, οἱ μὲν ταύτῃ ἀπικόμενοι καὶ φράξαντες αὐτῶν τὴν ὀπίσω φέρουσαν ὁδόν, σφεῖς δὲ ἐπισπόμενοι ἐξ ἐναντίης. ταῦτα βου-
15 λευσάμενοι ἀπέπεμπον τῶν νεῶν τὰς ταχθείσας, αὐτοὶ οὐκ ἐν νόῳ ἔχοντες ταύτης τῆς ἡμέρης τοῖσι Ἕλλησι ἐπιθήσεσθαι, οὐδὲ πρότερον ἢ τὸ σύνθημά σφι ἔμελλε φανήσεσθαι παρὰ τῶν περιπλωόντων ὡς ἡκόντων. ταύτας μὲν δὴ περιέπεμπον, τῶν δὲ
20 λοιπέων νεῶν ἐν τῇσι Ἀφετῇσι ἐποιεῦντο ἀριθμόν.

The Persian design is betrayed to the Greeks by the diver Skyllias of Skione.

VIII. Ἐν δὲ τούτῳ τῷ χρόνῳ, ἐν τῷ οὗτοι ἀριθμὸν ἐποιεῦντο τῶν νεῶν (ἦν γὰρ ἐν τῷ στρατοπέδῳ τούτῳ Σκυλλίης Σκιωναῖος δύτης τῶν τότε ἀνθρώπων ἄριστος, ὃς καὶ ἐν τῇ ναυηγίῃ τῇ κατὰ
25 τὸ Πήλιον γενομένῃ πολλὰ μὲν ἔσωσε τῶν χρημάτων τοῖσι Πέρσῃσι, πολλὰ δὲ καὶ αὐτὸς περιεβάλετο). οὗτος ὁ Σκυλλίης ἐν νόῳ μὲν εἶχε ἄρα καὶ πρότερον αὐτομολήσειν ἐς τοὺς Ἕλληνας, ἀλλ' οὐ γάρ οἱ

παρέσχε ὡς τότε. ὅτεῳ μὲν δὴ τρόπῳ τὸ ἐνθεῦτεν ἔτι ἀπίκετο ἐς τοὺς Ἕλληνας, οὐκ ἔχω εἶπαι ἀτρεκέως, θωυμάζω δέ, εἰ τὰ λεγόμενά ἐστι ἀληθέα. λέγεται γάρ, ὡς ἐξ Ἀφετέων δὺς ἐς τὴν θάλασσαν οὐ πρότερον ἀνέσχε, πρὶν ἢ ἀπίκετο ἐπὶ τὸ Ἀρτεμίσιον, 5 σταδίους μάλιστά κῃ τούτους ἐς ὀγδώκοντα διὰ τῆς θαλάσσης διεξελθών. λέγεται μέν νυν ἄλλα ψευδέσι ἴκελα περὶ τοῦ ἀνδρὸς τούτου, τὰ δὲ μετεξέτερα ἀληθέα. περὶ μέντοι τούτου γνώμη μοι ἀποδεδέχθω πλοίῳ μιν ἀπικέσθαι ἐπὶ τὸ Ἀρτεμίσιον. ὡς δὲ 10 ἀπίκετο, αὐτίκα ἐσήμηνε τοῖσι στρατηγοῖσι τήν τε ναυηγίην ὡς γένοιτο, καὶ τὰς περιπεμφθείσας τῶν νεῶν περὶ Εὔβοιαν.

The Greeks resolve to remain at Artemisium during that day, and in the night to go southward to meet the 200 Persian ships that were sailing round Euboea.

IX. Τοῦτο δὲ ἀκούσαντες οἱ Ἕλληνες λόγον σφίσι αὐτοῖσι ἐδίδοσαν. πολλῶν δὲ λεχθέντων ἐνίκα 15 τὴν ἡμέρην ἐκείνην αὐτοῦ μείναντάς τε καὶ αὐλισθέντας, μετέπειτεν νύκτα μέσην παρέντας πορεύεσθαι καὶ ἀπαντᾶν τῇσι περιπλωούσῃσι τῶν νεῶν. μετὰ δὲ τοῦτο, ὡς οὐδείς σφι ἐπέπλωε, δείλην ὀψίην γινομένην τῆς ἡμέρης φυλάξαντες αὐτοὶ ἐπανέπλωον ἐπὶ 20 τοὺς βαρβάρους, ἀπόπειραν αὐτῶν ποιήσασθαι βουλόμενοι τῆς τε μάχης καὶ τοῦ διεκπλόου.

First Day's Fighting. *Thirty ships of the Persian fleet are captured, but night-fall finds the battle still undecided.*

X. Ὁρέοντες δέ σφεας οἵ τε ἄλλοι στρατιῶται οἱ Ξέρξεω καὶ οἱ στρατηγοὶ ἐπιπλώοντας νηυσὶ ὀλίγῃσι, πάγχυ σφι μανίην ἐπενείκαντες ἀνῆγον καὶ 25 αὐτοὶ τὰς νέας, ἐλπίσαντές σφεας εὐπετέως αἱρήσειν, οἰκότα κάρτα ἐλπίσαντες. τὰς μέν γε τῶν Ἑλλήνων ὁρέοντες ὀλίγας νέας, τὰς δὲ ἑωυτῶν πλήθεί τε πολλαπλησίας καὶ ἄμεινον πλωούσας, καταφρονήσαντες ταῦτα ἐκυκλοῦντο αὐτοὺς ἐς μέσον. ὅσοι μέν νυν τῶν Ἰώνων ἦσαν εὔνοοι τοῖσι Ἕλλησι, ἀέκοντές τε ἐστρατεύοντο, συμφορήν τε ἐποιεῦντο μεγάλην, ὁρέοντες περιεχομένους αὐτοὺς καὶ ἐπιστάμενοι ὡς οὐδεὶς αὐτῶν ἀπονοστήσει· οὕτω ἀσθενέα σφι ἐφαίνετο εἶναι τὰ τῶν Ἑλλήνων πρήγματα. ὅσοισι δὲ καὶ ἡδομένοισι ἦν τὸ γινόμενον, ἅμιλλαν ἐποιεῦντο, ὅκως αὐτὸς ἕκαστος πρῶτος νέα Ἀττικὴν ἑλὼν δῶρα παρὰ βασιλέος λάμψεται. Ἀθηναίων γὰρ αὐτοῖσι λόγος ἦν πλεῖστος ἀνὰ τὰ στρατόπεδα. XI. Τοῖσι δὲ Ἕλλησι ὡς ἐσήμηνε, πρῶτα μὲν ἀντίπρωροι τοῖσι βαρβάροισι γενόμενοι ἐς τὸ μέσον τὰς πρύμνας συνήγαγον, δεύτερα δὲ σημήναντος ἔργου εἴχοντο, ἐν ὀλίγῳ περ ἀπολαμφθέντες καὶ κατὰ στόμα. ἐνθαῦτα τριήκοντα νέας αἱρέουσι τῶν βαρβάρων καὶ τὸν Γόργου τοῦ Σαλαμινίων βασιλέος ἀδελφεὸν Φιλάονα τὸν Χέρσιος, λόγιμον ἐόντα ἐν τῷ στρατοπέδῳ ἄνδρα. πρῶτος δὲ Ἑλλήνων νέα τῶν πολεμίων εἷλε ἀνὴρ Ἀθηναῖος Λυκομήδης Αἰσχραίου, καὶ τὸ ἀριστήιον ἔλαβε οὗτος. τοὺς δ' ἐν τῇ ναυμαχίῃ ταύτῃ ἑτεραλκέως ἀγωνιζομένους νὺξ ἐπελθοῦσα διέλυσε. οἱ μὲν δὴ Ἕλληνες ἐπὶ τὸ Ἀρτεμίσιον ἀπέπλωον, οἱ δὲ βάρβαροι ἐς τὰς Ἀφετάς, πολλὸν παρὰ δόξαν ἀγωνισάμενοι. ἐν ταύτῃ τῇ ναυμαχίῃ Ἀντίδωρος Λήμνιος μοῦνος τῶν σὺν βασιλέι Ἑλλήνων ἐόντων αὐτομολέει ἐς τοὺς Ἕλληνας, καὶ οἱ Ἀθηναῖοι διὰ τοῦτο τὸ ἔργον ἔδοσαν αὐτῷ χῶρον ἐν Σαλαμῖνι.

In the night there is a violent storm of rain and thunder, which terrifies and distresses the Persian fleet at Aphetae,

XII. Ὡς δὲ εὐφρόνη ἐγεγόνεε, ἦν μὲν τῆς ὥρης μέσον θέρος, ἐγίνετο δὲ ὕδωρ τε ἄπλετον διὰ πάσης τῆς νυκτὸς καὶ σκληραὶ βρονταὶ ἀπὸ τοῦ Πηλίου· οἱ δὲ νεκροὶ καὶ τὰ ναυήγια ἐξεφορέοντο ἐς τὰς Ἀφετάς, καὶ περί τε τὰς πρῴρας τῶν νεῶν εἰλέοντο καὶ ἐτάρασσον τοὺς ταρσοὺς τῶν κωπέων. οἱ δὲ στρατιῶται οἱ ταύτῃ ἀκούοντες ταῦτα ἐς φόβον κατιστέατο, ἐλπίζοντες πάγχυ ἀπολέεσθαι ἐς οἷα κακὰ ἧκον· πρὶν γὰρ ἢ καὶ ἀναπνεῦσαί σφεας ἔκ τε τῆς ναυηγίης καὶ τοῦ χειμῶνος τοῦ γενομένου κατὰ Πήλιον, ὑπέλαβε ναυμαχίη καρτερή, ἐκ δὲ τῆς ναυμαχίης ὄμβρος τε λάβρος καὶ ῥεύματα ἰσχυρὰ ἐς θάλασσαν ὁρμημένα βρονταί τε σκληραί.

and entirely destroys the detachment which was sailing round Euboea, driving the ships upon 'The Hollows.'

XIII. Καὶ τούτοισι μὲν τοιαύτη νὺξ ἐγίνετο· τοῖσι δὲ ταχθεῖσι αὐτῶν περιπλώειν Εὔβοιαν ἡ αὐτή περ ἐοῦσα νὺξ πολλὸν ἦν ἔτι ἀγριωτέρη, τοσούτῳ ὅσῳ ἐν πελάγεϊ φερομένοισι ἐπέπιπτε, καὶ τὸ τέλος σφι ἐγένετο ἄχαρι· ὡς γὰρ δὴ πλώουσι αὐτοῖσι χειμών τε καὶ τὸ ὕδωρ ἐπεγίνετο ἐοῦσι κατὰ τὰ Κοῖλα τῆς Εὐβοίης, φερόμενοι τῷ πνεύματι καὶ οὐκ εἰδότες τῇ ἐφέροντο, ἐξέπιπτον πρὸς τὰς πέτρας. ἐποιέετό τε πᾶν ὑπὸ τοῦ θεοῦ, ὅκως ἂν ἐξισωθείη τῷ Ἑλληνικῷ τὸ Περσικὸν μηδὲ πολλῷ πλέον εἴη. Οὗτοι μέν νυν περὶ τὰ Κοῖλα τῆς Εὐβοίης διεφθείροντο.

Second Day. *The Persians at Aphetae after their terrible night attempt no movement. The Greeks are reinforced by 53 Athenian ships, and attack and destroy some Kilikian vessels.*

XIV. Οἱ δὲ ἐν Ἀφετῆσι βάρβαροι, ὥς σφι ἀσμένοισι ἡμέρη ἐπέλαμψε, ἀτρέμας τε εἶχον τὰς νέας, καί σφι ἀπεχρᾶτο κακῶς πρήσσουσι ἡσυχίην ἄγειν ἐν τῷ παρεόντι. τοῖσι δὲ Ἕλλησι ἐπεβοήθεον 5 νέες τρεῖς καὶ πεντήκοντα Ἀττικαί. αὗταί τε δὴ σφεας ἐπέρρωσαν ἀπικόμεναι, καὶ ἅμα ἀγγελίη ἐλθοῦσα ὡς τῶν βαρβάρων οἱ περιπλώοντες τὴν Εὔβοιαν πάντες εἴησαν διεφθαρμένοι ὑπὸ τοῦ γενομένου χειμῶνος. φυλάξαντες δὴ τὴν αὐτὴν ὥρην πλώοντες 10 ἐπέπεσον νηυσὶ Κιλίσσῃσι, ταύτας δὲ διαφθείραντες, ὡς εὐφρόνη ἐγένετο, ἀπέπλωον ὀπίσω ἐπὶ τὸ Ἀρτεμίσιον.

Third Day (*the day of the fall of Leonidas at Thermopylae*). *The Persians advance with their ships arranged in a crescent, far outnumbering the Greeks. There is severe fighting, and the Greeks suffer heavily, but the losses of the Persians are still greater.*

XV. Τρίτῃ δὲ ἡμέρῃ δεινόν τι ποιησάμενοι οἱ στρατηγοὶ τῶν βαρβάρων νέας οὕτω σφι ὀλίγας 15 λυμαίνεσθαι καὶ τὸ ἀπὸ Ξέρξεω δειμαίνοντες οὐκ ἀνέμειναν ἔτι τοὺς Ἕλληνας μάχης ἄρξαι, ἀλλὰ παρακελευσάμενοι κατὰ μέσον ἡμέρης ἀνῆγον τὰς νέας. συνέπιπτε δὲ ὥστε τῇσι αὐτῇσι ἡμέρῃσι τὰς ναυμαχίας γίνεσθαι ταύτας καὶ τὰς πεζομαχίας τὰς 20 ἐν Θερμοπύλῃσι. ἦν δὲ πᾶς ὁ ἀγὼν τοῖσι κατὰ θάλασσαν περὶ τοῦ Εὐρίπου, ὥσπερ τοῖσι ἀμφὶ

Λεωνίδην τὴν ἐσβολὴν φυλάσσειν. οἱ μὲν δὴ παρεκελεύοντο ὅκως μὴ παρήσουσι ἐς τὴν Ἑλλάδα τοὺς βαρβάρους, οἱ δ' ὅκως τὸ Ἑλληνικὸν στράτευμα διαφθείραντες τοῦ πόρου κρατήσουσι. XVI. Ὡς δὲ ταξάμενοι οἱ Ξέρξεω ἐπέπλωον, οἱ Ἕλληνες ἀτρέμας εἶχον πρὸς τῷ Ἀρτεμισίῳ. οἱ δὲ βάρβαροι μηνοειδὲς ποιήσαντες τῶν νεῶν ἐκυκλέοντο, ὡς περιλάβοιεν αὐτούς. ἐνθεῦτεν οἱ Ἕλληνες ἐπανέπλωόν τε καὶ συνέμισγον. ἐν ταύτῃ τῇ ναυμαχίῃ παραπλήσιοι ἀλλήλοισι ἐγένοντο. ὁ γὰρ Ξέρξεω στρατὸς ὑπὸ μεγάθεός τε καὶ πλήθεος αὐτὸς ὑπ' ἑωυτοῦ ἔπιπτε, ταρασσομένων τε τῶν νεῶν καὶ περιπιπτουσέων περὶ ἀλλήλας· ὅμως μέντοι ἀντεῖχε καὶ οὐκ εἶκε· δεινὸν γὰρ χρῆμα ἐποιεῦντο ὑπὸ νεῶν ὀλίγων ἐς φυγὴν τράπεσθαι. πολλαὶ μὲν δὴ τῶν Ἑλλήνων νέες διεφθείροντο, πολλοὶ δὲ ἄνδρες, πολλῷ δ' ἔτι πλεῦνες νέες τε τῶν βαρβάρων καὶ ἄνδρες. Οὕτω δὲ ἀγωνιζόμενοι διέστησαν χωρὶς ἑκάτεροι.

The best in the fight.

XVII. Ἐν ταύτῃ τῇ ναυμαχίῃ Αἰγύπτιοι μὲν τῶν Ξέρξεω στρατιωτέων ἠρίστευσαν, οἳ ἄλλα τε ἔργα μεγάλα ἀπεδέξαντο καὶ νέας αὐτοῖσι ἀνδράσι εἷλον Ἑλληνίδας πέντε. τῶν δὲ Ἑλλήνων κατὰ ταύτην τὴν ἡμέρην ἠρίστευσαν Ἀθηναῖοι, καὶ Ἀθηναίων Κλεινίης ὁ Ἀλκιβιάδεω, ὃς δαπάνην οἰκηίην παρεχόμενος ἐστρατεύετο ἀνδράσι τε διηκοσίοισι καὶ οἰκηίῃ νηΐ·

The Greeks decide to retreat. Themistocles is the leading spirit. They first slaughter as much of the Euboean cattle as they can to prevent the enemy getting them.

XVIII. Ὡς δὲ διέστησαν ἄσμενοι ἑκάτεροι, ἐς ὅρμον ἠπείγοντο. οἱ δὲ Ἕλληνες ὡς διακριθέντες ἐκ τῆς ναυμαχίης ἀπηλλάχθησαν, τῶν μὲν νεκρῶν καὶ τῶν ναυηγίων ἐπεκράτεον, τρηχέως δὲ περιεφθέντες 5 καὶ οὐκ ἥκιστα Ἀθηναῖοι, τῶν αἱ ἡμίσεαι τῶν νεῶν τετρωμέναι ἦσαν, δρησμὸν δὴ ἐβούλευον ἔσω ἐς τὴν Ἑλλάδα. XIX. Νόῳ δὲ λαβὼν ὁ Θεμιστοκλέης, ὡς εἰ ἀπορραγείη ἀπὸ τοῦ βαρβάρου τό τε Ἰωνικὸν φῦλον καὶ τὸ Καρικόν, οἷοί τε εἴησαν ἂν τῶν λοιπῶν 10 κατύπερθε γενέσθαι, ἐλαυνόντων τῶν Εὐβοέων πρόβατα ἐπὶ τὴν θάλασσαν, ταύτῃ συλλέξας τοὺς στρατηγοὺς ἔλεγέ σφι, ὡς δοκέοι ἔχειν τινὰ παλάμην, τῇ ἐλπίζοι τῶν βασιλέος συμμάχων ἀποστήσειν τοὺς ἀρίστους. ταῦτα μέν νυν ἐς τοσοῦτο παρεγύμνου, 15 ἐπὶ δὲ τοῖσι κατήκουσι πρήγμασι τάδε ποιητέα εἶναί σφι ἔλεγε· τῶν τε προβάτων τῶν Εὐβοϊκῶν ὅσα τις ἐθέλοι καταθύειν (κρέσσον γὰρ εἶναι τὴν στρατιὴν ἔχειν ἢ τοὺς πολεμίους) παραίνεέ τε προειπεῖν τοῖσι ἑωυτῶν ἑκάστους πῦρ ἀνακαίειν· κομιδῆς δὲ πέρι τὴν 20 ὥρην αὐτῷ μελήσειν ὥστε ἀσινέας ἀπικέσθαι ἐς τὴν Ἑλλάδα. ταῦτα ἤρεσέ σφι ποιέειν καὶ αὐτίκα πῦρ ἀνακαυσάμενοι ἐτράποντο πρὸς τὰ πρόβατα.

A neglected Oracle.

XX. Οἱ γὰρ Εὐβοέες παραχρησάμενοι τὸν Βάκιδος χρησμὸν ὡς οὐδὲν λέγοντα, οὔτε τι ἐξεκομί- 25 σαντο οὐδὲν οὔτε προεσάξαντο ὡς παρεσομένου σφι πολέμου, περιπετέα τε ἐποιήσαντο σφίσι αὐτοῖσι τὰ πρήγματα. Βάκιδι γὰρ ὧδε ἔχει περὶ τούτων ὁ χρησμός·

Φράζεο, βαρβαρόφωνος ὅταν ζυγὸν εἰς ἅλα βάλλῃ
βίβλινον, Εὐβοίης ἀπέχειν πολυμηκάδας αἶγας.
τούτοισι δὲ οὐδὲν τοῖσι ἔπεσι χρησαμένοισι ἐν τοῖσι 5
τότε παρεοῦσί τε καὶ προσδοκίμοισι κακοῖσι παρῆν
σφι συμφορῇ χρᾶσθαι πρὸς τὰ μέγιστα.

In the evening a scout arrives with news of the disaster at Thermopylae. The Greek fleet accordingly start on their retreat.

XXI. Οἱ μὲν δὴ ταῦτα ἔπρησσον, παρῆν δὲ ὁ ἐκ Τρηχῖνος κατάσκοπος. ἦν μὲν γὰρ ἐπ᾽ Ἀρτεμισίῳ κατάσκοπος Πολύας, γένος Ἀντικυρεύς, τῷ προσετέ- 10 τακτο, καὶ εἶχε πλοῖον κατῆρες ἑτοῖμον, εἰ παλήσειε ὁ ναυτικὸς στρατός, σημαίνειν τοῖσι ἐν Θερμοπύλῃσι ἐοῦσι· ὣς δ᾽ αὕτως ἦν Ἁβρώνιχος ὁ Λυσικλέος Ἀθηναῖος καὶ παρὰ Λεωνίδῃ ἕτοιμος τοῖσι ἐπ᾽ Ἀρτεμισίῳ ἐοῦσι ἀγγέλλειν τριηκοντέρῳ, ἤν τι καταλαμβάνῃ 15 νεώτερον τὸν πεζόν. οὗτος ὦν ὁ Ἁβρώνιχος ἀπικόμενός σφι ἐσήμαινε τὰ γεγονότα περὶ Λεωνίδην καὶ τὸν στρατὸν αὐτοῦ. οἱ δὲ ὡς ἐπύθοντο ταῦτα, οὐκέτι ἐς ἀναβολὰς ἐποιεῦντο τὴν ἀποχώρησιν, ἐκομίζοντο δὲ ὡς ἕκαστοι ἐτάχθησαν, Κορίνθιοι πρῶτοι, ὕστατοι 20 δὲ Ἀθηναῖοι.

The plan of Themistocles for detaching the Ionian allies from Xerxes.

XXII. Ἀθηναίων δὲ νέας τὰς ἄριστα πλωούσας ἐπιλεξάμενος Θεμιστοκλέης ἐπορεύετο περὶ τὰ πότιμα ὕδατα· ἐντάμνων ἐν τοῖσι λίθοισι γράμματα, τὰ

Ἴωνες ἐπελθόντες τῇ ὑστεραίῃ ἡμέρῃ ἐπὶ τὸ Ἀρτεμίσιον ἐπελέξαντο. τὰ δὲ γράμματα τάδε ἔλεγε· "Ἄνδρες Ἴωνες, οὐ ποιέετε δίκαια ἐπὶ τοὺς πατέρας "στρατευόμενοι καὶ τὴν Ἑλλάδα καταδουλούμενοι. 5 "ἀλλὰ μάλιστα μὲν πρὸς ἡμέων γίνεσθε· εἰ δὲ ὑμῖν "ἐστὶ τοῦτο μὴ δυνατὸν ποιῆσαι, ὑμεῖς δὲ ἔτι καὶ νῦν "ἐκ τοῦ μέσου ἡμῖν ἔζεσθε καὶ αὐτοί, καὶ τῶν Καρῶν "δέεσθε τὰ αὐτὰ ὑμῖν ποιέειν· εἰ δὲ μηδέτερον τούτων "οἷόν τε γίνεσθαι, ἀλλ' ὑπ' ἀναγκαίης μέζονος κατέ-10 "ζευχθε ἢ ὥστε ἀπίστασθαι, ὑμεῖς γε ἐν τῷ ἔργῳ, "ἐπεὰν συμμίσγωμεν, ἐθελοκακέετε, μεμνημένοι ὅτι "ἀπ' ἡμέων γεγόνατε καὶ ὅτι ἀρχῆθεν ἡ ἔχθρη πρὸς "τὸν βάρβαρον ἀπ' ὑμέων ἡμῖν γέγονε." Θεμιστοκλῆς δὲ ταῦτα ἔγραψε, δοκέειν ἐμοί, ἐπ' ἀμφότερα νοέων, 15 ἵνα ἢ λαθόντα τὰ γράμματα βασιλέα Ἴωνας ποιήσῃ μεταβαλεῖν καὶ γενέσθαι πρὸς ἑωυτῶν, ἢ ἐπεί τε ἀνενειχθῇ καὶ διαβληθῇ πρὸς Ξέρξην, ἀπίστους ποιήσῃ τοὺς Ἴωνας καὶ τῶν ναυμαχιέων αὐτοὺς ἀπόσχῃ.

Fourth Day. *Next morning the Persians are informed of the retreat of the Greeks, and follow them as far as Histiaea, starting at noon.*

XXIII. Θεμιστοκλῆς μὲν ταῦτα ἐνέγραψε, τοῖσι 20 δὲ βαρβάροισι αὐτίκα μετὰ ταῦτα πλοίῳ ἦλθε ἀνὴρ Ἱστιαιεὺς ἀγγέλλων τὸν δρησμὸν τὸν ἀπ' Ἀρτεμισίου τῶν Ἑλλήνων. οἱ δ' ὑπ' ἀπιστίης τὸν μὲν ἀγγέλλοντα εἶχον ἐν φυλακῇ, νέας δὲ ταχέας ἀπέστειλαν προκατοψομένας. ἀπαγγειλάντων δὲ τούτων 25 τὰ ἦν, οὕτω δὴ ἅμα ἡλίῳ σκιδναμένῳ πᾶσα ἡ στρατιὴ ἔπλωε ἁλὴς ἐπὶ τὸ Ἀρτεμίσιον. ἐπισχόντες δὲ ἐν τούτῳ τῷ χώρῳ μέχρι μέσου ἡμέρης, τὸ ἀπὸ τούτου ἔπλωον ἐς Ἱστιαίην. ἀπικόμενοι δὲ τὴν πόλιν ἔσχον τῶν Ἱστιαιέων, καὶ τῆς Ἐλλοπίης μοίρης, γῆς δὲ τῆς Ἱστιαιήτιδος τὰς παραθαλασσίας κώμας πάσας ἐπέδραμον.

At Histiaea the men of the Persian fleet are invited by Xerxes to cross to the mainland to view the slaughtered Greeks at Thermopylae. Xerxes contrives to conceal the amount of his own loss.

XXIV. Ἐνθαῦτα δὲ τούτων ἐόντων Ξέρξης ἑτοιμασάμενος τὰ περὶ τοὺς νεκροὺς ἔπεμπε ἐς τὸν ναυτικὸν στρατὸν κήρυκα· προετοιμάσατο δὲ τάδε· ὅσοι τοῦ στρατοῦ τοῦ ἑωυτοῦ ἦσαν νεκροὶ ἐν Θερμοπύλῃσι (ἦσαν δὲ καὶ δύο μυριάδες), ὑπολιπόμενος τούτων ὡς χιλίους, τοὺς λοιποὺς τάφρους ὀρυξάμενος ἔθαψε, φυλλάδα τε ἐπιβαλὼν καὶ γῆν ἐπαμησάμενος, ἵνα μὴ ὀφθείησαν ὑπὸ τοῦ ναυτικοῦ στρατοῦ. ὡς δὲ διέβη ἐς τὴν Ἱστιαίην ὁ κῆρυξ, σύλλογον ποιησάμενος παντὸς τοῦ στρατοπέδου ἔλεγε τάδε· "Ἄνδρες "σύμμαχοι, βασιλεὺς Ξέρξης τῷ βουλομένῳ ὑμέων "παραδιδοῖ ἐκλιπόντα τὴν τάξιν καὶ ἐλθόντα θηή- "σασθαι, ὅκως μάχεται πρὸς τοὺς ἀνοήτους τῶν "ἀνθρώπων, οἳ ἤλπισαν τὴν βασιλέος δύναμιν ὑπερ- "βαλέεσθαι." XXV. Ταῦτα ἐπαγγειλαμένου, μετὰ ταῦτα οὐδὲν ἐγίνετο πλοίων σπανιώτερον. οὕτω πολλοὶ ἤθελον θηήσασθαι. διαπεραιωθέντες δὲ ἐθηεῦντο διεξιόντες τοὺς νεκρούς· πάντες δὲ ἠπιστέατο τοὺς κειμένους εἶναι πάντας Λακεδαιμονίους καὶ Θεσπιέας, ὁρέοντες καὶ τοὺς εἵλωτας. οὐ μὲν οὐδ' ἐλάνθανε τοὺς διαβεβηκότας Ξέρξης ταῦτα πρήξας περὶ τοὺς νεκροὺς τοὺς ἑωυτοῦ· καὶ γὰρ δὴ καὶ

γελοῖον ἦν· τῶν μὲν χίλιοι ἐφαίνοντο νεκροὶ κείμενοι,
οἱ δὲ πάντες ἐκέατο ἁλέες συγκεκομισμένοι ἐς τὠυτὸ
χωρίον, τέσσερες χιλιάδες. ταύτην μὲν τὴν ἡμέρην
πρὸς θέην ἐτράποντο, τῇ δ' ὑστεραίῃ οἱ μὲν ἀπέπλωον
5 ἐς Ἱστιαίην ἐπὶ τὰς νέας, οἱ δὲ ἀμφὶ Ξέρξην ἐς ὁδὸν
ὡρμέατο.

The Olympic Games [*July*, B.C. 480].

XXVI. Ἧκον δέ σφι αὐτόμολοι ἄνδρες ἀπ'
Ἀρκαδίης ὀλίγοι τινές, βίου τε δεόμενοι καὶ ἐνεργοὶ
βουλόμενοι εἶναι. ἄγοντες δὲ τούτους ἐς ὄψιν τὴν
10 βασιλέος ἐπυνθάνοντο οἱ Πέρσαι περὶ τῶν Ἑλλήνων τὰ ποιέοιεν· εἷς δέ τις πρὸ πάντων ἦν ὁ εἰρωτέων
αὐτοὺς ταῦτα. οἱ δέ σφι ἔλεγον, ὡς Ὀλύμπια
ἄγοιεν καὶ θεωρέοιεν ἀγῶνα γυμνικὸν καὶ ἱππικόν.
ὁ δὲ ἐπείρετο, ὅ τι τὸ ἄεθλον εἴη σφι κείμενον, περὶ
15 ὅτευ ἀγωνίζονται· οἱ δ' εἶπον τῆς ἐλαίης τὸν διδόμενον στέφανον. ἐνθαῦτα εἴπας γνώμην γενναιοτά-
την Τιγράνης ὁ Ἀρταβάνου δειλίην ὦφλε πρὸς
βασιλέος. πυνθανόμενος γὰρ τὸ ἄεθλον ἐὸν στέφανον, ἀλλ' οὐ χρήματα, οὔτε ἠνέσχετο σιγῶν εἶπέ τε
20 ἐς πάντας τάδε· "Παπαί, Μαρδόνιε, κοίους ἐπ' ἄνδρας
"ἤγαγες μαχεσομένους ἡμέας, οἳ οὐ περὶ χρημάτων
"τὸν ἀγῶνα ποιεῦνται, ἀλλὰ περὶ ἀρετῆς."

The quarrels of the Phocians and Thessalians. A Thessalian invasion repelled.

XXVII. Τούτῳ μὲν δὴ ταῦτα εἴρητο, ἐν δὲ τῷ
διὰ μέσου χρόνῳ, ἐπεί τε τὸ ἐν Θερμοπύλῃσι τρῶμα
25 ἐγεγόνεε, αὐτίκα Θεσσαλοὶ πέμπουσι κήρυκα ἐς Φωκέας, ἅτε σφι ἐνέχοντες αἰεὶ χόλον, ἀπὸ δὲ τοῦ

ὑστάτου τρώματος καὶ τὸ κάρτα. ἐσβαλόντες γὰρ
πανστρατιῇ αὐτοί τε οἱ Θεσσαλοὶ καὶ οἱ σύμμαχοι
αὐτῶν ἐς τοὺς Φωκέας οὐ πολλοῖσι ἔτεσι πρότερον
ταύτης τῆς βασιλέος στρατηλασίης ἐσσώθησαν ὑπὸ
τῶν Φωκέων καὶ περιέφθησαν τρηχέως. ἐπεί τε γὰρ 5
κατειλήθησαν ἐς τὸν Παρνησὸν οἱ Φωκέες ἔχοντες
μάντιν Τελλίην τὸν Ἠλεῖον, ἐνθαῦτα ὁ Τελλίης
οὗτος σοφίζεται αὐτοῖσι τοιόνδε· γυψώσας ἄνδρας
ἑξακοσίους τῶν Φωκέων τοὺς ἀρίστους, αὐτούς τε
τούτους καὶ τὰ ὅπλα αὐτῶν, νυκτὸς ἐπεθήκατο τοῖσι 10
Θεσσαλοῖσι, προείπας αὐτοῖσι, τὸν ἂν μὴ λευκανθί-
ζοντα ἴδωνται, τοῦτον κτείνειν. τούτους ὦν αἵ τε
φυλακαὶ τῶν Θεσσαλῶν πρῶται ἰδοῦσαι ἐφοβήθη-
σαν, δόξασαι ἄλλο τι εἶναι τέρας, καὶ μετὰ τὰς
φυλακὰς αὐτὴ ἡ στρατιὴ οὕτω ὥστε τετρακισχιλίων 15
κρατῆσαι νεκρῶν καὶ ἀσπίδων Φωκέας, τῶν τὰς μὲν
ἡμισέας ἐς Ἄβας ἀνέθεσαν, τὰς δὲ ἐς Δελφούς· ἡ δὲ
δεκάτη ἐγένετο τῶν χρημάτων ἐκ ταύτης τῆς μάχης
οἱ μεγάλοι ἀνδριάντες οἱ περὶ τὸν τρίποδα συνεστεῶτες ἔμπροσθε τοῦ νηοῦ τοῦ ἐν Δελφοῖσι, καὶ ἕτεροι 20
τοιοῦτοι ἐν Ἄβῃσι ἀνακέαται. XXVIII. Ταῦτα
μέν νυν τὸν πεζὸν ἐργάσαντο τῶν Θεσσαλῶν οἱ
Φωκέες, πολιορκέοντας ἑωυτούς, ἐσβαλοῦσαν δὲ ἐς
τὴν χώρην τὴν ἵππον αὐτῶν ἐλυμήναντο ἀνηκέστως.
ἐν γὰρ τῇ ἐσβολῇ, ἥ ἐστι κατὰ Ὑάμπολιν, ἐν ταύτῃ 25
τάφρον μεγάλην ὀρύξαντες ἀμφορέας κεινοὺς ἐς αὐτὴν κατέθηκαν, χοῦν δὲ ἐπιφορήσαντες καὶ ὁμοιώ-
σαντες τῷ ἄλλῳ χώρῳ ἐδέκοντο τοὺς Θεσσαλοὺς
ἐσβάλλοντας. οἱ δέ, ὡς ἀναρπασόμενοι τοὺς Φωκέας,
φερόμενοι ἐσέπεσον ἐς τοὺς ἀμφορέας. ἐνθαῦτα οἱ 30
ἵπποι τὰ σκέλεα διεφθάρησαν.

The Thessalians offer for a large indemnity to avert a Persian invasion from Phocis.

XXIX. Τούτων δὴ σφι ἀμφοτέρων ἔχοντες ἔγκοτον οἱ Θεσσαλοὶ πέμψαντες κήρυκα ἠγόρευον τάδε· "Ὦ Φωκέες, ἤδη τι μᾶλλον γνωσιμαχέετε μὴ "εἶναι ὁμοῖοι ἡμῖν. πρόσθε τε γὰρ ἐν τοῖσι Ἕλλησι,
5 "ὅσον χρόνον ἐκεῖνα ἡμῖν ἤνδανε, πλέον αἰεί κοτε "ὑμέων ἐφερόμεθα, νῦν τε παρὰ τῷ βαρβάρῳ τοσοῦτο "δυνάμεθα, ὥστε ἐπ' ἡμῖν ἐστι τῆς γῆς τε ἐστερῆσθαι "καὶ πρὸς ἠνδραποδίσθαι ὑμέας· ἡμεῖς μέντοι τὸ πᾶν "ἔχοντες οὐ μνησικακέομεν, ἀλλ' ἡμῖν γενέσθω ἀντ'
10 "αὐτῶν πεντήκοντα τάλαντα ἀργυρίου, καὶ ὑμῖν ὑπο- "δεκόμεθα τὰ ἐπιόντα ἐπὶ τὴν χώρην ἀποτρέψειν."

The Phocians refuse.

XXX. Ταῦτά σφι ἐπηγγέλλοντο οἱ Θεσσαλοί. οἱ γὰρ Φωκέες μοῦνοι τῶν ταύτῃ ἀνθρώπων οὐκ ἐμήδιζον, κατ' ἄλλο μὲν οὐδέν, ὡς ἐγὼ συμβαλλό-
15 μενος εὑρίσκω, κατὰ δὲ τὸ ἔχθος τὸ Θεσσαλῶν· εἰ δὲ Θεσσαλοὶ τὰ Ἑλλήνων αὖξον, ὡς ἐμοὶ δοκέειν, ἐμήδιζον ἂν οἱ Φωκέες. ταῦτα ἐπαγγελλομένων Θεσσαλῶν οὔτε δώσειν ἔφασαν χρήματα παρέχειν τέ σφισι Θεσσαλοῖσι ὁμοίως μηδίζειν, εἰ ἄλλως βου-
20 λοίατο· ἀλλ' οὐκ ἔσεσθαι ἑκόντες εἶναι προδόται τῆς Ἑλλάδος.

The Thessalians therefore guide the Persians into Phocis. The inhabitants retreat, some to Parnassus, others to the country of the Ozolian Locrians. The Persians lay waste Locris with fire and sword.

XXXI. Ἐπειδὴ δὲ ἀνηνείχθησαν οὗτοι οἱ λόγοι, οὕτω δὴ οἱ Θεσσαλοὶ κεχολωμένοι τοῖσι Φωκεῦσι

ΟΥΡΑΝΙΑ

ἐγένοντο ἡγεμόνες τῷ βαρβάρῳ τῆς ὁδοῦ. ἐκ μὲν δὴ τῆς Τρηχινίης ἐς τὴν Δωρίδα ἐσέβαλον. τῆς γὰρ Δωρίδος χώρης ποδεὼν στεινὸς ταύτῃ κατατείνει, ὡς τριήκοντα σταδίων μάλιστά κῃ εὖρος, κείμενος μεταξὺ τῆς τε Μηλίδος καὶ τῆς Φωκίδος χώρης, ἥ περ ἦν τὸ παλαιὸν Δρυοπίς· ἡ δὲ χώρη αὕτη ἐστὶ μητρόπολις Δωριέων τῶν ἐν Πελοποννήσῳ. ταύτην ὦν τὴν Δωρίδα γῆν οὐκ ἐσίναντο ἐσβαλόντες οἱ βάρβαροι· ἐμήδιζόν τε γὰρ καὶ οὐκ ἐδόκεε Θεσσαλοῖσι. XXXII. Ὡς δὲ ἐκ τῆς Δωρίδος ἐς τὴν Φωκίδα ἐσέβαλον, αὐτοὺς μὲν τοὺς Φωκέας οὐκ αἱρέουσι. οἱ μὲν γὰρ τῶν Φωκέων ἐς τὰ ἄκρα τοῦ Παρνησοῦ ἀνέβησαν (ἔστι δὲ καὶ ἐπιτηδέη δέξασθαι ὅμιλον τοῦ Παρνησοῦ ἡ κορυφή, κατὰ Νέωνα πόλιν κειμένη ἐπ' ἑωυτῆς, Τιθορέα οὔνομα αὐτῇ, ἐς τὴν δὴ ἀνηνείκαντο καὶ αὐτοὶ ἀνέβησαν), οἱ δὲ πλεῦνες αὐτῶν ἐς τοὺς Ὀζόλας Λοκροὺς ἐξεκομίσαντο, ἐς Ἄμφισσαν πόλιν τὴν ὑπὲρ τοῦ Κρισαίου πεδίου οἰκεομένην. οἱ δὲ βάρβαροι τὴν χώρην πᾶσαν ἐπέδραμον τὴν Φωκίδα· Θεσσαλοὶ γὰρ οὕτω ἦγον τὸν στρατόν· ὁκόσα δὲ ἐπέσχον, πάντα ἐπέφλεγον καὶ ἔκειρον, καὶ ἐς τὰς πόλις ἐνιέντες πῦρ καὶ ἐς τὰ ἱρά. XXXIII. Πορευόμενοι γὰρ ταύτῃ παρὰ τὸν Κηφισὸν ποταμὸν ἐδηίουν πάντα· καὶ κατὰ μὲν ἔκαυσαν Δρυμὸν πόλιν, κατὰ δὲ Χαράδρην καὶ Ἔρωχον καὶ Τεθρώνιον καὶ Ἀμφίκαιαν καὶ Νέωνα καὶ Πεδιέας καὶ Τριτέας καὶ Ἐλάτειαν καὶ Ὑάμπολιν καὶ Παραποταμίους καὶ Ἄβας, ἔνθα ἦν ἱρὸν Ἀπόλλωνος πλούσιον, θησαυροῖσί τε καὶ ἀναθήμασι πολλοῖσι κατεσκευασμένον· ἦν δὲ καὶ τότε καὶ νῦν ἐστὶ χρηστήριον αὐτόθι· καὶ τοῦτο τὸ ἱρὸν συλήσαντες ἐνέπρησαν. καί τινας

H. VIII.

διώκοντες εἷλον τῶν Φωκέων πρὸς τοῖσι οὔρεσι, καὶ γυναῖκάς τινας διέφθειραν.

The Persian army arrives at Panopeis on the frontier of Boeotia. There it divided into two columns; the stronger of the two with Xerxes himself advanced into Boeotia; the other took guides and wound round Parnassus with the view of attacking the temple of Delphi, wasting the country as they went.

XXXIV. Παραποταμίους δὲ παραμειβόμενοι οἱ βάρβαροι ἀπίκοντο ἐς Πανοπέας. ἐνθεῦτεν δὲ ἤδη διακρινομένη ἡ στρατιὴ αὐτῶν ἐσχίζετο. τὸ μὲν πλεῖστον καὶ δυνατώτατον τοῦ στρατοῦ ἅμα αὐτῷ Ξέρξῃ πορευόμενον ἐπ' Ἀθήνας ἐσέβαλε ἐς Βοιωτούς, ἐς γῆν τὴν Ὀρχομενίων. Βοιωτῶν δὲ πᾶν τὸ πλῆθος ἐμήδιζε, τὰς δὲ πόλις αὐτῶν ἄνδρες Μακεδόνες διατεταγμένοι ἔσωζον, ὑπὸ Ἀλεξάνδρου ἀποπεμφθέντες. ἔσωζον δὲ τῇδε, βουλόμενοι δῆλον ποιέειν Ξέρξῃ, ὅτι τὰ Μήδων Βοιωτοὶ φρονέοιεν. Οὗτοι μὲν δὴ τῶν βαρβάρων ταύτῃ ἐτράποντο. XXXV. ἄλλοι δὲ αὐτῶν ἡγεμόνας ἔχοντες ὡρμέατο ἐπὶ τὸ ἱρὸν τὸ ἐν Δελφοῖσι, ἐν δεξιῇ τὸν Παρνησὸν ἀπέργοντες. ὅσα δὲ καὶ οὗτοι ἐπέσχον τῆς Φωκίδος, πάντα ἐσιναμώρεον· καὶ γὰρ τῶν Πανοπέων τὴν πόλιν ἐνέπρησαν καὶ Δαυλίων καὶ Αἰολιδέων. ἐπορεύοντο δὲ ταύτῃ ἀποσχισθέντες τῆς ἄλλης στρατιῆς τῶνδε εἵνεκεν, ὅκως συλήσαντες τὸ ἱρὸν τὸ ἐν Δελφοῖσι βασιλέϊ Ξέρξῃ ἀποδέξαιεν τὰ χρήματα. πάντα δ' ἠπίστατο τὰ ἐν τῷ ἱρῷ ὅσα λόγου ἦν ἄξια Ξέρξης, ὡς ἐγὼ πυνθάνομαι, ἄμεινον ἢ τὰ ἐν τοῖσι οἰκίοισι ἔλιπε, πολλῶν αἰεὶ λεγόντων, καὶ μάλιστα τὰ Κροίσου τοῦ Ἀλυάττεω ἀναθήματα.

The God will protect his own. The Delphians send their women and children across to Achaia.

XXXVI. Οἱ δὲ Δελφοὶ πυνθανόμενοι ταῦτα ἐς πᾶσαν ἀρρωδίην ἀπίκατο, ἐν δείματι δὲ μεγάλῳ κατεστεῶτες ἐμαντεύοντο περὶ τῶν ἱρῶν χρημάτων, εἴτε σφέα κατὰ γῆς κατορύξωσι εἴτε ἐκκομίσωσι ἐς ἄλλην χώρην. ὁ δὲ θεός σφεας οὐκ ἔα κινέειν, φὰς 5 αὐτὸς ἱκανὸς εἶναι τῶν ἑωυτοῦ προκατῆσθαι. Δελφοὶ δὲ ταῦτα ἀκούσαντες σφέων αὐτῶν πέρι ἐφρόντιζον. τέκνα μέν νυν καὶ γυναῖκας πέρην ἐς τὴν Ἀχαιίην διέπεμψαν, αὐτῶν δὲ οἱ μὲν πλεῖστοι ἀνέβησαν ἐς τοῦ Παρνησοῦ τὰς κορυφὰς καὶ ἐς τὸ Κωρύκιον 10 ἄντρον ἀνηνείκαντο, οἱ δὲ ἐς Ἄμφισσαν τὴν Λοκρίδα ὑπεξῆλθον. πάντες δὲ ὦν οἱ Δελφοὶ ἐξέλιπον τὴν πόλιν πλὴν ἑξήκοντα ἀνδρῶν καὶ τοῦ προφήτεω.

The miraculous preservation of Delphi. The barbarians retreat towards Boeotia.

XXXVII. Ἐπεὶ δὲ ἀγχοῦ τε ἦσαν οἱ βάρβαροι ἐπιόντες καὶ ἀπώρεον τὸ ἱρόν, ἐν τούτῳ ὁ προφήτης, 15 τῷ οὔνομα ἦν Ἀκήρατος, ὁρᾷ πρὸ τοῦ νηοῦ ὅπλα προκείμενα ἔσωθεν ἐκ τοῦ μεγάρου ἐξενηνειγμένα ἱρά, τῶν οὐκ ὅσιον ἦν ἅπτεσθαι ἀνθρώπων οὐδενί. ὁ μὲν δὴ ἤιε Δελφῶν τοῖσι παρεοῦσι σημανέων τὸ τέρας, οἱ δὲ βάρβαροι ἐπειδὴ ἐγίνοντο ἐπειγόμενοι 20 κατὰ τὸ ἱρὸν τῆς Προνηίης Ἀθηναίης, ἐπιγίνεταί σφι τέρεα ἔτι μέζονα τοῦ πρὶν γενομένου τέρεος. θῶυμα μὲν γὰρ καὶ τοῦτο κάρτα ἐστί, ὅπλα ἀρήια αὐτόματα φανῆναι ἔξω προκείμενα τοῦ νηοῦ· τὰ δὲ δὴ ἐπὶ τούτῳ δεύτερα ἐπιγενόμενα καὶ διὰ πάντων 25 φασμάτων ἄξια θωυμάσαι μάλιστα. ἐπεὶ γὰρ δὴ ἦσαν ἐπιόντες οἱ βάρβαροι κατὰ τὸ ἱρὸν τῆς Προνηίης Ἀθηναίης, ἐν τούτῳ ἐκ μὲν τοῦ οὐρανοῦ κεραυνοὶ αὐτοῖσι ἐνέπιπτον, ἀπὸ δὲ τοῦ Παρνησοῦ ἀπορραγεῖσαι δύο κορυφαὶ ἐφέροντο πολλῷ πατάγῳ ἐς αὐτοὺς καὶ κατέλαβον συχνούς σφεων, ἐκ δὲ τοῦ ἱροῦ τῆς Προνηίης βοή τι καὶ ἀλαλαγμὸς ἐγίνετο. XXXVIII. Συμμιγέντων δὲ τούτων πάντων φόβος τοῖσι βαρβάροισι ἐνεπεπτώκεε. μαθόντες δὲ οἱ Δελφοὶ φεύγοντάς σφεας, ἐπικαταβάντες ἀπέκτειναν πλῆθός τι αὐτῶν. οἱ δὲ περιεόντες ἰθὺ Βοιωτῶν ἔφευγον. ἔλεγον δὲ οἱ ἀπονοστήσαντες οὗτοι τῶν βαρβάρων, ὡς ἐγὼ πυνθάνομαι, ὡς πρὸς τούτοισι καὶ ἄλλα ὥρεον θεῖα· δύο γὰρ ὁπλίτας μέζονας ἢ κατὰ ἀνθρώπων φύσιν ἔχοντας ἕπεσθαί σφι κτείνοντας καὶ διώκοντας. XXXIX. Τούτους δὲ τοὺς δύο Δελφοὶ λέγουσι εἶναι ἐπιχωρίους ἥρωας, Φύλακόν τε καὶ Αὐτόνοον, τῶν τὰ τεμένεά ἐστι περὶ τὸ ἱρόν, Φυλάκου μὲν παρ᾿ αὐτὴν τὴν ὁδὸν κατύπερθε τοῦ ἱροῦ τῆς Προνηίης, Αὐτονόου δὲ πέλας τῆς Κασταλίης ὑπὸ τῇ Ὑαμπείῃ κορυφῇ. οἱ δὲ πεσόντες ἀπὸ τοῦ Παρνησοῦ λίθοι ἔτι καὶ ἐς ἡμέας ἦσαν σῶοι, ἐν τῷ τεμένεϊ τῆς Προνηίης Ἀθηναίης κείμενοι, ἐς τὸ ἐνέσκηψαν διὰ τῶν βαρβάρων φερόμενοι. Τούτων μέν νυν τῶν ἀνδρῶν αὕτη ἀπὸ τοῦ ἱροῦ ἀπαλλαγὴ γίνεται.

Meanwhile the Greek fleet arrive at Salamis, where on the entreaty of the Athenians they anchor.

XL. Ὁ δὲ Ἑλλήνων ναυτικὸς στρατὸς ἀπὸ τοῦ Ἀρτεμισίου Ἀθηναίων δεηθέντων ἐς Σαλαμῖνα κατίσχει τὰς νέας. τῶνδε δὲ εἵνεκεν προσεδεήθησαν

αὐτῶν σχεῖν πρὸς Σαλαμῖνα Ἀθηναῖοι, ἵνα αὐτοὶ
παῖδάς τε καὶ γυναῖκας ὑπεξαγάγωνται ἐκ τῆς Ἀττικῆς, πρὸς δὲ καὶ βουλεύσωνται τὸ ποιητέον αὐτοῖσι
ἔσται. ἐπὶ γὰρ τοῖσι κατήκουσι πρήγμασι βουλὴν
ἔμελλον ποιήσεσθαι ὡς ἐψευσμένοι γνώμης. δοκέ- 5
οντες γὰρ εὑρήσειν Πελοποννησίους πανδημεὶ ἐν τῇ
Βοιωτίῃ ὑποκατημένους τὸν βάρβαρον τῶν μὲν εὗρον
οὐδὲν ἐόν, οἱ δὲ ἐπυνθάνοντο τὸν Ἰσθμὸν αὐτοὺς
τειχέοντας, τὴν Πελοπόννησον περὶ πλείστου τε
ποιευμένους περιεῖναι καὶ ταύτην ἔχοντας ἐν φυλακῇ, 10
τὰ δὲ ἄλλα ἀπιέναι. ταῦτα πυνθανόμενοι οὕτω δὴ
προσεδεήθησάν σφεων σχεῖν πρὸς τὴν Σαλαμῖνα.

The Athenian ships are employed in conveying their families to Troezen, Aegina and Salamis. The disappearance of the sacred serpent.

XLI. Οἱ μὲν δὴ ἄλλοι κατέσχον ἐς τὴν Σαλαμῖνα, Ἀθηναῖοι δὲ ἐς τὴν ἑωυτῶν. μετὰ δὲ τὴν
ἄπιξιν κήρυγμα ἐποιήσαντο, Ἀθηναίων τῇ τις δύνα- 15
ται σώζειν τὰ τέκνα τε καὶ τοὺς οἰκέτας. ἐνθαῦτα
οἱ μὲν πλεῖστοι ἐς Τροιζῆνα ἀπέστειλαν, οἱ δὲ ἐς
Αἴγιναν, οἱ δὲ ἐς Σαλαμῖνα. ἔσπευσαν δὲ ταῦτα
ὑπεκθέσθαι τῷ χρηστηρίῳ τε βουλόμενοι ὑπηρετέειν
καὶ δὴ καὶ τοῦδε εἵνεκεν οὐκ ἥκιστα· λέγουσι Ἀθη- 20
ναῖοι ὄφιν μέγαν φύλακον τῆς ἀκροπόλιος ἐνδιαι-
τᾶσθαι ἐν τῷ ἱρῷ. λέγουσί τε ταῦτα καὶ δὴ καὶ ὡς
ἐόντι ἐπιμήνια ἐπιτελέουσι προτιθέντες· τὰ δ᾽ ἐπιμήνια μελιτόεσσά ἐστι. αὕτη δ᾽ ἡ μελιτόεσσα ἐν τῷ
πρόσθε αἰεὶ χρόνῳ ἀναισιμουμένη τότε ἦν ἄψαυστος. 25
σημηνάσης δὲ ταῦτα τῆς ἰρείης μᾶλλόν τι οἱ Ἀθηναῖοι καὶ προθυμότερον ἐξέλιπον τὴν πόλιν ὡς καὶ

τῆς θεοῦ ἀπολελοιπυίης τὴν ἀκρόπολιν. ὡς δέ σφι πάντα ὑπεξεκέετο, ἔπλωον ἐς τὸ στρατόπεδον.

The Greek fleet at Salamis reinforced by contingents which had mustered at Troezen.

XLII. Ἐπεὶ δὲ οἱ ἀπ' Ἀρτεμισίου ἐς Σαλαμῖνα κατέσχον τὰς νέας, συνέρρεε καὶ ὁ λοιπὸς πυνθανόμενος ὁ τῶν Ἑλλήνων ναυτικὸς στρατὸς ἐκ Τροιζῆνος· ἐς γὰρ Πώγωνα τὸν Τροιζηνίων λιμένα προείρητο συλλέγεσθαι. συνελέχθησάν τε δὴ πολλῷ πλεῦνες νέες ἢ ἐπ' Ἀρτεμισίῳ ἐναυμάχεον, καὶ ἀπὸ πολίων πλεύνων. ναύαρχος μέν νυν ἐπῆν ὡυτὸς ὅς περ ἐπ' Ἀρτεμισίῳ, Εὐρυβιάδης Εὐρυκλείδεω ἀνὴρ Σπαρτιήτης, οὐ μέντοι γενεός γε τοῦ βασιληίου ἐών. νέας δὲ πολλῷ πλείστας τε καὶ ἄριστα πλωούσας παρείχοντο Ἀθηναῖοι.

The numbers of the ships contributed by each State.

XLIII. Ἐστρατεύοντο δὲ οἵδε· ἐκ μὲν Πελοποννήσου Λακεδαιμόνιοι ἑκκαίδεκα νέας παρεχόμενοι, Κορίνθιοι δὲ τὸ αὐτὸ πλήρωμα παρεχόμενοι τὸ καὶ ἐπ' Ἀρτεμισίῳ, Σικυώνιοι δὲ πεντεκαίδεκα παρείχοντο νέας, Ἐπιδαύριοι δὲ δέκα, Τροιζήνιοι δὲ πέντε, Ἑρμιονέες δὲ τρεῖς, ἐόντες οὗτοι πλὴν Ἑρμιονέων Δωρικόν τε καὶ Μακεδνὸν ἔθνος, ἐξ Ἐρινεοῦ τε καὶ Πίνδου καὶ τῆς Δρυοπίδος ὕστατα ὁρμηθέντες. οἱ δὲ Ἑρμιονέες εἰσὶ Δρύοπες, ὑπὸ Ἡρακλέος τε καὶ Μηλιέων ἐκ τῆς νῦν Δωρίδος καλεομένης χώρης ἐξαναστάντες.

[*Why the Plataeans were absent. The names borne by the Athenians at different epochs.*]

XLIV. Οὗτοι μὲν νυν Πελοποννησίων ἐστρατεύοντο, οἱ δὲ ἐκ τῆς ἔξω ἠπείρου, Ἀθηναῖοι μὲν πρὸς πάντας τοὺς ἄλλους παρεχόμενοι νέας ὀγδώκοντα καὶ ἑκατόν, μοῦνοι· ἐν Σαλαμῖνι γὰρ οὐ συνεναυμάχησαν Πλαταιέες Ἀθηναίοισι διὰ τοιόνδε τι πρῆγμα· ἀπαλλασσομένων τῶν Ἑλλήνων ἀπὸ τοῦ Ἀρτεμισίου, ὡς ἐγίνοντο κατὰ Χαλκίδα, οἱ Πλαταιέες ἀποβάντες ἐς τὴν περαίην τῆς Βοιωτίης χώρης πρὸς ἐκκομιδὴν ἐτράποντο τῶν οἰκετέων. οὗτοι μὲν νυν τούτους σώζοντες ἐλείφθησαν, Ἀθηναῖοι δὲ ἐπὶ μὲν Πελασγῶν ἐχόντων τὴν νῦν Ἑλλάδα καλεομένην ἦσαν Πελασγοί, οὐνομαζόμενοι Κραναοί, ἐπὶ δὲ Κέκροπος βασιλέος ἐπεκλήθησαν Κεκροπίδαι, ἐκδεξαμένου δὲ Ἐρεχθέος τὴν ἀρχὴν Ἀθηναῖοι μετουνομάσθησαν, Ἴωνος δὲ τοῦ Ξούθου στρατάρχεω γενομένου Ἀθηναίοισι ἐκλήθησαν ἀπὸ τούτου Ἴωνες·

The contributions of the various States continued.

XLV. Μεγαρέες δὲ τὠυτὸ πλήρωμα παρείχοντο καὶ ἐπ᾽ Ἀρτεμισίῳ, Ἀμπρακιῶται δὲ ἑπτὰ νέας ἔχοντες ἐπεβώθησαν, Λευκάδιοι δὲ τρεῖς, ἔθνος ἐόντες οὗτοι Δωρικὸν ἀπὸ Κορίνθου. XLVI. Νησιωτέων δὲ Αἰγινῆται τριήκοντα παρείχοντο. ἦσαν μέν σφι καὶ ἄλλαι πεπληρωμέναι νέες, ἀλλὰ τῇσι μὲν τὴν ἑωυτῶν ἐφύλασσον, τριήκοντα δὲ τῇσι ἄριστα πλωούσῃσι ἐν Σαλαμῖνι ἐναυμάχησαν. Αἰγινῆται δέ εἰσι Δωριέες ἀπὸ Ἐπιδαύρου· τῇ δὲ νήσῳ πρότερον οὔνομα ἦν Οἰνώνη. μετὰ δὲ Αἰγινήτας Χαλκιδέες τὰς ἐπ᾽ Ἀρτεμισίῳ εἴκοσι παρεχόμενοι καὶ Ἐρετριέες

τὰς ἑπτά· οὗτοι δὲ Ἴωνές εἰσι. μετὰ δὲ Κεῖοι τὰ
αὐτὰς παρεχόμενοι, ἔθνος ἐὸν Ἰωνικὸν ἀπὸ Ἀθηνέων.
Νάξιοι δὲ παρείχοντο τέσσερας, ἀποπεμφθέντες μὲν
ἐς τοὺς Μήδους ὑπὸ τῶν πολιητέων, κατά περ ὧλλοι
5 νησιῶται, ἀλογήσαντες δὲ τῶν ἐντολέων ἀπίκατο ἐς
τοὺς Ἕλληνας Δημοκρίτου σπεύσαντος, ἀνδρὸς τῶν
ἀστῶν δοκίμου καὶ τότε τριηραρχέοντος· Νάξιοι δέ
εἰσι Ἴωνες ἀπ' Ἀθηνέων γεγονότες. Στυρέες δὲ τὰς
αὐτὰς παρείχοντο νέας τὰς καὶ ἐπ' Ἀρτεμισίῳ, Κύθ-
10 νιοι δὲ μίαν καὶ πεντηκόντερον, ἐόντες συναμφότεροι
οὗτοι Δρύοπες. καὶ Σερίφιοί τε καὶ Σίφνιοι καὶ
Μήλιοι ἐστρατεύοντο· οὗτοι γὰρ οὐκ ἔδοσαν μοῦνοι
νησιωτέων τῷ βαρβάρῳ γῆν τε καὶ ὕδωρ. XLVII.
Οὗτοι μὲν ἅπαντες ἐντὸς οἰκημένοι Θεσπρωτῶν καὶ
15 Ἀχέροντος ποταμοῦ ἐστρατεύοντο· Θεσπρωτοὶ γάρ
εἰσι οἱ ὁμουρέοντες Ἀμπρακιήτῃσι καὶ Λευκαδίοισι,
οἳ ἐξ ἐσχατέων χωρέων ἐστρατεύοντο. τῶν δὲ ἐκτὸς
τούτων οἰκημένων Κροτωνιῆται μοῦνοι ἦσαν, οἳ ἐβώ-
θησαν τῇ Ἑλλάδι κινδυνευούσῃ νηῒ μιῇ, τῆς ἦρχε
20 ἀνὴρ τρὶς πυθιονίκης Φάϋλλος· Κροτωνιῆται δὲ γένος
εἰσὶ Ἀχαιοί. XLVIII. Οἱ μέν νυν ἄλλοι τριήρεας
παρεχόμενοι ἐστρατεύοντο, Μήλιοι δὲ καὶ Σίφνιοι
καὶ Σερίφιοι πεντηκοντέρους. Μήλιοι μὲν γένος ἐόντες ἀπὸ Λακεδαίμονος δύο παρείχοντο, Σίφνιοι δὲ καὶ
25 Σερίφιοι Ἴωνες ἐόντες ἀπ' Ἀθηνέων μίαν ἑκάτεροι.
ἀριθμὸς δὲ ἐγένετο ὁ πᾶς τῶν νεῶν, πάρεξ τῶν πεντηκοντέρων, τριηκόσιαι καὶ ἑβδομήκοντα καὶ ὀκτώ.

*A council of war. The captains of the Peloponnesian ships
wish to retire nearer the Isthmus.*

XLIX. Ὡς δὲ ἐς τὴν Σαλαμῖνα συνῆλθον οἱ
στρατηγοὶ ἀπὸ τῶν εἰρημένων πολίων, ἐβουλεύοντο

προθέντος Εὐρυβιάδεω γνώμην ἀποφαίνεσθαι τὸν βουλόμενον, ὅκου δοκέοι ἐπιτηδεότατον εἶναι ναυμαχίην ποιέεσθαι τῶν αὐτοὶ χωρέων ἐγκρατέες εἰσί· ἡ γὰρ Ἀττικὴ ἀπεῖτο ἤδη, τῶν δὲ λοιπέων πέρι προετίθεε. αἱ γνῶμαι δὲ τῶν λεγόντων αἱ πλεῖσται 5 συνεξέπιπτον πρὸς τὸν Ἰσθμὸν πλώσαντας ναυμαχέειν πρὸ τῆς Πελοποννήσου, ἐπιλέγοντες τὸν λόγον τόνδε, ὡς ἢν νικηθέωσι τῇ ναυμαχίῃ, ἐν Σαλαμῖνι μὲν ἐόντες πολιορκήσονται ἐν νήσῳ, ἵνα σφι τιμωρίη οὐδεμία ἐπιφανήσεται, πρὸς δὲ τῷ Ἰσθμῷ ἐς τοὺς 10 ἑωυτῶν ἐξοίσονται.

During the council news comes that Xerxes is in Attica wasting the land with fire and sword.

L. Ταῦτα τῶν ἀπὸ Πελοποννήσου στρατηγῶν ἐπιλεγομένων ἐληλύθεε ἀνὴρ Ἀθηναῖος ἀγγέλλων ἥκειν τὸν βάρβαρον ἐς τὴν Ἀττικὴν καὶ πᾶσαν αὐτὴν πυρπολέεσθαι. ὁ γὰρ διὰ Βοιωτῶν τραπό- 15 μενος στρατὸς ἅμα Ξέρξῃ, ἐμπρήσας Θεσπιέων τὴν πόλιν αὐτῶν ἐκλελοιπότων ἐς Πελοπόννησον καὶ τὴν Πλαταιέων ὡσαύτως· ἧκέ τε ἐς τὰς Ἀθήνας καὶ πάντα ἐκεῖνα ἐδηίου. ἐνέπρησε δὲ Θέσπειάν τε καὶ Πλάταιαν πυθόμενος Θηβαίων, ὅτι οὐκ ἐμήδιζον. 20

The occupation of Athens,—an empty city except for the treasurers of the temples and a few poor citizens.

LI. Ἀπὸ δὲ τῆς διαβάσιος τοῦ Ἑλλησπόντου, ἔνθεν πορεύεσθαι ἤρξαντο οἱ βάρβαροι, ἕνα αὐτοῦ διατρίψαντες μῆνα, ἐν τῷ διέβαινον ἐς τὴν Εὐρώπην, ἐν τρισὶ ἑτέροισι μησὶ ἐγένοντο ἐν τῇ Ἀττικῇ, Καλλιάδεω ἄρχοντος Ἀθηναίοισι. καὶ αἱρέουσι ἔρημον 25 τὸ ἄστυ, καί τινας ὀλίγους εὑρίσκουσι τῶν Ἀθηναίων

ἐν τῷ ἱρῷ ἐόντας, ταμίας τε τοῦ ἱροῦ καὶ πένητας
ἀνθρώπους, οἳ φραξάμενοι τὴν ἀκρόπολιν θύρῃσί τε
καὶ ξύλοισι ἠμύνοντο τοὺς ἐπιόντας, ἅμα μὲν ὑπ᾽
ἀσθενείης βίου οὐκ ἐκχωρήσαντες ἐς Σαλαμῖνα, πρὸς
5 δὲ αὐτοὶ δοκέοντες ἐξευρηκέναι τὸ μαντήϊον, τὸ ἡ
Πυθίη σφι ἔχρησε, τὸ ξύλινον τεῖχος ἀνάλωτον ἔσεσθαι, καὶ αὐτὸ δὴ τοῦτο εἶναι τὸ κρησφύγετον κατὰ
τὸ μαντήϊον, καὶ οὐ τὰς νέας.

The siege of the Acropolis.

LII. Οἱ δὲ Πέρσαι ἱζόμενοι ἐπὶ τὸν καταντίον
10 τῆς ἀκροπόλιος ὄχθον, τὸν Ἀθηναῖοι καλέουσι Ἀρή-
ϊον πάγον, ἐπολιόρκεον τρόπον τοιόνδε· ὅκως στυ-
πεῖον περὶ τοὺς ὀϊστοὺς περιθέντες ἅψειαν, ἐτόξευον
ἐς τὸ φράγμα. ἐνθαῦτα Ἀθηναίων οἱ πολιορκεό-
μενοι ὅμως ἠμύνοντο, καίπερ ἐς τὸ ἔσχατον κακοῦ
15 ἀπιγμένοι καὶ τοῦ φράγματος προδεδωκότος. οὐδὲ
λόγους τῶν Πεισιστρατιδέων προσφερόντων περὶ
ὁμολογίης ἐνεδέκοντο, ἀμυνόμενοι δὲ ἄλλα τε ἀντε-
μηχανέοντο καὶ δὴ καὶ προσιόντων τῶν βαρβάρων
πρὸς τὰς πύλας ὀλοιτρόχους ἀπίεσαν ὥστε Ξέρξην
20 ἐπὶ χρόνον συχνὸν ἀπορίῃσι ἐνέχεσθαι οὐ δυνάμενόν
σφεας ἑλεῖν.

*The Acropolis is stormed, the temples pillaged and burnt,
and a triumphant message despatched to Susa.*

LIII. Χρόνῳ δ᾽ ἐκ τῶν ἀπόρων ἐφάνη δή τις
ἔσοδος τοῖσι βαρβάροισι· ἔδεε γὰρ κατὰ τὸ θεοπρό-
πιον πᾶσαν τὴν Ἀττικὴν τὴν ἐν τῇ ἠπείρῳ γενέσθαι
25 ὑπὸ Πέρσῃσι. ἔμπροσθε ὦν πρὸ τῆς ἀκροπόλιος,
ὄπισθε δὲ τῶν πυλέων καὶ τῆς ἀνόδου, τῇ δὴ οὔτε τις
ἐφύλασσε οὔτ᾽ ἂν ἤλπισε μή κοτέ τις κατὰ ταῦτα

ἀναβαίη ἀνθρώπων, ταύτῃ ἀνέβησάν τινες κατὰ τὸ
ἱρὸν τῆς Κέκροπος θυγατρὸς Ἀγλαύρου, καίτοι περ
ἀποκρήμνου ἐόντος τοῦ χώρου. ὡς δὲ εἶδον αὐτοὺς
ἀναβεβηκότας οἱ Ἀθηναῖοι ἐπὶ τὴν ἀκρόπολιν, οἱ
μὲν ἐρρίπτεον ἑωυτοὺς κατὰ τοῦ τείχεος κάτω καὶ 5
διεφθείροντο, οἱ δὲ ἐς τὸ μέγαρον κατέφευγον. τῶν
δὲ Περσέων οἱ ἀναβεβηκότες πρῶτον μὲν ἐτράποντο
πρὸς τὰς πύλας, ταύτας δὲ ἀνοίξαντες τοὺς ἱκέτας
ἐφόνευον· ἐπεὶ δέ σφι πάντες κατέστρωντο, τὸ ἱρὸν
συλήσαντες ἐνέπρησαν πᾶσαν τὴν ἀκρόπολιν. LIV. 10
Σχὼν δὲ παντελέως τὰς Ἀθήνας Ξέρξης ἀπέπεμψε
ἐς Σοῦσα ἄγγελον ἱππέα Ἀρταβάνῳ ἀγγελέοντα τὴν
παρεοῦσάν σφι εὐπρηξίην.

The sacred olive shoots out afresh after its burning.

Ἀπὸ δὲ τῆς πέμψιος τοῦ κήρυκος δευτέρῃ ἡμέρῃ
συγκαλέσας Ἀθηναίων τοὺς φυγάδας, ἑωυτῷ δὲ ἑπο- 15
μένους, ἐκέλευε τρόπῳ τῷ σφετέρῳ θῦσαι τὰ ἱρὰ
ἀναβάντας ἐς τὴν ἀκρόπολιν, εἴτε δὴ ὦν ὄψιν τινὰ
ἰδὼν ἐνυπνίου ἐνετέλλετο ταῦτα, εἴτε καὶ ἐνθύμιόν οἱ
ἐγένετο ἐμπρήσαντι τὸ ἱρόν. οἱ δὲ φυγάδες τῶν
Ἀθηναίων ἐποίησαν τὰ ἐντεταλμένα. LV. Τοῦ δὲ 20
εἵνεκεν τούτων ἐπεμνήσθην, φράσω. ἔστι ἐν τῇ ἀκρο-
πόλι ταύτῃ Ἐρεχθέος τοῦ γηγενέος λεγομένου εἶναι
νηός, ἐν τῷ ἐλαίη τε καὶ θάλασσα ἔνι, τὰ λόγος παρ'
Ἀθηναίων Ποσειδέωνά τε καὶ Ἀθηναίην ἐρίσαντας
περὶ τῆς χώρης μαρτύρια θέσθαι. ταύτην ὦν τὴν 25
ἐλαίην ἅμα τῷ ἄλλῳ ἱρῷ κατέλαβε ἐμπρησθῆναι
ὑπὸ τῶν βαρβάρων· δευτέρῃ δὲ ἡμέρῃ ἀπὸ τῆς
ἐμπρήσιος Ἀθηναίων οἱ θύειν ὑπὸ βασιλέος κελευό-
μενοι ὡς ἀνέβησαν ἐς τὸ ἱρόν, ὥρεον βλαστὸν ἐκ τοῦ

στελέχεος ὅσον τε πηχυαῖον ἀναδεδραμηκότα. Οὗτοι μέν νυν ταῦτα ἔφρασαν.

The news of the fall of the Acropolis caused such terror in the fleet at Salamis that many of the captains hurried to their ships to set sail; and the council determine on the movement towards the Isthmus.

LVI. Οἱ δὲ ἐν Σαλαμῖνι Ἕλληνες, ὥς σφι ἐξηγγέλθη, ὡς ἔσχε τὰ περὶ τὴν Ἀθηνέων ἀκρόπολιν
5 ἐς τοσοῦτον θόρυβον ἀπίκοντο, ὥστε ἔνιοι τῶν στρατηγῶν οὐδὲ κυρωθῆναι ἔμενον τὸ προκείμενον πρῆγμα, ἀλλ' ἔς τε τὰς νέας ἐσέπιπτον καὶ ἱστία ἠείροντο ὡς ἀποθευσόμενοι. τοῖσί τε ὑπολειπομένοισι αὐτῶν ἐκυρώθη πρὸ τοῦ Ἰσθμοῦ ναυμαχέειν. νύξ τε ἐγί-
10 νετο, καὶ οἱ διαλυθέντες ἐκ τοῦ συνεδρίου ἐσέβαινον ἐς τὰς νέας.

Themistocles is persuaded to make another attempt to induce the Greeks to stay at Salamis.

LVII. Ἐνθαῦτα δὴ Θεμιστοκλέα ἀπικόμενον ἐπὶ τὴν νέα εἴρετο Μνησίφιλος ἀνὴρ Ἀθηναῖος, ὅ τι σφι εἴη βεβουλευμένον. πυθόμενος δὲ πρὸς αὐτοῦ,
15 ὡς εἴη δεδογμένον ἀνάγειν τὰς νέας πρὸς τὸν Ἰσθμὸν καὶ πρὸ τῆς Πελοποννήσου ναυμαχέειν, εἶπε· "Οὔ τοι "ἄρα, ἢν ἀπαείρωσι τὰς νέας ἀπὸ Σαλαμῖνος, περὶ οὐ-"δεμιῆς ἔτι πατρίδος ναυμαχήσεις. κατὰ γὰρ πόλις "ἕκαστοι τρέψονται, καὶ οὔτε σφέας Εὐρυβιάδης κατέ-
20 "χειν δυνήσεται οὔτε τις ἀνθρώπων ἄλλος ὥστε μὴ "οὐ διασκεδασθῆναι τὴν στρατιήν, ἀπολέεταί τε ἡ "Ἑλλὰς ἀβουλίῃσι. ἀλλ' εἴ τις ἔστι μηχανή, ἴθι καὶ "πειρῶ διαχέαι τὰ βεβουλευμένα, ἤν κως δύνῃ ἀνα-"γνῶσαι Εὐρυβιάδεα μεταβουλεύσασθαι ὥστε αὐτοῦ

"μενέειν." LVIII. Κάρτα δὴ τῷ Θεμιστοκλέϊ ἤρεσε ἡ ὑποθήκη, καὶ οὐδὲν πρὸς ταῦτα ἀμειψάμενος ἤϊε ἐπὶ τὴν νέα τὴν Εὐρυβιάδεω. ἀπικόμενος δὲ ἔφη ἐθέλειν οἱ κοινόν τι πρῆγμα συμμῖξαι. ὁ δ' αὐτὸν ἐς τὴν νέα ἐκέλευε ἐσβάντα λέγειν, εἴ τι ἐθέλοι. ἐν- ταῦτα ὁ Θεμιστοκλέης παριζόμενός οἱ καταλέγει ἐκεῖνά τε πάντα, τὰ ἤκουσε Μνησιφίλου, ἑωυτοῦ ποιεύμενος, καὶ ἄλλα πολλὰ προστιθείς, ἐς ὃ ἀνέγνωσε χρηΐζων ἔκ τε τῆς νεὸς ἐκβῆναι συλλέξαι τε τοὺς στρατηγοὺς ἐς τὸ συνέδριον.

The council reassembled. A sharp debate.

LIX. Ὡς δὲ ἄρα συνελέχθησαν, πρὶν ἢ τὸν Εὐρυβιάδεα προθεῖναι τὸν λόγον τῶν εἵνεκεν συνήγαγε τοὺς στρατηγούς, πολλὸς ἦν ὁ Θεμιστοκλέης ἐν τοῖσι λόγοισι οἷα κάρτα δεόμενος. λέγοντος δὲ αὐτοῦ ὁ Κορίνθιος στρατηγὸς Ἀδείμαντος ὁ Ὠκύτου εἶπε· "Ὦ Θεμιστόκλεες, ἐν τοῖσι ἀγῶσι οἱ προεξανιστά- "μενοι ῥαπίζονται." ὁ δὲ ἀπολυόμενος ἔφη· "Οἱ δέ γε "ἐγκαταλειπόμενοι οὐ στεφανεῦνται." LX. Τότε μὲν ἠπίως πρὸς τὸν Κορίνθιον ἀμείψατο, πρὸς δὲ τὸν Εὐρυβιάδεα ἔλεγε ἐκείνων μὲν οὐκέτι οὐδὲν τῶν πρότερον λεχθέντων, ὡς ἐπεὰν ἀπαείρωσι ἀπὸ Σαλαμῖνος, διαδρήσονται· παρεόντων γὰρ τῶν συμμάχων οὐκ ἔφερέ οἱ κόσμον οὐδένα κατηγορέειν· ὁ δὲ ἄλλου λόγου εἴχετο, λέγων τάδε.

The speech of Themistocles.

1. "Ἐν σοὶ νῦν ἐστὶ σῶσαι τὴν Ἑλλάδα, ἢν ἐμοὶ "πείθῃ ναυμαχίην αὐτοῦ μένων ποιέεσθαι, μηδὲ πει- "θόμενος τούτων τοῖσι λέγουσι ἀναζεύξῃς πρὸς τὸν

" Ἰσθμὸν τὰς νέας. ἀντίθες γὰρ ἑκάτερον ἀκούσας.
" πρὸς μὲν τῷ Ἰσθμῷ συμβάλλων ἐν πελάγεϊ ἀνα-
" πεπταμένῳ ναυμαχήσεις, τὸ ἥκιστα ἡμῖν σύμφορόν
" ἐστι νέας ἔχουσι βαρυτέρας καὶ ἀριθμὸν ἐλάσσονας,
5 " τοῦτο δὲ ἀπολέεις Σαλαμῖνά τε καὶ Μέγαρα καὶ
" Αἴγιναν, ἤν περ καὶ τὰ ἄλλα εὐτυχήσωμεν. ἅμα
" γὰρ τῷ ναυτικῷ αὐτῶν ἕψεται καὶ ὁ πεζὸς στρατός.
" καὶ οὕτω σφέας αὐτὸς ἄξεις ἐπὶ τὴν Πελοπόννησον,
" κινδυνεύσεις τε ἁπάσῃ τῇ Ἑλλάδι· 2. Ἢν δὲ τὰ ἐγὼ
10 " λέγω ποιήσῃς, τοσάδε ἐν αὐτοῖσι χρηστὰ εὑρήσεις·
" πρῶτα μὲν ἐν στεινῷ συμβάλλοντες νηυσὶ ὀλίγῃσι
" πρὸς πολλὰς, ἤν τὰ οἰκότα ἐκ τοῦ πολέμου ἐκβαίνῃ,
" πολλὸν κρατήσομεν,—τὸ γὰρ ἐν στεινῷ ναυμαχέειν
" πρὸς ἡμέων ἐστὶ, ἐν εὐρυχωρίῃ δὲ πρὸς ἐκείνων,—
15 " αὖτις δὲ Σαλαμὶς περιγίνεται, ἐς τὴν ἡμῖν ὑπεκκέεται
" τέκνα τε καὶ γυναῖκες. καὶ μὴν καὶ τόδε ἐν αὐτοῖσι
" ἔνεστι, τοῦ καὶ περιέχεσθε μάλιστα· ὁμοίως αὐτοῦ
" τε μένων προναυμαχήσεις Πελοποννήσου καὶ πρὸς
" τῷ Ἰσθμῷ, οὐδέ σφεας, εἴ περ εὖ φρονέεις, ἄξεις ἐπὶ
20 ' τὴν Πελοπόννησον. 3. Ἢν δέ γε καὶ τὰ ἐγὼ ἐλπίζω
" γένηται καὶ νικήσωμεν τῇσι νηυσὶ, οὔτε ὑμῖν ἐς τὸν
" Ἰσθμὸν παρέσονται οἱ βάρβαροι οὔτε προβήσονται
" ἑκαστέρω τῆς Ἀττικῆς, ἀπίασί τε οὐδενὶ κόσμῳ,
" Μεγάροισί τε κερδανέομεν περιεοῦσι καὶ Αἰγίνῃ καὶ
25 " Σαλαμῖνι, ἐν τῇ ἡμῖν καὶ λόγιόν ἐστι τῶν ἐχθρῶν
" κατύπερθε γενέσθαι. οἰκότα μέν νυν βουλευομένοισι
" ἀνθρώποισι ὡς τὸ ἐπίπαν ἐθέλει γίνεσθαι, μὴ δὲ
" οἰκότα βουλευομένοισι οὐκ ἐθέλει οὐδὲ ὁ θεὸς προσ-
" χωρέειν πρὸς τὰς ἀνθρωπηίας γνώμας."

A retort and a threat.

LXI. Ταῦτα λέγοντος Θεμιστοκλέος αὖτις ὁ Κορίνθιος Ἀδείμαντος ἐπεφέρετο, σιγᾶν τε κελεύων τῷ μὴ ἔστι πατρίς, καὶ Εὐρυβιάδεα οὐκ ἐῶν ἐπιψηφίζειν ἀπόλι ἀνδρί· πόλιν γὰρ τὸν Θεμιστοκλέα παρεχόμενον οὕτω ἐκέλευε γνώμας συμβάλλεσθαι. ταῦτα δέ οἱ προέφερε, ὅτι ἡλώκεσάν τε καὶ κατείχοντο αἱ Ἀθῆναι. τότε δὴ ὁ Θεμιστοκλέης ἐκεῖνόν τε καὶ τοὺς Κορινθίους πολλά τε καὶ κακὰ ἔλεγε, ἑωυτοῖσί τε ἐδήλου λόγῳ ὡς εἴη καὶ πόλις καὶ γῆ μέζων ἤπερ ἐκείνοισι, ἔστ' ἂν διηκόσιαι νέες σφι ἔωσι πεπληρωμέναι· οὐδαμοὺς γὰρ Ἑλλήνων αὐτοὺς ἐπιόντας ἀποκρούσεσθαι. LXII. Σημαίνων δὲ ταῦτα τῷ λόγῳ διέβαινε ἐς Εὐρυβιάδεα, λέγων μᾶλλον ἐπεστραμμένα· "Σὺ εἰ μενέεις αὐτοῦ καὶ μένων ἔσεαι "ἀνὴρ ἀγαθός· εἰ δὲ μή, ἀνατρέψεις τὴν Ἑλλάδα. τὸ "πᾶν γὰρ ἡμῖν τοῦ πολέμου φέρουσι αἱ νέες. ἀλλ' "ἐμοὶ πείθεο. εἰ δὲ ταῦτα μὴ ποιήσεις, ἡμεῖς μὲν, ὡς "ἔχομεν, ἀναλαβόντες τοὺς οἰκέτας κομιεύμεθα ἐς "Σῖριν τὴν ἐν Ἰταλίῃ, ἥ περ ἡμετέρη τέ ἐστι ἐκ "παλαιοῦ ἔτι, καὶ τὰ λόγια λέγει ὑπ' ἡμέων αὐτὴν "δέειν κτισθῆναι· ὑμεῖς δὲ συμμάχων τοιῶνδε μουνω-"θέντες μεμνήσεσθε τῶν ἐμῶν λόγων."

Eurybiades is persuaded.

LXIII. Ταῦτα δὲ Θεμιστοκλέος λέγοντος ἀνεδιδάσκετο Εὐρυβιάδης. δοκέειν δέ μοι, ἀρρωδήσας μάλιστα τοὺς Ἀθηναίους ἀνεδιδάσκετο, μή σφεας ἀπολίπωσι, ἢν πρὸς τὸν Ἰσθμὸν ἀνάγῃ τὰς νέας. ἀπολιπόντων γὰρ Ἀθηναίων οὐκέτι ἐγίνοντο ἀξιόμαχοι οἱ λοιποί. ταύτην δὲ αἱρέεται τὴν γνώμην αὐτοῦ μένοντας διαναυμαχέειν.

An earthquake. The Aeacidae, national heroes of Salamis, are sent for.

LXIV. Οὕτω μὲν οἱ περὶ Σαλαμῖνα ἔπεσι ἀκροβολισάμενοι, ἐπεί τε Εὐρυβιάδῃ ἔδοξε, αὐτοῦ παρεσκευάζοντο ὡς ναυμαχήσοντες. ἡμέρη τε ἐγίνετο καὶ ἅμα τῷ ἡλίῳ ἀνιόντι σεισμὸς ἐγένετο ἔν τε τῇ γῇ καὶ τῇ θαλάσσῃ. ἔδοξε δέ σφι εὔξασθαι τοῖσι θεοῖσι καὶ ἐπικαλέσασθαι τοὺς Αἰακίδας συμμάχους. ὡς δέ σφι ἔδοξε, καὶ ἐποίευν ταῦτα· εὐξάμενοι γὰρ πᾶσι τοῖσι θεοῖσι αὐτόθεν μὲν ἐκ Σαλαμῖνος Αἴαντά τε καὶ Τελαμῶνα ἐπεκαλέοντο, ἐπὶ δὲ Αἰακὸν καὶ τοὺς ἄλλους Αἰακίδας νέα ἀπέστελλον ἐς Αἴγιναν.

The mystic procession is seen coming along the Sacred way from Eleusis, and the sacred Bacchic shout is heard.

LXV. Ἔφη δὲ Δίκαιος ὁ Θεοκύδεος ἀνὴρ Ἀθηναῖος, φυγάς τε καὶ παρὰ Μήδοισι λόγιμος γενόμενος τοῦτον τὸν χρόνον, ἐπεί τε ἐκείρετο ἡ Ἀττικὴ χώρη ὑπὸ τοῦ πεζοῦ στρατοῦ τοῦ Ξέρξεω ἐοῦσα ἐρῆμος Ἀθηναίων, τυχεῖν τότε ἐὼν ἅμα Δημαρήτῳ τῷ Λακεδαιμονίῳ ἐν τῷ Θριασίῳ πεδίῳ, ἰδεῖν δὲ κονιορτὸν χωρέοντα ἀπὸ Ἐλευσῖνος ὡς ἀνδρῶν μάλιστά κῃ τρισμυρίων, ἀποθωυμάζειν τέ σφεας τὸν κονιορτὸν ὅτεων κοτε εἴη ἀνθρώπων, καὶ πρόκατε φωνῆς ἀκούειν, καί οἱ φαίνεσθαι τὴν φωνὴν εἶναι τὸν μυστικὸν ἴακχον. εἶναι δ' ἀδαήμονα τῶν ἱρῶν τῶν ἐν Ἐλευσῖνι γινομένων τὸν Δημάρητον, εἴρεσθαί τε αὐτόν, ὅ τι τὸ φθεγγόμενον εἴη τοῦτο· αὐτὸς δὲ εἶπαι· "Δημάρητε, οὐκ ἔστι ὅκως οὐ μέγα τι σίνος ἔσται τῇ

"βασιλέος στρατιῇ. τάδε γὰρ ἀρίδηλα ἐρήμου ἐούσης
"τῆς Ἀττικῆς, ὅτι θεῖον τὸ φθεγγόμενον, ἀπὸ Ἐλευ-
"σῖνος ἰὸν ἐς τιμωρίην Ἀθηναίοισί τε καὶ τοῖσι συμ-
"μάχοισι. καὶ ἢν μέν γε κατασκήψῃ ἐς τὴν Πελο-
"πόννησον, κίνδυνος αὐτῷ τε βασιλέϊ καὶ τῇ στρατιῇ
"τῇ ἐν τῇ ἠπείρῳ ἔσται, ἢν δὲ ἐπὶ τὰς νέας τράπηται
"τὰς ἐν Σαλαμῖνι, τὸν ναυτικὸν στρατὸν κινδυνεύσει
"βασιλεὺς ἀποβαλεῖν. τὴν δὲ ὁρτὴν ταύτην ἄγουσι
"Ἀθηναῖοι ἀνὰ πάντα ἔτεα τῇ Μητρὶ καὶ τῇ Κούρῃ,
"καὶ αὐτῶν τε ὁ βουλόμενος καὶ τῶν ἄλλων Ἑλλήνων
"μυεῖται καὶ τὴν φωνὴν, τῆς ἀκούεις, ἐν ταύτῃ τῇ ὁρτῇ
"ἰακχάζουσι." Πρὸς ταῦτα εἰπεῖν Δημάρητον· "Σίγα
"τε καὶ μηδενὶ ἄλλῳ τὸν λόγον τοῦτον εἴπῃς. ἢν γάρ
"τοι ἐς βασιλέα ἀνενειχθῇ τὰ ἔπεα ταῦτα, ἀποβαλέεις
"τὴν κεφαλὴν, καί σε οὔτε ἐγὼ δυνήσομαι ῥύσασθαι
"οὔτ' ἄλλος ἀνθρώπων οὐδὲ εἷς. ἀλλ' ἔχ' ἥσυχος,
"περὶ δὲ στρατιῆς τῆσδε θεοῖσι μελήσει." Τὸν μὲν δὴ
ταῦτα παραινέειν, ἐκ δὲ τοῦ κονιορτοῦ καὶ τῆς φωνῆς
γενέσθαι νέφος καὶ μεταρσιωθὲν φέρεσθαι ἐπὶ Σαλαμῖνος ἐπὶ τὸ στρατόπεδον τὸ τῶν Ἑλλήνων. οὕτω
δὲ αὐτοὺς μαθεῖν, ὅτι τὸ ναυτικὸν τὸ Ξέρξεω ἀπολέεσθαι μέλλοι. Ταῦτα μὲν Δίκαιος ὁ Θεοκύδεος ἔλεγε,
Δημαρήτου τε καὶ ἄλλων μαρτύρων καταπτόμενος.

The Persian navy meanwhile had left Histiaea and in six days arrived at Phalerum.

LXVI. Οἱ δὲ ἐς τὸν Ξέρξεω ναυτικὸν στρατὸν
ταχθέντες, ἐπειδὴ ἐκ Τρηχῖνος θηησάμενοι τὸ τρῶμα
τὸ Λακωνικὸν διέβησαν ἐς τὴν Ἱστιαίην, ἐπισχόντες
ἡμέρας τρεῖς ἔπλωον δι' Εὐρίπου, καὶ ἐν ἑτέρῃσι
τρισὶ ἡμέρῃσι ἐγένοντο ἐν Φαλήρῳ. ὡς μὲν ἐμοὶ

δοκέειν, οὐκ ἐλάσσονες ἐόντες ἀριθμὸν ἐσέβαλον ἐς
τὰς Ἀθήνας, κατά τε ἤπειρον καὶ τῇσι νηυσὶ ἀπικόμενοι, ἢ ἐπί τε Σηπιάδα ἀπίκοντο καὶ ἐς Θερμοπύλας. ἀντιθήσω γὰρ τοῖσί τε ὑπὸ τοῦ χειμῶνος
αὐτῶν ἀπολομένοισι καὶ τοῖσι ἐν Θερμοπύλῃσι καὶ
τῇσι ἐπ᾽ Ἀρτεμισίῳ ναυμαχίῃσι τούσδε τοὺς τότε
οὔκω ἑπομένους βασιλέϊ, Μηλιέας τε καὶ Δωριέας
καὶ Λοκροὺς καὶ Βοιωτοὺς πανστρατιῇ ἑπομένους
πλὴν Θεσπιέων τε καὶ Πλαταιέων καὶ μάλα Καρυστίους τε καὶ Ἀνδρίους καὶ Τηνίους τε καὶ τοὺς
λοιποὺς νησιώτας πάντας πλὴν τῶν πέντε πολίων,
τῶν ἐπεμνήσθην πρότερον τὰ οὐνόματα. ὅσῳ γὰρ
δὴ προέβαινε ἐσωτέρω τῆς Ἑλλάδος ὁ Πέρσης, τοσούτῳ πλέω ἔθνεά οἱ εἵπετο.

Xerxes holds a council of war with the naval commanders. Shall he fight or no?

LXVII. Ἐπεὶ ὦν ἀπίκατο ἐς τὰς Ἀθήνας
πάντες οὗτοι πλὴν Παρίων (Πάριοι δὲ ὑπολειφθέντες
ἐν Κύθνῳ ἐκαραδόκεον τὸν πόλεμον κῇ ἀποβήσεται),
οἱ δὲ λοιποὶ ὡς ἀπίκοντο ἐς τὸ Φάληρον, ἐνθαῦτα
κατέβη αὐτὸς Ξέρξης ἐπὶ τὰς νέας, ἐθέλων σφι
συμμῖξαί τε καὶ πυθέσθαι τῶν ἐπιπλωόντων τὰς
γνώμας. ἐπεὶ δὲ ἀπικόμενος προΐζετο, παρῆσαν μετάπεμπτοι οἱ τῶν ἐθνέων τῶν σφετέρων τύραννοι καὶ
ταξίαρχοι ἀπὸ τῶν νεῶν, καὶ ἵζοντο ὥς σφι βασιλεὺς
ἑκάστῳ τιμὴν ἐδεδώκεε, πρῶτος μὲν ὁ Σιδώνιος βασιλεύς, μετὰ δὲ ὁ Τύριος, ἐπὶ δὲ ὦλλοι. ὡς δὲ κόσμῳ
ἐπεξῆς ἵζοντο, πέμψας Ξέρξης Μαρδόνιον εἰρώτα,
ἀποπειρώμενος ἑκάστου, εἰ ναυμαχίην ποιέοιτο.

All answer yea except Artemisia.

LXVIII. Ἐπεὶ δὲ περιιὼν εἰρώτα ὁ Μαρδόνιος ἀρξάμενος ἀπὸ τοῦ Σιδωνίου, οἱ μὲν δὴ ἄλλοι κατὰ τωὐτὸ γνώμην ἐξεφέροντο, κελεύοντες ναυμαχίην ποιέεσθαι, Ἀρτεμισίη δὲ τάδε ἔφη.

Speech of Artemisia. She counsels delay, and an advance rather of the land forces.

1. "Εἰπαί μοι πρὸς βασιλέα, Μαρδόνιε, ὡς ἐγὼ
"τάδε λέγω οὔτε κακίστη γενομένη ἐν τῇσι ναυμα-
"χίῃσι τῇσι πρὸς Εὐβοίῃ οὔτε ἐλάχιστα ἀποδεξα-
"μένη. δέσποτα, τὴν δὲ ἐοῦσαν γνώμην με δίκαιόν
"ἐστιν ἀποδείκνυσθαι, τὰ τυγχάνω φρονέουσα ἄριστα
"ἐς πρήγματα τὰ σά. καί τοι τάδε λέγω, φείδεο τῶν
"νεῶν μηδὲ ναυμαχίην ποιέεο. οἱ γὰρ ἄνδρες τῶν
"σῶν ἀνδρῶν κρέσσονες τοσοῦτό εἰσι κατὰ θάλασσαν,
"ὅσον ἄνδρες γυναικῶν. τί δὲ πάντως δέει σε ναυμα-
"χίῃσι ἀνακινδυνεύειν; οὐκ ἔχεις μὲν τὰς Ἀθήνας,
"τῶν περ εἵνεκεν ὡρμήθης στρατεύεσθαι, ἔχεις δὲ τὴν
"ἄλλην Ἑλλάδα; ἐμποδὼν δέ τοι ἵσταται οὐδείς· οἱ
"δέ τοι ἀντέστησαν, ἀπήλλαξαν οὕτω, ὡς ἐκείνους
"ἔπρεπε. 2. Τῇ δὲ ἐγὼ δοκέω ἀποβήσεσθαι τὰ τῶν
"ἀντιπολέμων πρήγματα, τοῦτο φράσω· ἢν μὲν μὴ
"ἐπειχθῇς ναυμαχίην ποιεύμενος, ἀλλὰ τὰς νέας αὐτοῦ
"ἔχῃς πρὸς γῇ μένων, ἢ καὶ προβαίνων ἐς τὴν Πελο-
"πόννησον, εὐπετέως τοι, δέσποτα, χωρήσει τὰ νοέων
"ἐλήλυθας. οὐ γὰρ οἷοί τε πολλὸν χρόνον εἰσί τοι
"ἀντέχειν οἱ Ἕλληνες, ἀλλά σφεας διασκεδᾷς, κατὰ
"πόλις δὲ ἕκαστοι φεύξονται. οὔτε γὰρ σῖτος πάρα
"σφίσι ἐν τῇ νήσῳ ταύτῃ, ὡς ἐγὼ πυνθάνομαι, οὔτε
"αὐτοὺς οἰκός, ἢν σὺ ἐπὶ τὴν Πελοπόννησον ἐλαύνῃς

"τὸν πεζὸν στρατὸν, ἀτρεμιέειν τοὺς ἐκεῖθεν αὐτῶν
"ἥκοντας, οὐδέ σφι μελήσει πρὸ τῶν Ἀθηναίων ναυ-
"μαχέειν. 3. Ἢν δὲ αὐτίκα ἐπειχθῇς ναυμαχῆσαι,
"δειμαίνω, μὴ ὁ ναυτικὸς στρατὸς κακωθεὶς τὸν πεζὸν
5 "προσδηλήσηται. πρὸς δὲ, ὦ βασιλεῦ, καὶ τόδε ἐς
"θυμὸν βάλευ, ὡς τοῖσι μὲν χρηστοῖσι τῶν ἀνθρώπων
"κακοὶ δοῦλοι φιλέουσι γίνεσθαι, τοῖσι δὲ κακοῖσι
"χρηστοί. σοὶ δὲ ἐόντι ἀρίστῳ ἀνδρῶν πάντων κακοὶ
"δοῦλοι εἰσὶ, οἳ ἐν συμμάχων λόγῳ λέγονται εἶναι,
10 "ἐόντες Αἰγύπτιοί τε καὶ Κύπριοι καὶ Κίλικες καὶ
"Πάμφυλοι, τῶν ὄφελός ἐστι οὐδέν."

Xerxes, though agreeing with Artemisia, orders that the opinion of the majority should be followed.

LXIX. Ταῦτα λεγούσης πρὸς Μαρδόνιον, ὅσοι μὲν ἦσαν εὔνοοι τῇ Ἀρτεμισίῃ, συμφορὴν ἐποιεῦντο τοὺς λόγους ὡς κακόν τι πεισομένης πρὸς βασιλέος,
15 ὅτι οὐκ ἐᾷ ναυμαχίην ποιέεσθαι, οἱ δὲ ἀγαιόμενοί τε καὶ φθονέοντες αὐτῇ, ἅτε ἐν πρώτοισι τετιμημένης διὰ πάντων τῶν συμμάχων, ἐτέρποντο τῇ κρίσι ὡς ἀπολεομένης αὐτῆς. ἐπεὶ δὲ ἀνηνείχθησαν αἱ γνῶμαι ἐς Ξέρξην, κάρτα τε ἥσθη τῇ γνώμῃ τῆς Ἀρτε-
20 μισίης, καὶ νομίζων ἔτι πρότερον σπουδαίην εἶναι τότε πολλῷ μᾶλλον αἴνεε. ὅμως δὲ τοῖσι πλέοσι πείθεσθαι ἐκέλευε, τάδε καταδόξας, πρὸς μὲν Εὐβοίῃ σφέας ἐθελοκακέειν ὡς οὐ παρεόντος αὐτοῦ, τότε δὲ αὐτὸς παρεσκεύαστο θηήσασθαι ναυμαχέοντας.

The day before the battle. The Persian ships are brought up gradually into position opposite Salamis.

25 LXX. Ἐπειδὴ δὲ παρήγγελλον ἀναπλώειν, ἀνῆγον τὰς νέας ἐπὶ τὴν Σαλαμῖνα, καὶ παρεκρίθησαν

διαταχθέντες κατ' ἡσυχίην. τότε μέν νυν οὐκ ἐξέχρησέ σφι ἡ ἡμέρη ναυμαχίην ποιήσασθαι, νὺξ γὰρ ἐπεγένετο, οἱ δὲ παρεσκευάζοντο ἐς τὴν ὑστεραίην. τοὺς δὲ Ἕλληνας εἶχε δέος τε καὶ ἀρρωδίη, οὐκ ἥκιστα δὲ τοὺς ἀπὸ Πελοποννήσου. ἀρρώδεον δέ, 5 ὅτι αὐτοὶ μὲν ἐν Σαλαμῖνι κατήμενοι ὑπὲρ γῆς τῆς Ἀθηναίων ναυμαχέειν μέλλοιεν, νικηθέντες τε ἐν νήσῳ ἀπολαμφθέντες πολιορκήσονται, ἀπέντες τὴν ἑωυτῶν ἀφύλακτον.

The Persian land forces advance in the night towards the Isthmus. The Skironian pass had been already occupied by a large force under the Spartan Cleombrotus, and a wall was being hastily built across the Isthmus.

LXXI. Τῶν δὲ βαρβάρων ὁ πεζὸς ὑπὸ τὴν 10 παρεοῦσαν νύκτα ἐπορεύετο ἐπὶ τὴν Πελοπόννησον· καίτοι τὰ δυνατὰ πάντα ἐμεμηχάνητο, ὅκως κατ' ἤπειρον μὴ ἐσβάλοιεν οἱ βάρβαροι. ὡς γὰρ ἐπύθοντο τάχιστα Πελοποννήσιοι τοὺς ἀμφὶ Λεωνίδην ἐν Θερμοπύλῃσι τετελευτηκέναι, συνδραμόντες ἐκ 15 τῶν πολίων ἐς τὸν Ἰσθμὸν ἵζοντο, καί σφι ἐπῆν στρατηγὸς Κλεόμβροτος ὁ Ἀναξανδρίδεω, Λεωνίδεω δὲ ἀδελφεός. ἱζόμενοι δὲ ἐν τῷ Ἰσθμῷ καὶ συγχώσαντες τὴν Σκιρωνίδα ὁδόν, μετὰ τοῦτο ὥς σφι ἔδοξε βουλευομένοισι, οἰκοδόμεον διὰ τοῦ Ἰσθμοῦ τεῖχος. 20 ἅτε δὴ ἐουσέων μυριάδων πολλέων καὶ παντὸς ἀνδρὸς ἐργαζομένου ἤνετο τὸ ἔργον· καὶ γὰρ λίθοι καὶ πλίνθοι καὶ ξύλα καὶ φορμοὶ ψάμμου πλήρεες ἐσεφορέοντο, καὶ ἐλίννυον οὐδένα χρόνον οἱ βοηθήσαντες ἐργαζόμενοι, οὔτε νυκτὸς οὔτε ἡμέρης. LXXII. Οἱ 25 δὲ βοηθήσαντες ἐς τὸν Ἰσθμὸν πανδημεὶ οἵδε ἦσαν

Ἑλλήνων, Λακεδαιμόνιοί τε καὶ Ἀρκάδες πάντες καὶ Ἠλεῖοι καὶ Κορίνθιοι καὶ Σικυώνιοι καὶ Ἐπιδαύριοι καὶ Φλιάσιοι καὶ Τροιζήνιοι καὶ Ἑρμιονέες. οὗτοι μὲν ἦσαν οἱ βοηθήσαντες καὶ ὑπεραρρωδέοντες τῇ Ἑλλάδι κινδυνευούσῃ, τοῖσι δὲ ἄλλοισι Πελοποννησίοισι ἔμελε οὐδέν. Ὀλύμπια δὲ καὶ Κάρνεια παροιχώκεε ἤδη.

The nations inhabiting the Peloponnese.

LXXIII. Οἰκέει δὲ τὴν Πελοπόννησον ἔθνεα ἑπτά. τούτων δὲ τὰ μὲν δύο αὐτόχθονα ἐόντα κατὰ χώρην ἵδρυται νῦν τῇ καὶ τὸ πάλαι οἴκεον, Ἀρκάδες τε καὶ Κυνούριοι. ἓν δὲ ἔθνος τὸ Ἀχαϊκὸν ἐκ μὲν Πελοποννήσου οὐκ ἐξεχώρησε, ἐκ μέντοι τῆς ἑωυτῶν, οἰκέει δὲ τὴν ἀλλοτρίην. τὰ δὲ λοιπὰ ἔθνεα τῶν ἑπτὰ τέσσερα ἐπήλυδά ἐστι, Δωριέες τε καὶ Αἰτωλοὶ καὶ Δρύοπες καὶ Λήμνιοι. Δωριέων μὲν πολλαί τε καὶ δόκιμοι πόλιες, Αἰτωλῶν δὲ Ἦλις μούνη, Δρυόπων δὲ Ἑρμιόνη τε καὶ Ἀσίνη ἡ πρὸς Καρδαμύλῃ τῇ Λακωνικῇ, Λημνίων δὲ Παρωρεῆται πάντες. οἱ δὲ Κυνούριοι αὐτόχθονες ἐόντες δοκέουσι μοῦνοι εἶναι Ἴωνες, ἐκδεδωρίευνται δὲ ὑπό τε Ἀργείων ἀρχόμενοι καὶ τοῦ χρόνου, ἐόντες Ὀρνεῆται καὶ περίοικοι. Τούτων ὦν τῶν ἑπτὰ ἐθνέων αἱ λοιπαὶ πόλιες, πάρεξ τῶν κατέλεξα, ἐκ τοῦ μέσου κατέατο· εἰ δὲ ἐλευθέρως ἔξεστι εἰπεῖν, ἐκ τοῦ μέσου κατήμενοι ἐμήδιζον.

The movement of the Persian land forces renewed the determination of the Greek captains to retreat towards the Peloponnesus.

LXXIV. Οἱ μὲν δὴ ἐν τῷ Ἰσθμῷ τοιούτῳ πόνῳ συνέστασαν, ἅτε περὶ τοῦ παντὸς ἤδη δρόμον θέοντες

καὶ τῇσι νηυσὶ οὐκ ἐλπίζοντες ἐλλάμψεσθαι· οἱ δὲ
ἐν Σαλαμῖνι ὅμως ταῦτα πυνθανόμενοι ἀρρώδεον, οὐκ
οὕτω περὶ σφίσι αὐτοῖσι δειμαίνοντες, ὡς περὶ τῇ
Πελοποννήσῳ. τέως μὲν δὴ αὐτῶν ἀνὴρ ἀνδρὶ παρα-
στὰς σιγῇ λόγον ἐποιέετο, θῶυμα ποιεύμενοι τὴν 5
Εὐρυβιάδεω ἀβουλίην, τέλος δὲ ἐξερράγη ἐς τὸ μέσον.
σύλλογός τε δὴ ἐγίνετο, καὶ πολλὰ ἐλέγετο περὶ τῶν
αὐτῶν, οἱ μὲν, ὡς ἐς τὴν Πελοπόννησον χρεὸν εἴη
ἀποπλώειν καὶ περὶ ἐκείνης κινδυνεύειν, μηδὲ πρὸ
χώρης δοριαλώτου μένοντας μάχεσθαι, Ἀθηναῖοι δὲ 10
καὶ Αἰγινῆται καὶ Μεγαρέες αὐτοῦ μένοντας ἀμύνεσθαι.

The stratagem of Themistokles.

LXXV. Ἐνθαῦτα Θεμιστοκλέης ὡς ἐσσοῦτο τῇ
γνώμῃ ὑπὸ τῶν Πελοποννησίων, λαθὼν ἐξέρχεται ἐκ
τοῦ συνεδρίου, ἐξελθὼν δὲ πέμπει ἐς τὸ στρατόπεδον 15
τὸ Μήδων ἄνδρα πλοίῳ, ἐντειλάμενος τὰ λέγειν χρεὸν,
τῷ οὔνομα μὲν ἦν Σίκιννος, οἰκέτης δὲ καὶ παιδα-
γωγὸς ἦν τῶν Θεμιστοκλέος παίδων, τὸν δὴ ὕστερον
τούτων τῶν πρηγμάτων Θεμιστοκλέης Θεσπιέα τε
ἐποίησε, ὡς ἐπεδέκοντο οἱ Θεσπιέες πολιήτας, καὶ 20
χρήμασι ὄλβιον. ὃς τότε πλοίῳ ἀπικόμενος ἔλεγε
πρὸς τοὺς στρατηγοὺς τῶν βαρβάρων τάδε· "Ἔπεμ-
"ψέ με στρατηγὸς ὁ Ἀθηναίων λάθρῃ τῶν ἄλλων
"Ἑλλήνων (τυγχάνει γὰρ φρονέων τὰ βασιλέος καὶ
" βουλόμενος μᾶλλον τὰ ὑμέτερα κατύπερθε γίνεσθαι 25
"ἢ τὰ τῶν Ἑλλήνων πρήγματα) φράσοντα, ὅτι οἱ
"Ἕλληνες δρησμὸν βουλεύονται καταρρωδηκότες,
" καὶ νῦν παρέχει κάλλιστον ὑμέας ἔργον ἁπάντων
" ἐξεργάσασθαι, ἢν μὴ περιίδητε διαδράντας αὐτούς.
" οὔτε γὰρ ἀλλήλοισι ὁμοφρονέουσι οὔτ' ἔτι ἀντιστή- 30

"σονται ὑμῖν, πρὸς ἑωυτούς τε σφέας ὄψεσθε ναυμα-
"χέοντας τοὺς τὰ ὑμέτερα φρονέοντας καὶ τοὺς μή."

The Persians, believing that the Greeks intend to escape, first occupy the island Psyttaleia, and at midnight move their right wing forward close to Salamis so as to enclose the Greek fleet, and their left wing so as to block up the Strait between Salamis and Munychia.

LXXVI. Ὁ μὲν ταῦτά σφι σημήνας ἐκποδὼν ἀπαλλάσσετο, τοῖσι δὲ ὡς πιστὰ ἐγίνετο τὰ ἀγγελ-
5 θέντα, τοῦτο μὲν ἐς τὴν νησῖδα τὴν Ψυττάλειαν, μεταξὺ Σαλαμῖνός τε κειμένην καὶ τῆς ἠπείρου, πολλοὺς τῶν Περσέων ἀπεβίβασαν, τοῦτο δέ, ἐπειδὴ ἐγίνοντο μέσαι νύκτες, ἀνῆγον μὲν τὸ ἀπ' ἑσπέρης κέρας κυκλούμενοι πρὸς τὴν Σαλαμῖνα, ἀνῆγον δὲ οἱ
10 ἀμφὶ τὴν Κέον τε καὶ τὴν Κυνόσουραν τεταγμένοι, κατεῖχόν τε μέχρι Μουνυχίης πάντα τὸν πορθμὸν τῇσι νηυσί. τῶνδε δὲ εἵνεκεν ἀνῆγον τὰς νέας, ἵνα δὴ τοῖσι Ἕλλησι μηδὲ φυγεῖν ἐξῇ, ἀλλ' ἀπολαμφθέντες ἐν τῇ Σαλαμῖνι δοῖεν τίσιν τῶν ἐπ' Ἀρτεμισίῳ ἀγω-
15 νισμάτων. ἐς δὲ τὴν νησῖδα τὴν Ψυττάλειαν καλεομένην ἀπεβίβαζον τῶν Περσέων τῶνδε εἵνεκεν, ὡς ἐπεὰν γένηται ναυμαχίη, ἐνθαῦτα μάλιστα ἐξοισομένων τῶν τε ἀνδρῶν καὶ τῶν ναυηγίων (ἐν γὰρ δὴ πόρῳ τῆς ναυμαχίης τῆς μελλούσης ἔσεσθαι ἐκέετο
20 ἡ νῆσος), ἵνα τοὺς μὲν περιποιῶσι, τοὺς δὲ διαφθείρωσι. ἐποίευν δὲ σιγῇ ταῦτα, ὡς μὴ πυνθανοίατο οἱ ἐναντίοι. Οἱ μὲν δὴ ταῦτα τῆς νυκτὸς οὐδὲν ἀπυκοιμηθέντες παραρτέοντο.

An oracle fulfilled.

LXXVII. Χρησμοῖσι δὲ οὐκ ἔχω ἀντιλέγειν ὡς
25 οὐκ εἰσὶ ἀληθέες, οὐ βουλόμενος ἐναργέως λέγοντας

πειρᾶσθαι καταβάλλειν, ἐς τοιάδε πρήγματα ἐσβλέψας.

Ἀλλ' ὅταν Ἀρτέμιδος χρυσαόρου ἱερὸν ἀκτὴν
νηυσὶ γεφυρώσωσι καὶ εἰναλίην Κυνόσουραν,
ἐλπίδι μαινομένῃ λιπαρὰς πέρσαντες Ἀθήνας, 5
δῖα Δίκη σβέσσει κρατερὸν Κόρον, Ὕβριος υἱόν,
δεινὸν μαιμώοντα, δοκεῦντ' ἀνὰ πάντα πιθέσθαι.
Χαλκὸς γὰρ χαλκῷ συμμίξεται, αἵματι δ' Ἄρης
πόντον φοινίξει. τότ' ἐλεύθερον Ἑλλάδος ἦμαρ
εὐρύοπα Κρονίδης ἐπάγει καὶ πότνια Νίκη. 10

ἐς τοιαῦτα μὲν καὶ οὕτω ἐναργέως λέγοντι Βάκιδι ἀντιλογίης χρησμῶν πέρι οὔτε αὐτὸς λέγειν τολμῶ οὔτε παρ' ἄλλων ἐνδέκομαι.

During the night the Greek captains, not knowing what had happened, were still angrily debating, when Aristeides arrived from Aegina, bringing word of the Persian movement which he had actually seen.

LXXVIII. Τῶν δὲ ἐν Σαλαμῖνι στρατηγῶν ἐγίνετο ὠθισμὸς λόγων πολλός. ᾔδεσαν δὲ οὔκω, ὅτι 15 σφέας περιεκυκλέοντο τῇσι νηυσὶ οἱ βάρβαροι, ἀλλ' ὥσπερ τῆς ἡμέρης ὥρεον αὐτοὺς τεταγμένους, ἐδόκεον κατὰ χώρην εἶναι. LXXIX. Συνεστηκότων δὲ τῶν στρατηγῶν ἐξ Αἰγίνης διέβη Ἀριστείδης ὁ Λυσιμάχου, ἀνὴρ Ἀθηναῖος μέν, ἐξωστρακισμένος δὲ ὑπὸ 20 τοῦ δήμου, τὸν ἐγὼ νενόμικα, πυνθανόμενος αὐτοῦ τὸν τρόπον, ἄριστον ἄνδρα γενέσθαι ἐν Ἀθήνῃσι καὶ δικαιότατον. οὗτος ὡνὴρ στὰς ἐπὶ τὸ συνέδριον ἐξεκαλέετο Θεμιστοκλέα, ἐόντα μὲν ἑωυτῷ οὐ φίλον, ἐχθρὸν δὲ τὰ μάλιστα· ὑπὸ δὲ μεγάθεος τῶν παρεόν- 25
των κακῶν λήθην ἐκείνων ποιεύμενος ἐξεκαλέετο,

ἐθέλων αὐτῷ συμμῖξαι. προακηκόεε δὲ, ὅτι σπεύδοιεν οἱ ἀπὸ Πελοποννήσου ἀνάγειν τὰς νέας πρὸς τὸν Ἰσθμόν. ὡς δὲ ἐξῆλθέ οἱ Θεμιστοκλῆς, ἔλεγε Ἀριστείδης τάδε· "Ἡμέας στασιάζειν χρεόν ἐστι ἔν
5 "τε τῷ ἄλλῳ καιρῷ καὶ δὴ καὶ ἐν τῷδε περὶ τοῦ "ὁκότερος ἡμέων πλέω ἀγαθὰ τὴν πατρίδα ἐργάσεται. "λέγω δέ τοι, ὅτι ἴσόν ἐστι πολλά τε καὶ ὀλίγα λέγειν "περὶ ἀποπλόου τοῦ ἐνθεῦτεν Πελοποννησίοισι. ἐγὼ "γὰρ αὐτόπτης τοι λέγω γενόμενος, ὅτι νῦν οὐδ᾽ ἢν
10 "ἐθέλωσι Κορίνθιοί τε καὶ αὐτὸς Εὐρυβιάδης οἱοί τε "ἔσονται ἐκπλῶσαι· περιεχόμεθα γὰρ ὑπὸ τῶν πολε- "μίων κύκλῳ. ἀλλ᾽ ἐσελθὼν σφι ταῦτα σήμηνον."
LXXX. Ὁ δ᾽ ἀμείβετο τοισίδε· "Κάρτα τε χρηστὰ "διακελεύεαι καὶ εὖ ἤγγειλας. τὰ γὰρ ἐγὼ ἐδεόμην
15 "γενέσθαι, αὐτὸς αὐτόπτης γενόμενος ἥκεις. ἴσθι γὰρ "ἐξ ἐμέο τὰ ποιεύμενα ὑπὸ Μήδων. ἔδεε γάρ, ὅτε οὐκ "ἑκόντες ἤθελον ἐς μάχην κατίστασθαι οἱ Ἕλληνες, "ἀέκοντας παραστήσασθαι. σὺ δὲ ἐπεί περ ἥκεις "χρηστὰ ἀπαγγέλλων, αὐτός σφι ἄγγειλον. ἢν γὰρ
20 "ἐγὼ αὐτὰ λέγω, δόξω πλάσας λέγειν καὶ οὐ πείσω "ὡς οὐ ποιεύντων τῶν βαρβάρων ταῦτα. ἀλλά σφι "σήμηνον αὐτὸς παρελθών, ὡς ἔχει. ἐπεὰν δὲ σημή- "νῃς, ἢν μὲν πείθωνται, ταῦτα δὴ τὰ κάλλιστα, ἢν δὲ "αὐτοῖσι μὴ πιστὰ γένηται, ὁμοῖον ἡμῖν ἔσται. οὐ
25 "γὰρ ἔτι διαδρήσονται, εἴ περ περιεχόμεθα παντα- "χόθεν, ὡς σὺ λέγεις."

Aristeides fails to convince the captains;

LXXXI. Ταῦτα ἔλεγε παρελθὼν ὁ Ἀριστείδης, φάμενος ἐξ Αἰγίνης τε ἥκειν καὶ μόγις ἐκπλῶσαι λαθὼν τοὺς ἐπορμέοντας· περιέχεσθαι γὰρ πᾶν τὸ

στρατόπεδον τὸ Ἑλληνικὸν ὑπὸ τῶν νεῶν τῶν Ξέρ-
ξεω· παραρτέεσθαί τε συνεβούλευε ὡς ἀλεξησομένους.
Καὶ ὁ μὲν ταῦτα εἴπας μετεστήκεε, τῶν δὲ αὖτις
ἐγίνετο λόγων ἀμφισβασίη· οἱ γὰρ πλεῦνες τῶν
στρατηγῶν οὐκ ἐπείθοντο τὰ ἐξαγγελθέντα. 5

*but his news is confirmed by the arrival of a Tenian
trireme which had deserted from the Persian fleet.*

LXXXII. Ἀπιστεόντων δὲ τούτων ἧκε τριήρης
ἀνδρῶν Τηνίων αὐτομολέουσα, τῆς ἦρχε ἀνὴρ Παναί-
τιος ὁ Σωσιμένεος, ἥ περ δὴ ἔφερε τὴν ἀληθείην
πᾶσαν. διὰ δὲ τοῦτο τὸ ἔργον ἐνεγράφησαν Τήνιοι
ἐν Δελφοῖσι ἐς τὸν τρίποδα ἐν τοῖσι τὸν βάρβαρον 10
κατελοῦσι. σὺν δὲ ὦν ταύτῃ τῇ νηῒ τῇ αὐτομολησά-
σῃ ἐς Σαλαμῖνα καὶ τῇ πρότερον ἐπ' Ἀρτεμίσιον τῇ
Λημνίῃ ἐξεπληροῦτο τὸ ναυτικὸν τοῖσι Ἕλλησι ἐς
τὰς ὀγδώκοντα καὶ τριηκοσίας νέας· δύο γὰρ δὴ νεῶν
τότε κατέδεε ἐς τὸν ἀριθμόν. 15

*The Greeks therefore prepare to fight. Just as they are
putting off to sea the Aeacid Heroes arrive.*

LXXXIII. Τοῖσι δὲ Ἕλλησι ὡς πιστὰ δὴ τὰ
λεγόμενα ἦν τῶν Τηνίων ῥήματα, παρεσκευάζοντο ὡς
ναυμαχήσοντες. ἠώς τε δὴ διέφαινε, καὶ οἳ σύλλογον τῶν ἐπιβατέων ποιησάμενοι, προηγόρευε εὖ ἔχοντα μὲν ἐκ πάντων Θεμιστοκλέης, τὰ δὲ ἔπεα ἦν πάντα 20
κρέσσω τοῖσι ἕσσοσι ἀντιτιθέμενα. ὅσα δὲ ἐν ἀνθρώπου φύσι καὶ καταστάσι ἐγγίνεται, παραινέσας δὴ
τούτων τὰ κρέσσω αἱρέεσθαι, καὶ καταπλέξας τὴν
ῥῆσιν, ἐσβαίνειν ἐκέλευε ἐς τὰς νέας. Καὶ οὗτοι μὲν
δὴ ἐσέβαινον, καὶ ἧκε ἡ ἀπ' Αἰγίνης τριήρης, ἣ κατὰ 25

τοὺς Αἰακίδας ἀπεδήμησε. ἐνθαῦτα ἀνῆγον τὰς νέας ἁπάσας οἱ Ἕλληνες.

The fight. It is begun by the Athenian Ameinias charging and grappling a ship of the enemy. Both sides come to the rescue and the battle becomes general.

LXXXIV. Ἀναγομένοισι δέ σφι αὐτίκα ἐπεκέατο οἱ βάρβαροι. οἱ μὲν δὴ ἄλλοι Ἕλληνες [ἐπὶ] πρύμνην ἀνεκρούοντο καὶ ὤκελλον τὰς νέας, Ἀμεινίης δὲ Παλληνεὺς ἀνὴρ Ἀθηναῖος ἐξαναχθεὶς νηὶ ἐμβάλλει. συμπλακείσης δὲ τῆς νεὸς καὶ οὐ δυναμένων ἀπαλλαγῆναι, οὕτω δὴ οἱ ἄλλοι Ἀμεινίῃ βοηθέοντες συνέμισγον. Ἀθηναῖοι μὲν οὕτω λέγουσι τῆς ναυμαχίης γενέσθαι τὴν ἀρχήν, Αἰγινῆται δὲ τὴν κατὰ τοὺς Αἰακίδας ἀποδημήσασαν ἐς Αἴγιναν, ταύτην εἶναι τὴν ἄρξασαν. λέγεται δὲ καὶ τάδε, ὡς φάσμα σφι γυναικὸς ἐφάνη, φανεῖσαν δὲ διακελεύσασθαι ὥστε καὶ ἅπαν ἀκοῦσαι τὸ τῶν Ἑλλήνων στρατόπεδον ὀνειδίσασαν πρότερον τάδε· "Ὦ δαιμόνιοι, μέχρι "κόσου ἔτι πρύμνην ἀνακρούεσθε;" LXXXV. Κατὰ μὲν δὴ Ἀθηναίους ἐτετάχατο Φοίνικες (οὗτοι γὰρ εἶχον τὸ πρὸς Ἐλευσῖνός τε καὶ ἑσπέρης κέρας) κατὰ δὲ Λακεδαιμονίους Ἴωνες· οὗτοι δ' εἶχον τὸ πρὸς τὴν ἠῶ τε καὶ τὸν Πειραιέα. ἠθελοκάκεον μέντοι αὐτῶν κατὰ τὰς Θεμιστοκλέος ἐντολὰς ὀλίγοι, οἱ δὲ πλεῦνες οὔ. ἔχω μέν νυν συχνῶν οὐνόματα τριηράρχων καταλέξαι τῶν νέας Ἑλληνίδας ἑλόντων, χρήσομαι δὲ αὐτοῖσι οὐδὲν πλὴν Θεομήστορός τε τοῦ Ἀνδροδάμαντος καὶ Φυλάκου τοῦ Ἱστιαίου, Σαμίων ἀμφοτέρων. τοῦδε δὲ εἵνεκεν μέμνημαι τούτων μούνων, ὅτι Θεομήστωρ μὲν διὰ τοῦτο τὸ ἔργον Σάμου ἐτυράννευσε καταστησάντων τῶν Περσέων, Φύλακος δὲ εὐεργέτης βασιλέος ἀνεγράφη καὶ χώρῃ οἱ ἐδωρήθη πολλή. οἱ δ' εὐεργέται βασιλέος ὀροσάγγαι καλέονται Περσιστί. LXXXVI. Περὶ μὲν νυν τούτους οὕτω εἶχε, τὸ δὲ πλῆθος τῶν νεῶν ἐν τῇ Σαλαμῖνι ἐκεραΐζετο, αἱ μὲν ὑπ' Ἀθηναίων διαφθειρόμεναι, αἱ δὲ ὑπὸ Αἰγινητέων. ἅτε γὰρ τῶν μὲν Ἑλλήνων σὺν κόσμῳ ναυμαχεόντων κατὰ τάξιν, τῶν δὲ βαρβάρων οὐ τεταγμένων ἔτι οὔτε σὺν νόῳ ποιεόντων οὐδὲν, ἔμελλε τοιοῦτό σφι συνοίσεσθαι, οἷόν περ ἀπέβη. καίτοι ἦσάν γε καὶ ἐγένοντο ταύτην τὴν ἡμέρην μακρῷ ἀμείνονες αὐτοὶ ἑωυτῶν ἢ πρὸς Εὐβοίῃ, πᾶς τις προθυμεόμενος καὶ δειμαίνων Ξέρξην, ἐδόκεέ τε ἕκαστος ἑωυτὸν θηήσεσθαι βασιλέα.

A gallant feat of Queen Artemisia.

LXXXVII. Κατὰ μὲν δὴ τοὺς ἄλλους οὐκ ἔχω μετεξετέρους εἰπεῖν ἀτρεκέως ὡς ἕκαστοι τῶν βαρβάρων ἢ τῶν Ἑλλήνων ἠγωνίζοντο, κατὰ δὲ Ἀρτεμισίην τάδε ἐγένετο, ἀπ' ὧν εὐδοκίμησε μᾶλλον ἔτι παρὰ βασιλέϊ· ἐπειδὴ γὰρ ἐς θόρυβον πολλὸν ἀπίκετο τὰ βασιλέος πρήγματα, ἐν τούτῳ τῷ καιρῷ ἡ νηῦς ἡ Ἀρτεμισίης ἐδιώκετο ὑπὸ νεὸς Ἀττικῆς· καὶ ἣ οὐκ ἔχουσα διαφυγεῖν, ἔμπροσθε γὰρ αὐτῆς ἦσαν ἄλλαι νέες φίλιαι, ἡ δὲ αὐτῆς πρὸς τῶν πολεμίων μάλιστα ἐτύγχανε ἐοῦσα, ἔδοξέ οἱ τόδε ποιῆσαι, τὸ καὶ συνήνεικε ποιησάσῃ· διωκομένη γὰρ ὑπὸ τῆς Ἀττικῆς φέρουσα ἐνέβαλε νηῒ φιλίῃ ἀνδρῶν τε Καλυνδέων καὶ αὐτοῦ ἐπιπλώοντος τοῦ Καλυνδέων βασιλέος Δαμασιθύμου. εἰ μὲν καί τι νεῖκος πρὸς αὐτὸν ἐγεγόνεε ἔτι περὶ Ἑλλήσποντον ἐόντων, οὐ

μέντοι ἔγωγε ἔχω εἰπεῖν, οὔτε εἰ ἐκ προνοίης αὐτὰ
ἐποίησε, οὔτε εἰ συνεκύρησε ἡ τῶν Καλυνδέων κατὰ
τύχην παραπεσοῦσα νηῦς. ὡς δὲ ἐνέβαλέ τε καὶ
κατέδυσε, εὐτυχίῃ χρησαμένη διπλόα ἑωυτὴν ἀγαθὰ
5 ἐργάσατο· ὅ τε γὰρ τῆς Ἀττικῆς νεὸς τριήραρχος ὡς
εἰδέ μιν ἐμβάλλουσαν νηὶ ἀνδρῶν βαρβάρων, νομίσας
τὴν νέα τὴν Ἀρτεμισίης ἢ Ἑλληνίδα εἶναι ἢ αὐτο
μολέειν ἐκ τῶν βαρβάρων καὶ αὐτοῖσι ἀμύνειν, ἀπο
στρέψας πρὸς ἄλλας ἐτράπετο. LXXXVIII. Τοῦτο
10 μὲν τοιοῦτο αὐτῇ συνήνεικε γενέσθαι διαφυγεῖν τε καὶ
μὴ ἀπολέσθαι, τοῦτο δὲ συνέβη ὥστε κακὸν ἐργασα
μένην ἀπὸ τούτων αὐτὴν μάλιστα εὐδοκιμῆσαι παρὰ
Ξέρξῃ. λέγεται γὰρ βασιλέα θηεύμενον μαθεῖν τὴν
νέα ἐμβαλοῦσαν καὶ δή τινα εἶπαι τῶν παρεόντων·
15 "Δέσποτα, ὁρᾷς Ἀρτεμισίην, ὡς εὖ ἀγωνίζεται καὶ νέα
"τῶν πολεμίων κατέδυσε;" Καὶ τὸν ἐπείρεσθαι, εἰ
ἀληθέως ἐστὶ Ἀρτεμισίης τὸ ἔργον, καὶ τοὺς φάναι
σαφέως τὸ ἐπίσημον τῆς νεὸς ἐπισταμένους· τὴν δὲ
διαφθαρεῖσαν ἠπιστέατο εἶναι πολεμίην. τά τε γὰρ
20 ἄλλα, ὡς εἴρηται, αὐτῇ συνήνεικεν ἐς εὐτυχίην γενό
μενα καὶ τὸ τῶν ἐκ τῆς Καλυνδικῆς νεὸς μηδένα
ἀποσωθέντα κατήγορον γενέσθαι. Ξέρξην δὲ εἶπαι
λέγεται πρὸς τὰ φραζόμενα· "Οἱ μὲν ἄνδρες γεγό
"νασί μοι γυναῖκες, αἱ δὲ γυναῖκες ἄνδρες." Ταῦτα
25 μὲν Ξέρξην φασὶ εἶπαι.

The losses of either side.

LXXXIX. Ἐν δὲ τῷ πόνῳ τούτῳ ἀπὸ μὲν ἔθανε
ὁ στρατηγὸς Ἀριαβίγνης ὁ Δαρείου, Ξέρξεω ἐὼν
ἀδελφεός, ἀπὸ δὲ ἄλλοι πολλοί τε καὶ οὐνομαστοὶ
Περσέων καὶ Μήδων καὶ τῶν ἄλλων συμμάχων,

ὀλίγοι δέ τινες καὶ Ἑλλήνων. ἅτε γὰρ νέειν ἐπιστάμενοι, τοῖσι αἱ νέες διεφθείροντο, καὶ μὴ ἐν χειρῶν νόμῳ ἀπολλύμενοι ἐς τὴν Σαλαμῖνα διένεον. τῶν δὲ βαρβάρων οἱ πολλοὶ ἐν τῇ θαλάσσῃ διεφθάρησαν, νέειν οὐκ ἐπιστάμενοι. ἐπεὶ δὲ αἱ πρῶται ἐς 5 φυγὴν ἐτράποντο, ἐνθαῦτα αἱ πλεῖσται διεφθείροντο. οἱ γὰρ ὄπισθε τεταγμένοι, ἐς τὸ πρόσθε τῇσι νηυσὶ παριέναι πειρώμενοι ὡς ἀποδεξόμενοί τι καὶ αὐτοὶ ἔργον βασιλέϊ, τῇσι σφετέρῃσι νηυσὶ φευγούσῃσι περιέπιπτον. 10

Certain Phoenicians accuse the Ionians of treason, but are themselves executed. Xerxes watches the fight.

XC. Ἐγένετο δὲ καὶ τόδε ἐν τῷ θορύβῳ τούτῳ· τῶν τινὲς Φοινίκων, τῶν αἱ νέες διεφθάρατο, ἐλθόντες παρὰ βασιλέα διέβαλλον τοὺς Ἴωνας· ὡς δι' ἐκείνους ἀπολοίατο αἱ νέες, ὡς προδόντων. συνήνεικε ὦν οὕτω ὥστε Ἰώνων τε τοὺς στρατηγοὺς μὴ ἀπολέσθαι, Φοι- 15 νίκων τε τοὺς διαβάλλοντας λαβεῖν τοιόνδε μισθόν· ἔτι τούτων ταῦτα λεγόντων ἐνέβαλε νηῒ Ἀττικῇ Σαμοθρηϊκίη νηῦς. ἥ τε δὴ Ἀττικὴ κατεδύετο, καὶ ἐπιφερομένη Αἰγιναίη νηῦς κατέδυσε τῶν Σαμοθρηΐκων τὴν νέα. ἅτε δὴ ἐόντες ἀκοντισταὶ οἱ Σαμο- 20 θρήϊκες τοὺς ἐπιβάτας ἀπὸ τῆς καταδυσάσης νεὸς βάλλοντες ἀπήραξαν καὶ ἐπέβησάν τε καὶ ἔσχον αὐτήν. ταῦτα γενόμενα τοὺς Ἴωνας ἐρρύσατο· ὡς γὰρ εἶδέ σφεας Ξέρξης ἔργον μέγα ἐργασαμένους, ἐτράπετο πρὸς τοὺς Φοίνικας οἷα ὑπερλυπεόμενός 25 τε καὶ πάντας αἰτιώμενος, καὶ σφεων ἐκέλευσε τὰς κεφαλὰς ἀποταμεῖν, ἵνα μὴ αὐτοὶ κακοὶ γενόμενοι τοὺς ἀμείνονας διαβάλλωσι. ὅκως γάρ τινα ἴδοι

Ξέρξης τῶν ἑωυτοῦ ἔργον τι ἀποδεικνύμενον ἐν τῇ ναυμαχίῃ, κατήμενος ὑπὸ τῷ οὔρεϊ τῷ ἀντίον Σαλαμῖνος, τὸ καλέεται Αἰγάλεως, ἀνεπυνθάνετο τὸν ποιήσαντα, καὶ οἱ γραμματισταὶ ἀνέγραφον πατρόθεν τὸν τριήραρχον καὶ τὴν πόλιν. πρὸς δέ τι καὶ προσεβάλετο φίλος ἐὼν Ἀριαράμνης ἀνὴρ Πέρσης παρεὼν τούτου τοῦ Φοινικηΐου πάθεος.

The Persian fleet retires to Phalerum, harassed by the Aeginetan and Athenian ships.

XCI. Οἱ μὲν δὴ πρὸς τοὺς Φοίνικας ἐτράποντο, τῶν δὲ βαρβάρων ἐς φυγὴν τραπομένων καὶ ἐκπλεόντων πρὸς τὸ Φάληρον Αἰγινῆται ὑποστάντες ἐν τῷ πορθμῷ ἔργα ἀπεδέξαντο λόγου ἄξια. οἱ μὲν γὰρ Ἀθηναῖοι ἐν τῷ θορύβῳ ἐκεράϊζον τάς τε ἀντισταμένας καὶ τὰς φευγούσας τῶν νεῶν, οἱ δὲ Αἰγινῆται τὰς ἐκπλωούσας· ὅκως δέ τινες τοὺς Ἀθηναίους διαφύγοιεν, φερόμενοι ἐσέπιπτον ἐς τοὺς Αἰγινήτας.
XCII. Ἐνθαῦτα συνεκύρεον νέες ἥ τε Θεμιστοκλέος διώκουσα νέα, καὶ ἡ Πολυκρίτου τοῦ Κρίου ἀνδρὸς Αἰγινήτεω νηὶ ἐμβαλοῦσα Σιδωνίῃ, ἥ περ εἷλε τὴν προφυλάσσουσαν ἐπὶ Σκιάθῳ τὴν Αἰγιναίην, ἐπ' ἧς ἔπλεε Πυθέης ὁ Ἰσχενόου, τὸν οἱ Πέρσαι κατακοπέντα ἀρετῆς εἵνεκεν εἶχον ἐν τῇ νηὶ ἐκπαγλεόμενοι. τὸν δὴ περιάγουσα ἅμα Πέρσῃσι ἥλω νηῦς ἡ Σιδωνίη ὥστε Πυθέην οὕτω σωθῆναι ἐς Αἴγιναν. ὡς δὲ ἐσεῖδε τὴν νέα τὴν Ἀττικὴν ὁ Πολύκριτος, ἔγνω τὸ σημήϊον ἰδὼν τῆς στρατηγίδος, καὶ βώσας τὸν Θεμιστοκλέα ἐπεκερτόμησε ἐς τῶν Αἰγινητέων τὸν μηδισμὸν ὀνειδίζων. ταῦτα μέν νυν νηὶ ἐμβαλὼν ὁ

Πολύκριτος ἀπέρριψε ἐς Θεμιστοκλέα, οἱ δὲ βάρβαροι, τῶν αἱ νέες περιεγένοντο, φεύγοντες ἀπίκοντο ἐς Φάληρον ὑπὸ τὸν πεζὸν στρατόν.

The Aeginetans gained the first, the Athenians the second reputation for bravery in the battle. Artemisia escaped.

XCIII. Ἐν δὲ τῇ ναυμαχίῃ ταύτῃ ἤκουσαν Ἑλλήνων ἄριστα Αἰγινῆται, ἐπὶ δὲ Ἀθηναῖοι, ἀνδρῶν δὲ Πολύκριτός τε ὁ Αἰγινήτης καὶ Ἀθηναῖοι Εὐμένης τε ὁ Ἀναγυράσιος καὶ Ἀμεινίης Παλληνεὺς, ὃς καὶ Ἀρτεμισίην ἐπεδίωξε. εἰ μέν νυν ἔμαθε, ὅτι ἐν ταύτῃ πλέοι Ἀρτεμισίη, οὐκ ἂν ἐπαύσατο πρότερον ἢ εἷλέ μιν ἢ καὶ αὐτὸς ἥλω. τοῖσι γὰρ Ἀθηναίων τριηράρχοισι παρεκεκέλευστο, πρὸς δὲ καὶ ἄεθλον ἐκέετο μύριαι δραχμαί, ὃς ἄν μιν ζωὴν ἕλῃ· δεινὴν γάρ τι ἐποιεῦντο γυναῖκα ἐπὶ τὰς Ἀθήνας στρατεύεσθαι. αὕτη μὲν δὴ, ὡς πρότερον εἴρηται, διέφυγε, ἦσαν δὲ καὶ οἱ ἄλλοι, τῶν αἱ νέες περιεγεγόνεσαν, ἐν τῷ Φαλήρῳ.

The reported cowardice of the Corinthians.

XCIV. Ἀδείμαντον δὲ τὸν Κορίνθιον στρατηγὸν λέγουσι Ἀθηναῖοι αὐτίκα κατ' ἀρχὰς, ὡς συνέμισγον αἱ νέες, ἐκπλαγέντα τε καὶ ὑπερδείσαντα, τὰ ἱστία ἀειράμενον οἴχεσθαι φεύγοντα, ἰδόντας δὲ τοὺς Κορινθίους τὴν στρατηγίδα φεύγουσαν ὡσαύτως οἴχεσθαι. ὡς δὲ ἄρα φεύγοντας γίνεσθαι τῆς Σαλαμινίης κατὰ τὸ ἱρὸν Ἀθηναίης Σκιράδος, περιπίπτειν σφι κέλητα θείῃ πομπῇ, τὸν οὔτε πέμψαντα φανῆναι οὐδένα, οὔτε τι τῶν ἀπὸ τῆς στρατιῆς εἰδόσι προσ-

φέρεσθαι τοῖσι Κορινθίοισι. τῇδε δὲ σιμβάλλονται
εἶναι θεῖον τὸ πρῆγμα· ὡς γὰρ ἀγχοῦ γενέσθαι τῶν
νεῶν, τοὺς ἀπὸ τοῦ κέλητος λέγειν τάδε· "Ἀδείμαντε,
"σὺ μὲν ἀποστρέψας τὰς νέας ἐς φυγὴν ὥρμησαι
5 "καταπροδοὺς τοὺς Ἕλληνας· οἱ δὲ καὶ δὴ νικῶσι,
"ὅσον αὐτοὶ ἠρῶντο ἐπικρατῆσαι τῶν ἐχθρῶν." ταῦτα
λεγόντων, ἀπιστέειν γὰρ τὸν Ἀδείμαντον, αὖτις τάδε
λέγειν, ὡς αὐτοὶ οἷοί τε εἶεν ἀγόμενοι ὅμηροι ἀποθνῄ-
σκειν, ἢν μὴ νικῶντες φαίνωνται οἱ Ἕλληνες. οὕτω
10 δὴ ἀποστρέψαντα τὴν νέα αὐτόν τε καὶ τοὺς ἄλλους
ἐπ' ἐξεργασμένοισι ἐλθεῖν ἐς τὸ στρατόπεδον. τούτους
μὲν τοιαύτη φάτις ἔχει ὑπὸ Ἀθηναίων, οὐ μέντοι
αὐτοί γε Κορίνθιοι ὁμολογέουσι, ἀλλ' ἐν πρώτοισι
σφέας αὐτοὺς τῆς ναυμαχίης νομίζουσι γενέσθαι,
15 μαρτυρέει δέ σφι καὶ ἡ ἄλλη Ἑλλάς.

Aristides in Psyttaleia.

XCV. Ἀριστείδης δὲ ὁ Λυσιμάχου ἀνὴρ Ἀθηναῖος, τοῦ καὶ ὀλίγῳ τι πρότερον τούτων ἐπεμνήσθην
ὡς ἀνδρὸς ἀρίστου, οὗτος ἐν τῷ θορύβῳ τούτῳ τῷ
περὶ Σαλαμῖνα γενομένῳ τάδε ἐποίεε· παραλαβὼν
20 πολλοὺς τῶν ὁπλιτέων, οἳ παρατετάχατο παρὰ τὴν
ἀκτὴν τῆς Σαλαμινίης χώρης, γένος ἐόντες Ἀθηναῖοι,
ἐς τὴν Ψυττάλειαν νῆσον ἀπέβησε ἄγων, οἳ τοὺς
Πέρσας τοὺς ἐν τῇ νησῖδι ταύτῃ κατεφόνευσαν
πάντας.

*The Greeks collect the wrecks at Salamis; but some drift
upon the Attic coast.*

25 XCVI. Ὡς δὲ ἡ ναυμαχίη διελέλυτο, κατειρύσαντες ἐς τὴν Σαλαμῖνα οἱ Ἕλληνες τῶν ναυηγίων
ὅσα ταύτῃ ἐτύγχανε ἔτι ἐόντα, ἕτοιμοι ἦσαν ἐς

ἄλλην ναυμαχίην, ἐλπίζοντες τῇσι περιεούσῃσι νηυσὶ ἔτι χρήσεσθαι βασιλέα. τῶν δὲ ναυηγίων πολλὰ ὑπολαβὼν ἄνεμος ζέφυρος ἔφερε τῆς Ἀττικῆς ἐπὶ τὴν ἠϊόνα τὴν καλεομένην Κωλιάδα, ὥστε ἀποπλησθῆναι τὸν χρησμὸν τόν τε ἄλλον πάντα τὸν περὶ τῆς ναυμαχίης ταύτης εἰρημένον Βάκιδι καὶ Μουσαίῳ, καὶ δὴ καὶ κατὰ τὰ ναυήγια τὰ ταύτῃ ἐξενειχθέντα τὸ εἰρημένον πολλοῖσι ἔτεσι πρότερον τούτων ἐν χρησμῷ Λυσιστράτῳ Ἀθηναίῳ ἀνδρὶ χρησμολόγῳ, τὸ ἐλελήθεε πάντας τοὺς Ἕλληνας,

Κωλιάδες δὲ γυναῖκες ἐρετμοῖσι φρύξουσι·

τοῦτο δὲ ἔμελλε ἀπελάσαντος βασιλέος ἔσεσθαι.

The terror of Xerxes. He orders a bridge of boats to be made to Salamis.

XCVII. Ξέρξης δὲ ὡς ἔμαθε τὸ γεγονὸς πάθος, δείσας, μή τις τῶν Ἰώνων ὑπόθηται τοῖσι Ἕλλησι ἢ αὐτοὶ νοήσωσι πλέειν ἐς τὸν Ἑλλήσποντον λύσοντες τὰς γεφύρας καὶ ἀπολαμφθεὶς ἐν τῇ Εὐρώπῃ ἀπολέσθαι κινδυνεύσῃ, δρησμὸν ἐβούλευε· ἐθέλων δὲ μὴ ἐπίδηλος εἶναι μήτε τοῖσι Ἕλλησι μήτε τοῖσι ἑωυτοῦ ἐς τὴν Σαλαμῖνα χῶμα ἐπειρᾶτο διαχοῦν, γαυλούς τε Φοινικηΐους συνέδεε, ἵνα ἀντί τε σχεδίης ἔωσι καὶ τείχεος, ἀρτέετό τε ἐς πόλεμον ὡς ναυμαχίην ἄλλην ποιησόμενος. ὁρέοντες δέ μιν πάντες οἱ ἄλλοι ταῦτα πρήσσοντα εὖ ἠπιστέατο, ὡς ἐκ παντὸς νόου παρεσκεύασται μένων πολεμήσειν· Μαρδόνιον δ' οὐδὲν τούτων ἐλάνθανε ὡς μάλιστα ἔμπειρον ἐόντα τῆς ἐκείνου διανοίης. ταῦτά τε ἅμα Ξέρξης ἐποίεε, καὶ ἔπεμπε ἐς Πέρσας ἀγγελέοντα τὴν παρεοῦσάν σφι συμφορήν.

The Persian Courier post. Dismay at Susa.

XCVIII. Τούτων δὲ τῶν ἀγγέλων ἔστι οὐδὲν ὅ τι θᾶσσον παραγίνεται θνητὸν ἐόν· οὕτω τοῖσι Πέρσῃσι ἐξεύρηται τοῦτο. λέγουσι γάρ, ὡς ὅσων ἂν ἡμερέων ᾖ ἡ πᾶσα ὁδός, τοσοῦτοι ἵπποι τε καὶ ἄνδρες διεστᾶσι, κατὰ ἡμερησίην ὁδὸν ἑκάστην ἵππος τε καὶ ἀνὴρ τεταγμένος, τοὺς οὔτε νιφετός, οὐκ ὄμβρος, οὐ καῦμα, οὐ νὺξ ἔργει μὴ οὐ κατανύσαι τὸν προκείμενον ἑωυτῷ δρόμον τὴν ταχίστην. ὁ μὲν δὴ πρῶτος δραμὼν παραδιδοῖ τὰ ἐντεταλμένα τῷ δευτέρῳ, ὁ δὲ δεύτερος τῷ τρίτῳ· τὸ δὲ ἐνθεῦτεν ἤδη κατ' ἄλλον διεξέρχεται παραδιδόμενα, κατά περ Ἕλλησι ἡ λαμπαδηφορίη, τὴν τῷ Ἡφαίστῳ ἐπιτελέουσι. τοῦτο τὸ δράμημα τῶν ἵππων καλέουσι Πέρσαι ἀγγαρήιον. XCIX. Ἡ μὲν δὴ πρώτη ἐς Σοῦσα ἀγγελίη ἀπικομένη, ὡς ἔχοι Ἀθήνας Ξέρξης, ἔτερψε οὕτω δή τι Περσέων τοὺς ὑπολειφθέντας, ὡς τάς τε ὁδοὺς μυρσίνῃσι πάσας ἐστόρεσαν καὶ ἐθυμίων θυμιήματα καὶ αὐτοὶ ἦσαν ἐν θυσίῃσί τε καὶ εὐπαθείῃσι· ἡ δὲ δευτέρη σφι ἀγγελίη ἐπεξελθοῦσα συνέχεε οὕτω· ὥστε τοὺς κιθῶνας κατερρήξαντο πάντες, βοῇ τε καὶ οἰμωγῇ ἐχρέοντο ἀπλέτῳ, Μαρδόνιον ἐν αἰτίῃ τιθέντες. οὐκ οὕτω δὲ περὶ τῶν νεῶν ἀχθόμενοι ταῦτα οἱ Πέρσαι ἐποίευν, ὡς περὶ αὐτῷ Ξέρξῃ δειμαίνοντες.

Mardonius consoles Xerxes, and advises him to return home.

C. Καὶ περὶ Πέρσας μὲν ἦν ταῦτα τὸν πάντα μεταξὺ χρόνον γενόμενον, μέχρι οὗ Ξέρξης αὐτός σφεας ἀπικόμενος ἔπαυσε. Μαρδόνιος δὲ ὁρέων μὲν

Ξέρξην συμφορὴν μεγάλην ἐκ τῆς ναυμαχίης ποιεύμενον, ὑποπτεύων δὲ αὐτὸν δρησμὸν βουλεύειν ἐκ τῶν Ἀθηνέων, φροντίσας πρὸς ἑωυτὸν ὡς δώσει δίκην ἀναγνώσας βασιλέα στρατεύεσθαι ἐπὶ τὴν Ἑλλάδα, καί οἱ κρέσσον εἴη ἀνακινδυνεῦσαι ἢ κατεργάσασθαι τὴν Ἑλλάδα ἢ αὐτὸν καλῶς τελευτῆσαι τὸν βίον ὑπὲρ μεγάλων αἰωρηθέντα· πλέον μέντοι ἔφερέ οἱ ἡ γνώμη κατεργάσασθαι τὴν Ἑλλάδα· λογισάμενος ὦν ταῦτα προσέφερε τὸν λόγον τόνδε· "Δέσποτα, "μήτε λυπέεο μήτε συμφορὴν μηδεμίαν μεγάλην "ποιεῦ τοῦδε τοῦ γεγονότος εἵνεκεν πρήγματος. οὐ "γὰρ ξύλων ἀγὼν ὁ τὸ πᾶν φέρων ἐστὶ ἡμῖν, ἀλλ' "ἀνδρῶν τε καὶ ἵππων. σοὶ δὲ οὔτε τις τούτων τῶν "τὸ πᾶν σφι ἤδη δοκεόντων κατεργάσθαι ἀποβὰς "ἀπὸ τῶν νεῶν πειρήσεται ἀντιωθῆναι, οὔτ' ἐκ τῆς "ἠπείρου τῆσδε· οἵ τε ἡμῖν ἠντιώθησαν, ἔδοσαν "δίκας. εἰ μέν νυν δοκέει, αὐτίκα πειρώμεθα τῆς "Πελοποννήσου· εἰ δὲ καὶ δοκέει ἐπισχεῖν, παρέχει "ποιέειν ταῦτα. μὴ δὲ δυσθύμεε· οὐ γάρ ἐστι "Ἕλλησι οὐδεμία ἔκδυσις μὴ οὐ, δόντας λόγον τῶν "ἐποίησαν νῦν τε καὶ πρότερον, εἶναι σοὺς δούλους. "μάλιστα μέν νυν ταῦτα ποίεε· εἰ δ' ἄρα τοι βεβού-"λευται αὐτὸν ἀπελαύνοντα ἀπάγειν τὴν στρατιήν, "ἄλλην ἔχω καὶ ἐκ τῶνδε βουλήν. σὺ Πέρσας, 'βασιλεῦ, μὴ ποιήσῃς καταγελάστους γενέσθαι "Ἕλλησι. οὐδὲν γὰρ ἐν τοῖσι Πέρσῃσι δεδήληται "τῶν πρηγμάτων, οὐδὲ ἐρέεις ὅκου ἐγενόμεθα ἄνδρες "κακοί. εἰ δὲ Φοίνικές τε καὶ Αἰγύπτιοι καὶ Κύπριοι "τε καὶ Κίλικες κακοὶ ἐγένοντο, οὐδὲν πρὸς Πέρσας "τοῦτο προσήκει τὸ πάθος. ἤδη ὦν ἐπειδὴ οὐ Πέρσαι "τοι αἴτιοί εἰσι, ἐμοὶ πείθεο· εἴ τοι δέδοκται μὴ

"παραμένειν, σὺ μὲν ἐς ἤθεα τὰ σεωυτοῦ ἀπέλαυνε,
"τῆς στρατιῆς ἀπάγων τὸ πολλὸν, ἐμὲ δέ σοι χρὴ
"τὴν Ἑλλάδα παρασχεῖν δεδουλωμένην, τριήκοντα
"μυριάδας τοῦ στρατοῦ ἀπολεξάμενον."

A council of war. Artemisia gives the same advice as Mardonius.

CI. Ταῦτα ἀκούσας Ξέρξης ὡς ἐκ κακῶν ἐχάρη τε καὶ ἥσθη, πρὸς Μαρδόνιόν τε βουλευσάμενος ἔφη ὑποκρινέεσθαι ὁκότερον ποιήσει τούτων. ὡς δὲ ἐβουλεύετο ἅμα Περσέων τοῖσι ἐπικλήτοισι, ἔδοξέ οἱ καὶ Ἀρτεμισίην ἐς συμβουλίην μεταπέμψασθαι, ὅτι πρότερον ἐφαίνετο μούνη νοέουσα τὰ ποιητέα ἦν. ὡς δὲ ἀπίκετο ἡ Ἀρτεμισίη, μεταστησάμενος τοὺς ἄλλους, τούς τε συμβούλους Περσέων καὶ τοὺς δορυφόρους, ἔλεξε Ξέρξης τάδε· "Κελεύει με Μαρδόνιος μένοντα
"αὐτοῦ πειρᾶσθαι τῆς Πελοποννήσου, λέγων ὥς μοι
"Πέρσαι τε καὶ ὁ πεζὸς στρατὸς οὐδενὸς μεταίτιοι
"πάθεός εἰσι, ἀλλὰ βουλομένοισί σφι γένοιτ' ἂν ἀπό-
"δεξις. ἐμὲ ὦν ἢ ταῦτα κελεύει ποιέειν, ἢ αὐτὸς ἐθέλει
"τριήκοντα μυριάδας ἀπολεξάμενος τοῦ στρατοῦ
"παρασχεῖν μοι τὴν Ἑλλάδα δεδουλωμένην, αὐτὸν
"δ' ἐμὲ κελεύει ἀπελαύνειν σὺν τῷ λοιπῷ στρατῷ ἐς
"ἤθεα τὰ ἐμά. σὺ ὦν ἐμοὶ, καὶ γὰρ περὶ τῆς
"ναυμαχίης εὖ συνεβούλευσας τῆς γενομένης οὐκ
"ἐῶσα ποιέεσθαι, νῦν τε συμβούλευσον ὁκότερα
"ποιέων ἐπιτύχω εὖ βουλευσάμενος." CII. Ὁ μὲν ταῦτα συνεβουλεύετο, ἡ δὲ λέγει τάδε· "Βασιλεῦ,
"χαλεπὸν μέν ἐστι συμβουλευομένῳ τυχεῖν τὰ
"ἄριστα εἴπασαν, ἐπὶ μέντοι τοῖσι κατήκουσι πρήγ-
"μασι δοκέει μοι αὐτὸν μέν σε ἀπελαύνειν ὀπίσω,

"Μαρδόνιον δὲ, εἰ ἐθέλει τε καὶ ὑποδέκεται ταῦτα
"ποιήσειν, αὐτοῦ καταλιπεῖν σὺν τοῖσι ἐθέλει. τοῦτο
"μὲν γάρ, ἢν καταστρέψηται τά φησι ἐθέλειν καί οἱ
"προχωρήσῃ τὰ νοέων λέγει, σὸν τὸ ἔργον, ὦ δέσποτα,
"γίνεται, οἱ γὰρ σοὶ δοῦλοι κατεργάσαντο, τοῦτο δὲ, 5
"ἢν τὰ ἐναντία τῆς Μαρδονίου γνώμης γένηται,
"οὐδεμία συμφορὴ μεγάλη ἔσται σέο τε περιεόντος
"καὶ ἐκείνων τῶν πρηγμάτων περὶ οἶκον τὸν σόν. ἢν
"γὰρ σύ τε περιῇς καὶ οἶκος ὁ σὸς, πολλοὺς πολλάκις
"ἀγῶνας δραμέονται περὶ σφέων αὐτῶν οἱ Ἕλληνες. 10
"Μαρδονίου δὲ, ἤν τι πάθῃ, λόγος οὐδεὶς γίνεται·
"οὐδέ τι νικῶντες οἱ Ἕλληνες νικῶσι, δοῦλον σὸν
"ἀπολέσαντες· σὺ δὲ, τῶν εἵνεκεν τὸν στόλον ἐποι-
"ήσαο, πυρώσας τὰς Ἀθήνας ἀπελᾷς."

Xerxes commissions Artemisia to conduct his children to Ephesos under the charge of Hermotimos.

CIII. Ἥσθη τε δὴ τῇ συμβουλίῃ Ξέρξης· 15
λέγουσα γὰρ ἐπετύγχανε τά περ αὐτὸς ἐνόεε. οὐδὲ
γὰρ εἰ πάντες καὶ πᾶσαι συνεβούλευον αὐτῷ μένειν,
ἔμενε ἂν δοκέειν ἐμοί· οὕτω καταρρωδήκεε. ἐπαινέ-
σας δὲ τὴν Ἀρτεμισίην ταύτην μὲν ἀποστέλλει
ἄγουσαν αὐτοῦ τοὺς παῖδας ἐς Ἔφεσον· νόθοι γάρ 20
τινες παῖδές οἱ συνείποντο. CIV. Συνέπεμπε δὲ
τοῖσι παισὶ φύλακον Ἑρμότιμον, γένος μὲν ἐόντα
Πηδασέα, φερόμενον δὲ οὐ τὰ δεύτερα τῶν εὐνούχων
παρὰ βασιλέϊ. οἱ δὲ Πηδασέες οἰκέουσι ὑπὲρ Ἁλι-
καρνησοῦ. ἐν δὲ τοῖσι Πηδάσοισι τούτοισι τοιόνδε 25
φέρεται πρῆγμα γίνεσθαι· ἐπεὰν τοῖσι ἀμφικτυόσι
πᾶσι τοῖσι ἀμφὶ ταύτης οἰκέουσι τῆς πόλιος μέλλῃ
τι ἐντὸς χρόνου ἔσεσθαι χαλεπόν, τότε ἡ ἱρείη αὐτόθι

τῆς Ἀθηναίης φύει πώγωνα μέγαν. τοῦτο δέ σφι δὶς ἤδη ἐγένετο.

The terrible revenge of Hermotimos.

CV. Ἐκ τούτων δὴ τῶν Πηδασέων ὁ Ἑρμότιμος ἦν, τῷ μεγίστη τίσις ἤδη ἀδικηθέντι ἐγένετο πάντων τῶν ἡμεῖς ἴδμεν. ἁλόντα γὰρ αὐτὸν ὑπὸ πολεμίων καὶ πωλεόμενον ὠνέεται Πανιώνιος ἀνὴρ Χῖος, ὃς τὴν ζόην κατεστήσατο ἀπ᾽ ἔργων ἀνοσιωτάτων. ὅκως γὰρ κτήσαιτο παῖδας εἴδεος ἐπαμμένους, ἐκτάμνων ἀγινέων ἐπώλεε ἐς Σάρδις τε καὶ Ἔφεσον χρημάτων μεγάλων. παρὰ γὰρ τοῖσι βαρβάροισι τιμιώτεροί εἰσι οἱ εὐνοῦχοι πίστιος εἵνεκεν τῆς πάσης τῶν ἐνορχίων. ἄλλους τε δὴ ὁ Πανιώνιος ἐξέταμε πολλούς, ἅτε ποιεύμενος ἐκ τούτου τὴν ζόην, καὶ δὴ καὶ τοῦτον. καὶ, οὐ γὰρ τὰ πάντα ἐδυστύχεε ὁ Ἑρμότιμος, ἀπικνέεται ἐκ τῶν Σαρδίων παρὰ βασιλέα μετ᾽ ἄλλων δώρων, χρόνου δὲ προϊόντος πάντων τῶν εὐνούχων ἐτιμήθη μάλιστα παρὰ Ξέρξῃ. CVI. Ὡς δὲ τὸ στράτευμα τὸ Περσικὸν ὥρμα βασιλεὺς ἐπὶ τὰς Ἀθήνας ἐὼν ἐν Σάρδισι, ἐνθαῦτα καταβὰς κατά δή τι πρῆγμα ὁ Ἑρμότιμος ἐς γῆν τὴν Μυσίην, τὴν Χῖοι μὲν νέμονται, Ἀταρνεὺς δὲ καλέεται, εὑρίσκει τὸν Πανιώνιον ἐνθαῦτα. ἐπιγνοὺς δὲ ἔλεγε πρὸς αὐτὸν πολλοὺς καὶ φιλίους λόγους, πρῶτα μέν οἱ καταλέγων ὅσα αὐτὸς δι᾽ ἐκεῖνον ἔχοι ἀγαθά, δεύτερα δέ οἱ ὑπισχνεύμενος ἀντὶ τούτων ὅσα μιν ἀγαθὰ ποιήσει, ἢν κομίσας τοὺς οἰκέτας οἰκέῃ ἐκείνῃ, ὥστε ὑποδεξάμενον ἄσμενον τοὺς λόγους τὸν Πανιώνιον κομίσαι τὰ τέκνα καὶ τὴν γυναῖκα. ὡς δὲ ἄρα πανοικίῃ μιν περιέλαβε, ἔλεγε ὁ Ἑρμότιμος τάδε·

"Ὠ πάντων ἀνδρῶν ἤδη μάλιστα ἀπ' ἔργων ἀνοσιω-
"τάτων τὸν βίον κτησάμενε, τί σε ἐγὼ κακὸν ἢ αὐτὸς
"ἢ τῶν ἐμῶν τις ἐργάσατο, ἢ σὲ ἢ τῶν σῶν τινά, ὅτι
"με ἀντ' ἀνδρὸς ἐποίησας τὸ μηδὲν εἶναι; ἐδόκεές τε
"θεοὺς λήσειν οἷα ἐμηχανῶ τότε. οἵ σε ποιήσαντα 5
"ἀνόσια νόμῳ δικαίῳ χρεόμενοι, ὑπήγαγον ἐς χεῖρας
"τὰς ἐμάς, ὥστε σε μὴ μέμψασθαι τὴν ἀπ' ἐμέο τοι
"ἐσομένην δίκην." ὡς δέ οἱ ταῦτα ὠνείδισε, ἀχθέντων
τῶν παίδων ἐς ὄψιν ἠναγκάζετο ὁ Πανιώνιος τῶν
ἑωυτοῦ παίδων τεσσέρων ἐόντων τὰ αἰδοῖα ἀποτά- 10
μνειν, ἀναγκαζόμενος δὲ ἐποίεε ταῦτα. αὐτοῦ τε, ὡς
ταῦτα ἐργάσατο, οἱ παῖδες ἀναγκαζόμενοι ἀπέταμνον.
Πανιώνιον μέν νυν οὕτω περιῆλθε ἥ τε τίσις καὶ ὁ
Ἑρμότιμος.

The Persian fleet leaves Phalerum at night for the Hellespont.

CVII. Ξέρξης δὲ ὡς τοὺς παῖδας Ἀρτεμισίῃ 15
ἐπέτρεψε, ἀπάγειν ἐς Ἔφεσον, καλέσας Μαρδόνιον
ἐκέλευσέ μιν τῆς στρατιῆς διαλέγειν τοὺς βούλεται,
καὶ ποιέειν τοῖσι λόγοισι τὰ ἔργα πειρώμενον ὁμοῖα.
ταύτην μὲν τὴν ἡμέρην ἐς τοσοῦτο ἐγίνετο, τῆς δὲ
νυκτὸς κελεύσαντος βασιλέος τὰς νέας οἱ στρατηγοὶ 20
ἐκ τοῦ Φαλήρου ἀπῆγον ὀπίσω ἐς τὸν Ἑλλήσποντον,
ὡς τάχεος εἶχε ἕκαστος, διαφυλαξούσας τὰς σχεδίας
πορευθῆναι βασιλέϊ. ἐπεὶ δὲ ἀγχοῦ ἦσαν Ζωστῆρος
πλώοντες οἱ βάρβαροι, ἀνατείνουσι γὰρ ἄκραι λεπταὶ
τῆς ἠπείρου, ταύτας ἔδοξάν τε νέας εἶναι καὶ ἔφευγον 25
ἐπὶ πολλόν. χρόνῳ δὲ μαθόντες ὅτι οὐ νέες εἶεν,
ἀλλ' ἄκραι, συλλεχθέντες ἐκομίζοντο.

The Greek fleet pursues as far as Andros. 'Eurybiades, against the opinion of Themistokles, refuses to go farther.

CVIII. Ὡς δὲ ἡμέρη ἐγίνετο, ὁρέοντες οἱ Ἕλληνες κατὰ χώρην μένοντα τὸν στρατὸν τὸν πεζὸν ἤλπιζον καὶ τὰς νέας εἶναι περὶ Φάληρον, ἐδόκεόν τε ναυμαχήσειν σφέας, παραρτέοντό τε ὡς ἀλεξησόμενοι. ἐπεὶ δὲ ἐπύθοντο τὰς νέας οἰχωκυίας, αὐτίκα μετὰ ταῦτα ἐδόκεε ἐπιδιώκειν· τὸν μέν νυν ναυτικὸν τὸν Ξέρξεω στρατὸν οὐκ ἐπεῖδον διώξαντες μέχρι Ἄνδρου, ἐς δὲ τὴν Ἄνδρον ἀπικόμενοι ἐβουλεύοντο. Θεμιστοκλέης μέν νυν γνώμην ἀπεδείκνυτο διὰ νήσων τραπομένους καὶ ἐπιδιώξαντας τὰς νέας πλώειν ἰθέως ἐπὶ τὸν Ἑλλήσποντον λύσοντας τὰς γεφύρας. Εὐρυβιάδης δὲ τὴν ἐναντίην ταύτῃ γνώμην ἐτίθετο, λέγων, ὡς εἰ λύσουσι τὰς σχεδίας, τοῦτ' ἂν μέγιστον πάντων σφεῖς κακὸν τὴν Ἑλλάδα ἐργάσαιντο. εἰ γὰρ ἀναγκασθείη ἀπολαμφθεὶς ὁ Πέρσης μένειν ἐν τῇ Εὐρώπῃ, πειρῷτο ἂν ἡσυχίην μὴ ἄγειν, ὡς ἄγοντι μέν οἱ ἡσυχίην οὔτε τι προχωρέειν οἷόν τε ἔσται τῶν πρηγμάτων οὔτε τις κομιδὴ τὸ ὀπίσω φανήσεται, λιμῷ τέ οἱ ἡ στρατιὴ διαφθαρέεται, ἐπιχειρέοντι δὲ αὐτῷ καὶ ἔργου ἐχομένῳ πάντα τὰ κατὰ τὴν Εὐρώπην οἷά τε ἔσται προσχωρῆσαι κατὰ πόλιάς τε καὶ κατὰ ἔθνεα, ἤτοι ἁλισκομένων γε ἢ πρὸ τούτου ὁμολογεόντων. τροφήν τε ἕξειν σφέας τὸν ἐπέτειον αἰεὶ τῶν Ἑλλήνων καρπόν. ἀλλὰ δοκέειν γὰρ νικηθέντα τῇ ναυμαχίῃ οὐ μενέειν ἐν τῇ Εὐρώπῃ τὸν Πέρσην, ἐατέον ὦν εἶναι φεύγειν, ἐς ὃ ἔλθῃ φεύγων ἐς τὴν ἑωυτοῦ. τὸ ἐνθεῦτεν δὲ περὶ τῆς ἐκείνου ποιέεσθαι ἤδη τὸν ἀγῶνα ἐκέλευε. ταύτης δὲ εἴχοντο τῆς γνώμης καὶ Πελοποννησίων τῶν ἄλλων οἱ στρατηγοί.

The crafty speech of Themistokles.

CIX. Ὡς δὲ ἔμαθε ὅτι οὐ πείσει τούς γε πολλοὺς πλώειν ἐς τὸν Ἑλλήσποντον ὁ Θεμιστοκλέης, μεταβαλὼν πρὸς τοὺς Ἀθηναίους (οὗτοι γὰρ μάλιστα ἐκπεφευγότων περιημέκτεον, ὡρμέατό τε ἐς τὸν Ἑλλήσποντον πλώειν καὶ ἐπὶ σφέων αὐτῶν βαλλόμενοι, εἰ ὧλλοι μὴ βουλοίατο) ἔλεγέ σφι τάδε·
"Καὶ αὐτὸς ἤδη πολλοῖσι παρεγενόμην, καὶ πολλῷ
"πλέω ἀκήκοα τοιάδε γενέσθαι, ἄνδρας ἐς ἀναγκαίην
"ἀπειληθέντας νενικημένους ἀναμάχεσθαί τε καὶ
"ἀναλαμβάνειν τὴν προτέρην κακότητα. ἡμεῖς δὲ
"(εὕρημα γὰρ εὑρήκαμεν ἡμέας τε αὐτοὺς καὶ τὴν
"Ἑλλάδα, νέφος τοσοῦτο ἀνθρώπων ἀνωσάμενοι) μὴ
"διώκωμεν ἄνδρας φεύγοντας. τάδε γὰρ οὐκ ἡμεῖς
"κατεργασάμεθα, ἀλλὰ θεοί τε καὶ ἥρωες, οἳ ἐφθό-
"νησαν ἄνδρα ἕνα τῆς τε Ἀσίης καὶ τῆς Εὐρώπης
"βασιλεῦσαι ἐόντα ἀνόσιόν τε καὶ ἀτάσθαλον, ὃς τὰ
"ἱρὰ καὶ τὰ ἴδια ἐν ὁμοίῳ ἐποιέετο ἐμπιπράς τε καὶ
"καταβάλλων τῶν θεῶν τὰ ἀγάλματα, ὃς καὶ τὴν
"θάλασσαν ἀπεμαστίγωσε πέδας τε κατῆκε. ἀλλ'
"εὖ γὰρ ἔχει ἐς τὸ παρεὸν ἡμῖν νῦν μὲν ἐν τῇ Ἑλλάδι
"καταμείναντας ἡμέων τε αὐτῶν ἐπιμεληθῆναι καὶ
"τῶν οἰκετέων· καί τις οἰκίην τε ἀναπλασάσθω καὶ
"σπόρου ἀνακῶς ἐχέτω, παντελέως ἀπελάσας τὸν
"βάρβαρον· ἅμα δὲ τῷ ἔαρι καταπλέωμεν ἐπὶ Ἑλλησ-
"πόντου καὶ Ἰωνίης." ταῦτα ἔλεγε ἀποθήκην μέλλων ποιήσεσθαι ἐς τὸν Πέρσην, ἵνα ἢν ἄρα τί μιν καταλαμβάνῃ πρὸς Ἀθηναίων πάθος, ἔχῃ ἀποστροφήν· τά περ ὦν καὶ ἐγένετο.

Themistokles sends a message to Xerxes, asserting that he had restrained the Greeks from pursuit.

CX. Θεμιστοκλέης μὲν ταῦτα λέγων διέβαλλε, Ἀθηναῖοι δὲ ἐπείθοντο· ἐπειδὴ γὰρ καὶ πρότερον δεδογμένος εἶναι σοφὸς ἐφάνη ἐὼν ἀληθέως σοφός τε καὶ εὔβουλος, πάντως ἑτοῖμοι ἦσαν λέγοντι πείθεσθαι. ὡς δὲ οὗτοί οἱ ἀνεγνωσμένοι ἦσαν, αὐτίκα μετὰ ταῦτα ὁ Θεμιστοκλέης ἄνδρας ἀπέπεμπε ἔχοντας πλοῖον, τοῖσι ἐπίστευε σιγᾶν ἐς πᾶσαν βάσανον ἀπικνεομένοισι, τὰ αὐτὸς ἐνετείλατο βασιλέϊ φράσαι· τῶν καὶ Σίκιννος ὁ οἰκέτης αὖτις ἐγένετο. οἳ ἐπεί τε ἀπίκοντο πρὸς τὴν Ἀττικήν, οἱ μὲν κατέμενον ἐπὶ τῷ πλοίῳ, Σίκιννος δὲ ἀναβὰς παρὰ Ξέρξεα ἔλεγε τάδε· "Ἔπεμψέ με Θεμιστοκλέης ὁ Νεοκλέος, στρατηγὸς μὲν Ἀθηναίων, ἀνὴρ δὲ τῶν συμμάχων πάντων ἄριστος καὶ σοφώτατος, φράσοντά τοι ὅτι Θεμιστοκλέης ὁ Ἀθηναῖος, σοὶ βουλόμενος ὑπουργέειν, ἔσχε τοὺς Ἕλληνας τὰς νέας βουλομένους διώκειν καὶ τὰς ἐν Ἑλλησπόντῳ γεφύρας λύειν. καὶ νῦν κατ' ἡσυχίην πολλὴν κομίζεο."

Exaction of contributions from Andros, Karystos, Paros, and other islands.

CXI. Οἱ μὲν ταῦτα σημήναντες ἀπέπλωον ὀπίσω· οἱ δὲ Ἕλληνες· ἐπεί τέ σφι ἀπέδοξε μήτ' ἐπιδιώκειν ἔτι προσωτέρω τῶν βαρβάρων τὰς νέας, μήτε πλώειν ἐς τὸν Ἑλλήσποντον λύσοντας τὸν πόρον, τὴν Ἄνδρον περικατέατο, ἐξελεῖν ἐθέλοντες. πρῶτοι γὰρ Ἄνδριοι νησιωτέων αἰτηθέντες πρὸς Θεμιστοκλέος χρήματα οὐκ ἔδοσαν, ἀλλὰ προϊσχομένου Θεμιστοκλέος λόγον τόνδε, ὡς ἥκοιεν

Ἀθηναῖοι περὶ ἑωυτοὺς ἔχοντες δύο θεοὺς μεγάλους, Πειθώ τε καὶ Ἀναγκαίην, οὕτω τέ σφι κάρτα δοτέα εἶναι χρήματα, ὑπεκρίναντο πρὸς ταῦτα λέγοντες, ὡς κατὰ λόγον ἦσαν ἄρα αἱ Ἀθῆναι μεγάλαι τε καὶ εὐδαίμονες καὶ θεῶν χρηστῶν ἥκοιεν εὖ, ἐπεὶ Ἀνδρίους γε εἶναι γεωπείνας ἐς τὰ μέγιστα ἀνήκοντας, καὶ θεοὺς δύο ἀχρήστους οὐκ ἐκλείπειν σφέων τὴν νῆσον, ἀλλ' αἰεὶ φιλοχωρέειν, Πενίην τε καὶ Ἀμηχανίην, καὶ τούτων τῶν θεῶν ἐπηβόλους ἐόντας Ἀνδρίους οὐ δώσειν χρήματα· οὐδέκοτε γὰρ τῆς ἑωυτῶν ἀδυναμίης τὴν Ἀθηναίων δύναμιν εἶναι κρέσσω. οὗτοι μὲν δὴ ταῦτα ὑποκρινάμενοι καὶ οὐ δόντες χρήματα ἐπολιορκέοντο. CXII. Θεμιστοκλέης δέ, οὐ γὰρ ἐπαύετο πλεονεκτέων, ἐσπέμπων ἐς τὰς ἄλλας νήσους ἀπειλητηρίους λόγους αἴτεε χρήματα διὰ τῶν αὐτῶν ἀγγέλων, χρεόμενος λόγοισι τοῖσι καὶ πρὸς Ἀνδρίους ἐχρήσατο, λέγων ὡς εἰ μὴ δώσουσι τὸ αἰτεόμενον, ἐπάξει τὴν στρατιὴν τῶν Ἑλλήνων καὶ πολιορκέων ἐξαιρήσει. λέγων ὦν ταῦτα συνέλεγε χρήματα μεγάλα παρὰ Καρυστίων τε καὶ Παρίων, οἳ πυνθανόμενοι τήν τε Ἄνδρον ὡς πολιορκέοιτο διότι ἐμήδισε, καὶ Θεμιστοκλέα ὡς εἴη ἐν αἴνῃ μεγίστῃ τῶν στρατηγῶν, δείσαντες ταῦτα ἔπεμπον χρήματα. εἰ δὲ δή τινες καὶ ἄλλοι ἔδοσαν νησιωτέων, οὐκ ἔχω εἶπαι· δοκέω δέ τινας καὶ ἄλλους δοῦναι καὶ οὐ τούτους μούνους. καίτοι Καρυστίοισί γε οὐδὲν τούτου εἵνεκεν τοῦ κακοῦ ὑπερβολὴ ἐγένετο· Πάριοι δὲ Θεμιστοκλέα χρήμασι ἱλασάμενοι διέφυγον τὸ στράτευμα. Θεμιστοκλέης μέν νυν ἐξ Ἄνδρου ὁρμεόμενος χρήματα παρὰ νησιωτέων ἔκτητο λάθρῃ τῶν ἄλλων στρατηγῶν.

Retreat of Xerxes. Mardonius selects the troops who are to remain with him.

CXIII. Οἱ δ' ἀμφὶ Ξέρξεα ἐπισχόντες ὀλίγας ἡμέρας μετὰ τὴν ναυμαχίην ἐξήλαυνον ἐς Βοιωτοὺς τὴν αὐτὴν ὁδόν. ἔδοξε γὰρ Μαρδονίῳ ἅμα μὲν προπέμψαι βασιλέα, ἅμα δὲ ἀνωρίην εἶναι τοῦ ἔτεος
5 πολεμέειν, χειμερίσαι δὲ ἄμεινον εἶναι ἐν Θεσσαλίῃ, καὶ ἔπειτα ἅμα τῷ ἔαρι πειρᾶσθαι τῆς Πελοποννήσου. ὡς δὲ ἀπίκατο ἐς τὴν Θεσσαλίην, ἐνθαῦτα Μαρδόνιος ἐξελέγετο πρώτους μὲν Πέρσας πάντας τοὺς ἀθανάτους καλεομένους, πλὴν Ὑδάρνεος τοῦ
10 στρατηγοῦ (οὗτος γὰρ οὐκ ἔφη λείψεσθαι βασιλέος), μετὰ δὲ τῶν ἄλλων Περσέων τοὺς θωρηκοφόρους καὶ τὴν ἵππον τὴν χιλίην, καὶ Μήδους τε καὶ Σάκας καὶ Βακτρίους τε καὶ Ἰνδούς, καὶ τὸν πεζὸν καὶ τὴν ἄλλην ἵππον. ταῦτα μὲν ἔθνεα ὅλα εἵλετο, ἐκ δὲ τῶν ἄλλων
15 συμμάχων ἐξελέγετο κατ' ὀλίγους, τοῖσι εἰδεά τε ὑπῆρχε διαλέγων, καὶ εἴ τέοισί τι χρηστὸν συνῄδεε πεποιημένον· ἐν δὲ πλεῖστον ἔθνος Πέρσας αἱρέετο, ἄνδρας στρεπτοφόρους τε καὶ ψελιοφόρους, ἐπὶ δὲ Μήδους· οὗτοι δὲ πλῆθος μὲν οὐκ ἐλάσσονες ἦσαν
20 τῶν Περσέων, ῥώμῃ δὲ ἔσσονες· ὥστε σύμπαντας τριήκοντα μυριάδας γενέσθαι σὺν ἱππεῦσι.

The Spartans demand satisfaction for the death of Leonidas. Mardonius shall give it them.

CXIV. Ἐν δὲ τούτῳ τῷ χρόνῳ, ἐν τῷ Μαρδόνιός τε τὴν στρατιὴν διέκρινε καὶ Ξέρξης ἦν περὶ Θεσσαλίην, χρηστήριον ἐληλύθεε ἐκ Δελφῶν Λακεδαι-
25 μονίοισι, Ξέρξεα αἰτέειν δίκας τοῦ Λεωνίδεω φόνου καὶ τὸ διδόμενον ἐξ ἐκείνου δέκεσθαι. πέμπουσι δὴ

κήρυκα τὴν ταχίστην Σπαρτιῆται, ὃς ἐπειδὴ κατέλαβε ἐοῦσαν ἔτι πᾶσαν τὴν στρατιὴν ἐν Θεσσαλίῃ, ἐλθὼν ἐς ὄψιν τὴν Ξέρξεω ἔλεγε τάδε· "Ὦ βασιλεῦ · "Μήδων, Λακεδαιμόνιοί τέ σε καὶ Ἡρακλεῖδαι οἱ "ἀπὸ Σπάρτης αἰτέουσι φόνου δίκας, ὅτι σφέων τὸν "βασιλέα ἀπέκτεινας ῥυόμενον τὴν Ἑλλάδα." ὁ δὲ γελάσας τε καὶ κατασχὼν πολλὸν χρόνον, ὥς οἱ ἐτύγχανε παρεστεὼς Μαρδόνιος, δεικνὺς ἐς τοῦτον εἶπε· "Τοιγάρ σφι Μαρδόνιος ὅδε δίκας δώσει "τοιαύτας, οἵας ἐκείνοισι πρέπει."

Xerxes continues his retreat. His sacred chariot and horses are missing.

CXV. Ὁ μὲν δὴ δεξάμενος τὸ ῥηθὲν ἀπαλλάσσετο, Ξέρξης δὲ Μαρδόνιον ἐν Θεσσαλίῃ καταλιπὼν αὐτὸς ἐπορεύετο κατὰ τάχος ἐς τὸν Ἑλλήσποντον, καὶ ἀπικνέεται ἐς τὸν πόρον τῆς διαβάσιος ἐν πέντε καὶ τεσσεράκοντα ἡμέρῃσι, ἀπάγων τῆς στρατιῆς οὐδὲν μέρος ὡς εἰπεῖν. ὅκου δὲ πορευόμενοι γινοίατο καὶ κατ' οὕστινας ἀνθρώπους, τὸν τούτων καρπὸν ἁρπάζοντες ἐσιτέοντο, εἰ δὲ καρπὸν μηδένα εὕροιεν· οἱ δὲ τὴν ποίην τὴν ἐκ τῆς γῆς ἀναφυομένην καὶ τῶν δενδρέων τὸν φλοιὸν περιλέποντες καὶ τὰ φύλλα καταδρέποντες κατήσθιον, ὁμοίως τῶν τε ἡμέρων καὶ τῶν ἀγρίων, καὶ ἔλειπον οὐδέν· ταῦτα δ' ἐποίεον ὑπὸ λιμοῦ. ἐπιλαβὼν δὲ λοιμός τε τὸν στρατὸν καὶ δυσεντερίη κατ' ὁδὸν διέφθειρε. τοὺς δὲ καὶ νοσέοντας αὐτῶν κατέλειπε, ἐπιτάσσων τῇσι πόλισι, ἵνα ἑκάστοτε γίνοιτο ἐλαύνων, μελεδαίνειν τε καὶ τρέφειν, ἐν Θεσσαλίῃ τέ τινας καὶ ἐν Σίρι τῆς Παιονίης καὶ ἐν Μακεδονίῃ. ἔνθα καὶ τὸ ἱρὸν ἅρμα

καταλιπὼν τοῦ Διός, ὅτε ἐπὶ τὴν Ἑλλάδα ἤλαυνε, ἀπιὼν οὐκ ἀπέλαβε, ἀλλὰ δόντες οἱ Παίονες τοῖσι Θρήϊξι ἀπαιτέοντος Ξέρξεω ἔφασαν νεμομένας ἁρπασθῆναι ὑπὸ τῶν ἄνω Θρηίκων τῶν περὶ τὰς πηγὰς
5 τοῦ Στρυμόνος οἰκημένων.

Cruelty of the Thracian king.

CXVI. Ἔνθα καὶ ὁ τῶν Βισαλτέων βασιλεὺς γῆς τε τῆς Κρηστωνικῆς Θρῆϊξ, ἔργον ὑπερφυὲς ἐργάσατο. ὃς οὔτε αὐτὸς ἔφη τῷ Ξέρξῃ ἑκὼν εἶναι δουλεύσειν, ἀλλ' οἴχετο ἄνω ἐς τὸ οὖρος τὴν Ῥοδόπην,
10 τοῖσί τε παισὶ ἀπηγόρευε μὴ στρατεύεσθαι ἐπὶ τὴν Ἑλλάδα. οἱ δὲ ἀλογήσαντες, ἢ ἄλλως σφι θυμὸς ἐγένετο θηήσασθαι τὸν πόλεμον, ἐστρατεύοντο ἅμα τῷ Πέρσῃ. ἐπεὶ δὲ ἀνεχώρησαν ἀσινέες πάντες ἐξ ἐόντες, ἐξώρυξε αὐτῶν ὁ πατὴρ τοὺς ὀφθαλμοὺς διὰ
15 τὴν αἰτίην ταύτην.

Xerxes arrives at the Hellespont, and, finding the bridge destroyed, crosses to Abydos by ship.

CXVII. Καὶ οὗτοι μὲν τοῦτον τὸν μισθὸν ἔλαβον, οἱ δὲ Πέρσαι ὡς ἐκ τῆς Θρηίκης πορευόμενοι ἀπίκοντο ἐπὶ τὸν πόρον, ἐπειγόμενοι τὸν Ἑλλήσποντον τῇσι νηυσὶ διέβησαν ἐς Ἄβυδον· τὰς γὰρ
20 σχεδίας οὐκ εὗρον ἔτι ἐντεταμένας, ἀλλ' ὑπὸ χειμῶνος διαλελυμένας. ἐνθαῦτα δὲ κατεχόμενοι σιτία τε πλέω ἢ κατ' ὁδὸν ἐλάγχανον, οὐδένα τε κόσμον ἐμπιπλάμενοι καὶ ὕδατα μεταβάλλοντες ἀπέθνησκον τοῦ στρατοῦ τοῦ περιεόντος πολλοί. οἱ
25 δὲ λοιποὶ ἅμα Ξέρξῃ ἀπικνέονται ἐς Σάρδις.

According to another story he crossed from Eion, and was preserved by an act of wonderful devotion on the part of the Persians.

CXVIII. Ἔστι δὲ καὶ ἄλλος ὅδε λόγος λεγόμενος, ὡς ἐπειδὴ Ξέρξης ἀπελαύνων ἐξ Ἀθηνέων ἀπίκετο ἐπ᾽ Ἠιόνα τὴν ἐπὶ Στρυμόνι, ἐνθεῦτεν οὐκέτι ὁδοιπορίῃσι διεχρᾶτο, ἀλλὰ τὴν μὲν στρατιὴν Ὑδάρνεϊ ἐπιτράπει ἀπάγειν ἐς τὸν Ἑλλήσποντον, αὐτὸς δ᾽ ἐπὶ νεὸς Φοινίσσης ἐπιβὰς ἐκομίζετο ἐς τὴν Ἀσίην. πλώοντα δέ μιν ἄνεμον Στρυμονίην ὑπολαβεῖν μέγαν καὶ κυματίην. καὶ δή, μᾶλλον γάρ τι χειμαίνεσθαι γεμούσης τῆς νεὸς ὥστε ἐπὶ τοῦ καταστρώματος ἐπεόντων συχνῶν Περσέων τῶν σὺν Ξέρξῃ κομιζομένων, ἐνθαῦτα ἐς δεῖμα πεσόντα τὸν βασιλέα εἴρεσθαι βώσαντα τὸν κυβερνήτην, εἴ τις ἐστί σφι σωτηρίη. καὶ τὸν εἶπαι· "Δέσποτα, οὐκ ἔστι οὐδεμία, "ἢν μὴ τούτων ἀπαλλαγή τις γένηται τῶν πολλῶν "ἐπιβατέων." καὶ Ξέρξεα λέγεται ἀκούσαντα ταῦτα εἶπαι· "Ἄνδρες Πέρσαι, νῦν τις διαδεξάτω ὑμέων "βασιλέος κηδόμενος· ἐν ὑμῖν γὰρ οἶκε ἐμοὶ εἶναι ἡ "σωτηρίη." τὸν μὲν ταῦτα λέγειν, τοὺς δὲ προσκυνέοντας ἐκπηδᾶν ἐς τὴν θάλασσαν, καὶ τὴν νέα ἐπικουφισθεῖσαν οὕτω δὴ ἀποσωθῆναι ἐς τὴν Ἀσίην. ὡς δὲ ἐκβῆναι τάχιστα ἐς γῆν τὸν Ξέρξεα, ποιῆσαι τοιόνδε· ὅτι μὲν ἔσωσε βασιλέος τὴν ψυχήν, δωρήσασθαι χρυσέῃ στεφάνῃ τὸν κυβερνήτην, ὅτι δὲ Περσέων πολλοὺς ἀπώλεσε, ἀποταμεῖν τὴν κεφαλὴν αὐτοῦ. CXIX. Οὗτος δὲ ἄλλος λέγεται λόγος περὶ τοῦ Ξέρξεω νόστου, οὐδαμῶς ἔμοιγε πιστός, οὔτε ἄλλως οὔτε τὸ Περσέων τοῦτο πάθος. εἰ γὰρ δὴ ταῦτα

οὕτω εἰρέθη ἐκ τοῦ κυβερνήτεω πρὸς Ξέρξεα, ἐν
μυρίῃσι γνώμῃσι μίαν οὐκ ἔχω ἀντίξοον, μὴ οὐκ ἂν
ποιῆσαι βασιλέα τοιόνδε, τοὺς μὲν ἐκ τοῦ καταστρώματος καταβιβάσαι ἐς κοίλην νέα ἐόντας Πέρσας καὶ
5 Περσέων τοὺς πρώτους, τῶν δ' ἐρετέων ἐόντων
Φοινίκων ὅκως οὐκ ἂν ἴσον πλῆθος τοῖσι Πέρσῃσι
ἐξέβαλε ἐς τὴν θάλασσαν. ἀλλ' ὁ μὲν, ὡς καὶ
πρότερόν μοι εἴρηται, ὁδῷ χρεώμενος ἅμα τῷ ἄλλῳ
στρατῷ ἀπενόστησε ἐς τὴν Ἀσίην. CXX. Μέγα
10 δὲ καὶ τόδε μαρτύριον· φαίνεται γὰρ Ξέρξης ἐν τῇ
ὀπίσω κομιδῇ ἀπικόμενος ἐς Ἄβδηρα, καὶ ξεινίην τέ
σφι συνθέμενος καὶ δωρησάμενος αὐτοὺς ἀκινάκῃ τε
χρυσέῳ καὶ τιήρῃ χρυσοπάστῳ. καὶ ὡς αὐτοὶ
λέγουσι Ἀβδηρῖται, λέγοντες ἔμοιγε οὐδαμῶς πιστά,
15 πρῶτον ἐλύσατο τὴν ζώνην φεύγων ἐξ Ἀθηνέων
ὀπίσω, ὡς ἐν ἀδείῃ ἐών. τὰ δὲ Ἄβδηρα ἵδρυται
πρὸς τοῦ Ἑλλησπόντου μᾶλλον ἢ τοῦ Στρυμόνος
καὶ τῆς Ἠιόνος, ὅθεν δή μίν φασι ἐπιβῆναι ἐπὶ
τὴν νέα.

The Greek fleet return to Salamis and proceed to divide the spoil.

20 CXXI. Οἱ δὲ Ἕλληνες ἐπεί τε οὐκ οἷοί τε
ἐγένοντο ἐξελεῖν τὴν Ἄνδρον, τραπόμενοι ἐς Κάρυ-
στον καὶ δηϊώσαντες αὐτῶν τὴν χώρην ἀπαλλάσσοντο ἐς Σαλαμῖνα. πρῶτα μέν νυν τοῖσι θεοῖσι
ἐξεῖλον ἀκροθίνια ἄλλα τε καὶ τριήρεας τρεῖς
25 Φοινίσσας, τὴν μὲν ἐς Ἰσθμὸν ἀναθεῖναι, ἥ περ ἔτι
καὶ ἐς ἐμὲ ἦν, τὴν δὲ ἐπὶ Σούνιον, τὴν δὲ τῷ Αἴαντι
αὐτοῦ ἐς Σαλαμῖνα. μετὰ δὲ τοῦτο διεδάσαντο τὴν
ληΐην καὶ τὰ ἀκροθίνια ἀπέπεμψαν ἐς Δελφούς, ἐκ

τῶν ἐγένετο ἀνδριὰς ἔχων ἐν τῇ χειρὶ ἀκρωτήριον νεός, ἐὼν μέγαθος δυώδεκα πηχέων· ἕστηκε δὲ οὗτος τῇ περ ὁ Μακεδὼν Ἀλέξανδρος ὁ χρύσεος. CXXII. Πέμψαντες δὲ ἀκροθίνια οἱ Ἕλληνες ἐς Δελφοὺς ἐπειρώτεον τὸν θεὸν κοινῇ, εἰ λελάβηκε πλήρεα καὶ ἀρεστὰ 5 τὰ ἀκροθίνια. ὁ δὲ παρ᾽ Ἑλλήνων μὲν τῶν ἄλλων ἔφησε ἔχειν, παρ᾽ Αἰγινητέων δὲ οὔ, ἀλλὰ ἀπαίτεε αὐτοὺς τὰ ἀριστήϊα τῆς ἐν Σαλαμῖνι ναυμαχίης. Αἰγινῆται δὲ πυθόμενοι ἀνέθεσαν ἀστέρας χρυσέους, οἳ ἐπὶ ἱστοῦ χαλκέου ἑστᾶσι τρεῖς ἐπὶ τῆς γωνίης, 10 ἀγχοτάτω τοῦ Κροίσου κρητῆρος.

The chief prize of valour; all give their second votes to Themistokles.

CXXIII. Μετὰ δὲ τὴν διαίρεσιν τῆς ληίης ἔπλωον οἱ Ἕλληνες ἐς τὸν Ἰσθμὸν ἀριστήϊα δώσοντες τῷ ἀξιωτάτῳ γενομένῳ Ἑλλήνων ἀνὰ τὸν πόλεμον τοῦτον. ὡς δὲ ἀπικόμενοι οἱ στρατηγοὶ 15 διενέμοντο τὰς ψήφους ἐπὶ τοῦ Ποσειδέωνος τῷ βωμῷ, τὸν πρῶτον καὶ τὸν δεύτερον κρίνοντες ἐκ πάντων, ἐνθαῦτα πᾶς τις αὐτῶν ἑωυτῷ ἐτίθετο τὴν ψῆφον, αὐτὸς ἕκαστος δοκέων ἄριστος γενέσθαι, δεύτερα δὲ οἱ πολλοὶ συνεξέπιπτον Θεμιστοκλέα 20 κρίνοντες. οἱ μὲν δὴ ἐμουνοῦντο, Θεμιστοκλέης δὲ δευτερείοισι ὑπερεβάλλετο πολλόν.

His visit to Sparta; the honours given him there provoke jealousy at Athens.

CXXIV. Οὐ βουλομένων δὲ ταῦτα κρίνειν τῶν Ἑλλήνων φθόνῳ, ἀλλ᾽ ἀποπλωόντων ἑκάστων ἐς τὴν ἑωυτῶν ἀκρίτων, ὅμως Θεμιστοκλέης ἐβώσθη τε 25

καὶ ἐδοξώθη εἶναι ἀνὴρ πολλὸν Ἑλλήνων σοφώτατος ἀνὰ πᾶσαν τὴν Ἑλλάδα. ὅτι δὲ νικῶν οὐκ ἐτιμήθη πρὸς τῶν ἐν Σαλαμῖνι ναυμαχησάντων, αὐτίκα μετὰ ταῦτα ἐς Λακεδαίμονα ἀπίκετο ἐθέλων τιμηθῆναι.
5 καί μιν Λακεδαιμόνιοι καλῶς μὲν ὑπεδέξαντο, μεγάλως δὲ ἐτίμησαν. ἀριστήια μέν νυν ἔδοσαν Εὐρυβιάδῃ ἐλαίης στέφανον, σοφίης δὲ καὶ δεξιότητος Θεμιστοκλέι, καὶ τούτῳ στέφανον ἐλαίης. ἐδωρήσαντό τε μιν ὄχῳ τῷ ἐν Σπάρτῃ καλλιστεύοντι. αἰνέσαντες
10 δὲ πολλά, προέπεμψαν ἀπιόντα τριηκόσιοι Σπαρτιητέων λογάδες, οὗτοι οἵ περ ἱππέες καλέονται, μέχρι οὔρων τῶν Τεγεητικῶν, μοῦνον δὴ τοῦτον πάντων ἀνθρώπων τῶν ἡμεῖς ἴδμεν Σπαρτιῆται προέπεμψαν. CXXV. Ὡς δὲ ἐκ τῆς Λακεδαίμονος
15 ἀπίκετο ἐς τὰς Ἀθήνας, ἐνθαῦτα Τιμόδημος Ἀφιδναῖος, τῶν ἐχθρῶν μὲν τῶν Θεμιστοκλέος ἐών, ἄλλως δὲ οὐ τῶν ἐπιφανέων ἀνδρῶν, φθόνῳ καταμαργέων ἐνείκεε τὸν Θεμιστοκλέα, τὴν ἐς Λακεδαίμονα ἄπιξιν προφέρων, ὡς διὰ τὰς Ἀθήνας ἔχοι τὰ γέρεα τὰ
20 παρὰ Λακεδαιμονίων, ἀλλ' οὐ δι' ἑωυτόν. ὁ δέ, ἐπεί τε οὐκ ἐπαύετο ταῦτα λέγων ὁ Τιμόδημος, εἶπε· "Οὕτω ἔχει τοι· οὔτ' ἂν ἐγὼ ἐὼν Βελβινίτης ἐτιμήθην "οὕτω πρὸς Σπαρτιητέων, οὔτ' ἂν σύ, ὤνθρωπε, ἐὼν "Ἀθηναῖος.

Artabazus on his return from escorting Xerxes takes Olynthos and lays siege to Potidaea.

25 CXXVI. Ταῦτα μέν νυν ἐς τοσοῦτο ἐγένετο, Ἀρτάβαζος δὲ ὁ Φαρνάκεος ἀνὴρ ἐν Πέρσῃσι λόγιμος καὶ πρόσθε ἐών, ἐκ δὲ τῶν Πλαταιικῶν καὶ μᾶλλον ἔτι γενόμενος, ἔχων ἓξ μυριάδας στρατοῦ τοῦ

Μαρδόνιος ἐξελέξατο, προέπεμπε βασιλέα μέχρι τοῦ πόρου. ὡς δὲ ὁ μὲν ἦν ἐν τῇ Ἀσίῃ, ὁ δὲ ὀπίσω πορευόμενος κατὰ τὴν Παλλήνην ἐγίνετο, ἅτε Μαρδονίου τε χειμερίζοντος περὶ Θεσσαλίην τε καὶ Μακεδονίην καὶ οὐδέν κω κατεπείγοντος ἥκειν ἐς τὸ ἄλλο στρατόπεδον, οὐκ ἐδικαίου ἐντυχὼν ἀπεστεῶσι Ποτιδαιήτῃσι μὴ οὐκ ἐξανδραποδίσασθαί σφεας. οἱ γὰρ Ποτιδαιῆται, ὡς βασιλεὺς παρεξεληλάκεε καὶ ὁ ναυτικὸς τοῖσι Πέρσῃσι οἰχώκεε φεύγων ἐκ Σαλαμῖνος, ἐκ τοῦ φανεροῦ ἀπέστασαν ἀπὸ τῶν βαρβάρων· ὣς δὲ καὶ ὧλλοι οἱ τὴν Παλλήνην ἔχοντες. CXXVII. Ἐνθαῦτα δὴ ὁ Ἀρτάβαζος ἐπολιόρκεε τὴν Ποτίδαιαν. ὑποπτεύσας δὲ καὶ τοὺς Ὀλυνθίους ἀπίστασθαι ἀπὸ βασιλέος, καὶ ταύτην ἐπολιόρκεε. εἶχον δὲ αὐτὴν Βοττιαῖοι οἱ ἐκ τοῦ Θερμαίου κόλπου ἐξαναστάντες ὑπὸ Μακεδόνων. ἐπεὶ δέ σφεας εἷλε πολιορκέων, κατέσφαξε ἐξαγαγὼν ἐς λίμνην, τὴν δὲ πόλιν παραδιδοῖ Κριτοβούλῳ Τορωναίῳ ἐπιτροπεύειν καὶ τῷ Χαλκιδικῷ γένει, καὶ οὕτω Ὄλυνθον Χαλκιδέες ἔσχον.

The treason of Timoxenos discovered.

CXXVIII. Ἐξελὼν δὲ ταύτην ὁ Ἀρτάβαζος τῇ Ποτιδαίῃ ἐντεταμένως προσεῖχε, προσέχοντι δέ οἱ προθύμως συντίθεται προδοσίην Τιμόξεινος ὁ τῶν Σκιωναίων στρατηγός, ὅντινα μὲν τρόπον ἀρχήν, ἔγωγε οὐκ ἔχω εἰπεῖν (οὐ γὰρ ὦν λέγεται), τέλος μέντοι τοιάδε ἐγίνετο· ὅκως βιβλίον γράψειε ἢ Τιμόξεινος ἐθέλων παρὰ Ἀρτάβαζον πέμψαι ἢ Ἀρτάβαζος παρὰ Τιμόξεινον, τοξεύματος παρὰ τὰς

γλυφίδας περιειλίξαντες καὶ πτερώσαντες τὸ βιβλίον
ἐτόξευον ἐς συγκείμενον χωρίον. ἐπάϊστος δὲ ἐγένετο
ὁ Τιμόξεινος προδιδοὺς τὴν Ποτίδαιαν. τοξεύων γὰρ
ὁ Ἀρτάβαζος ἐς τὸ συγκείμενον, ἁμαρτὼν τοῦ χωρίου
5 τούτου βάλλει ἀνδρὸς Ποτιδαιήτεω τὸν ὦμον, τὸν δὲ
βληθέντα περιέδραμε ὅμιλος, οἷα φιλέει γίνεσθαι ἐν
πολέμῳ, οἳ αὐτίκα τὸ τόξευμα λαβόντες, ὡς ἔμαθον
τὸ βιβλίον, ἔφερον ἐπὶ τοὺς στρατηγούς· παρῆν δὲ
καὶ τῶν ἄλλων Παλληναίων συμμαχίη. τοῖσι δὲ
10 στρατηγοῖσι ἐπιλεξαμένοισι τὸ βιβλίον καὶ μαθοῦσι
τὸν αἴτιον τῆς προδοσίης ἔδοξε μὴ καταπλῆξαι
Τιμόξεινον προδοσίῃ τῆς Σκιωναίων πόλιος εἵνεκεν,
μὴ νομιζοίατο εἶναι Σκιωναῖοι ἐς τὸν μετέπειτεν
χρόνον αἰεὶ προδόται. ὁ μὲν δὴ τοιούτῳ τρόπῳ
15 ἐπάϊστος ἐγεγόνεε.

Artabazus loses two-fifths of his army in the sea while trying to get round the mole.

CXXIX. Ἀρταβάζῳ δὲ ἐπειδὴ πολιορκέοντι
ἐγεγόνεσαν τρεῖς μῆνες, γίνεται ἄμπωτις τῆς θαλάσσης μεγάλη καὶ χρόνον ἐπὶ πολλόν. ἰδόντες δὲ
οἱ βάρβαροι τέναγος γενόμενον παρήϊσαν ἐς τὴν
20 Παλλήνην. ὡς δὲ τὰς δύο μὲν μοίρας διοδοιπορή-
κεσαν, ἔτι δὲ τρεῖς ὑπόλοιποι ἦσαν, τὰς διελθόντας
χρῆν ἔσω εἶναι ἐν τῇ Παλλήνῃ, ἐπῆλθε πλημμυ-
ρὶς τῆς θαλάσσης μεγάλη, ὅση οὐδαμά κω, ὡς οἱ
ἐπιχώριοι λέγουσι, πολλάκις γενομένη. οἱ μὲν δὴ
25 νέειν αὐτῶν οὐκ ἐπιστάμενοι διεφθείροντο, τοὺς δὲ
ἐπισταμένους Ποτιδαιῆται ἐπιπλώσαντες πλοίοισι
ἀπώλεσαν. αἴτιον δὲ λέγουσι Ποτιδαιῆται τῆς τε

ρηχίης καὶ τῆς πλημμυρίδος καὶ τοῦ Περσικοῦ πάθεος γενέσθαι τόδε, ὅτι τοῦ Ποσειδέωνος ἐς τὸν νηὸν καὶ τὸ ἄγαλμα τὸ ἐν τῷ προαστείῳ ἠσέβησαν οὗτοι τῶν Περσέων, οἵ περ καὶ διεφθάρησαν ὑπὸ τῆς θαλάσσης. αἴτιον δὲ τοῦτο λέγοντες εὖ λέγειν ἔμοιγε δοκέουσι. 5 τοὺς δὲ περιγενομένους ἀπῆγε Ἀρτάβαζος ἐς Θεσσαλίην παρὰ Μαρδόνιον.

B.C. 479. *In the following spring the Persian fleet of 300 sail reassembles at Samos.*

CXXX. Οὗτοι μὲν οἱ προπέμψαντες βασιλέα οὕτω ἔπρηξαν· ὁ δὲ ναυτικὸς ὁ Ξέρξεω περιγενόμενος, ὡς προσέμιξε τῇ Ἀσίῃ φεύγων ἐκ Σαλαμῖνος καὶ 10 βασιλέα τε καὶ τὴν στρατιὴν ἐκ Χερσονήσου διεπόρθμευσε ἐς Ἄβυδον, ἐχειμέριζε ἐν Κύμῃ. ἔαρος δὲ ἐπιλάμψαντος πρώϊος συνελέγετο ἐς Σάμον· αἱ δὲ τῶν νεῶν καὶ ἐχειμέρισαν αὐτοῦ· Περσέων δὲ καὶ Μήδων οἱ πλεῦνες ἐπεβάτευον, στρατηγοὶ δέ σφι 15 ἐπῆλθον Μαρδόντης τε ὁ Βαγαίου καὶ Ἀρταΰντης ὁ Ἀρταχαίου· συνῆρχε δὲ τούτοισι καὶ ἀδελφιδέος αὐτοῦ Ἀρταΰντεω προσελομένου Ἰθαμίτρης. ἅτε δὲ μεγάλως πληγέντες, οὐ προῇσαν ἀνωτέρω τὸ πρὸς ἑσπέρης, οὐδ᾽ ἐπηνάγκαζε οὐδείς, ἀλλ᾽ ἐν τῇ Σάμῳ 20 κατήμενοι ἐφύλασσον τὴν Ἰωνίην μὴ ἀποστῇ, νέας ἔχοντες σὺν τῇσι Ἰάσι τριηκοσίας. οὐ μὲν οὐδὲ προσεδέκοντο τοὺς Ἕλληνας ἐλεύσεσθαι ἐς τὴν Ἰωνίην, ἀλλ᾽ ἀποχρήσειν σφι τὴν ἑωυτῶν φυλάσσειν, σταθμεύμενοι ὅτι σφέας οὐκ ἐπεδίωξαν φεύ- 25 γοντας ἐκ Σαλαμῖνος, ἀλλ᾽ ἄσμενοι ἀπαλλάσσοντο. κατὰ μέν νυν τὴν θάλασσαν ἑσσωμένοι ἦσαν τῷ θυμῷ, πεζῇ δὲ ἐδόκεον πολλὸν κρατήσειν τὸν Μαρδόνιον. ἐόντες δὲ ἐν Σάμῳ ἅμα μὲν ἐβουλεύοντο, εἴ τι δυναίατο κακὸν τοὺς πολεμίους ποιέειν, ἅμα δὲ καὶ ὠτακούστεον, ὅκῃ πεσέεται τὰ Μαρδονίου πρήγματα.

The Greek fleet assembles to the number of 110 at Aegina.

CXXXI. Τοὺς δὲ Ἕλληνας τό τε ἔαρ γινόμενον ἤγειρε καὶ Μαρδόνιος ἐν Θεσσαλίῃ ἐών. ὁ μὲν δὴ πεζὸς οὔκω συνελέγετο, ὁ δὲ ναυτικὸς ἀπίκετο ἐς Αἴγιναν, νέες ἀριθμὸν δέκα καὶ ἑκατόν. στρατηγὸς δὲ καὶ ναύαρχος ἦν Λευτυχίδης ὁ Μενάρεος τοῦ Ἡγησίλεω τοῦ Ἱπποκρατίδεω τοῦ Λευτυχίδεω τοῦ Ἀναξίλεω τοῦ Ἀρχιδήμου τοῦ Ἀναξανδρίδεω τοῦ Θεοπόμπου τοῦ Νικάνδρου τοῦ Χαρίλλου τοῦ Εὐνόμου τοῦ Πολυδέκτεος τοῦ Πρυτάνιος τοῦ Εὐρυφῶντος τοῦ Προκλέος τοῦ Ἀριστοδήμου τοῦ Ἀριστομάχου τοῦ Κλεοδαίου τοῦ Ὕλλου τοῦ Ἡρακλέος, ἐὼν τῆς ἑτέρης οἰκίης τῶν βασιλέων. οὗτοι πάντες, πλὴν τῶν δυῶν τῶν μετὰ Λευτυχίδην πρώτων καταλεχθέντων, οἱ ἄλλοι βασιλέες ἐγένοντο Σπάρτης. Ἀθηναίων δὲ ἐστρατήγεε Ξάνθιππος ὁ Ἀρίφρονος.

Envoys from the Ionians asking for help arrive at Sparta and Aegina. The Greek ships go as far as Delos.

CXXXII. Ὡς δὲ παρεγένοντο ἐς τὴν Αἴγιναν πᾶσαι αἱ νέες, ἀπίκοντο Ἰώνων ἄγγελοι ἐς τὸ στρατόπεδον τῶν Ἑλλήνων, οἳ καὶ ἐς Σπάρτην ὀλίγῳ πρότερον τούτων ἀπικόμενοι ἐδέοντο Λακεδαιμονίων ἐλευθεροῦν τὴν Ἰωνίην· τῶν καὶ Ἡρόδοτος ὁ Βασιληίδεω ἦν. οἳ στασιῶται σφίσι γενόμενοι

ἐπεβούλευον θάνατον Στράττι τῷ Χίου τυράννῳ,
ἐόντες ἀρχὴν ἑπτά· ἐπιβουλεύοντες δὲ ὡς φανεροὶ
ἐγένοντο ἐξενείκαντος τὴν ἐπιχείρησιν ἑνὸς τῶν
μετεχόντων, οὕτω δὴ οἱ λοιποὶ ἓξ ἐόντες ὑπεξέσχον
ἐκ τῆς Χίου, καὶ ἐς Σπάρτην τε ἀπίκοντο καὶ δὴ καὶ 5
τότε ἐς τὴν Αἴγιναν, τῶν Ἑλλήνων δεόμενοι καταπλῶσαι ἐς τὴν Ἰωνίην· οἳ προήγαγον αὐτοὺς μόγις
μέχρι Δήλου. τὸ γὰρ προσωτέρω πᾶν δεινὸν ἦν
τοῖσι Ἕλλησι οὔτε τῶν χώρων ἐοῦσι ἐμπείροισι,
στρατιῆς τε πάντα πλέα ἐδόκεε εἶναι· τὴν δὲ Σάμον 10
ἠπιστέατο δόξῃ καὶ Ἡρακλέας στήλας ἴσον ἀπέχειν.
συνέπιπτε δὲ τοιοῦτο ὥστε τοὺς μὲν βαρβάρους τὸ
πρὸς ἑσπέρης ἀνωτέρω Σάμου μὴ τολμᾶν καταπλῶσαι
καταρρωδηκότας, τοὺς δὲ Ἕλληνας χρηιζόντων Χίων
τὸ πρὸς τὴν ἠῶ κατωτέρω Δήλου. οὕτω δέος τὸ 15
μέσον ἐφύλασσέ σφεων.

Mardonius, before breaking up his winter quarters in Thessaly, consults the oracles by means of a man named Mus.

CXXXIII. Οἱ μὲν δὴ Ἕλληνες ἔπλωον ἐς τὴν
Δῆλον, Μαρδόνιος δὲ περὶ τὴν Θεσσαλίην ἐχείμαζε.
ἐνθεῦτεν δὲ ὁρμεόμενος ἔπεμπε κατὰ τὰ χρηστήρια
ἄνδρα Εὐρωπέα γένος, τῷ οὔνομα ἦν Μῦς, ἐντειλά- 20
μενος πανταχῇ μιν χρησόμενον ἐλθεῖν, τῶν οἷά τε
ἦν σφι ἀποπειρήσασθαι. ὅ τι μὲν βουλόμενος ἐκμα-
θεῖν πρὸς τῶν χρηστηρίων ταῦτα ἐνετέλλετο, οὐκ
ἔχω φράσαι· οὐ γὰρ ὦν λέγεται· δοκέω δ' ἔγωγε
περὶ τῶν παρεόντων πρηγμάτων καὶ οὐκ ἄλλων πέρι 25
πέμψαι. CXXXIV. Οὗτος ὁ Μῦς ἔς τε Λεβάδειαν
φαίνεται ἀπικόμενος καὶ μισθῷ πείσας τῶν ἐπιχωρίων

ἄνδρα καταβῆναι παρὰ Τροφώνιον, καὶ ἐς Ἄβας τὰς Φωκέων ἀπικόμενος ἐπὶ τὸ χρηστήριον. καὶ δὴ καὶ ἐς Θήβας πρῶτα ὡς ἀπίκετο, τοῦτο μὲν τῷ Ἰσμηνίῳ Ἀπόλλωνι ἐχρήσατο (ἔστι δὲ κατά περ ἐν Ὀλυμπίῃ
5 ἱροῖσι αὐτόθι χρηστηριάζεσθαι), τοῦτο δὲ ξεῖνόν τινα καὶ οὐ Θηβαῖον χρήμασι πείσας κατεκοίμησε ἐς Ἀμφιάρεω. Θηβαίων δὲ οὐδενὶ ἔξεστι μαντεύεσθαι αὐτόθι διὰ τόδε· ἐκέλευσέ σφεας ὁ Ἀμφιάρεως διὰ χρηστηρίων ποιεύμενος ὁκότερα βούλονται ἑλέσθαι
10 τούτων, ἑωυτῷ ἢ ἅτε μάντι χρέεσθαι ἢ ἅτε συμμάχῳ, τοῦ ἑτέρου ἀπεχομένους· οἱ δὲ σύμμαχόν μιν εἵλοντο εἶναι. διὰ τοῦτο μὲν οὐκ ἔξεστι Θηβαίων οὐδενὶ αὐτόθι ἐγκατακοιμηθῆναι. CXXXV. Τότε δὲ θῶμά μοι μέγιστον γενέσθαι λέγεται ὑπὸ Θηβαίων, ἐλθεῖν
15 ἄρα τὸν Εὐρωπέα Μῦν, περιστρωφώμενον πάντα τὰ χρηστήρια, καὶ ἐς τοῦ Πτώου Ἀπόλλωνος τὸ τέμενος. τοῦτο δὲ τὸ ἱρὸν καλέεται μὲν Πτῶον, ἔστι δὲ Θηβαίων, κέεται δὲ ὑπὲρ τῆς Κωπαΐδος λίμνης πρὸς οὔρεϊ ἀγχοτάτω Ἀκραιφίης πόλιος. ἐς τοῦτο τὸ ἱρὸν ἐπεί τε
20 παρελθεῖν τὸν καλεόμενον τοῦτον Μῦν, ἕπεσθαί οἱ τῶν ἀστῶν αἱρετοὺς ἄνδρας τρεῖς ἀπὸ τοῦ κοινοῦ ὡς ἀπογραψομένους τὰ θεσπιέειν ἔμελλε. καὶ πρόκατε τὸν πρόμαντιν βαρβάρῳ γλώσσῃ χρᾶν· καὶ τοὺς μὲν ἑπομένους τῶν Θηβαίων ἐν θώματι ἔχεσθαι ἀκούοντας
25 βαρβάρου γλώσσης ἀντὶ Ἑλλάδος, οὐδὲ ἔχειν ὅ τι χρήσονται τῷ παρεόντι πρήγματι· τὸν δὲ Εὐρωπέα Μῦν ἐξαρπάσαντα παρ' αὐτῶν τὴν ἐφέροντο δέλτον, τὰ λεγόμενα ὑπὸ τοῦ προφήτεω γράφειν ἐς αὐτήν, φάναι δὲ Καρίῃ μιν γλώσσῃ χρᾶν, συγγραψάμενον
30 δὲ οἴχεσθαι ἀπιόντα ἐς Θεσσαλίην.

Reassured by the answers he receives Mardonius sends Alexander of Makedon to Athens with a proposal of alliance.

CXXXVI. Μαρδόνιος δὲ ἐπιλεξάμενος ὅ τι δὴ λέγοντα ἦν τὰ χρηστήρια, μετὰ ταῦτα ἔπεμψε ἄγγελον ἐς Ἀθήνας Ἀλέξανδρον τὸν Ἀμύντεω ἄνδρα Μακεδόνα, ἅμα μὲν ὅτι οἱ προσκηδέες οἱ Πέρσαι ἦσαν (Ἀλεξάνδρου γὰρ ἀδελφεὴν Γυγαίην, Ἀμύντεω δὲ θυγατέρα, Βουβάρης ἀνὴρ Πέρσης ἔσχε, ἐκ τῆς οἱ ἐγεγόνεε Ἀμύντης ὁ ἐν τῇ Ἀσίῃ, ἔχων τὸ οὔνομα τοῦ μητροπάτορος, τῷ δὴ ἐκ βασιλέος τῆς Φρυγίης ἐδόθη Ἀλάβανδα πόλις μεγάλη νέμεσθαι), ἅμα δὲ ὁ Μαρδόνιος πυθόμενος ὅτι πρόξεινός τε εἴη καὶ εὐεργέτης ὁ Ἀλέξανδρος ἔπεμπε. τοὺς γὰρ Ἀθηναίους οὕτω ἐδόκεε μάλιστα προσκτήσεσθαι, λεών τε πολλὸν ἄρα ἀκούων εἶναι καὶ ἄλκιμον, τά τε κατὰ τὴν θάλασσαν συντυχόντα σφι παθήματα κατεργασαμένους μάλιστα Ἀθηναίους ἐπίστατο. τούτων δὲ προσγενομένων κατήλπιζε εὐπετέως τῆς θαλάσσης κρατήσειν, τά περ ἂν καὶ ἦν, πεζῇ τε ἐδόκεε πολλὸν εἶναι κρέσσων. οὕτω τε ἐλογίζετο κατύπερθέ οἱ τὰ πρήγματα ἔσεσθαι τῶν Ἑλληνικῶν. τάχα δ' ἂν καὶ τὰ χρηστήρια ταὐτά οἱ προλέγοι, συμβουλεύοντα σύμμαχον τὸν Ἀθηναῖον ποιέεσθαι· τοῖσι δὴ πειθόμενος ἔπεμπε.

How Perdiccas, the ancestor of Alexander, obtained the kingdom of Makedonia.

CXXXVII. Τοῦ δὲ Ἀλεξάνδρου τούτου ἕβδομος γενέτωρ Περδίκκης ἐστὶ ὁ κτησάμενος τῶν Μακεδόνων τὴν τυραννίδα τρόπῳ τοιῷδε· ἐξ Ἄργεος

ἔφυγον ἐς Ἰλλυριοὺς τῶν Τημένου ἀπογόνων τρεῖς ἀδελφεοί, Γαυάνης τε καὶ Ἀέροπος καὶ Περδίκκης, ἐκ δὲ Ἰλλυριῶν ὑπερβαλόντες ἐς τὴν ἄνω Μακεδονίην ἀπίκοντο ἐς Λεβαίην πόλιν. ἐνθαῦτα δὲ ἐθήτευον
5 ἐπὶ μισθῷ παρὰ τῷ βασιλέϊ, ὁ μὲν ἵππους νέμων, ὁ δὲ βοῦς, ὁ δὲ νεώτατος αὐτῶν Περδίκκης τὰ λεπτὰ τῶν προβάτων. ἦσαν δὲ τὸ πάλαι καὶ αἱ τυραννίδες τῶν ἀνθρώπων ἀσθενέες χρήμασι, οὐ μοῦνον ὁ δῆμος. ἡ δὲ γυνὴ τοῦ βασιλέος αὐτὴ τὰ σιτία σφι ἔπεσσε.
10 ὅκως δὲ ὀπτῷτο ὁ ἄρτος τοῦ παιδὸς τοῦ θητὸς τοῦ Περδίκκεω, διπλήσιος ἐγίνετο αὐτὸς ἑωυτοῦ. ἐπεὶ δὲ αἰεὶ τὠυτὸ τοῦτο ἐγίνετο, εἶπε πρὸς τὸν ἄνδρα τὸν ἑωυτῆς. τὸν δὲ ἀκούσαντα ἐσῆλθε αὐτίκα ὡς εἴη τέρας καὶ φέροι ἐς μέγα τι. καλέσας δὲ τοὺς θῆτας
15 προηγόρευέ σφι ἀπαλλάσσεσθαι ἐκ γῆς τῆς ἑωυτοῦ. οἱ δὲ τὸν μισθὸν ἔφασαν δίκαιοι εἶναι ἀπολαβόντες οὕτω ἐξιέναι. ἐνθαῦτα ὁ βασιλεὺς τοῦ μισθοῦ πέρι ἀκούσας, ἦν γὰρ κατὰ τὴν καπνοδόκην ἐς τὸν οἶκον ἐσέχων ὁ ἥλιος, εἶπε θεοβλαβὴς γενόμενος· "Μισ-
20 "θὸν δὲ ὑμῖν ἐγὼ ὑμέων ἄξιον τόνδε ἀποδίδωμι," δέξας τὸν ἥλιον. ὁ μὲν δὴ Γαυάνης τε καὶ ὁ Ἀέροπος οἱ πρεσβύτεροι ἔστασαν ἐκπεπληγμένοι, ὡς ἤκουσαν ταῦτα, ὁ δὲ παῖς, ἐτύγχανε γὰρ ἔχων μάχαιραν, εἶπας τάδε, "Δεκόμεθα, ὦ βασιλεῦ, τὰ διδοῖς,"
25 περιγράφει τῇ μαχαίρῃ ἐς τὸ ἔδαφος τοῦ οἴκου τὸν ἥλιον, περιγράψας δέ, ἐς τὸν κόλπον τρὶς ἀρυσάμενος τοῦ ἡλίου, ἀπαλλάσσετο αὐτός τε καὶ οἱ μετ' ἐκείνου.
CXXXVIII. Οἱ μὲν δὴ ἀπήϊσαν, τῷ δὲ βασιλέϊ σημαίνει τις τῶν παρέδρων, οἷόν τι χρῆμα ποιήσειε
30 ὁ παῖς καὶ ὡς σὺν νόῳ ἐκείνων ὁ νεώτατος λάβοι τὰ διδόμενα. ὁ δὲ ταῦτα ἀκούσας καὶ ὀξυνθεὶς πέμπει

ἐπ' αὐτοὺς ἱππέας ἀπολέοντας. ποταμὸς δέ ἐστι ἐν τῇ χώρῃ ταύτῃ, τῷ θύουσι οἱ τούτων τῶν ἀνδρῶν ἀπ' Ἄργεος ἀπόγονοι σωτῆρι. οὗτος, ἐπείτε διέβησαν οἱ Τημενίδαι, μέγας οὕτω ἐρρύη ὥστε τοὺς ἱππέας μὴ οἵους τε γενέσθαι διαβῆναι. οἱ δὲ ἀπικόμενοι 5 ἐς ἄλλην γῆν τῆς Μακεδονίης οἴκησαν πέλας τῶν κήπων τῶν λεγομένων· εἶναι Μίδεω τοῦ Γορδίεω, ἐν τοῖσι φύεται αὐτόματα ῥόδα, ἓν ἕκαστον ἔχον ἑξήκοντα φύλλα, ὀδμῇ τε ὑπερφέροντα τῶν ἄλλων. ἐν τούτοισι καὶ ὁ Σιληνὸς τοῖσι κήποισι ἥλω, ὡς λέγεται ὑπὸ 10 Μακεδόνων. ὑπὲρ δὲ τῶν κήπων οὖρος κέεται, Βέρμιον οὔνομα, ἄβατον ὑπὸ χειμῶνος. ἐνθεῦτεν δὲ ὁρμεόμενοι, ὡς ταύτην ἔσχον, κατεστρέφοντο καὶ τὴν ἄλλην Μακεδονίην. CXXXIX. Ἀπὸ τούτου δὴ τοῦ Περδίκκεω Ἀλέξανδρος ὧδε ἐγεγόνεε· Ἀμύντεω 15 παῖς ἦν Ἀλέξανδρος, Ἀμύντης δὲ Ἀλκέτεω, Ἀλκέτεω δὲ πατὴρ ἦν Ἀέροπος, τοῦ δὲ Φίλιππος, Φιλίππου δὲ Ἀργαῖος, τοῦ δὲ Περδίκκης ὁ κτησάμενος τὴν ἀρχήν.

The Speech of Alexander at Athens.

CXL. Ἐγεγόνεε μὲν δὴ ὧδε Ἀλέξανδρος ὁ 20 Ἀμύντεω, ὡς δὲ ἀπίκετο ἐς τὰς Ἀθήνας ἀποπεμφθεὶς ὑπὸ Μαρδονίου, ἔλεγε τάδε· "Ἄνδρες Ἀθηναῖοι, "Μαρδόνιος τάδε λέγει· ''Ἐμοὶ ἀγγελίη ἥκει παρὰ "'βασιλέος λέγουσα οὕτω· Ἀθηναίοισι τὰς ἁμαρτάδας "'τὰς ἐξ ἐκείνων ἐς ἐμὲ γενομένας πάσας μετίημι. νῦν 25 "'τε ὧδε, Μαρδόνιε, ποίεε. τοῦτο μὲν τὴν γῆν σφι "'ἀπόδος, τοῦτο δὲ ἄλλην πρὸς ταύτῃ ἑλέσθων αὐτοί, "'ἥντινα ἂν ἐθέλωσι, ἐόντες αὐτόνομοι. ἱρά τε πάντα "'σφι, ἢν δὴ βούλωνταί γε ἐμοὶ ὁμολογέειν, ἀνόρθω-

"'σον, ὅσα ἐγὼ ἐνέπρησα. Τούτων δὲ ἀπιγμένων
"'ἀναγκαίως ἔχει μοι ποιέειν ταῦτα, ἢν μὴ τὸ
"'ὑμέτερον ἀντίον γένηται. λέγω δὲ ὑμῖν τάδε νῦν·
"'Τί μαίνεσθε πόλεμον βασιλέϊ ἀνταειρόμενοι; οὔτε
5 "'γὰρ ἂν ὑπερβάλοισθε, οὔτε οἷοί τέ ἐστε ἀντέχειν
"'τὸν πάντα χρόνον. εἴδετε μὲν γὰρ τῆς Ξέρξεω
"'στρατηλασίης τὸ πλῆθος καὶ τὰ ἔργα, πυνθάνεσθε
"'δὲ καὶ τὴν νῦν παρ' ἐμοὶ ἐοῦσαν δύναμιν, ὥστε καὶ
"'ἢν ἡμέας ὑπερβάλησθε καὶ νικήσητε, τοῦ περ ὑμῖν
10 "'οὐδεμία ἐλπὶς εἴ περ εὖ φρονέετε, ἄλλη παρέσται
"'πολλαπλησίη. μὴ ὦν βούλεσθε παρισούμενοι
"'βασιλέϊ στέρεσθαι μὲν τῆς χώρης, θέειν δὲ αἰεὶ
"'περὶ ὑμέων αὐτῶν, ἀλλὰ καταλύσασθε. παρέχει
"'δὲ ὑμῖν κάλλιστα καταλύσασθαι βασιλέος ταύτῃ
15 "'ὡρμημένου. ἔστε ἐλεύθεροι, ἡμῖν ὁμαιχμίην συνθέ-
"'μενοι ἄνευ τε δόλου καὶ ἀπάτης.' Μαρδόνιος μὲν
"ταῦτα, ὦ Ἀθηναῖοι, ἐνετείλατό μοι εἰπεῖν πρὸς
"ὑμέας. ἐγὼ δὲ περὶ μὲν εὐνοίης τῆς πρὸς ὑμέας
"ἐούσης ἐξ ἐμεῦ οὐδὲν λέξω (οὐ γὰρ ἂν νῦν πρῶτον
20 "ἐκμάθοιτε), προσχρηίζω δὲ ὑμέων πείθεσθαι Μαρ-
"δονίῳ. ἐνορέω γὰρ ὑμῖν οὐκ οἵοισί τε ἐσομένοισι
"τὸν πάντα χρόνον πολεμέειν Ξέρξῃ. εἰ γὰρ ἐνώρων
"τοῦτο ἐν ὑμῖν, οὐκ ἄν κοτε ἐς ὑμέας ἦλθον ἔχων
"λόγους τούσδε· καὶ γὰρ δύναμις ὑπὲρ ἄνθρωπον ἡ
25 "βασιλέος ἐστὶ καὶ χεὶρ ὑπερμήκης. ἢν ὦν μὴ
"αὐτίκα ὁμολογήσητε, μεγάλα προτεινόντων ἐπ'
"οἷσι ὁμολογέειν ἐθέλουσι, δειμαίνω ὑπὲρ ὑμέων ἐν
"τρίβῳ τε μάλιστα οἰκημένων τῶν συμμάχων πάντων,
"αἰεί τε φθειρομένων μούνων, ἐξαίρετόν τι μεταίχμιον
30 "τὴν γῆν ἐκτημένων. ἀλλὰ πείθεσθε· πολλοῦ γὰρ
"ὑμῖν ἄξια ταῦτα, εἰ βασιλεύς γε ὁ μέγας μούνοισι

" ὑμῖν Ἑλλήνων τὰς ἁμαρτάδας ἀπιεὶς ἐθέλει φίλος
" γενέσθαι." Ἀλέξανδρος μὲν ταῦτα ἔλεξε.

The Spartans send envoys to counteract Alexander's influence at Athens.

CXLI. Λακεδαιμόνιοι δὲ, πυθόμενοι ἥκειν Ἀλέξανδρον ἐς Ἀθήνας ἐς ὁμολογίην ἄξοντα τῷ βαρβάρῳ Ἀθηναίους, ἀναμνησθέντες τῶν λογίων ὥς σφεας χρεών ἐστι ἅμα τοῖσι ἄλλοισι Δωριεῦσι ἐκπίπτειν ἐκ Πελοποννήσου ὑπὸ Μήδων τε καὶ Ἀθηναίων, κάρτα τε ἔδεισαν μὴ ὁμολογήσωσι τῷ Πέρσῃ Ἀθηναῖοι, αὐτίκα τέ σφι ἔδοξε πέμπειν ἀγγέλους. καὶ δὴ συνέπιπτε ὥστε ὁμοῦ σφέων γίνεσθαι τὴν κατάστασιν. ἐπανέμειναν γὰρ οἱ Ἀθηναῖοι διατρίβοντες, εὖ ἐπιστάμενοι ὅτι ἔμελλον Λακεδαιμόνιοι πεύσεσθαι ἥκοντα παρὰ τοῦ βαρβάρου ἄγγελον ἐπ' ὁμολογίῃ, πυθόμενοί τε πέμψειν κατὰ τάχος ἀγγέλους. ἐπίτηδες ὦν ἐποίευν, ἐνδεικνύμενοι τοῖσι Λακεδαιμονίοισι τὴν ἑωυτῶν γνώμην.

Speech of the Spartan envoys.

CXLII. Ὡς δὲ ἐπαύσατο λέγων Ἀλέξανδρος, διαδεξάμενοι ἔλεγον οἱ ἀπὸ Σπάρτης ἄγγελοι·
" Ἡμέας δὲ ἔπεμψαν Λακεδαιμόνιοι δεησομένους
" ὑμέων μήτε νεώτερον ποιέειν μηδὲν κατὰ τὴν
" Ἑλλάδα μήτε λόγους ἐνδέκεσθαι παρὰ τοῦ βαρ-
" βάρου. οὔτε γὰρ δίκαιον οὐδαμῶς, οὔτε κόσμον
" φέρον οὔ τί γε ἄλλοισι Ἑλλήνων οὐδαμοῖσι, ὑμῖν
" δὲ δὴ καὶ διὰ πάντων ἥκιστα πολλῶν εἵνεκεν·
" ἠγείρατε γὰρ τόνδε τὸν πόλεμον ὑμεῖς οὐδὲν ἡμέων
" βουλομένων, καὶ περὶ τῆς ὑμετέρης ἀρχῆς ὁ ἀγὼν

"ἐγένετο· νῦν δὲ φέρει καὶ ἐς πᾶσαν τὴν Ἑλλάδα.
"ἄλλως τε τούτων ἁπάντων αἰτίους γενέσθαι δουλο-
"σύνης τοῖσι Ἕλλησι Ἀθηναίους οὐδαμῶς ἀνασχετόν,
"οἵτινες αἰεὶ καὶ τὸ πάλαι φαίνεσθε πολλοὺς ἐλευ-
"θερώσαντες ἀνθρώπων. πιεζομένοισι μέντοι ὑμῖν
"συναχθόμεθα, καὶ ὅτι καρπῶν ἐστερήθητε διξῶν
"ἤδη, καὶ ὅτι οἰκοφθόρησθε χρόνον ἤδη πολλόν.
"ἀντὶ τούτων δὲ ὑμῖν Λακεδαιμόνιοί τε καὶ οἱ
"σύμμαχοι ἐπαγγέλλονται γυναῖκάς τε καὶ τὰ ἐς
"πόλεμον ἄχρηστα οἰκετέων ἐχόμενα πάντα ἐπι-
"θρέψειν, ἔστ' ἂν ὁ πόλεμος ὅδε συνεστήκῃ. μηδὲ
"ὑμέας Ἀλέξανδρος ὁ Μακεδὼν ἀναγνώσῃ, λεήνας
"τὸν Μαρδονίου λόγον. τούτῳ μὲν γὰρ ταῦτα
"ποιητέα ἐστί, τύραννος γὰρ ἐὼν τυράννῳ συγκα-
"τεργάζεται, ὑμῖν δέ γε οὐ ποιητέα, εἴ περ εὖ
"τυγχάνετε φρονέοντες, ἐπισταμένοισι ὡς βαρβά-
"ροισί ἐστι οὔτε πιστὸν οὔτε ἀληθὲς οὐδέν."

Answer of the Athenians: they will never make terms with Xerxes.

CXLIII. Ταῦτα ἔλεξαν οἱ ἄγγελοι. Ἀθηναῖοι δὲ πρὸς μὲν Ἀλέξανδρον ὑπεκρίναντο τάδε· "Καὶ
"αὐτοὶ τοῦτό γε ἐπιστάμεθα, ὅτι πολλαπλησίη ἐστὶ
"τῷ Μήδῳ δύναμις ἤπερ ἡμῖν, ὥστε οὐδὲν δέει τοῦτό
"γε ὀνειδίζειν. ἀλλ' ὅμως ἐλευθερίης γλιχόμενοι
"ἀμυνεύμεθα οὕτω, ὅκως ἂν καὶ δυνώμεθα. ὁμολο-
"γῆσαι δὲ τῷ βαρβάρῳ μήτε σὺ ἡμέας πειρῶ
"ἀναπείθειν οὔτε ἡμεῖς πεισόμεθα. νῦν δὲ ἀπάγ-
"γελλε Μαρδονίῳ, ὡς Ἀθηναῖοι λέγουσι, ἔστ' ἂν ὁ
"ἥλιος τὴν αὐτὴν ὁδὸν ἴῃ τῇ καὶ νῦν ἔρχεται, μήκοτε
"ὁμολογήσειν ἡμέας Ξέρξῃ· ἀλλὰ θεοῖσί τε συμ-

"μάχοισι πίσυνοί μιν ἐπέξιμεν ἀμυνόμενοι καὶ τοῖσι
"ἥρωσι, τῶν ἐκεῖνος οὐδεμίαν ὄπιν ἔχων ἐνέπρησε
"τούς τε οἴκους καὶ τὰ ἀγάλματα. σύ τε τοῦ λοιποῦ
"λόγους ἔχων τοιούσδε μὴ ἐπιφαίνεο Ἀθηναίοισι,
"μηδὲ δοκέων χρηστὰ ὑπουργέειν ἀθέμιστα ἔρδειν 5
"παραίνεε. οὐ γάρ σε βουλόμεθα οὐδὲν ἄχαρι πρὸς
"Ἀθηναίων παθεῖν, ἐόντα πρόξεινόν τε καὶ φίλον."

*Athenian address to the Spartan envoys urging instant
activity on the part of Sparta.*

CXLIV. Πρὸς μὲν Ἀλέξανδρον ταῦτα ὑπεκρίναντο, πρὸς δὲ τοὺς ἀπὸ Σπάρτης ἀγγέλους τάδε·
"Τὸ μὲν δεῖσαι Λακεδαιμονίους μὴ ὁμολογήσωμεν τῷ 10
"βαρβάρῳ κάρτα ἀνθρωπήϊον ἦν. ἀτὰρ αἰσχρῶς
"γε οἴκατε ἐξεπιστάμενοι τὸ Ἀθηναίων φρόνημα
"ἀρρωδῆσαι, ὅτι οὔτε χρυσός ἐστι γῆς οὐδαμόθι
"τοσοῦτος οὔτε χώρη κάλλεϊ καὶ ἀρετῇ μέγα ὑπερ-
"φέρουσα, τὰ ἡμεῖς δεξάμενοι ἐθέλοιμεν ἂν μηδίσαντες 15
"καταδουλῶσαι τὴν Ἑλλάδα. πολλά τε γὰρ καὶ
"μεγάλα ἐστὶ τὰ διακωλύοντα ταῦτα μὴ ποιέειν,
"μηδ' ἢν ἐθέλωμεν· πρῶτα μὲν καὶ μέγιστα τῶν
"θεῶν τὰ ἀγάλματα καὶ τὰ οἰκήματα ἐμπεπρησμένα
"τε καὶ συγκεχωσμένα, τοῖσι ἡμέας ἀναγκαίως ἔχει 20
"τιμωρέειν ἐς τὰ μέγιστα μᾶλλον ἤπερ ὁμολογέειν
"τῷ ταῦτα ἐργασαμένῳ, αὖτις δὲ τὸ Ἑλληνικὸν ἐὸν
"ὅμαιμόν τε καὶ ὁμόγλωσσον, καὶ θεῶν ἱδρύματά τε
"κοινὰ καὶ θυσίαι ἤθεά τε ὁμότροπα, τῶν προδότας
"γενέσθαι Ἀθηναίους οὐκ ἂν εὖ ἔχοι. ἐπίστασθέ τε 25
"οὕτω, εἰ μὴ πρότερον ἐτυγχάνετε ἐπιστάμενοι, ἔστ'
"ἂν καὶ εἷς περιῇ Ἀθηναίων, μηδαμὰ ὁμολογήσοντας
"ἡμέας Ξέρξῃ. ὑμέων μέντοι ἀγάμεθα τὴν πρόνοιαν

"τὴν ἐς ἡμέας ἔχουσαν, ὅτι προείδετε ἡμέων οἰκοφθο-
"ρημένων οὕτω ὥστε ἐπιτρέψαι ἐθέλειν ἡμέων τοὺς
"οἰκέτας. καὶ ὑμῖν μὲν ἡ χάρις ἐκπεπλήρωται,
"ἡμεῖς μέντοι λιπαρήσομεν οὕτω ὅκως ἂν ἔχωμεν,
5 "οὐδὲν λυπέοντες ὑμέας. νῦν δὲ, ὡς οὕτω ἐχόντων,
"στρατιὴν ὡς τάχιστα ἐκπέμπετε. ὡς γὰρ ἡμεῖς
"εἰκάζομεν, οὐκ ἑκὰς χρόνου παρέσται ὁ βάρβαρος
"ἐσβαλὼν ἐς τὴν ἡμετέρην, ἀλλ' ἐπειδὰν τάχιστα
"πύθηται τὴν ἀγγελίην ὅτι οὐδὲν ποιήσομεν τῶν
10 "ἐκεῖνος ἡμέων προσεδέετο. πρὶν ὦν παρεῖναι ἐκεῖ-
"νον ἐς τὴν Ἀττικὴν, ἡμέας καιρός ἐστι προβωθῆσαι
"ἐς τὴν Βοιωτίην." οἱ μὲν ταῦτα ὑποκριναμένων
Ἀθηναίων ἀπαλλάσσοντο ἐς Σπάρτην.

NOTES.

[*For persons and names of places see Historical and Geographical Index. G. refers to Goodwin's Greek Grammar, 1882. App. to the Appendix on the Ionic Dialect. Clyde to Clyde's Greek Syntax, 1870.*]

CHAPTER I.

The last book (VII) had described the fate of the contingent appointed to serve on land and guard Thermopylae; Herodotus now turns to the fleet.

1, 2. οἱ δὲ...ταχθέντες 'those whose assigned duty it was to serve afloat', that is assigned by their several states: cp. 7, 21 οἱ δὲ ἐς τὸν πεζὸν ἐτετάχατο. The general movements both of land force and fleet were directed by the national congress assembled in the Isthmus (7, 175).

4. Πλαταιέες. The Plataeans as an inland state without seaboard would have no ships; but they constantly followed and supported the Athenians as at Marathon (6, 108, 111). They were not however actually engaged at Salamis, see c. 44; though they afterwards pleaded their services at Artemisium as a proof of their Hellenic patriotism, see Thucyd. 3, 54, 3.

5. Κορίνθιοι. That the Corinthians should only send 40 ships when the Athenians sent 127 is a striking sign of the rapid advance of the latter. In B.C. 491 the Athenians had had to borrow, or rather purchase at a nominal price, 20 ships of Corinth wherewith to attack Aegina [6, 88, 89].

7. Χαλκιδέες. The Chalcidians manned Athenian ships probably because they were Athenians settled as cleruchs in the territory of Chalcis in Euboea [see 5, 77].

11, 12. **δύο τε νέας καὶ πεντηκοντέρους δύο** 'two triremes and two penteconters'. By νέες unqualified by any descriptive epithet understand triremes, or ships of war, ταχεῖαι: other triremes are called ὁπλιταγωγοί, ἱππαγωγοί etc. Penteconters were smaller vessels rowed by 50 men, 25 on each side sitting on the same level. The latter were the vessels almost universal in Greece until the decennium B.C. 490—80, when they were superseded by the triremes [Her. 1, 163, 4, Thucyd. 1, 14, 4]. The use of penteconters however still survived among more distant Greek states, as Rhodes [Thucyd. 6, 43, 1], as also among the Etruscans [id. 6, 103, 2]. The triremes carried an average of 200 men, see c. 17.

13. **Ὀπούντιοι**, see Hist. Ind. s. v. Locrians.
ἐπεβοήθεον, App. A. III. 8.

CHAPTER II.

15. **εἴρηταί δέ μοι**, that is in the preceding chapter. The numbers are:

Athenians	127	ships
Corinthians	40	,,
Megarians	20	..
Chalcidians	20	,,
Aeginetans	18	,,
Sicyonians	12	,,
Lacedaemonians	10	,,
Epidaurians	8	,,
Eretrians	7	
Troezenians	5	,,
Styrans	2	
Ceians	2	
	271	

16. **τῶν συλλεχθεισέων νεῶν**, that is 'of triremes', as above, l. 11.

20. **οἱ σύμμαχοι**, the members of the congress of the Isthmus, see above, l. 2.

1, 2. **οὐκ ἔφασαν...ἕψεσθαι** 'refused to serve under Athenians but would only do so if the Spartan leader took the command'.

Two clauses are compressed into one, οὐκ ἔφασαν ἔψεσθαι Ἀθηναίοις and ἔφασαν ἕψεσθαι μόνῳ τῷ Λάκωνι. Notice Ἀθηναίοις without article 'Athenians' = 'an Athenian commander', not the particular one.

2. ἀλλὰ λύσειν = ἀλλὰ ἔφασαν λύσειν.

τὸ μέλλον ἔσεσθαι 'which was about to take place'. The verb μέλλειν is regularly followed by the future infinitive and sometimes by the present, but not by the aorist infinitive, G. § 202, 3. Yet exceptions to this rule occasionally occur [see Rutherford *New Phrynichus* p. 420 sq.].

CHAPTER III.

4. κατ' ἀρχὰς 'originally', 'at first', cp. 9, 22. λόγος 'common talk'. πρὶν ἢ πέμπειν 'before they (the Greeks) sent'.

5. ἐπὶ συμμαχίην 'with a view of securing an alliance'. This refers to the embassy sent by the congress of the Isthmus to Gelo of Syracuse to induce him to join the alliance against the Persian invaders. In the discussion with Gelo the Spartans claimed the lead on land, the Athenians at sea, and Gelo refused help unless one or the other were conceded to him. Her. 7, 157—9.

7. μέγα πεποιημένοι 'because they regarded it as of first importance'. This use of ποιεῖσθαι [of which πεποιημένος is used as middle perf. part.] is common in Herod. see p. 6, l. 7, and cp. 9, 4 δεινὸν ποιησάμενοι. περιεῖναι 'survive', 'be saved'. Cp. p. 30, l. 15.

9—11. ὀρθὰ νοεῦντες 'and their sentiments were entirely right'.

πολέμου ὁμοφρονέοντος 'unanimous war', i.e. 'the war of a united country', an expression only justifiable by considering war to be personified. τοσούτῳ...ὅσῳ 'precisely as much worse as'.

12. οὐκ ἀντέτεινον 'they did not continue to make any counter-claim'.

13. μέχρι ὅσου 'as long as they (the Athenians) wanted them', i.e. the other Greeks. Cp. μέχρι κόσου p. 44, l. 15.

14, 15. περὶ τῆς ἐκείνου...ἐποιεῦντο 'they were going to attack the Persian's own territory'. Cp. p. 14, l. 14.

15, 16. τὴν Παυσανίεω ὕβριν 'the outrageous conduct of Pausanias'. Thucydides says he was βίαιος and that his mode of behaviour was a τυραννίδος μίμησις rather than a στρατηγία [1, 95]. And Plutarch [Aristid. 23] gives details of the roughness of his manners, the severity of his punishments, and the offensiveness of his manner of asserting the Spartan primacy.

ἀπείλοντο...Λακεδαιμονίους 'deprived the Lacedaemonians of the command'; for the double acc. see G. § 164.

The event referred to is the deposition of Pausanias in B.C. 478—7, and the selection of Aristeides to take the command of the allied fleet in the Northern Aegean, which is recounted by Thucydides [1, 94 sq.], and which led to the formation of the Confederacy of Delos.

CHAPTER IV.

18. τότε δὲ 'but at this time', opp. to ὕστερον μὲν l. 17. καὶ 'actually'.

19. καταχθείσας 'brought to land'.

21. παρὰ δόξαν...ἢ 'in an unexpectedly different manner than'. The phrase παρὰ δόξαν involves the idea of ἄλλως and is therefore followed by ἢ. Cp. 1, 79 ὥς οἱ παρὰ δόξαν ἔσχε τὰ πρήγματα ἢ ὡς αὐτὸς κατεδόκεε.

22. Notice the imperfect ἀπέβαινε 'were turning out'. κατεδόκεον, see p. 36, l. 22.

23. ἔσω, that is, South of the Euripus, towards the Peloponnesus, p. 10, l. 6.

2, 3. ἔστ' ἂν...ὑπεκθέωνται 'until they should have removed out of danger'. The construction represents the words used προσμεῖνον ἔστ' ἂν ὑπεκθεώμεθα, and is retained in Orat. Obliq. G. § 239, 2.

4. πείθουσι 'bribe'.

5. ἐπ' ᾧ τε 'on condition that'. For τε see on p. 10, l. 9.

6. πρὸ τῆς Εὐβοίης, that is, to the North of Euboea, in which direction the enemy were. Cp. p. 39, l. 9 and 9, 61 πρὸ τῆς πόλιος.

ποιήσονται, the infin. more commonly follows ἐπ' ᾧ τε, but the future indic. is also used *dramatically*. G. § 236, note 2. τὴν ναυμαχίην '*the* sea-fight', that is the fight which must inevitably come somewhere.

CHAPTER V.

9. ὡς παρ' ἑωυτοῦ δῆθεν 'as though out of his own pocket (*de suo*) as he pretended'. For παρ' ἑωυτοῦ cp. 2, 129 παρ' ἑωυτοῦ διδόντα. Cp. 7, 29 παρ' ἐμωυτοῦ δούς τὰς ἑπτὰ χιλιάδας. And for δῆθεν indicating the falseness of a pretext see 7, 211 φεύγεσκον δῆθεν 'they kept pretending to run away'; and combined with

ὡς, 9, 66 ὡς ἐς μάχην ἦγε δῆθεν 'he made a feint of leading them to the field'.

11. **ἤσπαιρε** 'struggled', properly 'panted', see 1, 111 ὁρέω παιδίον προκείμενον ἀσπαῖρόν τε καὶ κραυγανόμενον. 9, 120 ἤσπαιρον ὅκως περ ἰχθύες νεοάλωτοι. Very rarely found in Attic.

12. **ἀποπλώσεσθαι** from ἀποπλώω, Ionic and poetic form of -πλέω. [This form is used by the MSS. R and S, and I have retained it throughout, but in certain other MSS. the form is πλεύσεσθαι, πλέειν, πλέομεν κ.τ.λ. and Stein has adopted the latter.]

13. **πρὸς δὴ τοῦτον** 'to him he said'; the reason for the speech has been previously given by the clause 'Ἀδείμαντος γάρ. The logical order would be πρὸς Ἀδείμαντον εἶπε, οὗτος γὰρ ἤσπαιρε.

15, 16. **ἂν πέμψειε** 'will be likely to send you'. The plan of sending bribes round to the leading men in each state by the king of Persia is alluded to again in 9, 2, and 41; and we know from later authorities (Demosth. Phil. 3, 42) that it was actually done.

16. **ταὐτά τε ἅμα ἠγόρευε καὶ πέμπει.** The verb πέμπει is an historical present: 'He accompanied this speech by sending three talents to the ship of Adeimantus'. [For this use of τε—καὶ as expressing simultaneous action see on p. 28, l. 9.]

Plutarch, on the authority of the Lesbian Phanias, tells a story of Themistocles bribing an Athenian captain with one talent to stay at Artemisium [Themist. 7], but there is no reason why both stories may not be true.

18. **πάντες** 'both', cp. 5, 36; 6, 77 St. [Some few MSS. have πληγέντες with which Abicht compares Plutarch Demosth. 15 πληγεὶς ὑπὸ τῆς δωροδοκίας.]

19. **ἐκεχάριστο** is middle: 'And thus Themistocles had gratified the Euboeans while he secured a profit for himself at the same time'.

20—23. **ἐλάνθανε δὲ...χρήματα** 'and at the same time he was not suspected of having the balance of the money (the 30 talents, see c. 4), but the men who got their share of it believed that the money had been sent from Athens for this express purpose'.

21. **ἠπιστέατο** [App. D. II. a] 'believed', 'were given to understand'. Cp. p. 13, l. 22; p. 46, l. 19; p. 51, l. 20; p. 75, l. 15. We use the word to 'understand' in the same sense of 'belief'.

CHAPTER VI.

24. οὕτω δή 'it was thus', 'it was in these circumstances that'.

25. ἐγένετο δὲ ὧδε 'and how it came about was as follows', i.e. how the battle began and how it was carried on.

26. περὶ δείλην πρωΐην 'early in the afternoon', opposed to δείλην ὀψίην p. 5, l. 19.

27. ἔτι καὶ πρότερον 'already before this', cp. p. 36, l. 20.

4 1. αὐτοί 'with their own eyes'. ἐπιχειρέειν sc. ἑλεῖν. Cp. 9, 14 θέλων εἴ κως τούτους πρῶτον ἕλοι.

2. ἐκ μὲν δὴ τῆς ἀντίης 'straight down upon them', *ex adverso*. Cf. ἐκ τοῦ φανεροῦ (9, 1), ἐκ τῆς ἰθέης (9, 37). .

4, 5. ὁρμήσειαν...καταλαμβάνῃ. The coming down of night before they could get engaged is perhaps the contingency most present to their minds, but as the subj. after a past tense in the governing clause is as correct as the opt., on the *dramatic* principle of introducing the exact words of the person, the variation does not perhaps admit of any other explanation than the taste of the writer. For καταλαμβάνειν in this sense 9, 56 τοὺς δὲ ἐπεὶ ἠὼς κατελάμβανε.

5, 6. καὶ ἔμελλον δῆθεν ἐκφεύξεσθαι 'and then, as they thought, they were certain to escape'. For fut. inf. after ἔμελλον see above, p. 2, l. 2. The meaning of ἔμελλον here expressing certainty is found in common idiomatic phrases, such as, ἐμέλλετ' ἄρ' ἅπαντες ἀνασείειν βοήν 'I was certain you would shout', Arist. Ach. 347 ἔμελλον σ' ἄρα κινήσειν ἐγώ 'I was certain I should send you packing', id. Nub. 1301 ἆρ' ἐμέλλομέν ποθ' ὑμᾶς ἀποσοβήσειν τῷ χρόνῳ 'I was certain we should drive you off in time', id. Vesp. 464.

δῆθεν indicates the thoughts of another, which the writer discredits, see above, p. 3, l. 9.

6. μηδὲ πυρφόρον 'not even a sacred-fire bearer', i.e. not anyone at all. The πυρφόρος would be defended as long as anyone survived. Hence the phrase for total extinction. From Xenophon (Rep. Lac. XIII. 3) we learn that a lamp of sacred fire was carried with a Spartan host never to be extinguished. The person intrusted with this would be most carefully guarded.

6, 7. τῷ ἐκείνων λόγῳ 'according to their expressed purpose'.

CHAPTER VII.

7. **πρὸς ταῦτα** 'with a view to these contingencies'.

9. **ἔξωθεν Σκιάθου** 'to the East of Skiathos'. So as to have Skiathos between them and the Greeks.

10—12. **ἵνα δὴ περιλάβοιεν** 'that, as they intended (δή), they might enclose them'. Here the main purpose is expressed by the optative, while a secondary or subordinate purpose is expressed by a subjunctive clause (ὡς ἂν μὴ ὀφθέωσι 'in such a way that they might not be seen'), but see on l. 4 and cp. p. 40, ll. 13—15, Goodw. M. and T. § 44. 2. For **δή** almost equivalent to δῆθεν, shewing that the writer is representing the thoughts of others, see 9, 11 ἐν νόῳ δὴ ἔχοντες. 9, 59 ἦγε...κατὰ στίβον τῶν Ἑλλήνων ὡς δὴ ἀποδιδρησκόντων, infra p. 42, l. 25.

For the dramatic construction ὡς ἂν μὴ ὀφθέωσι after the historical περιέπεμπον cp. 9, 7 ἐκέλευσαν ὑμέας ἐκπέμπειν ὡς ἂν τὸν βάρβαρον δεκώμεθα. G. § 216, 2.

12—14. **οἱ μὲν...σφεῖς δὲ**. The party despatched round Euboea, and the main body remaining at Aphetae.

13. **τὴν ὀπίσω φέρουσαν ὁδὸν** 'their homeward course'.

14. **ἐξ ἐναντίης** 'from the opposite side', cp. ἐξ ἀντίης c. 6.

16. **ταύτης τῆς ἡμέρης** 'that day', the gen. of time within which. G. § 179.

17. **τὸ σύνθημα** 'the signal agreed upon', used of a 'watchword' in 9, 98. **ἔμελλε φανήσεσθαι** 'could appear', referring to the time it must necessarily take to get round the island. For ἔμελλε see p. 2, l. 2.

20. **ἐποιεῦντο ἀριθμὸν** 'held a muster of', cp. 7, 59. This was rendered necessary, as Stein observes, by the losses sustained by bad weather and attacks of enemies; see 7, 190, where 400 ships are said to have been lost on the coast of Magnesia.

CHAPTER VIII.

24, 25. **τῇ ναυαγίῃ τῇ κατὰ τὸ Πήλιον γενομένῃ** 'the shipwreck which had befallen them off Pelion', that mentioned in the last note.

26, 27. **περιβάλετο** 'possessed himself of', cp. 6, 25 πόλιν καλλίστην Ζάγκλην περιεβλέατο, see 9, 39. **ἄρα** 'as it appears', i.e. from what he did afterwards, p. 61, l. 4.

28. **αὐτομολήσειν**: notice the fut. inf. after ἐν νόῳ εἶχε on the analogy of the construction of μέλλω. The futurity implied in ἐν νόῳ εἶχε is expressed in the infinitive.

ἀλλ' οὐ γάρ 'but he [didn't do so then] for there was no opportunity', so we often find καὶ οὐ γάρ 9, 61, 87 etc. The negative belongs to the prevented action, γάρ introduces the cause of the prevention.

5   1. **πάρεσχε**, impers. p. 39, l. 27. Cp. Thucyd. 1, 120, 5; 5, 14, 2.

ὡς τότε 'at that time'. The meaning of ὡς here is hard to give by any English equivalent; it defines and limits the time indicated by τότε. Cobet proposes ἕως τότε 'up to that time'.

ὅτεῳ δὴ τρόπῳ 'now in what manner it actually happened'. δή here, like Lat. *adeo*, emphasizes and defines the word which it follows. **ἔτι** 'after all', that is after whatever attempts or exploits.

3, 4. **λέγεται γάρ**. The feat here mentioned is of course an impossible one, and is naturally disbelieved by Herodotus. The distance from Aphetae to Artemisium is about seven miles. It is possible perhaps that Skyllias made his way over this strait by swimming and diving at intervals. The natives of the Levant to this day are famous divers [Col. Leake quoted by Rawl.], and much greater distances have been swum in our own time.

5. **ἀνέσχε** 'came up to the surface'. ἔχω with its compounds is as often neuter as transitive. Abicht notices that in Odyss. 5, 320 ἀνασχεθέειν used in this sense is explained by the Scholiast by ἀναδῦναι.

8. **μετεξέτερα**=ἔνια. A word confined to the Ionic dialect. p. 45, l. 16.

9. **ἀποδεδέχθω** [δείκνυμι], App. E.

CHAPTER IX.

14, 15. **λόγον σφίσι αὐτοῖσι ἐδίδοσαν** 'took counsel among themselves', cp. 1, 97 συλλέχθησαν οἱ Μῆδοι ἐς τὠυτὸ καὶ ἐδίδοσαν σφίσι λόγον. Xen. Hell. 1, 1, 27 εἰ δὲ ἐπικαλοίη τι αὐτοῖς λόγον ἔφασαν χρῆναι διδόναι 'to discuss the matter'. Arist. Plut. 467 περὶ τούτου σφῶν ἐθέλω δοῦναι λόγον 'to argue the matter with you'.

15. ἐνίκα 'the decision was come to', 'the vote was passed'. For this impersonal use of νικᾶν see Soph. Antig. 233 τέλος δὲ μέν τοι δεῦρ' ἐνίκησεν μολεῖν: and again Her. 6, 101 ἐνίκα μὴ ἐκλιπεῖν τὴν πόλιν. A commoner usage is νικᾶν γνώμην 'to get one's view carried' [e.g. 1, 61].

16. αὐλισθέντας 'having encamped for the night'. Stein rightly explains that this refers to the camp on shore, where they were to pass the night; that the enemy might not be led to expect any unusual movement by seeing them spend the night on board.

17. παρέντας 'letting pass'.

18, 19. μετὰ δὲ τοῦτο 'but subsequently', i.e. on the same day as the Council. δείλην ὀψίην 'evening', opposed to δείλην πρωΐην 'afternoon' in c. 6.

20. αὐτοὶ *ultro* 'without being attacked', 'on their own account'. ἐπανέπλωον, notice the imperf. 'began putting to sea to attack'.

21, 22. ἀπόπειραν—διέκπλόου 'wishing to satisfy themselves as to the nature of their fighting and naval tactics'. αὐτῶν depends upon μάχης. The force of ἀπόπειρα as opposed to πεῖρα, like that of ἀποπειρᾶσθαι, is that of completion or satisfaction. See 2, 73; 3, 128; 9, 91. The διέκπλοος was a manoeuvre in naval warfare by which a single line of ships broke through the enemies' line, turned swiftly, and charged as they pleased, opposed to the ruder method of grappling and fighting from the decks. See 6, 12 where Dionysius is described as training the Ionian sailors, ὁ δὲ ἀνάγων ἑκάστοτε ἐπὶ κέρας ('in line') τὰς νέας, ὅκως τοῖσι ἐρέτῃσι χρήσαιτο διέκπλοον ποιεύμενος τῇσι νηυσὶ δι' ἀλληλέων καὶ τοὺς ἐπιβάτας ὁπλίσειε....

The manoeuvre required both swiftness and skill in working the vessel, so as to avoid charging prow to prow, and being charged on one's own broadside. See Thucyd. 1, 49, 3 διέκπλοι δ' οὐκ ἦσαν, ἀλλὰ θυμῷ καὶ ῥώμῃ τὸ πλέον ἐναυμάχουν ἢ ἐπιστήμῃ. The Athenians especially prided themselves on their skill in practising this manoeuvre, as well as another called the περίπλους, out-flanking the enemies' ship and charging it as one pleased,—see Thucyd. 7, 36, 3 τοῖς δὲ Ἀθηναίοις οὐκ ἔσεσθαι σφῶν ἐν στενοχωρίᾳ οὔτε περίπλουν οὔτε διέκπλουν, ᾧπερ τῆς τέχνης μάλιστα ἐπίστευον.

CHAPTER X.

25. **μανίην ἐπενείκαντες** [for the Ion. -ενείκας see App. E] 'thinking them mad'. Cp. 1, 131 τοῖσι ἀγάλματα ποιεῦσι μωρίην ἐπιφέρουσι. 6, 112 τοῖσι Ἀθηναίοισι μανίην ἐπέφερον.

2. **οἰκότα** [Ion. for εἰκότα App. E. f] 'what was reasonable and likely'.

3. **πολλαπλησίας**, App. A. II. (2).

4, 5. **καταφρονήσαντες ταῦτα** 'with these convictions': καταφρονέω in the common meaning of 'to despise' takes a genitive and is used by Herod. in 4, 134 [*and there only*, Abicht]. In the sense in which it is here employed it is only a strengthened form of φρονήσαντες, cp. 1, 66, and καταδοκεῖν in c. 4.

5. **ἐκυκλοῦντο...μέσον** [App. D. III. 3] 'began a movement to outflank them and get them within the circle of their ships'. ἐς μέσον is proleptic, 'so as to get them in the middle'.

7. **συμφορήν τε...μεγάλην** 'were exceedingly sorry for them', cp. p. 36, l. 13.

8. **ἐπιστάμενοι** 'feeling persuaded', cp. p. 3, l. 21.

11. **ἅμιλλαν ἐποιεῦντο** 'raced with each other', cp. 7, 196.

12. **δῶρα.** For the practice of giving rewards by the Persian king to those successful in war see Xen. Oecon. 4, 16.

For λάμψεται see App. E. II. 2. For the tense after ὅκως see G. § 217.

13. **λόγος** 'reputation', see 9, 78.

CHAPTER XI.

15. **ἐσήμηνε** sc. ὁ σαλπιγκτής. For the use of the σάλπιγξ see Aeschyl. Persae 397 σάλπιγξ δ' ἀϋτῇ πάντ' ἐκεῖν' ἐπέφλεγεν, Thucyd. 6, 32, 1 τῇ σάλπιγγι σιωπὴ ὑπεσημάνθη. Cp. Polyb. 16, 4, 7.

16. **ἐς τὸ μέσον τὰς πρύμνας συνήγαγον** 'drew their sterns together at a central point'. This manoeuvre, by which the ships were arranged so as to resemble an open fan, was for the purpose of preventing the enemy from practising the *diekplus*. Thus it was done by the Peloponnesians in the Gulf of Corinth when preparing to receive the attack of the Athenians [B.C. 429], see Thucyd. 2, 83, 5 οἱ δὲ Πελοποννήσιοι ἐτάξαντο κύκλον τῶν νεῶν ὡς μέγιστον· οἷοί τ' ἦσαν μὴ διδόντες διέκπλουν, τὰς πρώρας μὲν ἔξω εἴσω δὲ τὰς πρύμνας.

17. ἔργου εἴχοντο 'they set to work', p. 58, l. 20. ἐν ὀλίγῳ... ἀπολαμφθέντες 'though caught in a narrow part of the Strait', cp. 9, 51 ἐν τῷ Κιθαιρῶνι ἀπολελαμμένοι.

18. καὶ κατὰ στόμα, sc. ἐχόμενοί περ ἔργου (or some equivalent participle) 'and though they were engaged prow to prow', i.e. though they would have no opportunity in the narrow sea of practising the *diekplus* or *periplus*. Abicht however understands εἴχοντο after στόμα 'and they began the attack front to front'. I think the run of the sentence is conclusive in favour of the former construction, which is supported by Stein.

23. τὸ ἀριστήϊον 'the prize of valour', the recipient of which was formally decided upon after a battle, the various achievements and circumstances being fully discussed. See for instance what was done after the battle of Plataea, 9, 71.

27. πολλὸν παρὰ δόξαν ἀγωνισάμενοι 'after a battle the result of which much surprised them', for they had looked for an easy victory, see p. 5, l. 25. For παρὰ δόξαν cp. p. 2, l. 22.

31. χῶρον ἐν Σαλαμῖνι 'a farm in Salamis'.

CHAPTER XII.

1. εὐφρόνη 'the kindly one', a poetical word for νύξ, both of 7 which Herodotus uses with no apparent distinction. ἦν τῆς ὥρης μέσον θέρος 'it was midsummer', the gen. τῆς ὥρης is partitive, 'of the season it was full midsummer'; which is meant to emphasize the unusual occurrence of such a storm. The time was probably about the beginning of July, for the Olympic festival was going on, see c. 26, cp. 7, 206.

3. ἀπὸ τοῦ Πηλίου 'from the direction of Mt Pelion', that is from the North.

8. ἐς φόβον κατιστέατο 'began to be frightened'. App. D. 11.

6. ἐλπίζοντες 'expecting'. ἐς οἷα...ἧκον 'considering the amount of misfortunes into which they had fallen'; explained by the summary of their disasters in the next sentence.

10, 11. τοῦ χειμῶνος...κατὰ Πήλιον, see 7, 188. A storm of East wind caught the Persian fleet when off the shore of Magnesia and drove a large number of ships ashore on the promontory called the Ovens (Ἴπνοι) and other parts of the coast. ὑπέλαβε 'succeeded'. ἐκ 'after'. ῥεύματα 'swollen streams' or 'torrents'.

CHAPTER XIII.

15. **τοῖσι ταχθεῖσι**, see c. 7.

16. **πολλὸν**, App. C. 1, 2nd Decl. (4). **τοσούτῳ ὅσῳ** 'insomuch as'.

17. **ἐν πελάγεϊ** 'in the open sea', not under cover of headlands or bays.

18—20. **ὡς γὰρ δή...Εὐβοίης** 'for as the storm overtook them when actually sailing, just as they were opposite the Hollows of Euboea'. For the place see Hist. and Geogr. Index s.v. Hollows. **τῆς Εὐβοίης** is a topographical genitive, cp. 9, 27 τῆς ἡμετέρης ἐν Ἐλευσῖνι.

21. **ἐξέπιπτον** 'were cast ashore'. ἐκπίπτειν is used as a passive of ἐκβάλλειν. Cp. its meaning of 'to be banished' 'to be driven out'. See 6, 121 ὅκως Πεισίστρατος ἐκπέσοι ἐκ τῶν Ἀθηνέων.

22. **ὅκως ἂν ἐξισωθείη** 'that they might so be reduced to an equality', cp. 9, 22 ὡς ἂν ἀνέλοιατο. 9, 51 ὡς ἂν μὴ ἰδοίατο. When a final sentence expresses a conclusion in which another hypothesis is virtually contained ὡς and ὅπως take ἄν, and, after a past tense, an optative. We find also the subjunctive used dramatically with ὡς ἄν after a past tense in 9, 7, see p. 4, l. 10. The hypothesis involved in the present case may be thus expressed, 'That the Persian fleet might be reduced to an equality with the Greek fleet, as it would be *if these ships were lost*'.

CHAPTER XIV.

1. **ὥς σφι ἀσμένοισι...ἐπέλαμψε**, cp. p. 6, l. 10 ὅσοισι ἡδομένοισι ἦν.

3. **σφι ἀπεχρᾶτο** impers. 'it sufficed them', 'they were content to'.

6. **ἐπέρρωσαν** (ῥώννυμι) 'encouraged them'. This verb is somewhat rare. It is used as the opposite of ἐξέπληξε 'dismayed' in Thucyd. 4, 36, 2.

9. **τὴν αὐτὴν ὥρην** 'the same period of the day', that is the afternoon, as in their former attack, see p. 5, l. 19. ὥρη is not used for a definite division of time like our 'hour', see above p. 7, l. 1 where it means 'season of the year'. It is used here for the larger divisions of the day as morning, noon, afternoon. When Herodotus speaks of the *hours* he says τὰ δυώδεκα μέρεα τῆς ἡμέρης 2, 109.

CHAPTER XV.

13. **δεινόν τι ποιησάμενοι** 'ashamed', p. 2, l. 7. This phrase expresses any violent emotion of shame or anger or surprise. See 9, 5 and 7, the first of which refers to indignation, the second to shame.

15. **τὸ ἀπὸ Ξέρξεω** 'what Xerxes would do', thus 9, 7 τὸ ἀπ' ἡμέων = 'our conduct'.

17. **παρακελευσάμενοι** 'having passed round words of mutual exhortation'. So διακελευσαμένη γυνὴ γυναικί (9, 5). **ἀνῆγον** 'they *began* to launch'.

18. **συνέπιπτε δὲ ὥστε** 'and by a coincidence it so happened that'. Cp. p. 73, l. 12 συνέπιπτε τοιοῦτο ὥστε τοὺς μὲν βαρβάρους... μὴ καταπλῶσαι καταρρωδηκότας, τοὺς δὲ Ἕλληνας...κατωτέρω Δήλου (μὴ καταπλῶσαι). Thucyd. 5, 15 συνέβη τε εὐθὺς μετὰ τὴν μάχην... ὥστε πολέμου μηδὲν ἔτι ἅψασθαι μηδετέρους.

20. **ἐν Θερμοπύλῃσι**, see 7, 207 sq. The fighting at Thermopylae also extended over three days. On the 1st some Medes and Cissians were beaten back from the pass; on the 2nd a similar attempt was made with no better success; and on the 3rd the path over the mountain having been betrayed to Xerxes, Leonidas and his 300 were surrounded and fell.

2. **ὅκως μὴ παρήσουσι.** G. § 217.

9

CHAPTER XVI.

6. **μηνοειδὲς ποιησάντες** 'having formed a crescent with their ships'. μηνοειδὲς is used substantively for μηνοειδὲς σχῆμα. The crescent of ships must have presented its concave to the enemy, the object being that when the Greek fleet was tempted out to attack the centre, the two Persian wings might close round them.

7. **ἐκυκλέοντο** 'endeavoured to encircle them'. p. 6, l. 5.

8, 9. **ἐπανέπλωον** [see p. 3, l. 11] 'began to sail out to sea to attack them'. The ἀνά has the same sense as in ἀνῆγον p. 8, l. 17, and ἐπί gives the idea of hostility. **παραπλήσιοι** 'with no advantage on either side'.

11. **αὐτὸς ὑπ' ἑωυτοῦ ἔπιπτε** 'was self-destroyed'.

12. **περιπιπτουσέων...ἀλλήλας** 'fouling each other'.

14. **δεινὸν χρῆμα ἐποιεῦντο** [App. D. III. d], cp. p. 8, l. 14.

15. **τράπεσθαι** Ion. for τρέπεσθαι, App. A. II. 5.

πολλαὶ μὲν δή 'now it is true that many, etc.'

18. **ἀγωνιζόμενοι.** Stein remarks on the strangeness of the present participle instead of ἀγωνισάμενοι 'after contending', and compares 1, 76 τέλος οὐδέτεροι νικήσαντες διέστησαν νυκτὸς ἐπελθούσης· καὶ τὰ μὲν στρατόπεδα ἀμφότερα οὕτω ἠγωνίσατο. The present participle here may be explained by the consideration of the unfinished and undecided nature of the conflict, 'So they separated still fighting as I have described', i.e. without the affair being settled by a victory on either side.

CHAPTER XVII.

21. **αὐτοῖσι ἀνδράσι** 'crews and all', i.e. not after being abandoned by their crew. This dative of accompanying circumstance, or, as it is sometimes called, dative absolute, is very common in Greek writers, especially in this particular phrase. G. § 188, 5. See below l. 25.

24. **δαπάνην οἰκηΐην παρεχόμενος** 'defraying the expense out of his own resources'. This Clinias was father of the great Alcibiades, and was head of one of the richest families at Athens. This patriotic act of liberality in supplying a ship and crew was perfectly voluntary and must not be connected with the later trierarchies which the rich men were obliged to support; though this and similar acts may have suggested the system. The habit of keeping a private trireme however was maintained by Alcibiades, see Thucyd. 6, 61, 6.

25. **ἀνδράσι διηκοσίοισι.** This dative is similar to that commented upon on l. 21. For the number of 200 men, see on p. 1, l. 11, 12: and 7, 184 ὡς ἀνὰ διηκοσίους ἄνδρας λογίζομαι ἐν ἑκάστῃ νηί.

CHAPTER XVIII.

1. **ἄσμενοι** 'and glad to do so', 'to their great relief'. Cp. Odyss. 9, 62 ἔνθεν δὲ προτέρω πλέομεν ἀκαχήμενοι ἦτορ ἄσμενοι ἐκ θανάτοιο.

5. **οὐκ ἥκιστα** 'especially'.

6. **δρησμὸν δή** 'absolutely now a retreat', the δή like *tandem* indicating the outcome or result of previous events. 'They began to consider (and indeed it was time to do so) about retreating'. ἔσω, see p. 2, l. 23.

CHAPTER XIX.

9. **οἷοί τε εἴησαν ἄν** 'they would be able'. For this suffix τε see on 9, 23, and p. 3, l. 5 **ἐπ' ᾧ τε**. Compare ὅσον τε, ἅτε, ὥστε. 'The force of it is that of an undeclined τις', Monro *Homeric Gr.* § 108. [ἄν is absent from the MSS.]

10. **ἐλαυνόντων...ἐπὶ τὴν θάλασσαν** 'as the Euboeans were driving their sheep down to the sea'; that is, in order to transport them to a place of safety in accordance with their agreement with Themistocles, see cc. 4, 5. They apparently had not yet been able to complete the removal.

11. **ταύτῃ** 'at that place' i.e. where the flocks were collected. [St. reads ἐπὶ τὴν θάλασσαν ταύτην, i.e. to the sea of Artemisium where the fleet lay.]

12. **παλάμην** 'a contrivance', so in Pindar Olymp. 9, 26 it means 'art': properly and primarily it is the 'palm of the hand'.

14. **ἐς τοσοῦτο παρεγύμνου** 'he disclosed it so far', i.e. he didn't disclose it any further than this. Cp. 9, 44.

15. **ἐπὶ δὲ...πρήγμασι**, p. 21, l. 4 'in the immediate circumstances which had arisen'. For this meaning of ἐπί cp. the phrases ἐπ' ἐξεργασμένοις, ἐπ' Ἕλλησι ἀνδράσι (9, 17).

19. **κομιδῆς δὲ πέρι...μελήσειν** 'and as to their setting off, the proper season should be his own care'. That is the time in the night, see on p. 8, l. 9. **πῦρ ἀνακαίειν** to light the ordinary watchfires in the camp, that the enemy might be deceived and believe that they were remaining at Artemisium through the night.

22. **ἐτράποντο** [App. A. II. 5] **πρὸς τὰ πρόβατα** 'they set to work to slaughter the sheep'.

CHAPTER XX.

23, 4. **παραχρησάμενοι** 'having slighted' or 'neglected'. The force of παρά is that of the English *mis-* in composition. **ὡς οὐδὲν λέγοντα** 'as being worthless', 'having nothing in it'. Cp. the phrase λέγεις τι 'there is something in what you say', the opposite would be οὐδὲν λέγεις.

24. **οὔτε τι ἐξεκομίσαντο οὐδὲν οὔτε προεσάξαντο** 'they neither conveyed their families out of the islands nor took any precautionary measures for collecting corn into their forts'. Cp. 1, 190 of the

Babylonians expecting the attack of Cyrus προεσάξαντο σιτία ἐτέων κάρτα πολλῶν.

26. **περιπετέα τε...πρήγματα** 'and so they brought disasters upon themselves': they brought it about that the result was disastrous to themselves. περιπετής conveys the notion of a change, especially from good to bad [cp. περιπέτεια for the catastrophe of a tragedy]. It is a rare word in this sense, cp. Eurip. Andr. 982 νῦν οὖν ἐπειδὴ περιπετεῖς ἔχεις τύχας 'since your circumstances have suffered so disastrous a change'.

11 1. **ὧδε ἔχει** 'is in these terms'.

3. **βαρβαρόφωνος**, see another Oracle of Bakis in 9, 43. This compound of βάρβαρος is more ancient in usage than the simple βάρβαρος, and is the only form in which the word occurs in Homer (Il. 2, 867), and points to the difference of language as the great distinction between the Hellene and non-Hellene.

4. **βίβλινον**. In the bridge of ships made across the Hellespont the ships were fastened together by six cables, two made of flax, four of biblus [7, 36], a coarse variety of the same plant as that from which paper was made. **ἀπέχειν** infin. for imperative, G. § 269.

5. **οὐδὲν χρησαμένοισι** 'because they paid no attention to'. 5, 72 κληδόνι οὐδὲν χρεώμενος. **ἔπεσι** 'verses'.

7. **συμφορῇ χρᾶσθαι** 'to meet with disaster', a general phrase, used especially in legal language of losing one's citizenship (Demosth. 533); here it is explained by **πρὸς τὰ μέγιστα** 'in regard to their most vital interests'.

CHAPTER XXI.

8. **οἱ μὲν** i.e. the Greeks; he is continuing the narrative from c. 19.

9. **ὁ...κατάσκοπος** the look-out man stationed at Trachis. Thus we hear of ἡμερόσκοποι being stationed along the heights of Euboea (7, 182) as opposed to φρυκτωροί or the signallers by fire at night.

11. **κατῆρες** [Rt. ἀρ- apto] with oars all ready, fitted to start at any moment. **παλήσειε** 'should be engaged' [from πάλη 'wrestling'].

15. **τριηκοντέρῳ** a thirty-oared boat, cf. πεντεκόντερος p. 1, l. 11. **τι νεώτερον** 'any disaster'; cp. 6, 2 καταγνωσθεὶς πρὸς αὐτῶν νεώτερα πρήσσειν πρήγματα ἐς ἑωυτοὺς ἐκ Δαρείου.

18. οὐκέτι ἐς ἀναβολὰς ἐποιεῦντο τὴν ἀποχώρησιν 'no longer procrastinated about their departure', ἐς ἀναβολὰς ποιεῖσθαι = ἀναβάλλειν. Abicht quotes Thucyd. 7, 15 ὅτι δὲ μέλλετε ἅμα τῷ ἦρι εὐθὺς καὶ μὴ ἐς ἀναβολὰς πράσσειν.

CHAPTER XXII.

23. ἐπιλεξάμενος 'having selected for himself', i.e. to keep with him, waiting behind the others, which they could afterwards catch up by their superior speed.

2. ἐπελέξαντο 'read' from the notion of saying over to oneself, or perhaps of picking out for oneself the words, p. 70, l. 8.

3. ἐπὶ τοὺς πατέρας 'against the authors of your race', i.e. against the Athenians who were regarded as the parent stock of all Ionians, although the Athenians themselves were said to repudiate the name of Ionian, and to claim rather to be Pelasgians [Her. 1, 56, 103]. See however 7, 51, where Artabanus is represented as including the Athenians among the Ionians.

5. μάλιστα μέν...εἰ δὲ μή 'if possible'...'but if not'.

7. ἐκ τοῦ μέσου ἡμῖν ἕζεσθε 'remain out of the contest and take no part we beg of you'. ἡμῖν *dativus ethicus*.

τῶν Καρῶν. The Carians were not Hellenes, but they had before resisted the Persians and were therefore likely to be induced to desert. See 5, 117—120.

9. οἷόν τε, see p. 10, l. 9. ἀλλ' ὑπ' ἀναγκαίης...ἀπίστασθαι 'but have fallen under constraint too powerful to allow of your deserting'. For ὑπ' ἀναγκαίης cp. 9, 17. This use of κατέζευχθε is poetical, cp. Soph. Aj. 124 ἄτῃ συγκατέζευκται κακῇ (Ab.).

13. ἀπ' ὑμέων ἡμῖν γέγονε. An allusion to the fact of the Athenians having sent assistance to the revolting Ionians in B.C. 500, and having in their cause invaded Asia and burnt Sardis; see 5, 99—102.

14. δοκέειν ἐμοί 'in my opinion'. G. § 268. ἐπ' ἀμφότερα νοέων 'with an eye to the two alternatives'.

16. πρὸς ἑωυτῶν 'on their side' p. 30, l. 14.

ἐπεί τε ἀνενειχθῇ, for the subjunctive in a conditional relative sentence without ἄν see G. § 234. It is very rare except in Epic poetry: Ab. quotes c. 108 ἐς ὃ ἔλθῃ. Cp. Thucyd. 1, 137 μέχρι πλοῦς γένηται. διαβληθῇ 'represented in an invidious light'.

17. ἀπίστους *passive* 'distrusted'.

CHAPTER XXIII.

25. οὕτω δή *tum demum* 'then at last', or 'when they had been satisfied about *that*'. See p. 65, l. 20; p. 71, l. 17.

ἅμα ἡλίῳ σκιδναμένῳ 'as soon as the rays of the sun were spread abroad'. A poetical expression for 'at sunrise'. Stein quotes Aeschylus Pers. 504 πρὶν σκεδασθῆναι θεοῦ ἀκτῖνας. And Hom. Il. 7, 451 ὅσον τ' ἐπικίδναται ἠώς.

27. μέχρι μέσου, cp. p. 8, l. 17 κατὰ μέσον ἡμέρης. τὸ ἀπὸ τούτου 'thereafter', 9, 40; cp. τὸ ἐνθεῦτεν 9, 26.

CHAPTER XXIV.

9. καὶ δύο μυριάδες 'as many as twenty thousand'. The καί is used to emphasize the contrast.

11. φυλλάδα ἐπιβαλών 'having thrown leaves upon them' i.e. upon the corpses. Stein thinks it probable that this was some funeral custom, though we know of none such. Others would refer the scattering of the foliage to the τάφροι explaining the object to be the concealment of the recent digging. γῆν ἐπαμησάμενος 'having heaped up earth upon them', the usual word for the making of a grave or barrow, see Theognis 426—27 φύντα δ' ὅπως ὤκιστα πύλας Ἀΐδαο περῆσαι, καὶ κεῖσθαι πολλὴν γῆν ἐπαμησάμενον, as also other passages given by L. and Sc.

CHAPTER XXV.

20. οὐδὲν πλοίων σπανιώτερον 'boats were the most difficult things to get in the world', i.e. there was such a rush for the shore that all the boats were in use.

21. ἐθηεῦντο, App. D. III. 2 (b).

22. ἠπιστέατο, see p. 3, l. 21.

24. καὶ τοὺς εἵλωτας 'the Helots as well'. We know that each Spartan at Thermopylae had his Helot, see 7, 229; but it is not stated whether there was the same proportion as in the Spartan army which went to Plataea, viz. 7 helots to each Spartan, see 9, 10 and 28.

οὐ μὲν οὐδ' ἐλάνθανε 'not that he even escaped detection by'.

καὶ γὰρ δὴ καὶ γελοῖον ἦν 'for in point of fact it was absolutely ridiculous', explained by the next sentence, which might be expected to have been introduced by γάρ, the omission of which Stein illustrates by 7, 6 where τοῦτο μὲν and τοῦτο δὲ introduce explanatory clauses without this conjunction. For καὶ γὰρ δὴ καὶ cp. 7, 236.

3. **τέσσερες χιλιάδες.** The numbers originally accompanying Leonidas to Thermopylae were according to Herodotus [7, 202, 3] from the Peloponnesus (including the 300 Spartans) 3100, from Thespiae 700, from Thebes 400,—in all 4200. These were joined at Thermopylae by about 2000 Lokrians and Phokians,—making 6200. If we may reckon 7 helots for each of the 300 Spartans [p. 13, l. 24] the numbers will be raised to 8300. But Diodorus (11, 4) adds also 1000 Lakedaemonians [i.e. not Spartan citizens, probably Perioeci]:—the whole number will thus be 9300. But just before the final battle Leonidas sent away all the allies except the Thebans and Thespians [7, 219, 220]. The numbers engaged on the third day would therefore be

Spartans	300
Helots	2100
Lakedaemonians	1000
Thespians	700
Thebans	400
	4500

The Theban 400 deserted to the Persians, and therefore allowing for escapes, especially of Helots, and for any that fell on the two previous days, and adding 80 Mycenaeans [mentioned by Pausanias 2, 16, 5] the number of Greek corpses which Xerxes had to show may well have been about 4000. And this is the number mentioned in the Epitaph inscribed over them [7, 228],

Μυριάσιν ποτὲ τῇδε τριηκοσίαις ἐμάχοντο
ἐκ Πελοποννάσου χιλιάδες τέτορες.

CHAPTER XXVI.

8. **βίου δεόμενοι** 'in want of a livelihood'.

ἐνεργοί 'in active employment'.

12. **ὡς Ὀλύμπια ἄγοιεν.** The Olympic festival took place every fifth year, i.e. there were four clear years between each festival. It lasted five days and according to Böckh began on the

first full moon after the Summer solstice. It therefore varied by a few weeks, but may be considered to have usually taken place some time in the month Hecatombaeon (July).

14. κείμενον 'proposed for competition'.

15. τῆς ἐλαίης the garland given to the victors at the Olympic games was of wild olive (κότινος). Aristoph. Plut. 585 τοὺς νικῶντας στεφανώσας κοτίνῳ στεφάνῳ.

17. δειλίην ὦφλε 'was held guilty of cowardice', properly a legal term ὀφλεῖν δίκην 'to be cast in a suit', 'to incur the damages'. Then it is transferred to the matter of the charge itself, as μωρίαν ὀφλισκάνω 'I am held guilty of folly', Soph. Antig. 470.

19. οὔτε ἠνέσχετο σιγῶν 'he could not refrain from speaking'.

22. περὶ ἀρετῆς 'for honour', the valour is used for the result of valour—honour. So in Pindar αἰεὶ δ' ἀμφ' ἀρεταῖσι πόνος δαπάνα τε μάρναται πρὸς ἔργον Olymp. 5, 15; τίμα—ἄνδρα πὺξ ἀρετὰν εὑρόντα Ol. 7, 89; ξυναῖσι δ' ἀμφ' ἀρεταῖς τέταμαι Pyth. 11, 54. ἀρετὰν γε μὲν ἐκ Διὸς ἕξεις Theocr. Id. 17, 137.

CHAPTER XXVII.

1. καὶ τὸ κάρτα 'most especially', καί emphatic: p. 30, l. 7.

2. πανστρατιῇ, p. 21, l. 6.

3. οὐ πολλοῖσι ἔτεσι πρότερον. Neither the exact time nor the occasion of this invasion of Phokis is known: but the constant border warfare between the two nations had induced the Phokians to build a wall across the pass of Thermopylae for their protection [7, 176].

8. σοφίζεται τοιόνδε 'contrives the following trick against them'.   γυψώσας 'having smeared with chalk', cp. 7, 69; the object was to be able to distinguish each other from the enemy in the dim light without the necessity of shouting a pass-word, which was the cause of great confusion in night attacks, see Thucyd. 7, 44, 5.

14. ἄλλο τι εἶναι τέρας 'that it was something strange and supernatural'.

16. νεκρῶν καὶ ἀσπίδων '4000 dead bodies and shields'. That is, they killed 4000 men on the field. For if the men had escaped, the number of shields would have exceeded that of the dead bodies, cf. Thucyd. 7, 45, 2 ὅπλα μέντοι ἔτι πλείω ἢ κατὰ τοὺς νεκροὺς ἐλήφθη, many having thrown away their shields.

19. οἱ περὶ τὸν τρίποδα 'which are arranged round the tripod'. περί with acc. indicates a less close connexion than with gen. Cp. p. 20, l. 17: Stein quotes 9, 62 ἐγένετο δὲ πρῶτον περὶ τὰ γέρρα μάχη. This seems to be the tripod described by Pausanias (10, 13, 4) as being the centre of a group of gods; Hercules and Apollo are contending for it, while Latona is trying to restrain Apollo, and Athenè Hercules. It was dedicated by the Phokians as a thank-offering for their victory mentioned above (l. 3) under Tellias over the Thessalians. The colossal figures (οἱ μεγάλοι ἀνδριάντες) mentioned seem to have been placed round this work at some little distance, though grouped with some regularity (συνεστεῶτες).

20. ἔμπροσθε τοῦ νηοῦ, that is, outside the temple, in the τέμενος.

21. ἀνακέαται, App. D. II. 6.

CHAPTER XXVIII.

22, 23. τὸν πεζόν......πολιορκέοντας ἑωυτοὺς the land army which was besieging them. The plural participle with a singular noun of multitude. G. § 138, note 3.

24. τὴν ἵππον αὐτῶν 'their cavalry', in this meaning ἡ ἵππος is not used in the plural, but is a noun of multitude. Thessaly was full of rich plains, and was especially famous for its horses, and Thessalian cavalry were in request all through Greece.

26, 27. ἀμφορέας κεινοὺς 'empty wine-jars'. χοῦν is earth that has been moved. So συγχοῦν 'to fill up with earth' p. 37, l. 18.

29. ὡς ἀναρπασόμενοι 'believing that they were going to make short work of the Phokians': cf. 9, 59 οὗτοι μὲν βοῇ τε καὶ ὁμίλῳ ἐπήϊσαν ὡς ἀναρπασόμενοι τοὺς Ἕλληνας.

CHAPTER XXIX.

1. τούτων ἀμφοτέρων viz. the night surprise c. 27, and the stratagem which injured their horses c. 28.

2. ἔγκοτον 'grudge'. Cp. 3, 59 ἔγκοτον ἔχοντες Σαμίοισι.

3. γνωσιμαχέετε 'give way and confess', from the notion of differing and fighting with a former opinion. See 3, 25; 7, 130 and Aristoph. Aves 555

τὴν ἀρχὴν τὸν Δί' ἀπαιτεῖν,
κἂν μὲν μὴ φῇ μηδ' ἐθελήσῃ μηδ' εὐθὺς γνωσιμαχήσῃ
ἱερὸν πόλεμον πρωυδᾶν αὐτῷ.

5, 6. **πλέον αἰεί...ὑμέων ἐφερόμεθα** 'we always came off better than you', 'we were always more influential than you'. Cp. 8, 104 φερόμενος οὐ τὰ δεύτερα παρὰ τῷ βασιλέϊ 'being the most influential with the king'.   **ἐκεῖνα** 'that side'=τὰ ἐκείνων ['Ελλήνων] πράγματα.

7, 8. **ἐπ' ἡμῖν ἐστι** 'it is in our hands', 'it depends solely on us'.   **πρός** adverbial, 'besides', p. 26, l. 4.

8, 9. **τὸ πᾶν ἔχοντες** 'though we have the game absolutely in our hands', 'though we are all-powerful in the matter'. Cf. the use of ἕξεις 'you will control' in 9, 2.

10. **ἀντ' αὐτῶν** sc. κακῶν 'our wrongs' implied in μνησικακέομεν.

CHAPTER XXX.

16. **αὖξον** 'had been backing up', cp. 9, 31 καί τινες αὐτῶν τὰ Ἑλλήνων αὖξον.   **ὡς ἐμοὶ δοκέειν.** See p. 12, l. 14.

18. **παρέχειν τέ σφίσι** 'that it was open to them to medize as well as to the Thessalians if they chose'. For παρέχειν = παρεῖναι, cp. 8, 106 παρέχει ταῦτα ποιεῖν. See p. 5, l. 1. For οὔτε...τε cp. 6, 16.

19. **ἄλλως** 'otherwise than they were', or 'otherwise than rightly'.

20. **ἑκόντες εἶναι** 'with their own consent at least'. This phrase is generally used in a negative sentence. See 7, 104; 9, 7. An exception occurs in 7, 164.

CHAPTER XXXI.

23. **οὕτω δή**, p. 3, l. 24.

3. **ποδεών** properly 'the neck of a wine-skin', 2, 121; here it = 'a narrow tongue of land'.

ταύτῃ κατατείνει 'extends downwards in this direction'. It is the district 'of the upper valleys of the Kephisos and its main tributary, the Pindus'. Rawl. It stretches from Mt Oeta in a south-westerly direction, following the course of the Kephisos.

6. **μητρόπολις Δωριέων**, see 1, 56 where the Dorians are said to have moved first from Phthiotis to Histiaeotis, then to Pindos in Doris, thence to Dryopis, and thence to the Peloponnese.

CHAPTER XXXII.

12. **ἐς τὰ ἄκρα τοῦ Παρνησοῦ.** These Phokians collected in considerable force on Parnassus and did good service to the Greeks in this and the following years, see 9, 31.

14. **κειμένη ἐπ' ἑωυτῆς** 'being quite isolated', for ἐπ' ἑωυτῆς 'by itself' cp. 9, 17 ἐκέλευσέ σφεας ἐπ' ἑωυτῶν ἐν τῷ πεδίῳ ἵζεσθαι, cp. 9, 38.

15. **ἀνηνείκαντο** [App. E. 2. c. An Ionic form of 1 aor. mid. of ἀναφέρω, so in 1, 86 ἀνενεικάμενος] 'carried up their goods'. Stein refers to 9, 6 ὑπεξεκομίσαντό τε πάντα καὶ αὐτοὶ διέβησαν. See also p. 19, l. 11.

18. **ὑπὲρ τοῦ Κρισαίου πεδίου** 'on the heights above the Krisaean plain'. Strabo (4, 9) describes it as ἐπὶ τοῖς ἀκροῖς τοῦ Κρισαίου πέδου·

20. **οὕτω** 'by this route'.

21. **ἔκειρον** 'cut down its trees'. See 6, 75 ἔκειρε τὸ τέμενος: 9, 15 ἔκειρε τοὺς χώρους. See p. 32, l. 15. **ἐπέσχον** 'extended over', p. 18, l. 16; cp. 1, 108 τὴν ἄμπελον ἐπισχεῖν τὴν Ἀσίην πᾶσαν. Cp. 9, 31.

CHAPTER XXXIII.

24. **κατὰ μὲν ἔκαυσαν,** for this tmesis cp. 9, 5 κατὰ μὲν ἔλευσαν αὐτοῦ τὴν γυναῖκα, κατὰ δὲ τὰ τέκνα. See p. 34, l. 23. G. § 191 note 3, p. 241.

28. **θησαυροῖσί τε καὶ ἀναθήμασι.** The former refers to treasures in gold and silver money or plate, the latter to statues, tripods and other thank-offerings.

1. **πρὸς τοῖσι οὔρεσι** 'close to the hill country', that is, before 18 they could get high enough up to be safe.

CHAPTER XXXIV.

3. **Παραποταμίους** the name of a town in the valley of the Kephisos, which reaches the Boeotian frontier at Panopeis, or, as it was afterwards called, Phanoteus.

8. **πᾶν τὸ πλῆθος** 'the people in a body'. Yet exceptions have to be made to this statement in the case of the Plataeans and Thespians, and even in Thebes itself there seems to have been a division of opinion [9, 96-7]. The measure of Alexander in put-

ting Macedonian governors in the Boeotian cities looks as if they were not considered quite to be relied upon for medism, though Herodotos says the primary object was to satisfy Xerxes that Boeotia could be trusted.

11. τῇδε 'with this view'. βουλόμενοι 'because they wished'.

12. τὰ Μήδων, see p. 39, l. 24 φρονέων τὰ βασιλέος.

CHAPTER XXXV.

15. ἐν δεξιῇ τὸν Παρνησὸν ἀπέργοντες 'keeping Parnassus on their right'.

16. ἐπίσχον, p. 17, l. 21.

21. ἀποδέξαιεν [App. E. 2. e] τὰ χρήματα 'that they might display to Xerxes the wealth of the temple'. Not only was the temple of Delphi rich in gold and silver ornaments and works of art, but it possessed also a large treasury of money, and was a kind of bank for all Greece.

24. τὰ Κροίσου 'the offerings of Kroesos'. Kroesos, king of Lydia, having tested the skill of the various oracles of Greece, decided that the supremacy in prophetic power belonged to Delphi. He therefore offered there elaborate sacrifices of 3000 animals; and having made a pile of valuable objects of extraordinary magnificence,—couches overlaid with gold and silver, gold cups, and purple robes,—he burnt them in honour of the god, and from the molten gold made 117 bricks of solid metal, weighing 1½ talents each, and a figure of a lion in gold weighing 10 talents, and sent them to Delphi. Besides these he sent two large bowls of gold and silver, and many other articles of value. 1, 47—52. This was·in or about the year B.C. 555, when he was expecting the attack of Kyros.

CHAPTER XXXVI.

2. ἀπίκατο, App. D. II. a.

4. κατὰ γῆς κατορύξωσι 'whether they should bury them in the earth'. Cp. Arist. Plut. 237 εὐθὺς κατώρυξέν με κατὰ τῆς γῆς κάτω. σφέα, App. B. II. 1 (d).

6. προκατῆσθαι 'to defend'. Cp. 9, 106 ἀδύνατον γὰρ ἐφαίνετό σφι εἶναι ἑωυτοὺς Ἰώνων προκατῆσθαι φρουρέοντας.

8. πέρην App. A. II. 3 (d), 'across' the gulf of Corinth into Achaia.

11. ἀνηνείκαντο 'conveyed their goods', p. 17, l. 15.

13. τοῦ προφήτεω the Priest, or Interpreter, in charge of the temple, whose duty was to note down and hand over to the applicant the oracles delivered by the Pythia, when under the divine influence, *antistes templi*, Livy 7, 111. In later times when the number of visitors increased there were a larger number of priests.

CHAPTER XXXVII.

15. ἀπώρεον 'saw from a distance'. Cp. 9, 69 ἀπιδόντες σφέας οἱ τῶν Θηβαίων ἱππόται ἐπιφερομένους οὐδένα κόσμον ἤλαυνον ἐπ' αὐτούς.

17. ἐξενηνειγμένα, App. E. 2. c.

21. κατὰ τὸ ἱρὸν τῆς Προνηίης Ἀθηναίης 'opposite the temple of Athenè Pronaia'. Pausanias (10, 8, 4) says that on entering the town of Delphi one passed several temples one after the other, the fourth of which was that of Athenè Pronaia.

25. καὶ διὰ πάντων φασμάτων 'quite above all other prodigies'. For the sense of διὰ cp. p. 36, l. 17; and for the emphatic καὶ p. 30, l. 17.

3, 4. ἀπὸ δὲ τοῦ Παρνησοῦ...ἐφέροντο. This phenomenon is **20** by no means improbable, as the huge boulders scattered about on the site of Delphi testify. The frequency of earthquakes in the region of Parnassus is well described by Professor Mahaffy in his description of another town, Arachova, in the same district [*Rambles and Studies in Greece*, p. 261]:

> 'The town has a curious, scattered appearance, owing not
> 'only to the extraordinary nature of the site, but to the fact that
> 'huge boulders, I might say rocks, have been shaken loose by
> 'earthquakes from above, and have come tumbling into the
> 'middle of the town. They crush a house or two, and stand
> 'there in the middle of a street. Presently someone comes and
> 'builds a house up against the side of this rock; others venture
> 'in their turn, and so the town recovers itself, till another earth-
> 'quake makes another rent. Since 1870 these earthquakes have
> 'been very frequent. At first they were very severe, and ruined
> 'almost all the town; but now they are very slight, and so
> 'frequent that we were assured that they happened at some time
> '*every day*.'

6. ἀλαλαγμὸς a shouting of *alalai*, a war-cry. Aeschyl. Pers. 392 κέλαδος Ἑλλήνων...ὄρθιον δ' ἅμα Ἀντηλάλαξε νησιώτιδος πέτρας ἠχώ.

CHAPTER XXXVIII.

7. τούτων πάντων 'all these wonders'. It is difficult to determine what foundation of truth there may be to such tales. The storm and the sudden detachment of the great boulders from the mountain are facts in themselves credible enough, see the passage quoted from Prof. Mahaffy above; and in a sudden panic among men, whose minds were already predisposed to superstitious awe, because attacking a place whose sanctity was so renowned, the appearance of superhuman warriors may easily have been imagined. So at Marathon the Athenian Epizelos fancied that he saw one [6, 117]; and at Salamis a form of a goddess was believed to have appeared to the Athenians as they backed out of the fight [c. 84]; and at the battle of Leuctra the national hero, Aristomenes, was said to have cheered on his Messenian countrymen [Paus. 4, 32, 4]; and Phylakos appeared again at Delphi on the attack of the Gauls [Paus. 10, 23, 2]. Mr Grote seems however to hold that this attack on Delphi was withdrawn on the news of the defeat at Salamis. 'On this occasion the real protectors of the treasures were the conquerors at Salamis and Plataea'. *Hist. of Greece*, vol. 4, p. 463.

10. ἰθὺ Βοιωτῶν 'straight to Boeotia'. So ἰθὺ τοῦ ἱεροῦ· ἰθὺ τῆς Θρηικίης, 9, 69, 89.

13. μέζονας ἢ κατὰ ἀνθρώπων φύσιν 'of superhuman size'. φύσις is used of the outward form bestowed by nature, whether in regard to appearance or size. See Arist. Vesp. 1071 τὴν ἐμὴν ἰδὼν φύσιν. In Homer the more common word in this sense is φυή.

CHAPTER XXXIX.

16. ἐπιχωρίους ἥρωας 'heroes of the place'. Every Greek state had its heroes, i.e. certain of its citizens whose public services had seemed to deserve apotheosis, either in founding the state or defending it. The worship paid to them was different in kind from that paid to the god [ὡς ἥρωϊ ἐναγίζουσιν ὡς θεῷ θύουσι Paus. 2, 11, 7], though the two were apt to be confounded. Instances of such national heroes are the Aeakidae of Aegina (8, 64); Harmodios and Aristogeiton at Athens; Androkrates at Plataea (9, 25). Dr Arnold [Thucyd. 5, 11] compares the worship paid to such heroes to the adoration of Saints.

17. τὰ τεμένεα the sacred enclosures round the temples, cut off (τέμνω) from the profane ground. **περὶ τὸ ἱρόν** 'in the neighbourhood of *the* temple', i.e. of the great temple of Apollo, p. 15, l. 19.

18. **παρ' αὐτὴν τὴν ὁδόν** 'abutting on the road itself', i.e. 'the sacred road' from Daulis up to the great temple, on which stood also the temple of Athenè Pronaia, see p. 19, l. 21.

'The road from Daulis to the S.-W. leads along a rugged valley to Delphi, and falls in with another from Ambryssus on the S., at a point halfway between the two. This place was called the σχιστὴ ὁδός, or the Divided Way'. Wordsworth, *Athens and Attica*, p. 237.

21. **ἐς ἡμέας** 'to my day'.

23. **διὰ τῶν βαρβάρων** 'through the ranks of the Barbarians'.

CHAPTER XL.

21 1. **σχεῖν πρὸς Σαλαμῖνα** 'to come to anchor near Salamis'. The more usual construction is σχεῖν ἐς, see below l. 13 and above p. 20, l. 27. Thucyd. 3, 34, 1 ἔσχε ἐς Νότιον, 4, 3, 1 ἐς τὴν Πύλον σχόντας. Thucydides also uses the dative 7, 1, 2 σχόντες Ῥηγίῳ καὶ Μεσσήνῃ. But the use of πρὸς is to indicate not the actual putting on shore *at* Salamis, but near it, either on the island or the opposite coast.

3. **πρὸς δὲ** *adverbial* 'and besides', see p. 16, l. 8. τὸ = τί *quid*, cp. 9, 54 ἐπείρεσθαι τὸ χρεὸν εἴη ποιέειν, 9, 71 γενομένης λέσχης ὃς γένοιτο ἄριστος.

4. **ἐπὶ καὶ τοῖσι κατήκουσι**, p. 10, l. 15.

βουλὴν ἔμελλον ποιήσεσθαι 'they had to reconsider their plans in view of the disappointment of their expectations'. For the construction of ἔμελλον see on p. 2, l. 3.

6. **πανδημεί** 'with all their available forces', cp. 6, 108; 9, 37: whereas πανστρατιῇ [p. 15, l. 2: p. 34, l. 8] seems properly to mean 'with a full levy of all arms'—hoplites, cavalry, light-armed; which would consist of two-thirds of all available. Cp. Thucyd. 4, 94.

8. **οἱ δέ**, 'whereas on the contrary they learnt'.

τὸν Ἰσθμὸν τειχέοντας. This wall was built from sea to sea, about seven miles east of the town of Corinth, and can still be traced. It was completed early next year [B.C. 479]. See 9, 7—8.

9. **περὶ πλείστου ποιευμένους**, 'regarding as the matter of first importance.' p. 8, l. 14.

10, 11. **περιεῖναι** 'should be saved', cp. p. 2, l. 8. **ἀπιέναι** [ἀπ—ἵημι]. **οὕτω δή**, p. 3, l. 24: p. 16, l. 22.

CHAPTER XLI.

15. **τῇ τις δύναται**, 'in whatever direction each found it possible', i.e. it was left to individuals to go where they pleased; the population was not moved en masse.

17. **ἐς Τροιζῆνα.** According to Plutarch the people of Troezen received them with great kindness; voted a public provision of two obols a day for each adult, and gave a general permission to the children to pick fruit. Plutarch Themist. c. 10.

19. **τῷ χρηστηρίῳ**, the two oracles which had been given to the Athenian envoys in the early part of the year. The first (7, 140) had announced utter destruction to Athens and other Greek towns, and had warned the Athenians to fly to the ends of the earth: the second (7, 141) had been less alarming, and had prophesied that when all else was lost 'a wooden wall alone' should be left uncaptured to Athenè. Some interpreted this of a wooden palisade round the Acropolis, but Themistocles had persuaded his fellow-citizens that it meant the fleet; and moreover encouraged them by the interpretation of the last two lines of the second oracle,

> ὦ θείη Σαλαμίς, ἀπολεῖς δὲ σὺ τέκνα γυναικῶν
> ἤ που σκιδναμένης Δημήτερος ἢ συνιούσης.

For he remarked that had the god meant to prophesy destruction to the Athenians at Salamis the epithet would not have been θείη but σχετλίη. The people had therefore been fully persuaded to abandon their town and trust to their fleet. Professor Mahaffy takes the view that the priests of Delphi were playing a double game in view of what they thought was the certain success of Persia: 'I cannot but suspect', he says, 'that they hoped to gain the favour of Xerxes, and remain under him what they had hitherto been, a wealthy and protected corporation'. [*Rambles and Studies in Greece* p. 272.] Perhaps, without attributing to them feelings so unpatriotic, we may conclude that being usually under Spartan influence they took the Peloponnesian view,—that to save Northern Greece was impossible, and that the only hope was to abandon it and defend the Isthmus.

20. **οὐκ ἥκιστα** 'especially', p. 37, l. 4.

21. **ὄφιν μέγαν.** This serpent, emblem of the earthborn Erechtheus, was supposed to be kept in the Ancient Temple of Athenè Polias, which in its subsequently restored state formed the eastern

portion of the Erechtheum on the Acropolis. This temple also contained the old olive-wood statue of Athenè Polias to which the *peplus* was yearly brought; the sacred olive from which all the other sacred olives (μορίαι) were taken; and the golden lamp always burning, from which emigrants lit the lamp which they took to their new home.

φύλακον. Ionic form of φύλακα, cp. 1, 84. The serpent was sometimes called ὄφις οἰκουρός, cf. Aristoph. Lys. 758 ἀλλ' οὐ δύναμαι 'γωγ' οὐδὲ κοιμᾶσθ' ἐν πόλει, ἐξ' οὗ τὸν ὄφιν εἶδον τὸν οἰκουρόν ποτε.

22. ἐν τῷ ἱρῷ 'in the temple' sc. of Athenè Polias, see above. καὶ δὴ καὶ ὡς ἰόντι 'and moreover as though it actually existed'. Herodotos evidently doubts the existence of the serpent : and Plutarch [Themist. 10], though apparently believing in the existence of the serpent, looked upon the whole affair as a trick got up between the priests and Themistocles. Rawlinson well compares the story of the priests in Babylon contained in the book of Daniel 'Bel and the Dragon'. See also the scene in the temple of Aesculapius Arist. Plut. 678 where the priest goes round with a bag collecting the eatables from the altars. ἐπιμήνια that is on the day of every new moon.

24. μελιτόεσσα 'a honey-cake', apparently the proper offering to subterranean powers. Thus Strepsiades before going in the den of the Sophists, as if he were going into the cave of Trophonius, says, ἐς τὼ χειρέ νυν Δός μοι μελιτοῦτταν πρότερον (Aristoph. Nub. 506). Thus too Aeneas gives Cerberus *melle soporatam et medicatis frugibus offam* (Aen. 6, 420).

25. ἀναισιμουμένη 'used up'. ἀναισιμόω is a verb confined almost entirely to Herodotus, who uses it frequently for ἀναλίσκω or δαπανάω.

26. τῆς ἱρείης 'the priestess'. Plutarch Themist. 10 says οἱ ἱερεῖς εἰσήγγελλον εἰς τοὺς πολλούς, but insinuates that it was by the instigation of Themistocles.

1. ὡς καὶ τῆς θεοῦ ἀπολελοιπυίης τὴν ἀκρόπολιν 'because they **22** believed that the goddess too had abandoned the Acropolis'. The gods were believed to abandon a conquered town. Cp. Vergil Aen. 2, 351 *Excessere omnes adytis arisque relictis | Di quibus imperium hoc steterat.* Aeschyl. S. c. Th. 207 ἀλλ' οὖν θεοὺς | τοὺς τῆς ἁλούσης πόλεως ἐκλείπειν λόγος. So Tacitus (Hist. 5, 13) says that when the temple at Jerusalem was on fire *audita major humana vox*,

excedere deos; simul ingens motus excedentium. A passage in Euripides [Troad. 23] gives a reason ἐρημία γὰρ πόλιν ὅταν λάβῃ κακή | νοσεῖ τὰ τῶν θεῶν οὐδὲ τιμᾶσθαι θέλει.

2. **στρατόπεδον** here='the fleet', cp. p. 43, l. 1. Plutarch (Them. c. 10) gives a full description of the scene of the departure, the tears, and touching adieus, not the least moving part being the leaving behind of domestic animals, especially the dogs. He also tells us that the Council of the Areopagus supplied each man fighting on board with 8 drachmae.

CHAPTER XLII.

7. **προείρητο** 'they had been ordered beforehand', i.e. by the congress at the Isthmus, see on p. 1, l. 1.

8. **πλεῦνες**. App. B. 1. c.

11. **οὐ μέντοι...βασιλητίου.** The two kings at the time of the 3 days of Artemisium were Leonidas and Leotychides. Both kings could not go out with the army together, and as Leonidas was at Thermopylae the other king is kept at home. In the next year Leotychides took the command of the Spartan ships, while the son of Leonidas, Pleistarchus, was a child and kept at home, being represented by his cousin Pausanias.

CHAPTER XLIII.

16. **τὸ αὐτὸ πλήρωμα** 'the same complement of ships', i.e. forty. See c. 2.

20. **Δωρικόν τε καὶ Μακεδνόν** 'Doric or Makednian' [old Makedonian], two names belonging to the same tribe, see on p. 40, l. 11.

23, 24. **ἐκ τῆς νῦν Δωρίδος**. See p. 17, l. 7. **ἐξαναστάντες** 'having been driven out'.

CHAPTER XLIV.

2. **πρὸς πάντας...παρεχόμενοι** sc. ἐστρατεύοντο 'supplying the largest number in comparison with any of the other Greeks', πλείστας must be understood, its place being taken by the numerals. The numbers,—Athenians 180, total 378 (or 366 as it really is),— would almost justify the sense 'as many as all the rest put together'. We must remember also that Athens supplied the 20 ships which the Chalkidians manned [c. 1]. For a preposition with acc. taking the place of a genitive after a comparative clause cp. Thuc. 1, 23

ἡλίου ἐκλείψεις πυκνότεραι παρὰ τὰ ἐκ τοῦ πρὶν χρόνου μνημονευόμενα.

4. **μοῦνοι** 'by themselves', without the Plataeans, as is explained by the next sentence, see p. 1, l. 5.

8. **ἐς περαίην τῆς Βοιωτίης χώρης** 'to the opposite shore, namely that of Boeotia', a genitive in apposition, or of definition. περαίην sc. γῆν. For the use of the word in the relation of one shore to another, cp. p. 19, l. 8.

ἐκκομιδήν, cp. ἐξεκομίσαντο p. 10, l. 24. The Plataeans were in double danger, for their fidelity to the Hellenic cause and especially to the Athenians, and from the enmity of the Thebans.

9. **τῶν οἰκετέων** 'of their families', includes all members of the household, women, children and slaves, p. 56, l. 26.

10. **ἐπὶ...ἐχόντων** 'at the period of the occupation by the Pelasgi of what is now called Hellas'. G. § 191, VI. 1. For a discussion of these names see *Historical Index*, and cp. 1, 56.

14. **Ἀθηναῖοι μετουνομάσθησαν** 'changed their name to that of Athenians'.

15, 16. **στρατάρχεω** [-χης App. C. I. 4] 'general'. 'A designedly indefinite expression instead of the usual βασιλεύς' (St.). Ἴωνες though the Athenians repudiated the term 1, 143. Cp. what is said in Ἀθ. πολ. 3 of the origin of the Polemarch.

CHAPTER XLV.

17. **τὠυτὸ πλήρωμα** p. 22, l. 15, 'the same complement', i.e. twenty ships, see p. 1, l. 6. **τὠυτὸ καὶ** 'the same as'; for καί introducing the second term of a comparison, cp. Thucyd. 7, 71 παραπλήσια οἱ Ἀθηναῖοι ἐπεπόνθεσαν ἐν Συρακούσαις καὶ ἔδρασαν αὐτοὶ ἐν Πύλῳ.

19. **ἐπεβώθησαν**· App. A. III. 8.

CHAPTER XLVI.

20. **Νησιωτέων** 'islanders', as opposed to people of the continent, and therefore without article. Cp. νῆσοι 6, 49; 9, 3.

23. **τὴν ἑωυτῶν** sc. γῆν.

25. **Δωριέες ἀπὸ Ἐπιδαύρου**, see 5, 83, where to this connexion is traced the commencement of a war between Athens and Aegina.

4. **ἐς τοὺς Μήδους**. Plutarch [de malign. Herod. xxxvi] declares this statement to be false, and that the Naxians as a state supported the Hellenic side; and moreover that, according to Hellanicus, they

sent 6, according to Ephoros 5 ships. They appear on the Delphian Serpent stand and on the Olympic Column. Simonides records that their squadron sank 5 of the enemy's ships, and rescued a Greek ship.

Δημόκριτος τρίτος ἦρξε μάχης, ὅτε παρ Σαλαμῖνα
Ἕλληνες Μήδοις σύμβαλον ἐν πελάγει·
πέντε δὲ νῆας ἕλεν δηΐων, ἕκτην δ' ὑπὸ χεῖρα
ῥύσατο βαρβαρικὴν Δωρίδ' ἁλισκομένην.

κατά περ ἄλλοι νησιῶται 'just as the other islanders had been'. Since the suppression of the Ionic revolt in the year B.C. 497—5 the Persian power had been supreme in the Cyclades, except in a few of the islands near the main-land; and as yet no Hellenic fleet held the Aegean.

5. ἀπίκατο, App. D. II. a.

6. σπεύσαντος sc. αὐτοὺς 'having urged them on'. Cp. l. 1, 38 τὸν γάμον τοι τοῦτον ἔσπευσα.

9. τὰς καὶ ἐπ' Ἀ. 'the same number as at Artemisium', that is *two*. See p. 1, l. 11. πεντηκόντερον, see on p. 1, l. 12.

13. νησιωτέων, see on p. 23, l. 19. γῆν τε καὶ ὕδωρ 'earth and water' as symbols of the ownership of the Great King over the entire country. This had been twice demanded: once in B.C. 492 by Dareios when all the Islanders had submitted (6, 49); a second time by Xerxes in the early part of this year [B.C. 480], which latter appears to be the occasion here alluded to, although when speaking of it [7, 133] Herodotos says nothing about the Islanders.

CHAPTER XLVII.

14. ἐντὸς οἰκημένοι Θεσπρωτῶν that is 'South and East of Thresprotia', which is the S.-W. part of Epirus.

16. ὁμουρέοντες 'coterminous', for οὖρος = ὅρος see App. A. III. 7.

17. ἐκτὸς to the west. The island of Leucas sent three ships, but no state west of that, except Krotona in Magna Graecia.

19. τῇ Ἑλλάδι. Herodotus does not mean to exclude Krotona from Hellas, rather to mark that her sending this ship was in consequence of a feeling that she belonged to Hellas.

20. τρὶς πυθιονίκης 'who had thrice been victor at the Pythian games'; i.e. twice in the pentathlum and once in the stadium [Paus. 10, 9, 1] see Hist. Ind. *Phayllos*. The Pythian games were celebrated, in the third year of each Olympiad, on the Cnossaean plain near Delphi, in honour of Apollo, Artemis, and Latona.

CHAPTER XLVIII.

21. **τριήρεας...πεντηκοντέρους**, see on p. 1, l. 12.

26. **ἀριθμὸς...ὁ πᾶς τῶν νεῶν**...Herodotus gives a wrong total—by 12—of the items enumerated in cc. 43—48. He reckons 378; the true result being 366 triremes. The easiest explanation is that he has made a mistake, as is the case in several other places when he gives a series of numbers; or that some error has found its way among the symbols for numbers in the MSS.

Some editors however have accounted for the 12 additional ships by supposing Herodotos to reckon in those ships of the Aeginetans which were ready and fully manned but left to guard the island [p. 23, l. 21]. It is impossible to say with certainty that this is so, but it may be noticed that at Artemisium the Aeginetans supplied 18 ships [p. 1, l. 8] and at Salamis 30, an addition of 12; supposing then that at Salamis *half* their reserve fleet of 24 was sent, the 12 would be accounted for. But this must remain mere conjecture. Aeschylos, who was himself present, reckons the number as 310, Persae 342 ὁ πᾶς ἀριθμὸς εἰς τριακάδας δέκα | ναῶν δεκὰς δ' ἦν τῶνδε χωρὶς ἔκκριτος. And other authors have given different numbers, varying from 271 to 700. See Introduction.

πάρεξ τῶν πεντηκοντέρων 'without counting the penteconters'. The number of penteconters is 7, viz. Keos 2, Kythnos, Seriphos and Siphnos 1 each, and Melos 2.

CHAPTER XLIX.

1. **προθέντος** sc. ἀποφαίνεσθαι, 'Eurybiades having proposed that any one that chose should express his opinion'. Cf. 9, 27 προέθηκε λέγειν. Demosth. 317 ἀεὶ δ' ἐν κοινῷ τὸ συμφέρον ἡ πόλις προυτίθει σκοπεῖν. See on p. 29, l. 12.

2. **τὸν βουλόμενον** 'whoever chose', the regular expression in public meetings and laws for unrestricted license of speech, or of freedom of action in prosecuting etc.

ὅκου...ποιέεσθαι 'where he thought was the most suitable place to fight the sea-fight'. Cp. 9, 2 οὐκ εἴη χῶρος ἐπιτηδεότερος ἐνστρατοπεδεύεσθαι. The construction is ὅκου χωρέων 'in whichever of the localities' τῶν ἐγκρατέες εἰσί 'of which they had the command', i.e. whether in the gulf of Salamis or further south-west, and nearer the coast of the Isthmus.

4. Ἀττικὴ 'the coast of Attica'. ἀπεῖτο [ἀπ ἵημι], had been abandoned', 'was out of the question now'.

6. συνεξέπιπτον 'appeared to agree in recommending'. Stein notices the use of the imperfect here as referring to the fact that this decision was not final, and in fact was reversed. See l. 13.

7. ἐπιλέγοντες τὸν λόγον τόνδε 'they urging the following arguments', the nominative masculine (*nominativus pendens*) is used as though αἱ γνῶμαι τῶν λεγόντων were οἱ λέγοντες τὰς γνώμας. ἐπιλέγειν = 'urge in addition to what has been said', 'to allege as an additional argument'. Cp. 7, 147 ἐπιλέγων τὸν λόγον τόνδε 'alleging the following argument' i.e. as an explanation.

9. ἵνα σφι τιμωρίη οὐδεμία ἐπιφανήσεται 'where no help could make its appearance'. Cp. 7, 169 ἔσχοντο τῆς τιμωρίης 'they abstained from giving help': Herod. does not use the word in the sense of 'vengeance'.

10. ἐς τοὺς ἑωυτῶν ἐξοίσονται 'they could land and find themselves among their own men': cp. p. 40, l. 17.

CHAPTER L.

12. ταῦτα...ἐπιλεγομένων 'while they were engaged in these considerations'. Cp. with the use of the active ἐπιλέγοντες above in l. 7. The whole body are said ἐπιλέγεσθαι (mid.) to have said over to them and so to 'take into consideration', though individuals ἐπιλέγουσι. Cp. the distinction between ἀπογράφειν and ἀπογράφεσθαι in 7, 100: cp. ποιήσασθαι 9, 15.

14. ἐς τὴν Ἀττικὴν continuing from c. 34.

17. αὐτῶν ἐκλελοιπότων ἐς Πελοπόννησον 'the inhabitants having abandoned it and fled to the Peloponnese', seven hundred of the Thespians were at Thermopylae and fell there, see c. 25 and 7, 222—6: the rest fled to the Peloponnese, and 1800 were at Plataea in the following year, but were unable to procure ὅπλα, 9, 30.

18. ἐς τὰς Ἀθήνας i.e. 'into *Attica*'. Cp. p. 34, l. 15; 9, 1, 17; so ἐς τὰς Θήβας 'into the Thebaid' 9, 13.

CHAPTER LI.

21. ἀπὸ τῆς διαβάσιος. The passage of the Persian army over the Hellespont took place at the beginning of spring, ἅμα τῷ ἔαρι, 7, 37: if we take this to mean the middle of April, the arrival of the

Persians in Attica will be dated as in the latter part of August. The battle itself took place in the Attic month Boedromion [Aug.—Sept.] for the time for the solemn procession to Eleusis had come, see c. 65.

24. **Καλλιάδεω ἄρχοντος** 'in the archonship of Kalliades'. The first of the nine archons (Ἄρχων ἐπώνυμος) gave his name to the year.

25. **ἐρῆμον** [in Attic always ἔρημον] 'deserted by its inhabitants'. See c. 41.

26. **τὸ ἄστυ** properly used here of 'the town' as composed of buildings, πόλις being a town as composed of citizens (πολῖται). So also when Mardonius took Athens next year αἱρέει ἐρῆμον τὸ ἄστυ, 9, 3. Stein however regards it as applying to the Acropolis. **καί τινας ὀλίγους** 'and only some few'.

1. **ταμίας τοῦ ἱροῦ** 'the stewards of the treasury of the temple', 26 that is of the public money (τῆς κοινῆς προσόδου) kept in the temple of Athene Polias, whom Demosthenes (1075) calls ταμίαι τῶν τῆς θεοῦ. Although no doubt all public money was withdrawn at this time for the exigencies of the fleet, there would be objects of religious reverence or artistic value still left in the temple, which these stewards declined to abandon. There were ten of them.

2. **φραξάμενοι...θύρῃσί τε καὶ ξύλοισι** 'having barricaded the Acropolis with planks and boards': that is, on the west side of the Acropolis where it slopes down towards the Areopagus. The other sides of the Acropolis were either fortified by the Pelasgic wall [5, 64; 6, 137], or were looked upon as safe from the abruptness and steepness of the rock.

3. **ἠμύνοντο** 'tried to keep off'. **ὑπ' ἀσθενείης βίου** 'from want of means', cp. 2, 88 τοὺς χρήμασι ἀσθενεστέρους. See also 2, 47.

4. **πρὸς δέ** 'and besides', p. 16, l. 8.

5. **ἐξευρηκέναι** 'that they had discovered the meaning of'. **τὸ μαντήϊον.** See 7, 141,

τεῖχος Τριτογενεῖ ξύλινον διδοῖ εὐρύοπα Ζεὺς
μοῦνον ἀπόρθητον τελέθειν, τό σε τέκνα τ' ὀνήσει.

This some interpreted of the fortifications of the Acropolis, others on the suggestion of Themistocles of the fleet, p. 21, l. 19.

7. **καὶ αὐτὸ δὴ τοῦτο εἶναι** 'and that this was in their ideas [δή, cp. p. 4, l. 12] the actual refuge meant'. The infinitive εἶναι depends on ἐξευρηκέναι or some word implied in it.

κρησφύγετον 'place of refuge', cp. 9, 15, 96. The derivation of the word is uncertain. The explanation accepted by the ancient Grammarians was 'a place of refuge from the Cretan' [Κρής].

CHAPTER LII.

9. ἱζόμενοι ἐπί 'having gone up and stationed themselves upon'. Cp. p. 37, l. 16 ἐς τὸν Ἰσθμὸν ἵζοντο. καταντίον. The Areopagus is separated from the western end of the Acropolis by a dip in the ground only a few yards wide.

11, 12. ὅκως...ἄψειαν 'as often as they had set a light to': the optative is *iterative*, or as it is sometimes called of *indefinite frequency*. Cp. 1, 17 ὅκως εἴη ἐν τῇ γῇ καρπὸς ἁδρὸς τηνικαῦτα ἐσέβαλλε τὴν στρατιήν, p. 56, l. 7; p. 63, l. 17.

15. προδεδωκότος 'had betrayed them', that is, had failed to withstand the assaults of the enemy and had fallen. The barricade therefore was in addition to whatever permanent fortification was already existing at this point, and which still admitted of defence.

16. λόγους 'proposals', 9, 14.

17—19. ἄλλα τε...καὶ δὴ καὶ 'among other measures to which they had recourse they rolled down upon the Barbarians as they approached the gates huge masses of rock'. ὁλοίτροχος see Xenoph. Anab. 4, 2, 2. [εἴλω *volvo*, or according to others ὅλος τρέχω.] τὰς πύλας the gates in the Pelasgic ring wall facing the Areopagus in front of which the Propylaea afterwards stood.

20. ἐπὶ χρόνον συχνόν, cp. 9, 62 χρόνον ἐπὶ πολλόν. Also with definite numbers, 9, 8 ἐπὶ δέκα ἡμέρας.

ἀπορίῃσι ἐνέχεσθαι 'was in perplexity', 'was at a stand'. Cp. 9, 98 ἐν ἀπορίῃ εἴχοντο.

CHAPTER LIII.

22. χρόνῳ 'at length'. Cp. 9, 62 ὡς δὲ χρόνῳ κοτὲ ἐγένετο τὰ σφάγια χρηστά. ἐκ τῶν ἀπόρων 'in these difficulties', p. 53, l. 24.

23. δή *tandem*, p. 10, l. 6. ἔδεε 'it was fated'.

24. τὴν Ἀττικὴν τὴν ἐν τῇ ἠπείρῳ 'Attica on the mainland' as opposed to the Islands, such as Salamis and others. He is again referring to the two oracles given in 7, 140—1.

25. ἔμπροσθε...πρό, that is on the northern side, still called the front of the Acropolis.

26. ὄπισθε 'on the side remote from'. τῆς ἀνόδου 'the regular pathway up' the Acropolis.

27. μή...ἀναβαίη. For the construction after ἂν ἤλπισε, which is equivalent to a verb of fearing, see G. § 218. κατὰ ταῦτα ' at that spot'. Ab. quotes 3, 64 ἐτρωματίσθη κατὰ τοῦτο τῇ αὐτὸς πρότερον τὸν θεὸν Ἆπιν ἔπληξε.

1. κατὰ τὸ ἱρὸν 'by way of the temple of Aglauros', which was 27 on the northern side of the Acropolis near the cave of Pan.

4. ἐπὶ τὴν ἀκρόπολιν. Cobet would omit these words; but they indicate that the Barbarians had not only climbed up to the wall but were actually on the plateau of the Acropolis; see p. 26, l. 9.

5. κατὰ τοῦ τείχεος 'down from the wall'.

6. τὸ μέγαρον 'the shrine of the temple'.

7. ἐτράποντο πρὸς τὰς πύλας, cp. p. 10, l. 22.

8. ταύτας...ἐφόνευον 'and when they had opened these gates they then began slaughtering the suppliants' i.e. in the temple. The gates are those of the wall.

CHAPTER LIV.

12. Ἀρταβάνῳ. He sends to Artabanus because he had at first dissuaded the enterprise [see 7, 10—18] and had been sent back to Susa in charge of the realm in the absence of the king [7, 52-3.]

15. τοὺς φυγάδας the family of the Peisistratidae and their adherents; p. 26, l. 16.

18. ἐνθύμιον 'a religious scruple'. Cp. 2, 175 ἐνθυμιστὸν ποιησάμενον. Cp. Thucyd. 7, 50, 4 ἐνθύμιον ποιούμενοι. So also the verb ἐνθυμεῖσθαι id. 7, 18, 2. Id. 5, 16 ἐς ἐνθυμίαν 'by way of exciting a religious scruple'.

CHAPTER LV.

22. Ἐρεχθέος...νηός. See on p. 21, l. 22.

23. ἐλαίη. The sacred olive from which the other sacred olives in Attica were supposed to be cuttings. θάλασσα according to Pausanias [1, 26, 6; 8, 10, 3] was a salt well on the Acropolis which communicated with the Aegean and in which the roar of the ocean could be heard. λόγος 'story' or 'myth'. The story is thus given in Apollodorus [3, 14, 1—3]. "In the time of Cecrops the gods determined to select each a city in which to be separately and

specially honoured. Poseidon came first to Attica, struck the Acropolis with his trident and opened a well (θάλασσα) which is now called the well of Erechtheus. Afterwards came Athenè and, calling Cecrops to witness that she took possession of the place, planted an olive. The god and goddess then disputed for the possession of the land. Zeus referred the question to a jury of 12 gods: Cecrops was summoned as a witness to prove that Athene had planted her olive first. The verdict was in her favour: she called the place after her Athens, while Poseidon in wrath flooded the Thriasian plain and submerged Attica." Soph. O. C. 711.

25. **μαρτύρια θέσθαι** 'alleged as evidence', see above.

26. **κατέλαβε** 'it was the fate of this olive to be burnt'. Cp. 6, 103 τὸν Κίμωνα κατέλαβε φυγεῖν. Except in this passage Herodotus seems always to use it of *persons*.

28 1. **στελέχεος**, 'trunk' or 'stump'. So in Pindar Nem. 10, 62 δρυὸς ἐν στελέχει ἡμένοι.

The shooting out of the burnt stump of the Sacred Olive may well have seemed to the Athenians, when they heard of it, as an omen of their future restoration sent by the guardian goddess of the city. The length of the shoot may have grown with the telling, but there is nothing incredible in the main fact. The olive is a tree very tenacious of life and will survive burning in a wonderful manner. Thus Pliny [N. H. 7, 241] says *oliva in totum ambusta revixit*. Cp. Vergil Georg. 2, 303—313. Accordingly the sacred olives (μορίαι) standing in various parts of Attica were protected from destruction even when reduced to stumps by fire or lightning, and were then called σηκοί. See Lysias, Orat. 7 περὶ τοῦ σηκοῦ.

CHAPTER LVI.

4. **ὡς ἴσχε τὰ περί...** 'what had happened to the Acropolis'.

6. **τὸ προκείμενον πρῆγμα** 'the proposal before them', i.e. that of abandoning Attica to its fate and removing the fleet close to the Isthmus, see c. 49.

7. **ἠείροντο** 'began hoisting their sails'.

9, 10. **νύξ τε ἐγίνετο, καὶ οἱ διαλυθέντες...ἐσέβαινον** 'after leaving the council they were just going on board their ships as the night was falling': or 'night was just falling as those who had broken up from the council were going on board'. For τε and καὶ thus indicating simultaneousness see p. 3, l. 16; p. 47, l. 17; 9, 55 ἐς νεῖκεά τε ἀπίκατο καὶ ὁ κῆρυξ παρίστατο. 9, 57 οἵ τε ἀμφὶ Ἀμομφάρετον παρεγίνοντό σφι καὶ ἡ ἵππος προσεκέετο πᾶσα.

CHAPTER LVII.

12. **ἐνθαῦτα δή** 'it was in that position of affairs', p. 67, l. 18.

17. **περὶ οὐδεμιῆς ἔτι πατρίδος ναυμαχήσεις** 'you will not have any longer a united country to fight for', or 'any country to fight for in future which may be looked upon as one'. He means, 'it will be no longer a question of defending Hellas as such, but each squadron will have to fight separately for its own city'.

20. **ὥστε μὴ οὐ διασκεδασθῆναι** 'from being scattered in every direction'. The double negative accompanies the infinitive after a negative sentence. G. § 263, 2 note.

22. **ἀβουλίῃσι** a poetical use of the plural in abstract nouns, cp. ἀπορίῃσι p. 26, l. 20. Abicht also compares the frequent Homeric ἀτασθαλίῃσι.

23. **διαχέαι** 'to rescind', 'to annul', as opposed to ἐκυρώθη l. 9; lit. 'to pour different ways', and thus 'to obliterate'. In Xenoph. Cyr. 5, 3 of the effect of wet upon the tracks of animals (τὰ ἴχνη) opposed to συνίστησι.

ἀναγνῶσαι 'to persuade', both this meaning of ἀναγινώσκειν (7, 11) and this form of the 1st aorist are peculiar to the Ionic dialect. This form only occurs in composition, see p. 29, l. 8; p. 53, l. 4.

CHAPTER LVIII.

2. **ἡ ὑποθήκη** 'the suggestion', cp. 1, 156 ἡσθεὶς τῇ ὑποθήκῃ. 29

4. **συμμῖξαι** 'to communicate', p. 34, l. 20. This rare meaning is illustrated by various commentators from Theognis 64

ἀλλὰ δόκει μὲν πᾶσιν ἀπὸ γλώσσης φίλος εἶναι
χρῆμα δὲ συμμίξῃς μηδενὶ μηδ' ὁτιοῦν
σπουδαῖον.

7. **ἑωυτοῦ ποιεύμενος** 'pretending that they (the arguments) were his own', 'adopting as his own'. Cp. 4, 180 τὸν Δία ἑωυτοῦ μιν ποιήσασθαι θυγατέρα.

8. **ἀνέγνωσε**, p. 28, l. 23.

CHAPTER LIX.

12. **προθεῖναι τὸν λόγον** 'introduced the discussion', 'explained for what he had summoned them'. The president of an assembly in opening a debate was said λόγον προτιθέναι [Xen. Mem. 4, 2, 3 τῆς πόλεως λόγον περί τινος προτιθείσης] or προτιθέναι followed by infinitive [p. 25, l. 1]: or προτιθέναι γνώμας [Thucyd. 6, 14 καὶ σὺ, ὦ Πρύτανι, γνώμας προτίθει αὖθις Ἀθηναίοις]. Cobet therefore wishes to omit τόν, *Variae Lect.* p. 353.

13. **πολλὸς ἦν** 'was very urgent', 'said much', cp. the Lat. *creber fuisti* 'you often said' Cic. pro Planc. § 83. Cp. 9, 91 ὡς δὲ πολλὸς ἦν λισσόμενος, 1, 98 ἦν πολλὸς ὑπὸ παντὸς ἀνδρὸς καὶ προβαλλόμενος καὶ αἰνεόμενος. Cp. also 3, 46 ἔλεγον πολλὰ οἷα κάρτα δεόμενοι.

17. **ῥαπίζονται** 'are struck with the wands of the keepers of the course' (ῥαβδοῦχοι or Ἑλλανοδίκαι Paus. 6, 2, 1). In Thucydides 5, 50 one Lichas ὑπὸ τῶν ῥαβδούχων πληγὰς ἔλαβε for some breach of the rules. See Holden's note on Plutarch Themist. 11. This anecdote is repeated by Plutarch, as well as the still more celebrated answer to Eurybiades on his raising his stick, 'Strike but hear me', πάταξον μὲν ἄκουσον δέ.

ἀπολυόμενος 'by way of excusing himself'. Sometimes with an acc., Thucyd. 8, 87 βουλόμενος πρὸς αὐτοὺς ἀπολύεσθαι τὰς διαβολάς.

CHAPTER LX.

20. **ἐκείνων** p. 28, l. 17.

23. **οὐκ ἔφερέ οἱ κόσμον οὐδένα** 'it had not been becoming in him'. See on p. 31, l. 27. **κατηγορέειν** sc. τῶν συμμάχων.

24. **εἴχετο**, see p. 6, l. 17.

§ 1.

25. **ἐν σοὶ νῦν ἐστί** 'it is in your hands', 'it depends on you'. Cp. Soph. Aj. 519 ἐν σοὶ πᾶσ' ἔγωγε σώζομαι, p. 65, l. 17; 6. 108.

27. **ἀναζεύξῃς...τὰς νέας** 'remove the ships to the Isthmus'. ἀναζευγνύναι is properly 'to harness again'. Elsewhere Herod. has τὸν στρατόν (9, 41) or τὸ στρατόπεδον (9, 58) as the object. Its use with ships shews that its original meaning was quite merged in that of 'removal'.

30. 1. **ἀντίθες...ἀκούσας** 'listen to the alternative courses and contrast their advantages against each other'.

3. **τὸ ἥκιστα ἡμῖν σύμφορόν ἐστι** 'which is as far as possible from being to our advantage considering that the ships which we have are heavier and fewer in number than the enemy'. [The MSS. have ἐς τό. I have ventured to omit ἐς which it seems difficult if not impossible to construe. Stein imagines that the copyist may have left out some such verb as ἀνάγειν 'to put out into which open sea'.]

4. **βαρυτέρας.** According to Plutarch [Them. 14] the Persian ships were heavier and more cumbrous than those of the Greeks. It has been proposed to read βραχυτέρας.

ἀριθμὸν ἐλάσσονας. The number of the Greek fleet as given in c. 48 was 378, that of the Persian ships [7, 184] was originally 1207; and though that number had been reduced by shipwreck and losses in battle, they were still as vastly superior in numbers to the Greeks as before, owing to reinforcements. See c. 66.

5. **τοῦτο δέ** 'and in the next place'. For the phrase τοῦτο μέν ...τοῦτο δέ see p. 40, l. 6 and 7, 6; 9, 7 and 27. Here the first antithetical sentence is introduced simply by μέν in l. 2, cp. 5, 45.

8. **αὐτὸς ἄξεις** 'you yourself will be the instrument of bringing them against the Peloponnese'.

9. **κινδυνεύσεις...Ἑλλάδι** 'and what you will stake on the event will be the safety of the whole of Greece'. **κινδυνεύειν** 'to be in danger' may stand (1) with infin. κινδυνεύσει ἀποβαλεῖν τὸν ναυτικὸν στρατὸν p. 33, l. 7, (2) with prep. περὶ ἐκείνης κινδυνεύειν 8, 74, (3) as here with dat. of object risked, cp. 7, 209 κινδυνεύειν τῇ ψυχῇ.

§ 2.

10. **τοσάδε χρηστά** 'the advantages which I will enumerate'.

12. **τὰ οἰκότα** [οἰκώς=εἰκώς App. E. (f)] 'what we have a right to expect'.

14. **πρὸς ἡμέων** 'on our side', 'in our favour'. Cf. Eurip. Alc. 57 πρὸς τῶν ἐχόντων, Φοῖβε, τὸν νόμον τίθης. Cf. p. 12, l. 16.

15. **περιγίνεται** present for certain future, 'will be saved'. For the meaning cp. περιεῖναι p. 2, l. 8.

ὑπεκκέεται [=ὑπ-εκ-κεῖται used as pass. of ὑπεκτιθέναι 'have been removed'] see c. 41.

16. **καὶ μήν** 'again'. **καὶ τόδε** 'even the point which you care most for', i.e. the safety of the Peloponnesus.

17. **τοῦ καὶ περιέχεσθε** 'which you actually cleave to', 'which

you value'. Cp. 7, 160 τῆς ἡγεμονίης περιέχεσθε, but in 9, 57 it is used without any case following. καὶ emphatic, p. 19, l. 25.

ὁμοίως...Ἰσθμῷ 'if you stay where you are you will be quite as much fighting for the Peloponnesus as (καὶ) you would near the isthmus'. For καὶ cp. p. 23, l. 17.

19. σφέας i.e. the Persians, cp. l. 8.

§ 3.

21. ὑμῖν *ethic dative* 'you won't have them coming to the isthmus'. For παρεῖναι ἐς cp. 6, 24 παρῆν ἐς τὴν Ἀσίην, Arist. Plut. 411 κατακλίνειν αὐτὸν εἰς Ἀσκληπιοῦ.

23. ἑκαστέρω τῆς Ἀττικῆς may mean 'farther than Attica', or, 'farther into Attica', cp. 9, 14 ἑκαστάτω τῆς Εὐρώπης.

24. κερδανέομεν 'we shall be the gainers by the survival of Megara, Salamis, and Aegina'. κερδαίνειν is the opposite of ζημιοῦσθαι.

25. λόγιον 'an oracle', referring again to the oracle given in 7, 141 and especially to the line ὦ θείη Σαλαμίς, ἀπολεῖς δὲ σὺ τέκνα γυναικῶν. See on p. 21, l. 19.

27. ὡς τὸ ἐπίπαν 'as a general rule'. The full sentence is οἰκότα βουλευομένοισι οἰκότα ἐθέλει γίνεσθαι 'to reasonable plans reasonable success usually comes'. ἐθέλει 'is wont', cp. 7, 157 τῷ εὖ βουλευθέντι πρήγματι τελευτὴ ὡς τὸ ἐπίπαν χρηστὴ ἐθέλει ἐπιγίνεσθαι.

28. οὐδὲ ὁ θεὸς...γνώμας 'but when men counsel ill heaven itself is not wont either to further human designs'. προσχωρέειν πρὸς 'to join as an ally', cp. Thucyd. 1, 103, 4 προσεχώρησαν καὶ Μεγαρῆς Ἀθηναίοις ἐς συμμαχίαν. Id. 3, 61, 3 προσεχώρησαν πρὸς Ἀθηναίους καὶ μετ' αὐτῶν πολλὰ ἡμᾶς ἔβλαπτον.

CHAPTER LXI.

2. ἐπεφέρετο 'attacked', 'inveighed against'. In the literal sense of 'attack' cp. p. 47, l. 19, Thucyd. 4, 67, 4 τοῖς τῶν Ἀθηναίων ὁπλίταις ἐπιφερομένοις βεβαίους τὰς πύλας παρέσχον.

3. οὐκ ἐῶν 'forbidding', cp. 9, 2. ἐπιψηφίζειν 'to put the vote to', i.e. 'to allow a vote to a cityless man'. This word is applied to him who puts a subject to the vote, the president of an assembly, cp. Thucyd. 6, 14, 1 σύ, ὦ πρύτανι, ταῦτα ἐπιψήφιζε καὶ γνώμας προτίθει αὖθις Ἀθηναίοις. There does not seem any example of its use

with dative of those to whom the vote is put earlier than Lucian. Many therefore interpret this 'Don't put this to the vote for a cityless man', i.e. at his instance. This construction is quite as difficult as the other, and produces a less satisfactory sense.

4, 5. **πόλιν γάρ...συμβάλλεσθαι** 'for he bade Themistocles not deliver a vote with the rest unless he could show that he had a city', i.e. unless he could show that he appeared for some existing city as its envoy. For **οὕτω** after a participle cp. p. 12, l. 25.

For **γνώμας συμβάλλεσθαι** *sententias dicere* see 5, 92, 1 εἴχετε ἂν περὶ αὐτοῦ γνώμας ἀμείνονας συμβαλέσθαι ἤπερ νῦν. (St.)

6. **κατείχοντο** ' was actually in possession of the enemy'.

10. **ἔστ' ἂν διηκόσιαι νέες**...'as long as they had 200 ships'. The point of Themistocles' retort is shown more at length by Plutarch. 'If you go away and desert us a second time, it will soon be heard in Greece that the Athenians have possession of a free city and a territory as good as that which they lost'. Plutarch however seems to combine the two councils of Herodotos into one meeting [Them. 11].

CHAPTER LXII.

14. **ἐπεστραμμένα** sc. *ἔπη*, 'earnestly', cp. 1, 30 εἴρετο ἐπιστρεφέως. Cf. 7, 160 ἐπειδὴ ὥρα ἀπεστραμμένους τοὺς λόγους τοῦ Συάγρου [where some read ἐπεστρ., but the analogy of ἀποβλέπειν 'to look earnestly at' from the notion of looking away from everything else will serve to justify the ἀπεστρ.].

σύ...εἰ δὲ μή...'If you will remain and act like a brave man,—well and good, but if not'—for this *aposiopesis* followed by εἰ δὲ μή cf. Aristoph. Plut. 468

κἂν μὲν ἀποφήνω μόνην
ἀγαθῶν ἁπάντων οὖσαν αἰτίαν ἐμὲ
ὑμῖν, δι' ἐμέ τε ζῶντας ὑμᾶς· εἰ δὲ μὴ
ποιεῖτον ἤδη τοῦθ' ὅτι ἂν ὑμῖν δοκῇ.

'If I prove to you that I am the author of all blessings to you, and that it is by me you live,—well: otherwise do what you please to me'. See Goodwin's *Moods and Tenses*, p. 112, note 2.

15, 16. **τὸ πᾶν τοῦ πολέμου** 'the whole fate of the war'. **ἀλλά** p. 78, l. 30.

18. **τοὺς οἰκέτας** 'our families', see p. 23, l. 9.

19. Σῖριν τὴν ἐν Ἰταλίῃ, for Siris see Historical Index. The idea of finding in the west a new home and new prosperity more than once reappeared in Athenian history. This perhaps influenced Pericles in promoting the colony of Thurii in B.C. 444, and caused the readiness of the Athenians to interfere in the quarrels of Syracuse and Leontini in Sicily in B.C. 427, which eventually led to such disasters. A reported migration of Ionians to Siris was probably the ground on which Themistocles based the claim of Athens to a hold upon Siris. The notion of a whole Hellenic community migrating *en masse* to the west was not a new one in Hellenic history, see the Story of the people of Phokaea 1, 163—7.

20. λόγια, another instance of the use made by Themistocles of the popular belief in oracles, noticed by Plutarch, when he was inducing the Athenians to leave their town: Them. 10 σημεῖα δαιμόνια καὶ χρησμοὺς ἐπῆγεν αὐτοῖς. We cannot tell to what particular oracles he refers: but the collection which went by the name of Bakis contained oracular verses referring to a large number of different matters and in all probability some referring to Italy and Sicily.

CHAPTER LXIII.

23. ἀνεδιδάσκετο 'began to be convinced'.

24. δοκέειν δέ μοι. See p. 12, l. 14.

27. ἐγίνοντο. The words ἀπολιπόντων Ἀθηναίων 'if the Athenians abandoned them', form the protasis of a condition, the apodosis is ἐγίνοντο without ἄν. This omission of ἄν gives a more emphatic expression to the certainty of the result; just as in Latin the corresponding tenses of the indicative are used for the subjunctive as in Verg. Aen. 2, 54 *si mens non laeva fuisset Impulerat* (for impulisset); and just as we say, 'I had done so' for 'I should have done so'. We must also note that although the sentence is in the form of a *past condition* it is so by anticipation: the contingency is really one of the future.

32 1, 2. ταύτην...διαναυμαχέειν 'he decides upon (selects) this decision, namely, that he should remain there and fight the battle out'. Like διαμάχεσθαι [Xen. Oecon. 1, 23] διαναυμαχέειν means 'to fight to the end', and so is rightly used of the main battle as opposed to any skirmish.

CHAPTER LXIV.

3. **ἔπεσι ἀκροβολισάμενοι** 'after this skirmish of words'. The meaning of ἀκροβολίζεσθαι is to skirmish as opposed to coming to close quarters, see Thucyd. 3, 73; the metaphor is similar to that in p. 41, l. 15 ὠθισμὸς λόγων.

5, 6. **τε...καί** see p. 3, l. 16. **σεισμός.** See on p. 20, l. 4.

8. **ἐπικαλέσασθαι** 'to summon the Aeakidae to come as allies to their aid'. For the worship of Heroes see on p. 20, l. 16.

9. **ἔδοξε...ἐποίευν.** Notice the tenses, the aorist of a single complete act, the imperfect of the beginning of a series: 'when they had once determined on these things they also set about doing them'. Ab. and St. compare 7, 128 ὡς δὲ ἐπεθύμησε καὶ ἐποίεε ταῦτα.

11. **ἐπὶ Αἰακόν** 'to fetch Aeakos'. Cf. Arist. Ranae 111 ἡνίκ' ἦλθες ἐπὶ τὸν Κέρβερον. See on 9, 44.

CHAPTER LXV.

14. **φυγάς**, of the Athenian exiles with Xerxes, see p. 27, l. 15.

15. **ἐκείρετο.** See p. 17, l. 21.

16. **ἐρῆμος Ἀθηναίων.** See p. 25, l. 25.

19. **ἀπὸ Ἐλευσῖνος...τρισμυρίων.** On the sixth day of the great Eleusinia a solemn procession went from Athens to Eleusis, carrying a statue of Iacchus (Bacchus) adorned with myrtle and torch in hand, along the sacred road which traversed the Thriasian plain, raising joyous shouts of Iacche! oh Iacche! [See Arist. Ran. 316.] Not only Athenians, but all other Greeks also might share in the ceremonies at these mysteries, and possibly a crowd of 30,000 persons might at times have been present at them. If the story is in any way true, it shews how important they were considered, if even at this time of danger and national disaster some worshippers were found to keep up the celebration as best they might; just as for several years during the Peloponnesian war, when the inroads of the Spartans made it dangerous or impossible to go along the sacred way as usual, the Athenians who wished to join in the initiations were conveyed by sea to Eleusis, until in B.C. 407 Alcibiades on his recall escorted the sacred pro-

cession once more by land at the head of an army [Xen. Hellen. I, 4, 21]. We must regard the number (τρισμυρίων) as not meant to be exact but to indicate a large crowd.

21. **πρόκατε** 'forthwith' [πρό], for the suffix τε see on p. 10, l. 9.

23. **ἀδαήμονα τῶν ἱρῶν**, that is, he had not been initiated, and did not know the sacred song which was sung only by the initiated.

For the discussion of the ceremonies at and meaning of the Eleusinian Mysteries a dictionary of antiquities must be consulted. It is enough to say that as they were probably connected with a more ancient form of religion than prevailed in Greece, so they were almost the last of all heathen ceremonies to die out before the advance of Christianity. They embraced a mystic worship of Nature-powers as represented by corn and wine [Demeter and Iacchus], and initiation in them was held not only in some way to purify the character, but to speak to the devout of another life of hope beyond the grave. This may be illustrated by two of the very numerous passages referring to them in ancient literature. 'Blessed is he' (says Pindar, fr. 102) 'whoso shall not go beneath the hollow earth until he hath beheld them! He knoweth of the end of life that by God's grace it is but a beginning'. 'They who share in these initiations' (says Isocrates, Panegyr. 6) 'have sweeter hopes concerning life's end and all time to come'.

83 2. **θεῖον** 'supernatural'.

3. **ἐς τιμωρίην Ἀθηναίοισι** 'to protect the Athenians', see on p. 25, l. 9.

4. **κατασκήψῃ**. Cf. ἐνέσκηψαν p. 20, l. 23.

7. **κινδυνεύσει ἀποβαλεῖν**. For constructions of κινδυνεύειν see p. 30, l. 9.

9. **τῇ Μητρὶ καὶ τῇ Κούρῃ** 'to Demeter and Persephonè'. [Cobet would read Δήμητρι in which he is supported by the best MS.] One of the objects of the Eleusinian mysteries was supposed to be that of celebrating the wanderings of Demeter in search of her daughter (ἡ κόρη).

10. **ὁ βουλόμενος**, see on p. 25, l. 2.

18. **ἐκ** 'after', p. 7, l. 10.

19, 20. **ἐπὶ Σαλαμῖνος ἐπὶ τὸ στρατόπεδον** 'in the direction of Salamis, so as to rest over the camp of the Greeks'. For this juxtaposition of ἐπί with different cases cp. 9, 47 ὀπίσω ἦγε τοὺς Σπαρτιήτας ἐπὶ τὸ δεξιὸν κέρας· ὡς δ' αὔτως καὶ ὁ Μαρδόνιος ἐπὶ τοῦ εὐωνύμου, where the distinction of meaning is the same '*to* the left wing' and '*towards* the left wing'. The Greeks who were not on board were encamped in Salamis.

22. μέλλοι 'was destined', p. 2, l. 3.

23. καταπτόμενος 'appealing to', cp. 6, 68 θεῶν καταπτόμενος.

CHAPTER LXVI.

25. θηησάμενοι, see c. 24.

28. ὡς ἐμοὶ δοκέειν, p. 12, l. 14. For the numbers see on p. 30, l. 4.

2. ἐς τὰς Ἀθήνας 'into Attica', p. 25, l. 18.

4. ὑπὸ τοῦ χειμῶνος cc. 12—13.

8. πανστρατιῇ. See p. 15, l. 2.

11. πλὴν τῶν πέντε...οὐνόματα [App. A. III. 7]. The five islands mentioned in c. 46, Naxos, Melos, Kythnos, Seriphos, Siphnos. Notice that Herod. speaks of these small islands as πόλεις 'states'.

13. ἐσωτέρω 'further south', cp. ἔσω p. 2, l. 23. For the gen. τῆς Ἑλλάδος see on p. 30, l. 23.

CHAPTER LXVII.

15. ἀπίκατο. App. D. II. a. ἐς τὰς Ἀθήνας see p. 25, l. 18.

17. ἐκαραδόκεον 'were watching', cf. 7, 163 καραδοκήσοντα τὴν μάχην ᾗ πεσέεται, cp. ib. 168; properly 'to watch with outstretched head', like a combatant looking out for his enemy's blow, cp. Eurip. I. T. 133 καραδοκῶν τἀπιόντα τραύματα.

19. κατέβη...ἐπὶ τὰς νέας 'went down to the shore (from the town) to where the ships lay'.

20. συμμίξαι 'to converse with', p. 29, l. 4.

21. προΐζετο 'he sat down in state', 'in a conspicuous place'.

23. ταξίαρχοι, used generally by Herodotos of officers in the land force, see 9, 42, 53: but in 7, 99 it is also used of naval officers. He uses a Greek title for a certain rank, though that may not have been the exact title used in the several fleets. In Athens the taxiarchs were tribal officers next in rank to the Strategi.

ὥς σφι βασιλεὺς...ἐδεδώκεε 'according to the rank the king had assigned to each'. One of the special ways in which an

Eastern king rewarded his subjects was by assigning a place more or less near himself. Cf. Xen. Oecon. 4, 8 οὓς μὲν ἂν αἰσθάνηται τῶν ἀρχόντων συνοικουμένην τε τὴν χώραν παρεχομένους καὶ ἐνεργὸν οὖσαν τὴν γῆν...τούτοις μὲν χώραν τε ἄλλην προστίθησι...καὶ ἕδραις ἐντίμοις γεραίρει. Many references in the Old Testament to this custom will occur to the reader. The kings of Sidon and Tyre are in the place of honour here because the Phoenicians were the most important providers of ships. See 7, 96.

25. **μετά...ἐπί** adverbial, p. 17, l. 24; p. 62, l. 18. Herodotos very often uses μετά in this way. The different grades indicated by the two prepositions also should be noticed, 'next', and 'following in order'.

27. **ἀποπειρώμενος** 'by way of ascertaining the opinion of each'. See p. 5, l. 22 and 9, 21.

CHAPTER LXVIII.

2. **κατὰ τὠυτὸ γνώμην ἐξεφέροντο** 'were unanimous in the opinion which they expressed'. The force of the middle in this phrase is that of producing as their own; cp. 5, 36 where the same expression is used under similar circumstances.

§ 1.

5. **εἶπαι**, App. E. 2. The infinitive for imperative, cp. p. 11, l. 4. [Stein reads εἰπεῖν with the MSS.]

6. **κακίστη** 'the most cowardly', cp. ἐθελοκακεῖν p. 12, l. 11.

8. **δέσποτα, τὴν δὲ ἐοῦσαν** 'My lord, I on the other hand must declare my real opinion'. For the reading of this passage see notes on next. The δέ at the beginning of such a speech implies a contrast with what has gone before. Stein shews its force by quoting 1, 32; 3, 82; 8, 137, 142, in which passages it as here introduces a similar speech, and comes immediately after the vocative of the person addressed.

For the meaning of **ἐοῦσαν** 'real' cp. 1, 95 τὸν ἐόντα λόγον λέγειν. Artemisia hints that the others have not spoken their *real* opinion.

9. **τὰ τυγχάνω φρονέουσα ἄριστα** in apposition to γνώμην, 'namely the ideas which I actually entertain as being best calculated to promote your wishes'.

10. καί τοι τάδε 'well then, this is what I say'.
11. ποιέω (al. ποίεε), see App. D. III. footnote 8.
13, 14. πάντως 'at all'. ἀνακινδυνεύειν 'to undergo a risk', implying that such action is superfluous or at least voluntary. See 9, 26 χρεόν...τὸν στρατὸν τῷ στρατῷ μὴ ἀνακινδυνεύειν συμβάλλοντα.
17. ἀπήλλαξαν 'came off', 'fared', a common use of ἀπαλλάσσειν, cp. 5, 63 ὁ στόλος οὕτως ἀπήλλαξε, still more common in the mid. and pass. Cp. Aristoph. Plut. 271 μῶν ἀξιοῖς ἀπαλλαγῆναι ἀζήμιος.

§ 2.

19. ἀντιπολέμων = πολεμίων, cp. 7, 236. It is a word not used by Attic writers.
20. τὰς νέας αὐτοῦ ἔχῃς πρὸς γῇ. The policy of keeping the fleet entire and in close proximity to the army had been urged on Xerxes before by Achaemenes, see 7, 236.
24. διασκεδᾷς fut. σκεδά[σ]ω. κατὰ πόλις. Cp. the fears expressed by Mnesiphilos, p. 28, l. 18—22.
25. πάρα = πάρεστι.
26. νήσῳ, Salamis.
1. ἀτρεμιέειν 'that they will remain where they are'. App. D, 36 III. d, note 2.
ἐκεῖθεν that is from the Peloponnese.

§ 3.

5. προσδηλήσηται 'may damage the land force besides'
πρός adverb. See p. 16, l. 8. τόδε ἐς θυμὸν βάλευ 'reflect upon this truth', cp. 7, 51 ἐς θυμὸν βαλεῦ τὸ παλαιὸν ἔπος. For βάλευ see App. D, footnote 9.
8. σοί, note emphatic position of pronoun. ἐν συμμάχων λόγῳ 'in the category of allies'; 6, 19 ἐν ἀνδροπέδων λόγῳ. Artemisia does not venture to speak against the Persians, but has a real contempt for these other non-Hellenes; though the Egyptians are said to have borne off the prize of valour at Artemisium [c. 17].

CHAPTER LXIX.

13. συμφορὴν ἐποιεῦντο. See p. 6, l. 7.
15. οὐκ ἐᾷ 'dissuades', p. 31, l. 3. ἀγαιόμενοί [ἀγάομαι] τε

καὶ φθονέοντες 'who were ill disposed to and jealous of her'. Cf. 6, 61 φθόνῳ καὶ ἄγῃ χρεόμενος.

16. ἅτε ἐν πρώτοισι τετιμημένης 'because she enjoyed the highest position in the king's esteem'. The introduction of the gen. abs. with ἅτε, instead of a participle agreeing with αὐτῇ, shows that the writer is giving his own explanation of their jealousy. Cp. p. 47, l. 14. ἐν πρώτοισι may be either masc. or neut. cp. Thuc. 4, 105 δύνασθαι ἐν τοῖς πρώτοις τῶν ἠπειρωτῶν and id. 7, 27, 4 ἐν το῀ς πρώτοις ἐκάκωσε τὰ πράγματα [ἡ Δεκέλεια]. For omission of article in this idiom see instances in L. and Sc.

17. διά 'above', cp. p. 19, l. 25. τῇ κρίσι 'this expression of opinion', *sententia* [but Stein reads ἀνακρίσι 'contradiction', 'opposition', quoting Plato 176 and 277. See note on text].

21. τοῖσι πλέοσι 'the majority'.

22. καταδόξας seems only a strengthened δόξας, 'having made up his mind', cp. p. 2, l. 22 and 9, 57.

23. τότε δέ 'whereas on this occasion'. ἐθελοκακέειν, p. 12, l. 11: the present is here used as an historical tense.

CHAPTER LXX.

25. παρήγγελλον 'when they (the leaders) passed the word round to put to sea'.

26. παρεκρίθησαν 'were ranged in line of battle', the forces of the two parts of the word are—ἐκρίθησαν 'they were separated', παρά 'in lateral order': so that it is a proleptic word,—'they were so separated as to be in line'.

37   3. ἐπεγένετο 'came down upon them while thus engaged', 'overtook them'.

4. οὐκ ἥκιστα, p. 21, l. 20.

5, 6. ἀρρώδεον ὅτι...ναυμαχέειν μέλλοιεν...πολιορκήσονται 'But they were alarmed (at the thought) that they were going to fight for Attica while fixed at Salamis, and that if conquered they would be caught in the Island and subjected to a siege'. 'Verbs of fearing as they imply *thought* sometimes take the construction of ordinary indirect discourse', and with ὅτι introducing a *causal* sentence cp. Xen. Cyr. 3, 1, 1 ἐφοβεῖτο ὅτι ὀφθήσεσθαι ἔμελλε τὰ βασίλεια οἰκοδομεῖν ἀρχόμενος. Goodwin, *Moods and Tenses*, p. 85, 6. The expression ναυμαχέειν μέλλοιεν is to be noted as equivalent to a future coordinate with πολιορκήσονται, the optative is used as representing the thoughts of another, just as the future optative is used for the indic. fut. in oblique oration. The variation to the indicative in the second clause is a matter of idiom like the variation of the moods in two final clauses, both being grammatically admissible; see p. 4, l. 11; p. 40, l. 12.

8. ἀπολαμφθέντες 'cut off from retreat'.

CHAPTER LXXI.

11. ἐπὶ τὴν Πελοπόννησον 'to invade the Peloponnese': but they got no farther than the Megarid, see 9, 14.

16. ἐς τὸν Ἰσθμὸν ἵζοντο. See p. 26, l. 9.

18. συγχώσαντες 'having blocked up with earthworks', see on p. 15, l. 27.

20. οἰκοδόμεον 'they began to build'. The wall which crossed the Isthmus at a point about seven miles east of Corinth was finished in the following spring, see 9, 8. The distance across is about five miles.

22. ἤνετο 'was being wrought to perfection'. The verb ἄνω is nearly confined to poetry, the more common form ἀνύω being generally used by Attic prose writers.

23. φορμοί 'baskets' [Rt. φερ, φέρω, φορέω, φορός], it was also used as a measure of corn about equal to a medimnus. ψάμμου. The sand, as Stein remarks, was for the double purpose of making mortar and filling up the space left between the two sides of the wall to be made into a solid mass of rubble.

24, 25. ἔλίνυον 'rested', cf. 1, 67. A verb confined to poetry and Ionic prose. νυκτός...ἡμέρης, p. 4, l. 16.

CHAPTER LXXII.

26. πανδημεί 'with every available man', see πανστρατιῇ p. 15, l. 2; p. 21, l. 6.

4. ὑπεραρρωδέοντες τῇ Ἑλλάδι. Stein regards this dat. as anomalous quoting Eurip. Suppl. 344 ἡ τεκοῦσα χὑπερορρωδοῦσ' ἐμοῦ, but it may be looked upon as a case of a dative of advantage, like the converse ἐλπίδα ἔχων σωτηρίας τῇ Ἑλλάδι. G. § 184, 3.

6. Κάρνεια. This Spartan festival [see Hist. Index] began on the 7th of the month Metageitnion [the Spartan Karneios] and

lasted to the 16th. It was therefore late in August. παροιχώκεε ἤδη 'had been concluded by this time', and therefore—Herodotus means—the other Peloponnesian states had no excuse for not appearing. The Karneia had before been alleged at Sparta as an excuse for delay, see 7, 206.

CHAPTER LXXIII.

9. αὐτόχθονα opposed to ἐπήλυδα in l. 14. Those people, of whose coming to a land no history or tradition existed, were considered to be αὐτόχθονες 'natives of the soil', in this case the Pelasgi. Thus the Karians claimed to be autochthonous of Asia Minor (1, 171), and the Athenians of Attica, of which the symbol was the grasshopper formerly worn by them [Thucyd. 1, 6, 3]. So too the Sikani are said to be αὐτόχθονες of Sicily [id. 6, 2, 2]. In 9, 73 αὐτόχθων is used just like our 'native'.

12. οὐκ ἐξεχώρησε did not quit the Peloponnesus, that is at the coming of the Dorians. See Historical Index s. v. *Dorians*.

13. τὴν ἀλλοτρίην 'the land of others'. The Achaioi, a name which in Homer is used often as a general appellation for Greeks, seem to have lived in southern Peloponnese, and retreating before the conquering Dorians settled in the district along the north coast of the Peloponnese, hence called Achaia, anciently named Aegialos [Paus. 5, 1, 1].

14. ἐπήλυδα 'subsequent immigrations'.

18. Παρωρεῆται πάντες 'to the Lemnians belong all the towns of the Paroreats', that is the 'mountain peoples' of the district Triphylia in Elis. The word only means 'dwellers by the mountains', but came to be used as a geographical term for this district, cp. 4, 148.

οἱ δὲ Κυνούριοι...Ἴωνες 'The Kynurii seem to be the only people who are at once Ionians and autochthonous'. As Stein says, two ideas are involved in the sentence: 'the Kynurii seem to be Ionians, and in that case are the only ones still remaining in the Peloponnese'.

20. ἐκδεδωρίευνται...χρόνου 'have been thoroughly Doricised both by being under the rule of Argives and by the lapse of time'. The difficulty of the sentence lies in the fact that ὑπὸ has to be supplied before τοῦ χρόνου from the previous line, and yet is in a different sense; ὑπὸ Ἀργείων is a genitive of the agent depending

upon ἀρχόμενοι, while ὑπὸ τοῦ χρόνου is instrumental. Cobet [*Variae Lect.* p. 424] proposes therefore to omit ἀρχόμενοι as having been a gloss explaining ὑπὸ Ἀργείων, [sc. ἀρχόμενοι,] which was then introduced into the text.

21. **ἰόντες Ὀρνεῆται καὶ περίοικοι** 'being in the position of Orneats *or* perioeki'. The inhabitants of Orneae resisting the Dorian conquerors were reduced to the position of the Spartan *perioeki* or unenfranchised farmers; and thence the name was applied to all others remaining in the country in the same position. Cp. the derivation given by some of the word Helotes, viz. from Helos on the Laconian gulf, and of *Caerites* in Roman polity. The Argives seem to have destroyed Orneae in B.C. 416 [Thucyd. 6, 7, 2].

23. **πάρεξ τῶν**, by attraction for πάρεξ ἐκείνων ἅς. **ἐκ τοῦ μέσου κατέατο** [App. D. II. a] 'held aloof from the war'. Cp. p. 12, l. 7.

24. **κατήμενοι** 'by so holding aloof they were really medizing'.

CHAPTER LXXIV.

25. **τοιούτῳ πόνῳ συνέστασαν** 'were engrossed in the active labour I have described', i.e. in building the wall. Cp. 9, 89 λιμῷ συστάντας καὶ καμάτῳ. Cf. 7, 170.

26. **ἅτε περὶ τοῦ παντὸς ἤδη δρόμον θέοντες** 'seeing that their all was now at stake'. Herodotos is fond of this metaphor from the race-course, see 9, 37 ὥστε τρέχων περὶ τῆς ψυχῆς. 7, 57 περὶ ἑωυτοῦ τρέχειν. Cf. Aristoph. Vesp. 376 ποιήσω περὶ ψυχῆς δρόμον δραμεῖν. p. 55, l. 26; p. 78, l. 12.

1. **ἐλλάμψεσθαι** 'that they would distinguish themselves'. Cp. 39 1, 80 τῷ ἱππικῷ ἐλλάμπεσθαι.

2. **ταῦτα** refers to the facts mentioned in cc. 71—3, viz. the advance of the Persians towards the Peloponnese, the abstention of many of the Peloponnesian states, and yet the comparative security of the peninsula by the rapid completion of the wall; in spite of this reassuring circumstance however the fleet were still (ὅμως) alarmed for the safety of the Peloponnese. [The comparative obscurity of this train of thought has suggested to some the reading ὁμῶς, while Abicht thinks that we should probably read ὁμοίως.]

5. **σιγῇ λόγον ἐποιέετο** 'began saying under his breath', or 'secretly', cp. 2, 140 σιγῇ τοῦ Αἰθίοπος 'without the knowledge

of Aethiops', *clam Aethiope*. The use of σιγῇ in this adverbial sense of 'secretly' accounts for its employment in what seems a kind of bull in such an expression as σιγῇ λόγον ποιεῖσθαι [=λέγειν].

θῶυμα ποιεύμενοι = θαυμάζοντες 'expressing their surprise at', cp. p. 41, l. 25. For ποιεῖσθαι 'regard' see p. 2, l. 7.

6. **ἐξερράγη** 'it (the discontent) burst out'. Cp. 6, 129 οὐ βουλόμενος ἐκραγῆναι ἐς αὐτόν.

7. **σύλλογός τε δή** 'and a meeting for debate actually took place'.

8. **οἱ μὲν** sc. ἔλεγον. For this construction St. compares Soph. Ant. 259 λόγοι δ' ἐν ἀλλήλοισιν ἐρρόθουν κακοί, | φύλαξ ἐλέγχων φύλακα.

9. **περὶ ἐκείνης κινδυνεύειν** 'and to fight in defence of it'. This is not a construction of κινδυνεύειν with preposition = 'to hazard' [see p. 30, l. 9], but κινδυνεύειν here = μάχεσθαι and περί 'in behalf of', cp. Il. 12, 243 εἷς οἰωνὸς ἄριστος ἀμύνεσθαι περὶ πάτρης.

πρὸ, p. 3, l. 6.

'Αθηναῖοι δὲ, sc. ἐκέλευον.

CHAPTER LXXV.

13. **ἑσσοῦτο τῇ γνώμῃ** 'was outvoted', for the opposite νικᾶν see on p. 5, l. 15.

19. **Θεσπιέα ἐποίησε** 'caused him to be admitted citizen of Thespiae'. **ὡς ἐπεδέκοντο** 'when they were admitting new citizens'. Of the Thespians 700 had fallen at Thermopylae [7, 222], the Persians had burnt their town [c. 50], and we find afterwards that they were so reduced that they could not supply themselves with arms at Plataea [9, 30]: that they should enrol new citizens therefore when the troubles were over was natural; and Themistocles was so influential in Greece in the period immediately following, that his recommendation would be enough to obtain admission of his friend.

21. **ἔλεγε...τάδε**. The whole incident is graphically described in the Persae of Aeschylos, 351 sq. See Introduction.

24. **φρονέων τὰ βασιλέος** 'well disposed to the king's interests'. p. 18, l. 12. Notice the omission of the article with βασιλέος. The king of Persia is spoken of as βασιλεύς.

25. **κατύπερθε**, p. 30, l. 26.

27. **παρέχει** 'you have an opportunity', for this impersonal use see p. 5, l. 1.

1. **τὰ ὑμέτερα φρονέοντας.** See above p. 39, l. 25 and 7, 102 40 τὰ σὰ φρονέειν.

CHAPTER LXXVI.

4. **ἀπαλλάσσετο** 'departed', though the act. is used in p. 35, l. 17 in sense of 'came off'.

5, 7. **τοῦτο μὲν...τοῦτο δὲ** 'in the first place', 'in the second place', see on p. 30, l. 5.

7. **ἐπειδὴ ἐγίνοντο μέσαι νύκτες** 'towards midnight'. According to Aeschylos [Pers. 366] the orders were to do this εὖτ' ἂν φλέγων ἀκτῖσιν ἥλιος χθόνα λήξῃ. For **νύκτες** 'the night hours', cp. Arist. Nub. 2 τὸ χρῆμα τῶν νυκτῶν ὅσον ἀπέραντον. This particular phrase 'midnight' is always without the article, see Arist. Vesp. 218 ἀπὸ μέσων νυκτῶν γε παρακαλοῦσ' ἀεί.

8. **τὸ ἀπ' ἑσπέρης κέρας** 'the western or *right* wing'. The sense of ἀπὸ like that of ἐκ in p. 26, l. 22 is 'on the side of'.

9. **κυκλούμενοι** 'by way of encircling the Greeks or 'circling round towards Salamis', but Her. elsewhere always uses this word transitively, p. 6, l. 5; 3, 157. The Persian ships were stationed all along the Attic coast from Phalerum as well as on the S. coast of Salamis. This extreme left wing was now brought up the Saronic gulf so as to rest upon the east coast of Salamis, while, according to Aeschylos (Pers. 374), a detachment went to the west of the island to close up the passage between it and the Megarid, though Herod. does not mention this movement directly; the right wing was moved closer to the Peiraeus, and the islet (νησίς) of Psyttaleia, between Salamis and the mainland, was occupied by 4000 troops (Paus. 1, 36, 2; Persae 439).

10. **Κέον τε καὶ τὴν Κυνόσουραν.** Stein suggests that these names apply to the same place, see Hist. Index. For this use of τε...καί cp. p. 22, l. 20 Δωρικόν τε καὶ Μακεδνὸν ἔθνος.

13. **ἀνῆγον...ἵνα δὴ...ἐξῇ...δοῖεν.** For the change of mood see on p. 4, ll. 4 and 10.

14. **δοῦναι τίσιν** 'to give satisfaction', on the analogy of δίκην δοῦναι. Elsewhere τίσις is used in the sense of 'punishment inflicted': see 1, 86; 8, 106; or of 'revenge taken', 8, 105.

16—21. ὡς belongs to ἐνθαῦτα μάλιστα ἐξοισομένων 'on the ground that, whenever the sea fight did take place, the men and wrecks would be sure to be washed ashore there more than anywhere', p. 42, l. 21. The final clause after ἀπεβίβαζον is ἵνα... περιποιῶσι, and for the subj. mood used *dramatically* (that is, as representing the actual thoughts of the person concerned) after historic tense see G. § 216, 2.

For the meaning of ἐξοισομένων see p. 25, l. 10.

22. τῆς νυκτός 'that night', the gen. of time within which, p. 37, l. 25, G. § 179. οὐδὲν ἀποκοιμηθέντες 'without taking any interval of sleep'. The meaning of the compound ἀποκοιμᾶσθαι seems to be that of sleeping as a relief from other employments, 'to get a snatch of sleep', and thus to be naturally used of the sleep taken in the midst of military duties. See Arist. Vesp. 211, where the old man's servants have been keeping watch for Philocleon when besieged by his son ('as though he were the town of Skione'),—Sosias says, 'since we have driven this enemy away' τί οὐκ ἀπεκοιμήθημεν ὅσον ὅσον στίλην; 'why shouldn't we snatch just a wee drop of sleep?' Stein, however, regards ἀπό as intensive, 'without getting any sound sleep'. Polyb. 3, 79, 10 βραχὺ μέρος τῆς νυκτὸς ἀπεκοιμῶντο.

CHAPTER LXXVII.

1. καταβάλλειν 'to bring into contempt', used as the opp. of ἐξαίρειν 'to exalt' in 9, 79.

3. Ἀρτέμιδος...ἀκτήν. The coast of Salamis on which stood a temple of Artemis.

4. Κυνόσουραν p. 40, l. 10, 'dog's-tail', seems a common name for a peninsula. The particular place here meant is uncertain. See Index and Introduction.

5. λιπαράς 'shining' [lit. oily], either from the clearness of its air, of which the Athenians were proud [Eur. Med. 829 ἀεὶ διὰ λαμπροτάτου βαίνοντες ἁβρῶς αἰθέρος], or from its groves of olives; though Aristophanes [Ach. 637] said it was an epithet better suited to sardines,

εἰ δέ τις ὑμᾶς ὑποθωπεύσας λιπαρὰς καλέσειεν Ἀθήνας
εὕρετο πᾶν ἂν διὰ τὰς λιπαράς, ἀφύων τιμὴν περιάψας.

6. σβέσσει = σβέσει, a form rarely if ever found elsewhere; for meaning, see 5, 77 ἔσβεσαν ὕβριν. Κόρον 'Presumption' resulting

from over-great success or wealth. For the birth of κόρος from ὕβρις 'unchecked impulse', cp. Pind. Ol. 13, 13 ὕβριν κόρου μάτερα θρασύ μυθον.

7. **δοκεῦντ' ἀνὰ πάντα πιθέσθαι** 'expecting to be obeyed in everything', 'expecting to rule the world'. For **δοκεῦντα** see App. D. footnote (9).

9. **ἐλεύθερον ἦμαρ** 'the day of freedom,' sc. 'freedom', cp. Hom. Il. 22, 490 ἦμαρ ὀρφανικόν 'the day of orphanhood', = 'orphanhood'.

11—13. **ἐς τοιαῦτα...ἐνδέκομαι.** The syntax of this sentence is much dislocated, though the meaning is clear. The ἐς stands in the way as it did in p. 30, l. 3; and, if we understand ἐσβλέψας after ἐς τοιαῦτα [see l. 1], we are met with the difficulty of coupling two participles ἐσβλέψας and λέγοντι by the conjunction καί, which are in different cases and refer to different people. Of this latter anomaly however Abicht quotes another example in Herodotus (7, 9). All would be made easy by omitting ἐς; but if this is to stand we must understand ἐσβλέψας as above, and translate 'Looking at such facts and considering that Bakis speaks thus clearly I dare neither venture on an argument against oracles myself, nor can I admit any such from others'.

Or we might possibly combine ἐς τοιαῦτα with οὕτω ἐναργέως and translate 'Now against Bakis when he speaks in regard to such facts and so clearly I dare neither' etc.

The dative **Βάκιδι** depends upon the verbal subst. ἀντιλογίης, which is itself a partitive gen. for ἀντιλογίης τι, if indeed this latter particle has not dropped from the text; finally ἀντιλογίης is followed by a preposition περὶ χρησμῶν as though it were a verb: for which Stein compares 7, 237 κακολογίης...ξείνου πέρι.

CHAPTER LXXVIII.

15. **ὠθισμὸς λόγων** 'a sharp combat of words', cp. p. 32, l. 3. ὠθισμὸς (a pushing)='a hand to hand engagement', 'a personal encounter', see 9, 62.

16. **περικυκλέοντο** 'were actually engaged in surrounding them'. See p. 40, l. 9.

18. **κατὰ χώρην** 'unmoved', '*in statu quo*'.

CHAPTER LXXIX.

18. συνεστηκότων...τῶν στρατηγῶν 'while the generals were contending'. Cp. Thucyd. 1, 1, 1 τὸ ἄλλο Ἑλληνικὸν ὁρῶν συνιστάμενον πρὸς ἀλλήλους. Cf. Her. 7, 142 συνεστηκυῖαι γνῶμαι 'opposed', 1, 208 γνῶμαι μὲν αὗται συνέστασαν.

20. ἐξωστρακισμένος 'who had been banished by a sentence of ostracism' two years before; he was residing at Argos.

[The institution of ostracism is explained by Grote, *History of Greece* pt. II. ch. xxxii. It was peculiar to Athens and a few other states, though a somewhat similar process called *petalism* (from the votes being inscribed on leaves πέταλα) existed in Syracuse [Diod. 11, 87]. It was instituted by Cleisthenes as a means of preventing civil disturbances (στάσεις) from the excessive power of one man, or the keen rivalry of two statesmen. The Ecclesia was first asked without mention of names whether there was occasion for such a proceeding: if the answer was in the affirmative, the agora was arranged for the voting of the ten tribes, and the ostracism was inflicted upon a man on the condition (1) that 6000 in all voted, (2) that the majority of such named him. The votes were written on bits of earthenware or shells [ὄστρακα], hence the name. The sentence so passed consisted of an order to a man to reside for 10 years out of Attica; but it did not involve permanent loss of citizenship or any loss of property. The institution lasted until B.C. 420 when it seems to have been discredited by being employed against a mean person named Hyperbolos [Plut. Arist. 7; Nic. 11].

Ostracism prevailed also, it is said, in Argos, Miletos, and Megara. Some hold—against Plutarch—that 6000 votes were required against a man before he could be banished.

23. στὰς ἐπὶ τὸ συνέδριον 'appearing at the council', not entering it, in the sense of taking part in it, as the next word ἐξεκαλέετο shows. Cp. 3, 46 καταστάντες ἐπὶ τοὺς ἄρχοντας, 9, 5 ἀπικόμενος ἐπὶ τὴν βουλήν. According to Plutarch [Them. 12, 3] the last council was held in the tent of Themistokles.

25. ἐχθρὸν see Plut. Themist. 3 'Themistokles early took up a position of hostility to the leading men, and especially towards Aristides, whose political course was diametrically opposite to his own. Various motives are assigned to this enmity; but the fact is that the difference of their habits and character accounts for it. For Aristides was by nature gentle and high minded; his political conduct was never inspired by the desire of popularity, nor could he refrain from opposing Themistokles in the wild schemes to which for the sake of his own advancement he was continually inciting the people'.

ὑπό, cp. p. 1, l. 3. λήθην...ποιεύμενος 'forgetting', ἀπολανθανόμενος, cf. p. 39, l. 5 where θῶυμα ποιεύμενοι = θαυμάζοντες.

1. συμμῖξαι 'to communicate with him'. p. 29, l. 4; p. 34, l. 20.

5. καὶ δὴ καί 'and especially of course'. p. 26, l. 18.

7. ὅτι ἴσον...λέγειν 'that it matters nothing whether they talked much or little'.

9. αὐτόπτης 'an eye-witness'. Aristides had seen and understood the movement of the Persian ships as he was himself coming from Aegina.

CHAPTER LXXX.

16. ἐξ ἐμέο 'by my instigation'. ὅτε 'since'.

18. παραστήσασθαι 'to bring them over to our view'.

21. ὡς οὐ ποιεύντων 'from a belief that the Barbarians are not so acting', p. 47, l. 14.

23. δή 'of course'.

25. εἴ περ 'if, as is no doubt the case'.

CHAPTER LXXXI.

27. παρελθών 'having come before the council'.

1. στρατόπεδον 'fleet' p. 22, l. 2.

2. παραρτέεσθαι = παρασκευάζεσθαι (l. 17) 'to make the preparations for battle', 'to clear the decks for action'. One of these preparations appears to have been to unship if practicable the great sails, that the ships might be as light and convenient as possible. [Xen. Hell. 1, 1, 13.]

5. οὐκ ἐπείθοντο τὰ ἐξαγγελθέντα 'did not credit the news'. The natural construction of πείθεσθαι is (1) with the dat. whether of person or thing, or (2) with acc. of thing dat. of person ταῦτά σοι πείθομαι. But Herodotus has two varieties of construction besides the ordinary one (1) with gen. of person—πείθεσθαι ἐμέο 1, 126; cp. 5, 29, 33; (2) as here with a neuter accusative, cp. 2, 12 τὰ περὶ Αἴγυπτον ὧν καὶ τοῖσι λέγουσιν αὐτὰ πείθομαι.

CHAPTER LXXXII.

10. **ἐς τὸν τρίποδα.** That is on the tripod dedicated at Delphi from the spoils taken in the following year at the battle of Plataea. It stood on a stand made of three twisted serpents, the three heads affording places for the three legs of the tripod; which stand still exists at Constantinople, whither it was taken by the Emperor Constantine. The inscription was on the stand, not on the tripod, and can still be deciphered. See 9, 81; Thucyd. 1, 132.

12. **τῇ Δημνίῃ**, see p. 6, l. 28.

13. **ἐς τὰς ὀγδώκοντα καὶ τριηκοσίας.** See above p. 24, l. 26 where the total (a wrong one according to the items) is given as 378.

15. **κατέδεε** impersonal 'there were wanting two ships to complete the number'.

CHAPTER LXXXIII.

17. **παρεσκευάζοντο.** See on l. 2.

18. **ἠώς τε δὴ διέφαινε καὶ οἱ...ποιησάμενοι** 'and as soon as day began to break they (the commanders) summoned a meeting of the armed marines, and Themistokles made the best speech of all'. For τε...καὶ expressing simultaneousness see p. 3, l. 16. The plural ποιησάμενοι refers to all the commanders of whom Themistokles is one, and the construction, though halting, is intelligible: 'having assembled the men (they made speeches), Themistokles best of them all'. For a participle not followed by a verb see p. 23, l. 1. And for **ἐκ πάντων** cf. 1, 134 τιμῶσι δὲ ἐκ πάντων τοὺς ἄγχιστα ἑωυτῶν οἰκέοντας, 'especially'. Aeschylos also [Pers. 387] represents the start of the Greek fleet as being at daybreak.

20, 21. **τὰ δὲ ἔπεα—ἀντιτιθέμενα** 'and his expressions were all a contrasting of things base with things noble'.

21—3. **ὅσα δὲ...αἱρέεσθαι** 'and advised them, to use his own words (δή), in all that the nature and constitution of a man admitted of, to choose the nobler. The participle παραινέσας agreeing with Θεμιστοκλέης takes the place of a verb. For κατάστασις cp. 2, 173 οὕτω δὴ καὶ ἀνθρώπου κατάστασις. For δή introducing the words as the thought of another see p. 4, l. 12.

23. **καταπλέξας** 'having thus finished', a metaphor apparently from weaving, 'to wind up', cp. 4, 205 οὐκ εὖ τὴν ζόην κατέπλεξε.

So also διαπλέκειν, see 5, 92 διαπλέξαντος τὸν βίον εὖ. Pind. Nem. 7, 99 βίοτον ἁρμόσαις ἥβᾳ λιπαρῷ τε γήραϊ διαπλέκοις εὐδαίμον' ἐόντα.

25. **δή** 'accordingly'. **καί** 'and simultaneously', cp. p. 4, l. 12; p. 26, l. 7.

κατά 'in the matter of' p. 45, l. 15. See for the calling in the Aeakidae c. 64.

1. **ἐνθαῦτα** 'thereupon', **ἀνῆγον** 'began putting out to sea'. **44**

CHAPTER LXXXIV.

3. **ἀναγομένοισι** 'as they were in the act of leaving land'.

5. **ἐπὶ πρύμνην ἀνεκρούοντο** 'began to back water', the preposition is omitted in l. 16. **ἀνακρούεσθαι** 'to push oneself backwards', i.e. to row backward; cp. 6, 115 ἐξανακρουσάμενοι. **ὦκελλον** 'were *nearly* running aground'.

6. **ἐξαναχθείς** 'having got clear off shore'.

8. **οὕτω δή** 'it was in these circumstances', p. 3, l. 24. Aeschylos (*Pers.* 411) says that the enemy's ship thus attacked was a Phoenikian, and we see in the next chapter that the Athenians were opposed by the Phoenikians.

12. **λέγεται.** Notice the double construction after this word, first an indirect clause introduced by ὡς, and then an ordinary acc. and infin. φανεῖσαν διακελεύσασθαι. This is another instance of idiomatic variety in two clauses essentially coordinate.

13. **διακελεύσασθαι...ὀνειδίσασαν** 'encouraged them to go on after first uttering the following taunt', cp. 9, 5 διακελευσαμένη γυνὴ γυναικί.

14. **στρατόπεδον** 'fleet', p. 2, l. 2.

15. **ὦ δαιμόνιοι.** This form of address seems to be meant to express surprise and some angry contempt, see 7, 48: but like other kindred expressions its meaning would doubtless be modified by the tone in which it was uttered.

μέχρι κόσου 'how far?', or 'how long?', see p. 2, l. 13.

CHAPTER LXXXV.

16. **κατά** 'opposite', see 9, 46 etc. **ἐτετάχατο**, App. D. II. a.

18. **τὸ πρὸς Ἐλευσῖνος...κέρας** 'the wing towards Eleusis and the west', p. 45, l. 23. There does not seem however any appreciable difference between the meaning of πρὸς with the gen. here and

with the accus. in l. 19, 20. The same variation occurs elsewhere, see 4, 37 τὸ πρὸς Ἑσπέρης...τὰ πρὸς Βορέην. See the remark on l. 12, and cp. ἐπί used with gen. and acc. in 9, 47. See above, p. 33, l. 19. Stein observes that ἑσπέρη and ἠώς here stand for North-West and South-East.

20. ἠθελοκάκεον, p. 12, l. 11.
22. συχνῶν οὐνόματα 'the names of several', i.e. Ionians.
27. ἐτυράννευσε 'became absolute ruler of'.

45 1. καταστησάντων τῶν Περσέων 'on the appointment of the Persians'. In B.C. 492 Mardonios had been sent down to Asia Minor by Darius to supersede Artaphernes, and with instructions to put down the *tyranni* in the Ionian towns, which seems to have been a measure intended to conciliate Hellenic feeling to the Persian over-lordship [Her. 6, 43]. But such a measure was much at variance with the interests of the Persians and was not likely to have been long maintained, and indeed Herodotos indicates that it would seem incredible in his day.

2. εὐεργέτης...πολλή 'was entered in the records as a "benefactor" of the king and a large quantity of land was given him'. The custom of keeping a record of such as had done good service to the king is referred to in Esther c. vi. 'On that night could not the king sleep, and he commanded to bring the book of records of the chronicles; and they were read before the king. And it was found written, that Mordecai had told of Bigthana and Teresh...who sought to lay hold on the king Ahasuerus'. The word εὐεργέτης by which Herodotus here translates the Persian title was well known in Greek polity, and was bestowed by states on leading men in other states in return for good services received. See Thucyd. 1, 129, 2 where Xerxes tells Themistokles κεῖταί σοι εὐεργεσία ἐν τῷ ἡμετέρῳ οἴκῳ εἰσαεὶ ἀνάγραπτος. Cp. id. 1, 137, 7. And for the practice among the Greeks of giving this title accompanied by fixed privileges see Xen. Vect. 3, 11; Demosth. Lept. 466; Fals. Leg. 446. Sometimes the title and certain privileges were given to all the citizens of a state, as to the Syracusans by the people of Antandros [Xen. Hell. 1, 1, 26].

3. ὀροσάγγαι. 'This word is interpreted by Photios and Hesychios as σωματοφύλακες βασιλέως "body-guards of the king", and in this sense is used by Sophocles fr. 185'. Stein. Persian scholars seem divided as to its derivation.

CHAPTER LXXXVI.

6. **ἐκεραΐζετο** 'were entirely demolished', used here and in c. 91 to indicate the breaking up of the ships by the charges of the enemy. Elsewhere Herodotos uses it of plundering a town or destroying persons or things, 1, 88 κ. ἄστυ. 7, 125 οἱ λέοντες τὰς καμήλους ἐκεράϊζον μούνας. [It is from the Rt. κερ, from which we have had κείρω p. 32, l. 15.]

7. **ἅτε**, p. 38, l. 26.

8. **κατὰ τάξιν** 'in regular order of naval war'. Cobet would omit these words as being merely equivalent to σὺν κόσμῳ. But the two clauses balance; σὺν κόσμῳ is opposite to οὐ τεταγμένων, κατὰ τάξιν to οὔτε σὺν νόῳ.

10. **ἔμελλε.** p. 2, l. 3.

11. **ἦσάν γε καὶ ἐγένοντο,** 'were and showed themselves to be'.

12. **ἀμείνονες ἑωυτῶν ἤ** 'their valour was even greater than at Euboea', i.e. at Artemisium. The phrase ἀμείνονες ἑωυτῶν is regarded as making one comparative adjective. Cp. 2, 25 ὁ Νεῖλος ἑωυτοῦ ῥέει πολλῷ ὑποδεέστερος ἢ τοῦ θέρεος.

πᾶς τις προθυμεόμενος. For the singular participle clause after plural verb cp. the construction of *quisque*: and for the converse see p. 43, l. 9.

13. **δειμαίνων Ξέρξην.** Cp. p. 8, l. 15. For ἐδόκεε τε following participial clause cp. p. 75, l. 11.

CHAPTER LXXXVII.

15. **κατά** 'in regard to', p. 43, l. 25.
16. **μετεξετέρους.** See on p. 5, l. 8.
18. **μᾶλλον ἔτι.** p. 36, l. 20.
23. **πρὸς τῶν πολεμίων** 'on the side nearest the enemy'. See p. 44, l. 18; p. 66, l. 16.
25. **συνήνεικε** 'turned out successful'. Cp. 9, 37 οὐ μέντοι ἔς γε τέλος οἱ συνήνεικε τὸ ἔχθος τὸ ἐς Λακεδαιμονίους.
26. **φέρουσα** 'full tilt', cp. Æschin. in Ctes. § 82 εἰς τοῦτο φέρων περιέστησε τὰ πράγματα 'in his violent haste'.
29. **ἔτι...ἰόντων** 'while they (Artemisia and the king) were in the vicinity of the Hellespont'. περί with acc. cp. p. 15, l. 19.

1. **ἐκ προνοίης** 'on purpose', 'of malice aforethought', opposed to κατὰ τύχην, cp. 3, 121.

8. αὐτοῖσι, sc. the Greeks, as is implied by the subject τριήραρχος, a Greek trierarch. This pursuing trierarch is said in c. 93 to have been Ameinias of Pallene.

9. πρὸς ἄλλας ἐτράπετο 'turned his attention to attacking other ships'. p. 10, l. 22.

CHAPTER LXXXVIII.

9, 10. τοῦτο μὲν...τοῦτο δὲ 'in the first place'...'in the second place', p. 40, l. 6.

συνήνεικε 'happened fortunately', p. 45, l. 25.

13, 14. θηεύμενον 'surveying the battle'. See p. 47, l. 28 sq.
καὶ δὴ 'and thereupon'.

17, 18. φάναι 'said yes'. τὸ ἐπίσημον 'her ensign', that is the design on her ship's prow. Such a design is mentioned in 3, 59 where certain ships are said to have had the figure of wild boars on their prows. The position of this figurehead would make it plain to a spectator from shore, but it would not be seen by the Athenian captain pursuing.

19. ἠπιστέατο 'they believed', p. 3, l. 21.

21. καὶ τὸ...κατήγορον γενέσθαι 'and the fact that no one was saved from the Calyndian vessel to be her accuser'.

CHAPTER LXXXIX.

26. πόνῳ 'engagement'.

26—8. ἀπὸ μὲν ἔθανε...ἀπὸ δὲ sc. ἔθανον, cp. p. 17, l. 24; p. 34, l. 23.

2. καὶ μὴ ἐν χειρῶν νόμῳ ἀπολλύμενοι 'and if they did not perish in actual fighting'. Cf. 9, 48 ἐς χειρῶν νόμον ἀπικέσθαι. For μὴ with participle in conditional sense cp. 7, 101 οὐκ ἀξιόμαχοί εἰσι ἐμὲ ἐπιόντα προσμεῖναι μὴ ἐόντες ἄρθμιοι.

3. διένεον, see on p. 5, l. 3, 4.

6. ἐνθαῦτα 'it was at that point'.

CHAPTER XC.

12. διεφθάρατο App. D. II. (a).

14. ὡς προδόντων 'on the ground that they (the Ionians) had played traitors'. For the change of case cp. p. 36, l. 16.

18. κατεδύετο 'became water-logged'. That this does not mean entirely sunk is shown by the passage immediately following, and by

Thucyd. 1, 50, 1 οἱ Κορίνθιοι τὰ σκάφη οὐχ εἷλκον ἀναδούμενοι τῶν νεῶν ἃς καταδύσειαν, πρὸς δὲ τοὺς ἀνθρώπους φονεύειν ἐτράποντο, 'The Corinthians did not set to work to tow off the hulls of such vessels as they had disabled (water-logged), but turned to slaughtering the men'.

19. ἐπιφερομένη 'charging'. See on p. 31, l. 2.

23. ἐρρύσατο sufficed to save the Ionians from the danger in which they stood from the accusation of the Phoenikians.

28. ἵνα...διαβάλλωσι dramatic subj. after a past tense in the main clause, 'that they may not (he said) after playing the coward themselves slander men better than themselves'. See p. 40, l. 17.

2. κατήμενος ὑπὸ τῷ οὔρεϊ 'sitting under the crest of the hill opposite Salamis which is called Aegaleos'. Rawlinson from a personal survey believes that he discovered the exact position of Xerxes' seat on a small eminence beneath the N.W. extremity of Aegaleos (*Scaramagna*), which commands a view of the narrowest part of the bay. Aeschylos (Persae 464) says that Xerxes was 'on a high hill near the beach, which commanded a view of the whole fleet'. And Plutarch (Them. 13) describes it as being 'above the Heracleum, where the channel is narrowest'.

3. ἀνεπυνθάνετο 'he always asked the name of the man who did it'.

4. ἀνέγραφον 'entered it in the book'. See on p. 45, l. 2. And for the γραμματισταί 'king's secretaries' thus accompanying the king, see the account of the review of the army at the mouth of the Strymon, 7, 100, διεξελαύνων ἐπὶ ἅρματος παρὰ ἔθνος ἓν ἕκαστον ἐπυνθάνετο, καὶ ἀπέγραφον οἱ γραμματισταί.

πατρόθεν 'with the name of his father'. Cp. Xen. Oecon. 7, 3 ὀνομάζοντές με Ἰσχόμαχον πατρόθεν προσκαλοῦνται.

5, 6. πρὸς δέ τι καὶ προσεβάλετο...πάθεος 'and what contributed also something to the punishment of the Phoenikians was the fact that Ariaramnes a Persian was there who was on friendly terms with the Ionians'. Cp. Thucyd. 3, 36, 1 καὶ πρὸς ξυνεβάλετο οὐκ ἐλάχιστον τῆς ὁρμῆς αἱ Πελοποννησίων νῆες ἐς Ἰωνίαν ἐκείνοις βοηθοὶ τολμήσασαι παρακινδυνεῦσαι 'And what contributed more than anything to their passionate determination was the fact that the Peloponnesian ships had ventured boldly into Ionia to assist these men'.

CHAPTER XCI.

10. ὑποστάντες 'having thrown themselves in their way'. The Aeginetan ships were in the position of a reserve; but there is no need to translate here 'laid in wait for them', as if they had intentionally concealed themselves.

ἐν τῷ πορθμῷ seems to mean the narrowest point, that namely, between Psyttaleia and the Attic coast which is less than 4000 feet. Plut. Arist. c. 9.

12. ἐκεράϊζον 'kept destroying', see p. 45, l. 6.

14. ὅκως 'whenever', with optative of indefinite repetition, cp. p. 26, l. 11; 6, 31 ὅκως δὲ λάβοι. 6, 61 ὅκως δὲ ἐνείκειε. G. § 213, 3.

15. φερόμενοι ἐσέπιπτον 'as they were running at full speed they fell in with the Aeginetans'. Notice the masculine participle referring to the crews instead of the ships. p. 45, l. 26. For the meaning of φερόμενος indicating rapidity, cf. Aesch. in Ctes. 89 πάλιν ἧκε φερόμενος εἰς τὴν ἑαυτοῦ φύσιν. For ἐσέπιπτον cp. 7, 210.

CHAPTER XCII.

16. συνεκύρεον 'came alongside each other'.

18. ᾗ περ εἷλε, see 7, 179—181. Biogr. Ind. s. v. *Pytheas.*

20. κατακοπέντα 'cut to pieces'. He fought so determinedly that he was 'almost hacked to pieces' (κατεκρεουργήθη ἅπας, 7, 181), and yet was not killed.

22. τὸν δή...Σιδωνίη 'and it was with this man still on board that the Sidonian vessel was captured'.

23. σωθῆναι ἐς 'escaped to Aegina', 'got safe back to' p. 65, l. 20.

25. τὸν...μηδισμόν 'he shouted out to Themistokles in taunting terms as to the charge of medizing which had been brought against the Aeginetans'. In B.C. 491 the Aeginetans had been charged with medizing because of their having given earth and water to the king, and Krios, father of this Polykritos, had been one of the persons in Aegina who had put himself forward to resist the consequent demand of hostages by Kleomenes. See 6, 50, 73. Polykritos now asks Themistokles ironically whether he thinks the Aeginetans still medize?

1. ἀπέρριψε 'threw out tauntingly', cp. 6, 69 ἐκεῖνος τοῦτο ἀπέρριψε τὸ ἔπος. 1, 153; 7, 13.

3. ὑπὸ τὸν πεζὸν στρατόν 'under cover of the land force', cp.

9, 96 ἐς τὴν ἤπειρον ἀπέπλεον ὅκως ἔωσι ὑπὸ τὸν πεζὸν στρατὸν τὸν σφέτερον ἐόντα ἐν τῇ Μυκάλῃ.

CHAPTER XCIII.

4. ἤκουσαν...ἄριστα 'gained the best renown', cp. 6, 86; 9, 79.
5. ἐπὶ δὲ 'but next to them'.
8. ὃς καὶ...ἐπεδίωξε 'who, among other things, was the man who chased Artemisia', p. 45, l. 21. In mentioning the high credit gained by these men Herodotos cannot be referring to the formal ἀριστεία, which was a subject of vote afterwards, see c. 123. Yet Diodorus (11, 27) says that it was assigned to Ameinias.
10. ἢ καί. The second of two alternative or conditional clauses is frequently accompanied by καί. See p. 27, l. 18; p. 53, l. 17; 1, 19; 3, 33; 9, 5 etc.
11. πρὸς δὲ 'and besides', p. 16, l. 8; p. 48, l. 5.
12. ἐκέετο 'was publicly offered'. μύριαι δραχμαί about £400.
13. δεινήν...ἐποιεῦντο 'they were indignant', p. 8, l. 13.
14. δή sums up and dismisses the subject, cp. on 6, 52.

CHAPTER XCIV.

18. αὐτίκα κατ' ἀρχάς 'at the very beginning of the battle'.
19. τὰ ἱστία δειράμενον 'having spread his sails'. The sails were furled for action, during which only the oars would be used; in fact the greater sails were if possible put ashore. See 6, 13.
22. τῆς Σαλαμινίης sc. γῆς, topographical genitive 'in Salamis', p. 7, l. 20; p. 20, l. 27. γίνεσθαι see note p. 50, l. 2.
24. θείῃ πομπῇ 'by the guidance of Providence'.
τὸν relative. οὔτε...οὔτε These negatives are used instead of the simple οὐ to mark the logical antithesis between the sender and the recipient, and yet the clauses are not grammatically co-ordinate. The first οὔτε qualifies strictly φανῆναι, the second belongs to εἰδόσι 'but there was no appearance of anyone having sent it, nor were the Korinthians to whom it came acquainted at all with what had happened to those actually engaged'. τῶν ἀπὸ τῆς στρατιῆς 'of the state of affairs *in* the army',—a common way to speak of something distant, *from* which news must come to the speaker, cf. Aeschyl. Agam. 521 κῆρυξ Ἀχαιῶν, χαῖρε, τῶν ἀπὸ στρατοῦ. Eur. I. T. 540 τίς εἶ ποθ'; ὡς εὖ πυνθάνει τἀφ' Ἑλλάδος.

50 2. ὡς...γενέσθαι 'for when it got near'. The infinitive is often kept even in subordinate clauses of *oratio obliqua*. So above p. 49, l. 22: cp. 9, 41. See Clyde § 97. It is not confined to conjunctions of time or relative pronouns. In 9, 41 it is used after ἔνθα, in Thucyd. 4, 98, 4 after εἰ, and in Xen. Cyrop. 1, 6, 18 after ὅτι. See also Thucyd. 1, 92, 5; and note on Aeschines in Ctes. § 96. Goodwin *M. and T.* § 92, 2 note 3.

3. τοὺς ἀπὸ 'those on board the boat', see p. 49 l. 24.

5. καὶ δή 'already'. Cp. 9, 6 καὶ δὴ ἐν Βοιωτίῃ ἐλέγετο εἶναι.

7. τάδε 'as follows'.

8—9. ὡς αὐτοί...οἱ Ἕλληνες 'that the Korinthians might take them (the speakers) as hostages and put them to death if the Greeks should not turn out to be in the midst of victory'. For ἄγεσθαι in this sense see 6, 73, 85.

9. ἢν μή...φαίνωνται. A subjunctive clause is dramatically used instead of the optative in *oratio obliqua*, as being the very words employed by the speakers οἷοί τε εἶμεν...ἢν μὴ φαίνωνται.

οὕτω δή 'it was in these circumstances', i.e. after hearing these words. See on 6, 36.

11. ἐπ' ἐξεργασμένοισι 'when all was over', i.e. when the battle was finished. Cp. 9, 77 αὐτίκα μετὰ ταῦτα ἀπίκοντο Μαντινέες ἐπ' ἐξεργασμένοισι.

τούτους...φάτις ἔχει 'are credited with conduct of this kind', cp. the converse phrase with a similar meaning 9, 84 ἔχει τινὰ φάτιν ...ἀνὴρ Ἐφέσιος θάψαι Μαρδόνιον 'is credited by some'. Thus λόγος ἔχει τινὰ or ἔχει τις λόγον, and αἰτίη τινὰ ἔχει, or αἰτίην ἔχει τις in the same chapter 5, 70.

15. μαρτυρέει...Ἑλλάς. The epigram of Simonides is quoted in all editions in illustration of this statement (fr. 100):

ὦ ξεῖν' εὔυδρόν ποτ' ἐναίομεν ἄστυ Κορίνθου·
νῦν δ' ἅμμ' Αἴαντος νᾶσος ἔχει Σαλαμίς·
ῥεῖα δὲ φοινίσσας νῆας καὶ Πέρσας ἑλόντες
καὶ Μήδους ἱερὰν Ἑλλάδα ῥυσάμεθα.

And also an epitaph of the same poet (fr. 103) on Adeimantos:

οὗτος Ἀδειμάντου κείνου τάφος, οὗ διὰ βουλὰς
Ἑλλὰς ἐλευθερίας ἀμφέθετο στέφανον.

The enmity between Athens and Korinth which existed from B.C. 460 to the outbreak of the Peloponnesian war, and the efforts made by the Korinthians to form a counterpoise to the growing naval power of Athens by an alliance with Epidauros, would account for the attempt on the part of Athenian patriots to decry the services of the Korinthians at the time of the Persian invasion, and would explain the ease with which anything to their discredit would be believed at Athens and communicated to Herodotos. [Thucyd. 1, 103—106.] Adeimantos is represented throughout as backward in the war, and as hostile to Themistokles, cf. 5, 59, 61. Plutarch accuses Herodotos of being influenced by a bribe from Athens; and Dion Chrysostom has a story that he asked for pay at Korinth and was refused.

CHAPTER XCV.

17. τοῦ καὶ...ἐπεμνήσθην, see c. 79. ὡς ἀνδρὸς ἀρίστου 'as a man of the highest character', including of course 'courage'; but Herodotos had no occasion in the previous mention of him to say anything of his prowess in the fight.

18. θορύβῳ, p. 47, l. 11.

20. παρατετάχατο, App. D. II. a. They had been stationed on board ships along the coast of Psyttaleia to prevent the Persian troops there [c. 76] from giving help to their comrades in difficulties. Aesch. Pers. 454.

22. ἀπέβησε ἄγων 'took them with him and disembarked them'.

23. τῇ νησῖδι: See p. 40, l. 5.

CHAPTER XCVI.

25. κατειρύσαντες 'having dragged on shore'.

27. ταύτῃ 'in that direction', 'in that part of the bay'; for many of the ships were wrecked while trying to escape along the Attic coast towards Phalerum; and many more were drifted away by the W. wind mentioned in the next sentence.

3. τῆς Ἀττικῆς the topographical genitive, see p. 49, l. 22.   51

4. Κωλιάδα the Kolian beach was 20 stades (about 2¼ miles) from Phalerum. Pausan. 1, 1, 5. Col. Leake identified it with the point called now the 'Three towers' (τρεῖς πύργοι) and Stein accepts this without comment; but recent authorities have decided upon a point more S.E. *Cape St Kosmas.*

9. Λυσιστράτῳ dat. of agent after perfect pass. so Βάκιδι and Μουσαίῳ above. G. § 188. p. 62, l. 16.

11. φρύξουσι 'shall roast', the women are to use the driftwood from the wrecks, oars, spars and other fragments for firewood. The MSS. have φρίξουσι 'shall shudder at'; and some have explained that there is an intentional ambiguity between the two words. The simple meaning is quite forcible enough.

12. ἀπελάσαντος βασιλέος 'after the king had marched away', i.e. when the inhabitants returned in the autumn of 480 after the Persian army had evacuated Attica.

ἔμελλε ἔσεσθαι 'was destined to be'. Cp. p. 2, l. 2.

CHAPTER XCVII.

14—17. μὴ ὑπόθηται...κινδυνεύσῃ. For the subjunctive in a clause depending on a verb in a secondary tense (δείσας...ἐβούλευε) see Goodw. *M. and T.* p. 80, 1. Cp. on p. 4, l. 10; p. 40, l. 17.

17. κινδυνεύσῃ 'lest he should be in danger'. For the change of subject of two verbs grammatically co-ordinate, see 6, 30. ἐβούλευε 'he began to think over'.

19. ἐπειρᾶτο 'he pretended to be proceeding with his attempt', 'he went on with it'.

20. διαχοῦν 'to make a causeway across'. This distance was nearly a mile at the narrowest part, where a service of ferry boats was afterwards established under strict supervision. See Aesch. in Ctes. § 158. The object of the causeway would be to enable the Persian land army to cross to Salamis and take the Athenian refugees prisoners, without fear of the terrible fleet by which theirs had just been conquered. Rawlinson notices that Alexander took the Island of Tyre by a similar construction, but there the distance was only half and the depth of water much less. Ktesias (Pers. 26) and Strabo (9, 1, 13) assign the formation of this plan and the beginning of the embankment to a period before the battle, as the various editors point out; but the words of Herodotos do not preclude this,—nay rather confirm it; the imperfect ἐπειρᾶτο means 'he went on trying', as though nothing had happened.

γαύλους of Phœnikian transport vessels see 3, 136; 6, 17. The line of ships lashed together was independent of the χοῦς and meant to protect the men working at it, as well as to give a passage to men crossing; and this may very well have been begun after the battle.

21. ἀρτέετο, cp. 5, 120 οἱ δὲ αὖτις πολεμέειν ἀρτέοντο.

23. εὖ ἠπιστέατο 'were fully persuaded'. See p. 3, l. 21.

24. ὡς...παρεσκεύασται 'that he was fully determined and prepared'. The perfect is used dramatically for the pluperfect. Xerxes would have said παρεσκεύασμαι. For the future infinitive after a verb expressing intention, cp. the construction of μέλλω, p. 79, l. 12. ἐκ παντὸς νόου 'in real earnest'.

26. ἔμπειρον...διανοίης 'acquainted with his character'. διανοία opp. to the παιδεία and λόγος of a statesman in Aesch. in Ctes. § 170.

ἅμα...καὶ, cp. 4, 150 ἅμα τε ἔλεγε ταῦτα καὶ ἐδείκνυε ἐς τὸν Βάττον: and 3, 65; 4, 67. (Abicht.)

27. ἔπεμπε ἐς Πέρσας i.e. to Susa, see p. 27, l. 12.

CHAPTER XCVIII.

2. ὅ τι παραγίνεται 'which arrives at the destination', so 6, 95 52 παρεγίνοντο δὲ καὶ αἱ ἱππαγωγοὶ νέες.

θνητὸν ἐὸν 'I mean anything less than divine'. Herodotos uses θνητὸν as equivalent to ζῶον in 2, 68 πάντων τῶν ἴδμεν θνητῶν τοῦτο ἐξ ἐλαχίστου μέγιστον γίνεται (of the crocodile); 1, 216 πάντων τῶν θνητῶν τὸ τάχιστον (the horse). And Xenophon (Cyrop. 8, 6, 18) says of these ἀγγαρήϊοι that some people declared that they went faster than cranes, but that at any rate they went faster than anything human on land (ἀνθρωπίνων πεζῇ). οὕτω without conjunction, see 6, 15, 21.

3. ὅσων...ὁδός that is, as Xenophon explains, a day's journey of a horse. The American pony posts are made with shorter relays.

5. διεστᾶσι 'are posted at intervals'.

7. μὴ οὐ generally after a verb containing a negative idea, which is itself negatived, cp. 6, 88; 9, 18; G. § 283, 6—7 and § 263 note, cp. p. 28, l. 20; but also following any negatived verb, see p. 69, l. 7. τὸν προκείμενον 'the distance allotted to him'.

10. τὸ δὲ ἐνθεῦτεν 'and thenceforth', cp. 9, 11.

11. κατά περ...λαμπαδηφορίη. On the torch races see note on 6, 105, where they are mentioned as being used in the worship of Pan. Of the two kinds of torch racing the Persian courier-post is comparable to that in which the contest was between two or more lines of men stationed at intervals, each man carrying the

torch to the man in front of him,—and especially to those races which, as was sometimes the case, were run on horseback.

13. ἀγγαρήϊον n. 'an express'. Rawlinson mentions two derivations of the word,—angáreh 'an account book', and so 'registered'; and harkáreh 'a common drudge' or 'workman'. The verb ἀγγαρεύειν 'to requisition' is well-known from its use in St Matt. 5, 41; 27, 32 etc., cp. Esther 8, 10 'he...sent letters by posts on horseback.'

CHAPTER XCIX.

15. οὕτω δή τι. The δή has a certain sense of irony, 'to such a strange degree!', as though Herodotos were thinking of the groundlessness of their rejoicing.

16. ὡς for ὥστε.

μυρσίνῃσι...ἱστόρεσαν. For this custom of expressing gladness in connexion with religious rites see 7, 54. The scene on the entry of our Lord into Jerusalem will of course occur to our minds.

17. ἐθυμίων θυμιήματα 'and were burning incense'. θυμιᾶν here has a cognate accusative. It is used with other words which indicate something used in the same way as incense. See 3, 107; 4, 75; 6, 97.

καὶ αὐτοί...εὐπαθείῃσι 'and were universally engaging in sacrifices and feastings'. The αὐτοί emphasises the distinction between the people at large and the special class who would conduct the religious services. For ἐν θυσίῃσι κ.τ.λ. cp. 3, 27 ἦσαν ἐν θαλίῃσι. 1, 24 ἰδὼν...τοὺς ἀνθρώπους ἐν εὐπαθείῃσι ἐόντας.

19. ἐπεξελθοῦσα 'which arrived on the heels of the first'.

συνέχεε οὕτω 'threw them into such consternation'. Cp. 7, 142 συνεχέοντο αἱ γνῶμαι τῶν φαμένων. It is more common in poetry.

τοὺς κιθῶνας κατερρήξαντο. This sign of mourning, rendered familiar to us by the writers of the Old and New Testament, was common to all Eastern peoples. Thus Aeschylos describes Xerxes as watching the fight at Salamis,—ῥήξας δὲ πέπλους κἀνακωκύσας λιγύ (Pers. 470). Herodotos uses a very strong expression 'they tore their inner garments to pieces'. Cp. 3, 66 πάντες τὰ ἐσθῆτος ἐχόμενα εἶχον, ταῦτα κατηρείκοντο.

21. Μαρδόνιον ἐν αἰτίῃ τιθέντες 'laying the blame on Mardonius'. So αἰτίη is said ἔχειν τινα (5, 70). Cp. 5, 106 ὅρα μὴ ἐξ ὑστέρης σεωυτὸν ἐν αἰτίῃ σχῇς.

CHAPTER C.

1. **συμφορήν...ποιεύμενον** 'much distressed in consequence of the sea-fight'. Cp. 9, 77.

3—5. **ὡς δώσει...καὶ οἱ κρέσσον εἴη.** The future indicative is used in preference to the future optative, but in the second clause the ordinary optative of the *oratio obliqua* is used. The change of mood is perhaps only another instance of the taste for variety evidenced in the use of subj. and optative in final clauses [see on 9, 51]. But notice that here and at p. 56, l. 24—5, as well as in 9, 69 (ἀγγέλλεται...ὅτι μάχη τε γέγονε καὶ νικῷεν οἱ μετὰ Παυσανίεω) the *time* of the action is different. In p. 61, l. 3 the infinitive is used by a similar variation, and in ll. 4 and 5 of the same page the indicative and optative. Abicht says that the optative 'gives the thought a more subjective colouring'; but in the instances before us, as in p. 56, l. 24, the reverse seems to be the case.

4. **ἀναγνώσας** 'for having overpersuaded', p. 28, l. 23; p. 80, l. 12: referring to his speech given in 8, 9.

5. **ἀνακινδυνεῦσαι** 'to stake everything again on the risk', see p. 35, l. 14; 9, 26. ἀνακινδυνεύειν is constructed with a participle in 9, 26, 41; but κινδυνεύειν is followed by an infinitive in p. 51, l. 17; p. 33, l. 7. See note on 6, 9. Cp. the double construction of πειρᾶσθαι.

7. **ὑπὲρ μεγάλων αἰωρηθέντα** 'having played for high stakes', 'endangered himself for great objects'. Cp. Thucyd. 7, 77, 2 ἐν τῷ αὐτῷ κινδύνῳ τοῖς φαυλοτάτοις αἰωροῦμαι.

πλέον...ἔφερε 'his opinion inclined more to'. Cp. 5, 118 τούτου τοῦ ἀνδρὸς ἡ γνώμη ἔφερε...συμβάλλειν. 6, 110 τῶν ἡ γνώμη ἔφερε συμβάλλειν.

9. **προσέφερε** 'he propounded the following proposal'. Cp. 5, 40 προσέφερον αὐτῷ τάδε. Cp. 3, 74, 134; 5, 30.

12. **ὁ τὸ πᾶν φέρων** 'the decisive contest'. Cp. p. 31, l. 15 τὸ πᾶν τοῦ πολέμου.

15. **πειρήσεται ἀντιωθῆναι** 'will make the experiment of facing you'. πειρᾶσθαι is constructed by Herodotos both with participle and infinitive: with the former it generally refers to an attempt actually made, see 6, 5, 50; 9, 26, 53; with the latter to a future possibility, cp. 6, 138. Yet in 6, 9 τοὺς ἑωυτοῦ ἕκαστος ὑμέων

πολιήτας πειράσθω ἀποσχίζων ἀπὸ τοῦ λοιποῦ συμμαχικοῦ this distinction appears to be neglected. There is the same indefiniteness in our use of 'to try'. The two phrases 'I will try swimming', and, 'I will try to swim', may sometimes approach each other so nearly as to be hardly distinguishable.

17. νυν 'then', 'accordingly'.

πειρώμεθα τῆς Πελοποννήσου 'let us make an attempt on'. In this sense πειρᾶν is used in 6, 82. The middle is elsewhere used with persons. See 1, 76; 2, 163; 7, 125; 9, 46.

18. εἰ δὲ καὶ 'and if also on the other hand'. For this use of καί with an alternative clause cp. p. 49, l. 10; 9, 91 εἴρετο εἴτε κληδόνος ἕνεκεν...εἴτε καὶ κατὰ συντυχίην...

παρέχει impersonal = πάρεστι, cp. p. 5, l. 1; p. 16, l. 18.

20. Ἕλλησι...δούλους 'for the Greeks there can be no escape from becoming your slaves, after having given account for what they have done now and on former occasions'. οὐδεμία ἔκδυσις......μὴ οὐ...εἶναι. After an expression implying difficulty or impossibility μὴ οὐ is pretty frequently found with the infinitive, and οὐδεμία ἔκδυσις = ἀδύνατόν ἐστιν ἐκδῦναι. Cp. 1, 187 δεινὸν ἐδόκεε εἶναι μὴ οὐ συσπουδάζειν. 3, 82 Δήμου ἄρχοντος ἀδύνατα μὴ οὐ κακότητα ἐγγίνεσθαι. The accusative δόντας, in spite of the dative Ἕλλησι, arises from the influence of the infinitive, by an attraction fairly common in Greek writers; cp. p. 60, l. 22. τῶν is attracted into the case of an antecedent unexpressed, for ἐκείνων ἅ.

21. πρότερον. Though the reference is to the Peloponnesians primarily, yet we may understand various events in previous Persian expeditions, such as the battle of Marathon, to be included. But the special reference is rather to the treatment of the Persian envoys at Sparta (7, 133).

22. εἰ δ' ἄρα *quodsi forte*, see p. 59, l. 28.

24. καὶ ἐκ τῶνδε 'in this case also', 'in these circumstances'. Cp. Dem. de Cor. § 256 ἐκ τῶν ἐνόντων 'in the existing circumstances'. p. 26, l. 22.

25. καταγελάστους sc. by causing them to give up the attempt to subjugate Greece.

26. ἐν τοῖσι Πέρσῃσι 'as far as the Persians are concerned'.

οὐδὲν...πρηγμάτων 'it is not by the fault of the Persians that any of your affairs have been brought to confusion'. There is a parallel use of ἐν in Eurip. Hippol. 324 ἐν σοὶ λελείψομαι 'it will be your fault if I fail'. Soph. Aj. 510 ἐν σοὶ πᾶσ' ἔγωγε σώζομαι 'my salvation depends wholly on you'.

27. ὅκου 'in what respect', 'at what point'.

28. Φοίνικες...Αἰγύπτιοι...Κύπριοι...Κίλικες without definite article, 'mere Phoenikians, Egyptians etc.' Cp. 9, 28 Ἀθηναίους ἀξιονικωτέρους εἶναι ἔχειν τὸ κέρας ἤπερ Ἀρκάδας.

30. τοῦτο τὸ πάθος 'this defeat', p. 51, l. 13. So τὸ τρῶμα 6, 132. ἤδη ὦν introduces a necessary consequence of what has been said before, as in 6, 53.

1. ἤθεα 'home'. Cp. 1, 15, 157; 4, 80; 5, 14.

2. ἐμὲ δὲ emphatic and opp. to σὺ μέν, 'but on me should fall the duty'.

CHAPTER CI.

5. ὡς ἐκ κακῶν a joy great in proportion to the distress which it followed, lit. 'considering that it was after misery'. Cp. Thucyd. 7, 42, 2 τῷ δὲ προτέρῳ στρατεύματι τῶν Ἀθηναίων, ὡς ἐκ κακῶν, ῥώμη τις ἐγεγένητο. ἐκ 'after', cp. Eurip. Hipp. 109 ἐκ κυναγίας 'after hunting'.

6. βουλευσάμενος goes with ὑποκρινέεσθαι 'he said that he would answer, after consideration, which of these two courses he would adopt'. The future indicative ποιήσει retained in oblique narration dramatically, by a very common idiom.

7. ὡς...ἐβουλεύετο 'while he was consulting'.

8. ἐπικλήτοισι 'those summoned to council', 9, 42.

10. πρότερον, see c. 68.

11. μεταστησάμενος 'having caused to withdraw'. The middle, because (1) the action is done by the agency of others, cf. 6, 46 ναυπηγεῖσθαι, ib. 48 ποιέεσθαι, and (2) because the action affects the subject, cp. 1, 8 [Κῦρος] μεταστησάμενος τοὺς ἄλλους εἴρετο Κροῖσον...

15. μεταίτιοι 'involved in a share of the blame for any disaster'.

16. βουλομένοισί σφι γένοιτ' ἄν 'they will be glad to have'.

ἀπόδεξις 'an opportunity of shewing it', i.e. that they were not to blame for the disaster.

21—23. καὶ...νῦν τε, in the former clause περὶ τῆς ναυμαχίης, serving as a kind of date, is opposed to νῦν.

23. **οὐκ ἐῶσα ποιέεσθαι** 'advising against my allowing it be fought'. For **ποιέεσθαι** see note above l. 11.

24. **ἐπιτύχω εὖ βουλευσάμενος** 'I may succeed in taking the right decision'. 9, 12 τύγχανε εὖ βουλευόμενος. **ἐπιτύχω** is a deliberative subjunctive. Cp. p. 55, l. 16.

CHAPTER CII.

25. **συνεβουλεύετο** 'consulted her', notice the middle contrasted with συνεβούλευσας above l. 22. So **συμβουλευομένῳ** 'to one who consults me'.

27. **ἐπὶ...πρήγμασι** 'seeing, however, that matters have come to this pass', 'in the circumstances which have arisen'. Cp. p. 10, l. 15.

2. **τοῦτο μὲν...τοῦτο δέ.** See p. 40, l. 5.

4. **τὰ νοέων λέγει** 'what he speaks of as in his mind', lit. 'designing which he speaks'.

σὸν τὸ ἔργον 'the credit of the achievement is yours'. For this use of ἔργον cp. 6, 29 τὸ δὲ δὴ ἔργον τῆς ἵππου τοῦτο ἐγένετο. 9, 102 ὅκως ἑαυτῶν γένηται τὸ ἔργον καὶ μὴ Λακεδαιμονίων.

8. **ἐκείνων τῶν πρηγμάτων** sc. περιεόντων 'while that empire which you have in Asia remains'. Stein joins περὶ οἶκον τὸν σὸν to συμφορή, but the next sentence seems rather to point to its belonging to πρηγμάτων, 'there will be no great disaster as long as you and the power you possess in your native country survive' i.e. in Asia as opposed to Europe. περί is not local, but the ἐκείνων practically justifies the translation given. Baehr '*te quidem salvo salvisque tuae domus rebus*'. The king's house and the kingdom are identical, *l'état c'est moi*. For the sense of **πρήγματα** 'power' or 'empire' cp. 6, 13 τὰ βασιλέος πρήγματα. ib. 39 καταλαμψόμενος τὰ πρήγματα. Abicht brackets περὶ οἶκον τὸν σόν.

10. **ἀγῶνας δραμέονται περὶ σφέων αὐτῶν** 'will at many times and in many ways find themselves in danger'. A metaphor from the race-course. Cp. p. 38, l. 26. 9, 37 ὥστε τρέχων περὶ τῆς ψυχῆς. 7, 58 περὶ ἑωυτοῦ δραμεῖν.

11. **ἤν τι πάθῃ** i.e. 'if he is defeated and killed', a common euphemism.

λόγος 'account'. Cp. 4, 135 τῶν ἦν ἐλάχιστος ἀπολλυμένων λόγος.

9, 70 οὗτοι ἐν οὐδενὶ λόγῳ ἀπώλοντο. Ib. 80 ἐσθῆτος ποικίλης λόγος ἐγίνετο οὐδὲ εἷς. See p. 6, l. 13.

14. **πυρώσας**, see c. 53. For his purpose see 7, 8, 2 μέλλω ζεύξας τὸν Ἑλλήσποντον ἐλᾶν στρατὸν διὰ τῆς Εὐρώπης ἐπὶ τὴν Ἑλλάδα, ἵνα Ἀθηναίους τιμωρήσαιμι.

CHAPTER CIII.

16. **ἐπετύγχανε** 'she succeeded in expressing exactly what he had in his own mind'. Cp. p. 54, l. 24.

18. **δοκέειν ἐμοί**, see p. 12, l. 14.

19. **ταύτην μὲν** corresponds to συνέπεμπε δέ in c. 104. For this coupling of different parts of two clauses, cp. Aesch. in Ctes. 53 δοκεῖν μὲν ἀληθῆ λέγειν, ἀρχαῖα δέ.

20. **ἐς Ἔφεσον** that they might be sent thence to Sardis and then up the country to Susa; for the road began from Ephesos, see p. 56, l. 9; 5, 54. **νόθοι** born of παλλακαί.

CHAPTER CIV.

23. **φερόμενον...οὐ τὰ δεύτερα** sc. τὰ πρῶτα 'was the most influential of the eunuchs', or 'the highest in rank'. Cp. 7, 211 οὐδὲν πλέον ἐφέροντο 'they succeeded no better'. For the litotes cp. 1, 23 οὐδενὸς δεύτερος.

26. **ἐπεάν** 'whenever' (ἐπεὶ ἄν), usually ἐπὴν in Attic poetry and prose before Xenophon. Yet ἐπὴν is really Ionic. See Meisterhans *Gramm. der Att. Inschr.* p. 210. In 4, 134 four MSS. have ἐπήν.

27. **ἀμφὶ...πόλιος.** The genitive of place after ἀμφί is very rare, if not unexampled.

28. **τι χαλεπόν** 'a misfortune'. **ἐντὸς χρόνου** 'shortly', 'within a short time', opp. to ἐκὰς χρόνου, p. 82, l. 7.

1. **πώγωνα**, see 1, 175, where Herodotos says that it happened three times. Stein and Abicht bracket the clause from οἱ δὲ Πηδασέες to Ἑρμότιμος ἦν as an interpolation from the 1st book written by some scholar as an explanation on the margin, and thence taken into the text. It had long ago been condemned by Valknaer; but is defended by Baehr.

CHAPTER CV.

4. ἤδη emphasises μεγίστη like δή 'the very greatest ever known'. Cp. p. 57, l. 1.

6. τὴν ζόην κατεστήσατο 'secured his livelihood' [Cobet would read κατεκτήσατο, cp. p. 57, l. 1—2]. For ἀπό cp. 2, 36 ποιεύμενος ἀπὸ τούτων τὴν ζόην.

7. ὅκως...κτήσαιτο, the optative of repeated action, p. 26, l. 11; p. 48, l. 14.

8. εἴδεος ἐπαμμένοις 'that had reached their time of beauty', 'full-grown boys'. Cp. 1, 139 ὅσαι δὲ εἰδέος δὲ ἐπαμμένοι εἰσὶ καὶ μεγάθεος.

9. ἐς Σάρδις τε καὶ Ἔφεσον, that is, for export into Upper Asia: the road going through those places. See p. 55, l. 20.

11. πίστιος...τῆς πάσης 'entire confidence'.

13. καὶ δὴ καί. Cp. p. 21, l. 22.

καὶ οὐ γάρ. The reason is given by anticipation. Cp. p. 57, l. 24; 9, 61, 87.

15. παρὰ βασιλέα to the king's palace at Susa.

CHAPTER CVI.

18. ὥρμα 'was engaged in starting'. ἐπί 'to attack'.

20. κατὰ δή τι πρῆγμα, *negotii nescio cujus causa*, cp. the force of δή in δή ποτε, εἰ δή ποτε, ὅτι δή ποτε, ὁπόθεν δή ποτε and the like. τὴν Χῖοι νέμονται 'which is inhabited by Chians'. See 1, 160. Note the absence of the definite article, cp. p. 53, l. 28.

24—26. ἔχοι...ποιήσει, for the variation of moods see p. 53, l. 3—5. In both cases the future indicative expresses a more certain result than would be conveyed by the optative.

26. ἐκείνῃ 'there' i.e. at Sardis. τοὺς οἰκέτας 'his family', including wife, children and servants. Cp. p. 3, l. 2; p. 23, l. 9.

28. ἄρα 'accordingly', 'as a natural result'. There is an ironic consciousness of the coming tragedy conveyed by the word.

29. πανοικίῃ 'with his entire family', cp. 9, 109 τῇ δὲ κακῶς γὰρ ἔδεε πανοικίῃ γενέσθαι.

περιέλαβε 'got him into his hands'. Cp. 5, 23 ἐπεὰν αὐτὸν περιλάβῃς.

1. ἤδη μάλιστα...ἀνοσιωτάτων. For the emphatic ἤδη see 57 on p. 56, l. 4. Thus we find it used to mark a climax, see 7, 35 ἤδη δὲ ἤκουσα 'and I have even heard'. Aeschines in Ctesiph. § 52 καὶ ταῦτα ἤδη τὰ περὶ Μειδίαν 'and, above all, there was the affair of Midias'.

4. ἐδόκεές τε 'and you expected!'

7. ὥστε σε μὴ μέμψασθαι 'that you may have no occasion to undervalue', 'to find fault with', or 'think insufficient'. The word is bitterly ironical. So μεμπτοί 'inadequate' Thucyd. 7, 15, 1. ἐμεμψάμην 'I spoke disparagingly of', id. 1, 143, 3. There is a similar ironical use of the verb in Xenophon Hell. 6, 2, 34 εἰ δέ τις μὴ ἀκολουθήσοι, προεῖπε μὴ μέμψεσθαι τὴν δίκην.

13. περιῆλθε 'returned upon him', 'overtook him' as by a heaven-sent fate and vengeance which lay in wait for him; generally with the notion of 'outwitting', as in 3, 4 σοφίῃ μιν περιῆλθε ὁ Φάνης. Sometimes it merely expresses a final result, 7, 88 ἐς φθίσιν περιῆλθε ἡ νοῦσος.

CHAPTER CVII.

17. διαλέγειν 'to select', the notion of comparison between the persons offered for selection is conveyed by διά. Cp. p. 62, l. 16.

18. ποιέειν...πειρώμενον ὁμοῖα 'and to do his best to make his deeds tally with his professions'. Herodotos varies the construction of πειρᾶσθαι with infinitive and participle (see p. 53, l. 15 compared with ἐπειρᾶτο κατιών 6, 5); this is the third variation,—in which the word expressing 'the attempt' is put in the participle—'to make as far as trying was concerned'.

19. ταύτην τὴν ἡμέρην 'during this day', i.e. of the fight. The battle had begun at daybreak. Aeschyl. Pers. 388.

τῆς δὲ νυκτὸς 'but in the course of the night', p. 37, l. 25; p. 40, l. 22.

21. ἀπῆγον 'began to start their ships'.

22. ὡς τάχεος εἶχε ἕκαστος 'as quickly as they each could', cp. 6, 116 ὡς ποδῶν εἶχον. 9, 59 ὡς ποδῶν ἕκαστος εἶχον.

23. πορευθῆναι βασιλεῖ 'for the king to go over on foot'. The purpose or epexegetic infinitive depending on διαφυλαξούσας. Cp. § 265. Madv. § 148 Rem. 3.

24. **γάρ** introducing the reason by anticipation, cp. p. 56, l. 14.

26. **ἐπὶ πολλόν** 'for a long distance'. So ἐπί of extension of time 9, 62 χρόνον ἐπὶ πολλόν, p. 70, l. 18: of space 2, 32 νέμεται... τὴν πρὸς ἠῶ χώρην τῆς Σύρτιος οὐκ ἐπὶ πολλόν.

27. **ἐκομίζοντο** 'they continued their voyage'.

CHAPTER CVIII.

58   2. **κατὰ χώρην**, cp. p. 38, l. 9.

3. **περὶ Φάληρον**, see c. 92 end.

7. **διώξαντες** 'after chasing them', or, 'though they chased them'.

10. **διὰ νήσων** 'from island to island', taking the island course instead of coasting along the shore of the mainland. In this technical sense the phrase is always without article, see 6, 95 παρά τε Ἰκάριον καὶ διὰ νήσων τὸν πλοῦν ἐποιεῦντο. 9, 3 ἅμα δὲ πύρσοισι διὰ νήσων ἐδόκεε βασιλέϊ δηλώσειν κ.τ.λ.

11. **ἐπί** 'up to', p. 33, l. 19.

12. **γνώμην ἐτίθετο** 'gave an opinion'. The expression seems derived from the idea of actually depositing a voting pebble or tablet. Cp. 3, 81; 7, 82.

13. **τοῦτ' ἄν.** The ἄν is so placed to emphasise τοῦτο 'that this was the very worst thing they could do to Greece'.

16. **ἡσυχίην μὴ ἄγειν** '*not* to keep quiet', as we wish him to do. It is a litotes for ἐπιχειρέειν τι (6, 20). Cp. 7, 11 εἰ ἡμεῖς ἡσυχίην ἄγομεν, ἀλλ' οὐκ ἐκεῖνοι, ἀλλὰ καὶ μάλα στρατεύσονται ἐπὶ τὴν ἡμετέραν.

18. **τὸ ὀπίσω** 'back home again', cp. 4, 134. The neuter article τό is frequently used in such adverbial phrases. Cp. τὸ ἐνθεῦτεν, τὸ ἐπὶ τοῦτο.

20. **ἔργου ἐχομένῳ**, cp. p. 6, l. 17.

22. **ἤτοι...γε** 'either, of course'.

25. **οὐ μενέειν.** The infinitive in indirect discourse with οὐ. See 9, 58; G. p. 308.

26. **ἐς ὃ ἔλθῃ** 'till he shall have come'. Without ἄν, see on p. 12, l. 16.

27. **ἤδη** belongs to τὸ ἐνθεῦτεν and introduces a necessary

consequence, 'and so from that time forward'. Cp. p. 52, l. 10; ἤδη ὦν p. 53, l. 30.

28. ποιέεσθαι...τὸν ἀγῶνα 'to take care that the fight is for his (the king's) territory'.

εἴχοντο 'they held to'.

CHAPTER CIX.

3. τούς γε πολλούς 'the main body at least' i.e. of the allies. 59 The Athenians were ready to follow his advice and commands.

5. μεταβαλών...Ἀθηναίους 'turning from them to the Athenians'. The word is used intransitively meaning 'to change plans' or 'feelings'. Cp. 1, 65 μετέβαλον ὧδε ἐς εὐνομίην, ib. 66 μεταβαλόντες εὐνομήθησαν. 7, 170 μεταβαλόντας ἀντὶ μὲν Κρητῶν γενέσθαι Ἰήπυγας. But the middle in 5, 75 of physical movement μετεβάλλοντό τε καὶ ἀπαλλάσσαντο 'they faced round and marched off'.

6. ἐκπεφευγότων sc. τῶν βαρβάρων 'at their having escaped'.

7. ἐπὶ σφέων αὐτῶν βαλλόμενοι 'deliberating by themselves'. Cf. 3, 155 ἐπ᾽ ἐμεωυτοῦ βαλόμενος. For ἐπί with gen. defining connexion with an object distinct from others cp. 9, 17 ἐπ᾽ ἑωυτῶν ἵζεσθαι and note.

9. πολλοῖσι neuter 'many cases'.

10. ἐς ἀναγκαίην ἀπειληθέντας 'when brought to bay'.

12. ἀναλαμβάνειν...κακότητα 'repair their former misfortune'. Cp. 5, 121 τοῦτο τὸ τρῶμα ἀνέλαβον. For κακότης cp. 6, 67 τοῦτο ἀρξεῖν...ἢ μυρίης κακότητος ἢ μυρίης εὐδαιμονίης. The abstract word used for the concrete κακόν.

13. εὕρημα γὰρ εὑρήκαμεν...ἀνωσάμενοι 'we ourselves as well as Hellas have had an unexpected stroke of luck in having repelled so vast a cloud of men'. Grammatically ἡμᾶς τε καὶ τὴν Ἑλλάδα are in apposition with εὕρημα 'we have been fortunate enough to save ourselves and Greece, a stroke of luck, by repelling'. Or we may regard εὕρημα εὑρήκαμεν as a single compound verb governing an accusative 'we have fortunately managed'; cp. Aesch. in Ctes. 181 Μιλτιάδης μάχην τοὺς βαρβάρους νικήσας and other examples quoted by Madv. § 26, 6. For εὕρημα see 7, 10; 7, 155 μετὰ τοῦτο τὸ εὕρημα. Thucyd. 5, 46, 1 ἐκείνοις δὲ δυστυχοῦσιν ὅτι τάχιστα εὕρημα εἶναι διακινδυνεῦσαι.

11—2

14. **νέφος**, cp. Polyb. 9, 37, 10 (of the threatened Roman invasion) λεληθασιν αὐτοῖς ἐπισπασάμενοι τηλικοῦτο νέφος ἀπὸ τῆς ἑσπέρας.

16. **ἐφθόνησαν**. The φθόνος of the gods against everything too great or powerful is a doctrine frequently appearing in Herodotos. 1, 32 τὸ θεῖον πᾶν ἐὸν φθονερόν τε καὶ ταραχῶδες. 3, 40 ἐπισταμένῳ τὸ θεῖον ὡς ἔστι φθόνερον. 7, 10 § 5 φιλεῖ γὰρ ὁ θεὸς τὰ ὑπερέχοντα πάντα κολούειν...οὐ γὰρ ἐᾷ φρονέειν μέγα ὁ θεὸς ἄλλον ἢ ἑωυτόν.

18. **ἀτάσθαλον** 'presumptuous', 'blindly impious'. The word is poetical. Cp. 7, 35 ἐνετέλλετο δὴ ὦν ῥαπίζοντας λέγειν βάρβαρά τε καὶ ἀτάσθαλα. 9, 18 μὴ ὑπάρχειν ἔργα ἀτάσθαλα ποιέων.

ὃς τὰ ἱρα...ἀγάλματα. The Persians burnt the Greek temples, says Herodotos, on the plea of revenge for the burning of the temple of Kybebe in Sardis in B.C. 500, see p. 77, l. 28 f.; 5, 102; 7, 8, 2. Aesch. Pers. 805

οἳ γῆν μολόντες Ἑλλάδ' οὐ θεῶν βρέτη
ᾐδοῦντο συλᾶν οὐδὲ πιμπράναι νεώς·
βωμοὶ δ' ἄϊστοι, δαιμόνων θ' ἱδρύματα
πρόρριζα φύρδην ἐξανέστραπται βάθρων.

21. **ἀπεμαστίγωσε**, see 7, 35. The ἀπό is intensive, 'violently scourged'.

22. **γὰρ** anticipatory, cp. p. 57, l. 24. **νῦν μὲν** 'at this time of the year', answered by ἅμα δὲ τῷ ἔαρι in l. 26.

24. **τῶν οἰκετέων** 'our families', see p. 56, l. 26. **τις** 'let each man'. Cp. p. 65, l. 16; 6, 9 νῦν τις ὑμέων εὖ ποιήσας φανήτω τὸν βασιλέος οἶκον. **ἀναπλασάσθω** 'restore', 'rebuild'. **σπόρου ἀνακῶς ἐχέτω** 'let him give his whole attention to sowing', cp. 1, 24 ἀνακῶς εἶχε τῶν πορθμέων.

25. **παντελέως ἀπελάσας** 'as having entirely driven off the Persians', 'in the conviction that he has entirely driven off', i.e. as far as Attica was concerned, for the Persians were still in Greece.

26. **ἐπὶ** p. 33, l. 19.

27. **ἀποθήκην** sc. χάριτος 'a store of gratitude', 'with a view of securing for himself a claim on the gratitude of the Persians'. Cp. 6, 41 χάριτα μεγάλην καταθήσεσθαι. 7, 178 χάριν ἀθάνατον κατέθεντο, 9, 60, 78; Aeschin. in Ctes. § 42 πολλὴν χάριν καταθέμενοι.

28. ἦν ἄρα 'if after all', 'if by any chance', p. 53, l. 22. Cp. Demosth. 3 Olynth. § 26 εἴ τις ἄρα οἶδεν ὑμῶν ὁποία ποτ' ἐστιν. Lycurg. § 136 εἴ τις ἄρα ἐστιν αἴσθησις τοῖς ἐκεῖ περὶ τῶν ἐνθάδε γιγνομένων. Cp. Plato Phaedr. 255 B ἐὰν ἄρα καὶ ἐν τῷ πρόσθεν... διαβεβλημένος ᾖ.

30. τά περ ὦν καὶ ἐγένετο 'just what in fact did actually happen'.

CHAPTER CX.

1. διέβαλλε 'was using deceit', or 'was putting them off the scent'. Cp. 5, 107 λέγων ταῦτα διέβαλλε. With an accusative 5, 50 διαβάλλων ἐκεῖνον εὖ. 9, 116 λέγων δὲ τοιάδε Ξέρξεα διεβάλετο. Arist. Thesm. 1214 διέβαλέ μ' ὦ γραῦς. See Thompson on Phaedr. 255 B ὑπὸ συμφοιτητῶν ἤ τινων ἄλλων διαβεβλημένος.

3. δεδογμένος εἶναι σοφός, cp. p. 68, l. 1.

ἐφάνη ἐών 'he had been proved to be', i.e. by the result of his policy in regard to fighting the Persians at Salamis.

σοφός τε καὶ εὔβουλος. Cf. the estimate of Themistokles by Thucydides (1, 138) τῶν τε παραχρῆμα δι' ἐλαχίστης βουλῆς κράτιστος γνώμων καὶ τῶν μελλόντων ἐπὶ πλεῖστον τοῦ γενησομένου ἄριστος εἰκαστής. σοφός is especially applicable to natural ability or genius.

6. ἄνδρας ἀπέπεμπε according to Plutarch (Them. c. 16) he sent Arnaces one of the king's eunuchs who had been a prisoner of war. πλοῖον 'a transport', opp. to a ναῦς μακρά or τριήρης.

7. ἐς πᾶσαν βάσανον ἀπικνεομένοισι 'no matter to what torture they might be put'. Spies and traitors when caught were put to the rack. See Demosth. de Cor. § 133.

9. αὖτις, see p. 39, l. 17.

16. ἴσχε 'prevented', 'kept back'. Cp. 9, 12 ὑποδεξάμενοι σχήσειν τὸν Σπαρτιήτην μὴ ἐξιέναι.

18. κομίζεο 'proceed on your journey', p. 11, l. 19; p. 57, l. 27.

CHAPTER CXI.

20. σφι ἀπέδοξε 'they had decided against pursuing'. The negative ἀπέδοξε is followed by μή, as words containing negative ideas often are, though this μή cannot be translated in English. Goodw. § 283, 6. Cp. 1, 152 ἀπέδοξέ σφι μὴ τιμωρέειν Ἴωσι.

22. λύσοντας, the accusative after ἔδοξέ σφι is caused by the influence of the infinitive. See 6, 22 ἐδόκεε δέ...βουλευομένοισι...ἐς ἀποικίην ἐκπλέειν μηδὲ μένοντας Μήδοισι δουλεύειν. p. 53, l. 20.

23, 24. ἐξελεῖν cp. 9, 86. νησιωτέων 'of all Island Greece', in this sense always without the definite article. Cp. p. 23, l. 20. So νῆσοι 5, 31.

24. αἰτηθέντες...χρήματα. These demands upon the islanders for money Themistokles no doubt regarded as founded on natural equity. The combined Greek squadron had been and were fighting for their deliverance, and it was but fair, as they could not give help, that they should contribute in money. It may perhaps be regarded as the beginning of what became the organized exaction of φόρος instituted in B.C. 476 in virtue of the confederacy of Delos, and which (under this name or, in the new league, under that of σύνταξις) was continually increased by special exactions of the ἀργυρολόγοι νῆες, whenever Athens was in need, or could find a decent pretext for doing so, down to the time of the battle of Chaeroneia (B.C. 338).

61 2. Πειθώ τε καὶ Ἀναγκαίην. In Plutarch (Them. 21) they are given as Πειθώ and Βία, and the two gods in the reply of the Andrians as Πενία καὶ Ἀπορία. See the same chapter for the discontent and hostility roused by Themistokles in these proceedings.

4. κατὰ λόγον ἄρα 'naturally, as it appeared from what he said', p. 4, l. 27.

4—5. ἦσαν...ἥκοιεν for the change of mood, see 6, 3; 5, 97.

5. θεῶν χρηστῶν ἥκοιεν εὖ 'and were well off for beneficent gods'. Cp. 5, 62 ἄνδρες χρημάτων εὖ ἥκοντες. 1, 31 τοῦ βίου εὖ ἥκοντι. 1, 149 χώρην ὡρέων ἥκουσαν οὐκ ὁμοίως. 7, 157 σὺ δὲ δυνάμιος ἥκεις μεγάλης. The genitive is one of respect, ἥκειν is constructed like ἔχειν. Madv. § 49 b R. 2. Schweigh. sees an ironical allusion to the ruined state of Athens at the time.

ἐπεί...εἶναι 'for the Andrians were' said they. The infinitive is often preserved in the subordinate clauses of the *oratio obliqua*. Cp. p. 49, l. 22; 6, 137 ταύτην ὡς ἰδεῖν τοὺς Ἀθηναίους ἐξεργασμένην εὖ. G. § 260 note 2.

6. γεωπείνας [πένομαι, πένης] 'poorly off for land', cp. 2, 6 ὅσοι μὲν γεωπεῖναί εἰσι ἀνθρώπων...οἱ δὲ πολλὴν ἔχουσι. Andros, in spite of this complaint, was and is a fertile island. ἐς τὰ μέγιστα

ἀνήκοντας takes the place of a superlative adverb, 'to the highest degree', p. 81, l. 21, cp. 7, 13 φρενῶν γὰρ ἐς τὰ ἐμωυτοῦ πρῶτα οὐ ἀνήκω.

7. ἀχρήστους 'unkindly', cp. 9, 111 λόγος ἄχρηστος.

8. Ἀμηχανίην 'inability', 'helplessness', a rare word, cp. an inscription apud Aesch. in Ctes. § 184 πρῶτοι δυσμενέων εὗρον ἀμηχανίην (of starving out Eion). Alkaios Fr. 92 ἀργαλέον πενίαν, κακὸν ἄσχετον, ἃ μέγα δάμνησι λᾶον ἀμαχανίᾳ σὺν ἀδελφέᾳ.

9. ἐπηβόλους 'being in possession of these gods'. 9, 94 τούτων ἐπήβολος γενόμενος, cp. Soph. Ant. 492 λευσῶσαν οὐδ' ἐπήβολον φρενῶν. It is a poetical word, and a metrical variation of ἐπίβολος. For its active use, cp. Aeschyl. Ag. 528 τερπνῆς ἆρ' ἦτε τῆσδ' ἐπήβολοι νόσου.

10. οὐδέκοτε...κρέσσω. That is, the Athenian power can never do impossibilities,—it cannot make them pay what they have not got. The present εἶναι of what is existing at the time and will exist: 'Neither now nor ever can the Athenian power overcome their inability'. 7, 172 οὐδαμὰ γὰρ ἀδυνασίης ἀνάγκη κρέσσων ἔφυ (quoted by Stein).

11. δή sums up and dismisses the subject. Cp. 6, 52 τὴν μὲν δὴ Πυθίην ταῦτά σφι ἀνελεῖν κ.τ.λ.

CHAPTER CXII.

16. τοῖσι καὶ 'in the same words as'. So τὠυτὸ καὶ p. 23, l. 16. ταὐτὰ καὶ τὰ 6, 102.

19. ἐξαιρήσει see p. 60, l. 23. In this connexion the word probably refers to the notion of removing the inhabitants from a conquered place. Cp. 5, 16 τοὺς ἐν τῇ λίμνῃ κατοικημένους ἐξαιρέειν. See on 6, 33. λέγων ὧν...συνέλεγε 'by the use then of these threats he succeeded in collecting great sums'. The imperfect of continued action.

22. τῶν στρατηγῶν i.e. of the ten Athenian Strategi, who managed foreign affairs. Themistokles would, therefore, they thought, be able to wield the whole power of Athens against them. αἴνῃ 'reputation', 'respect', a poetical word. Cp. 3, 74; 9, 16.

23. εἰ δὲ δή 'but whether as a fact'. νησιωτέων, see on p. 60, l. 24.

27. τοῦ κακοῦ ὑπερβολή 'a postponement of misfortune'. That

is, apparently, they were punished all the same for medizing by being forced to submit to the presence of the fleet and the violence and extortion of the other commanders besides Themistokles.

28. **διέφυγον τὸ στράτευμα** 'avoided a visit from the fleet'.

29. **μέν νυν** 'so then', introducing the conclusion of a series of facts. Cp. 6, 22, 45, 47 etc.

ἐξ Ἄνδρου ὁρμεόμενος 'starting from Andros', 'using Andros as his base of operations'. Cp. 5, 94 ἐπολέμεον γὰρ ἔκ τε Ἀχιλληίου πόλιος ὁρμεόμενοι καὶ Σιγείου χρόνον ἐπὶ συχνὸν Μυτιληναῖοί τε καὶ Ἀθηναῖοι.

30. **παρὰ νησιωτέων**, see p. 60, l. 24. **λάθρῃ** 'without the knowledge of the other nine strategi'. See the violent attack upon Themistokles by the poet Timokreon of Rhodes quoted in Plutarch, Them. 2, who calls him ἀργυρίων ὑπόπλεως, and asserts that he got large sums from individuals accused of medizing. It is certain that by some means Themistokles became possessed of great wealth. Plut. Them. 25; Aelian V. H. 10, 17. Grote, vol. v. p. 140.

CHAPTER CXIII.

1. **οἱ δ' ἀμφὶ Ξέρξεα** 'Xerxes and his army'. Thucydides (8, 65, 1) uses ἀμφί in a similar phrase in one of the two places in which he has this preposition, οἱ ἀμφὶ τὸν Πείσανδρον. Elsewhere Thucydides uses περί: and though ἀμφί is fairly frequent in Herodotos, it soon disappeared in Attic prose. See on 6, 62.

3. **τὴν αὐτὴν ὁδὸν** 'by the same route by which they had come'. See c. 50. The army seems to have come from Plataea over Dryoskephalae.

4. **ἀνωρίην τοῦ ἔτεος** 'too late in the year', 'an unseasonable time'. It seems to be an ἅπ. λεγ. Aristophanes (Ach. 23) has ἀωρίαν sero. For the construction cp. ἀωρὶ τῶν νυκτῶν [Aelian ap. Suid. s. v. ἀωρία]. p. 82, l. 7 ἑκὰς χρόνου.

6. **πειρᾶσθαι**, p. 53, l. 17.

7. **ἀπίκατο** 'when they had arrived'. App. D. II. (a).

9. **τοὺς ἀθανάτους**, cp. 7, 211 οἱ δὲ Πέρσαι ἐκδεξάμενοι ἐπήϊσαν, τοὺς ἀθανάτους ἐκάλεε βασιλεύς. The explanation of their name is given in 7, 83. They were always exactly 10,000.

10. **λείψεσθαι βασιλέος** 'said that he would not be separated

from the king'. Cp. 9, 66 λειπομένου Μαρδονίου ἀπὸ βασιλέος. 9, 19 λείπεσθαι τῆς ἐξόδου Λακεδαιμονίων.

11. **τοὺς θωρηκοφόρους** the Persians,—who wore περὶ τὸ σῶμα κιθῶνας χειριδωτοὺς ποικίλους λεπίδος σιδηρέης (7, 61), 'sleeved tunics of various colours covered with iron scales'. In 9, 22 Masistius wears a θώρηξ χρύσεος λεπιδωτὸς under a purple tunic.

12—13. **τὴν ἵππον τὴν χιλίην.** The 1000 cavalry picked from the whole army who headed the king's guard on the march (7, 40). For ἡ ἵππος see 9, 14.

Μήδους (7, 62). **Σάκας** (7, 64; 9, 31, 71). **Βακτρίους** (7, 64; 9, 31). **Ἰνδοὺς** (7, 65; 9, 31; 3, 94).

15. **κατ' ὀλίγους** 'in small groups', 'taking a few from each', opp. to ἔθνεα ὅλα.

εἴδεα see p. 56, l. 8.

16. **διαλέγων**, p. 57, l. 17. **τέοισι** (τισὶ)...**πεποιημένον**, dat. of agent, see p. 51, l. 16.

17. **ἓν δὲ πλεῖστον ἔθνος Πέρσας αἱρέετο** 'but of a single race the Persians were those from whom he selected the largest number'. Lit. 'but one race he chose in greatest number,—Persians'. ἓν and πλεῖστον are placed together to bring out the contrast more clearly: grammatically ἔθνος and Πέρσας are in apposition [Abicht reads ἓν δέ]. The imperfect (αἱρέετο) is used of a process that continued for some time.

18. **στρεπτοφόρους...ψελιοφόρους**, see 7, 88; 9, 25. The Persians commonly wore such chains and bracelets. Plutarch Them. 18 describes the corpses on the shore after the battle of Salamis as περικείμενοι ψέλια χρυσᾶ καὶ στρεπτούς. Cp. also Xenophon Oeconom. 4, 23.

ἐπὶ δὲ 'and next to them', p. 34, l. 25.

20. **ῥώμῃ δὲ ἔσσονες.** For this view of the superiority of the Persians as soldiers, see 9, 68.

CHAPTER CXIV.

24. **ἐληλύθεε** Ionic pluperf., 5, 98.

26. **τὸ διδόμενον** 'whatever was offered'. For ἐκ instead of ὑπὸ (common in Herodotos), see 5, 21 ζήτησις μεγάλη ἐκ τῶν Περσέων ἐγίνετο. 6, 22 τὸ ἐκ τῶν στρατηγῶν τῶν σφετέρων ποιηθέν.

63 1. κατέλαβε 'overtook', p. 4, l. 5.

4. Ἡρακλεῖδαι οἱ ἀπὸ Σπάρτης 'the Heraclids of Sparta', that is, the kings, see c. 131. For ἀπό see p. 49, l. 25.

7. κατασχών 'after pausing', 'having remained silent', generally ἐπισχών in this sense, cp. p. 33, l. 26; p. 62, l. 1. But cp. 5, 19 οὐδαμῶς ἔτι κατέχειν οἷός τε ἦν 'he could by no means restrain himself any longer' (ὥστε δὲ βαρέως φέρων εἶπε πρὸς Ἀμύντην τάδε). In the passive, see p. 64, l. 21.

8. δεικνὺς ἐς τοῦτον 'pointing to him'. δείκνυσθαι 'to stretch out the hand', Hom. Il. 9, 196 τώ καὶ δεικνύμενος προσέφη πόδας ὠκὺς Ἀχιλλεύς. Herm. 367 δείξατο δ' εἰς Κρονίωνα. But Herodotos uses the active in this sense, cp. 4, 150 ἐδείκνυε ἐς τὸν Βάττον. 5, 49 δεικνὺς ἐς τὴν γῆς περίοδον. 9, 82 δεικνύντα ἐς ἑκατέρην τοῦ δείπνου τὴν παρασκευήν.

9. Μαρδόνιος...δίκας δώσει. For the fulfilment of this in the contrary sense to that intended by Xerxes, see 9, 64.

CHAPTER CXV.

11. δεξάμενος τὸ ῥηθὲν 'having accepted the words' (as of good omen), cp. 9, 91 δέκομαι τὸν οἰωνὸν τὸν Ἡγησίστρατον. See p. 62, l. 26.

16. ὡς εἰπεῖν 'so to speak', modifying the preceding statement. G. § 268.

17. ὅκου...γινοίατο 'wherever they come from time to time' optative of indefinite frequency, cp. p. 26, l. 12. So the indefinite εὕροιεν in l. 19.

19—21. οἱ δὲ...κατήσθιον. For δὲ in apodosis cp. 9, 70 ἕως μὲν γὰρ ἀπῆσαν οἱ Ἀθηναῖοι, οἱ δ' ἠμύνοντο.

19—24. οἱ δὲ...διέφθειρε. See Grote IV. p. 489. Aeschylos gives a dreadful picture of this retreat, which Grote criticises as exaggerated. Thirlwall (2, p. 316) seems to accept it as authentically supplementing the narrative of Herodotos. The passage of Aeschylos (Persae 485—513) seems to contain only the same statement, expressed in somewhat heightened language, as that of Herodotos, except in the particular of the disaster on the Strymon (496).

νυκτὶ δ' ἐν ταύτῃ θεὸς
χειμῶν' ἄωρον ὦρσε, πήγνυσιν δὲ πᾶν

ῥέεθρον ἁγνοῦ Στρυμόνος· θεοὺς δέ τις
τὸ πρὶν νομίζων οὐδαμοῦ, τότ' ηὔχετο
λιταῖσι γαῖαν οὐρανόν τε προσκυνῶν.
ἐπεὶ δὲ πολλὰ θεοκλυτῶν ἐπαύσατο
στρατός, περᾷ κρυσταλλοπῆγα διὰ πόρον·
χὥστις μὲν ἡμῶν πρὶν σκεδασθῆναι θεοῦ
ἀκτῖνας ὡρμήθη σεσωσμένος κυρεῖ.
φλέγων γὰρ αὐγαῖς λαμπρὸς ἡλίου κύκλος
μέσον πόρον διῆκε θερμαίνων φλογί.
'πῖπτον δ' ἐπ' ἀλλήλοισιν· ηὐτύχει δέ τοι
ὅστις τάχιστα πνεῦμ' ἀπέρρηξεν βίου.

To this Grote objects the impossibility of a sudden frost of one night in November freezing the Strymon sufficiently to induce the army to venture on the ice, and for a certain part to get over; and further observes that the army was not in so great a hurry, as no enemy was on their rear. Rawlinson agrees with Grote, and refers to the fact that a bridge of boats had been thrown across the Strymon for the downward march, which probably was used again (7, 24, 114). Some editors of Aeschylos doubt the genuineness of the passage altogether. Many rumours doubtless reached Athens of the king's disastrous retreat; and some accident may have occurred on the Strymon of which it suited the purpose of Aeschylos to make the most. But it is evident that nothing certain was known at the time; for late in the next year, after the battle of Mykale, the Greeks had not heard of the destruction of the Hellespontine bridge, see 9, 106. See also on p. 65, l. 1.

26. ἵνα...γίνοιτο 'wherever he was', cp. supr. l. 17.

μελεδαίνειν *curare*, a poetical word, cp. Theogn. 1129 ἐμπίομαι πενίης θυμοφθόρου οὐ μελεδαίνων. Theocr. 10, 52 εὐκτὸς ὁ τῷ βατράχῳ, παῖδες, βίος· οὐ μελεδαίνει τὸν τὸ πιεῖν ἐγχεῦντα, but apparently used in this medical sense in Ionic, as Hippocr. 598, 26 is quoted. Cauer *Tit. Ion.* p. 319. Roberts *Epigr.* p. 78.

28. τὸ ἱρὸν ἅρμα see 7, 40; drawn by the Nisaean mares, 9, 20.

2. ἀπέλαβε 'got back', 1, 61 ἀπολαβὼν τὴν τυραννίδα.

3. νεμομένας 'as they were grazing', only used again by Herod. in a metaphorical sense 5, 101 τὰ περιέσχατα νεμομένου τοῦ πυρός.

4. τῶν ἄνω Θρηίκων 'the up-land Thracians', i.e. those living inland. Cp. 1, 130 τῆς ἄνω Ἅλυος Ἀσίης.

CHAPTER CXVI.

7. **ὑπερφυὲς** 'of unnatural cruelty'. It is used in a good sense in 9, 78 ἔργον ἔργασταί τοι ὑπερφυὲς μέγαθός τε καὶ κάλλος. It is a neutral word meaning anything beyond the ordinary course of nature, whether for good or bad, and came to be used colloquially somewhat as are 'awful', 'tremendous' in modern conversational English. See Arist. Eq. 141 ὑπερφυᾶ τέχνην ἔχων. Nub. 76 μίαν εὗρον ἀτραπὸν δαιμονίως ὑπερφυᾶ. Pax 229 ὑπερφυὴς τὸ μέγεθος. (Plut. 734). Plut. 750 ὑπερφυὴς ὅσος. Thesm. 830 πόλλ' ἂν γυναῖκες... μεμψαίμεθ' ἂν τοῖσιν ἀνδράσιν δικαίως· ἓν δ' ὑπερφυέστατον.

8—10. οὔτε...τε cp. 6, 16 οὔτε προακηκοότες ὡς εἶχε περὶ τῶν Χίων, ἰδόντες τε στρατὸν κτλ.; ib. 30; ib. 92 Αἰγινῆται δὲ οὔτε συνεγινώσκοντο, ἦσάν τε αὐθαδέστεροι.

10. **ἀπηγόρευε μὴ στρατεύεσθαι** 'forbade them to go on an expedition'. G. p. 308, § 6, cp. p. 60, l. 20.

11—12. **οἱ δὲ ἀλογήσαντες ἤ...θυμὸς ἐγένετο** 'but they because they despised his command or because they had a longing to see the war'. For two coordinate clauses one with a participle and the other with the indicative, see p. 27, l. 17 εἴτε δὴ ὄψιν τινὰ ἰδών...εἴτε καὶ ἐνθύμιον ἐγένετο. 9, 5 εἴτε δὴ δεδεγμένος χρήματα παρὰ Μαρδονίου, εἴτε καὶ ταῦτά οἱ ἥνδανε. 1, 19 εἴτε δὴ συμβουλεύσαντός τευ, εἴτε καὶ αὐτῷ ἔδοξε. For **θυμὸς** 'wish', 'longing' cp. 1, 1 ὠνέεσθαι τῶν φορτίων τῶν σφι ἦν θυμὸς μάλιστα.

CHAPTER CXVII.

18. **ἐπὶ τὸν πόρον** That is, to the channel between Sestos and Abydos.

19. **τῇσι νηυσὶ** 'on board the ships'. Herodotos seems certainly to mean the fleet which had been despatched immediately after the battle of Salamis, p. 57, l. 21—22. And, if that is so, there is no ground for the remark of Trogus (Justin. 2, 13, 10) *ubi cum solutum pontem hibernis tempestatibus offendisset, piscatoria scapha trajecit.*

20. **ἐντεταμένας** lit. 'tightly stretched'. The ships were lashed together with ropes to form a bridge. See 7, 34.

21. **κατεχόμενοι** 'halting there', and so having leisure to eat, as they had not when ἐπειγόμενοι (l. 18). Herodotos does not seem

to use this passive or middle in this sense elsewhere; but cp. the use of κατασχών in 5, 19 and p. 63, l. 7. [Gebhardt wished to change it to καταγόμενοι, and ἐλάγχανον to ἐλάμβανον].

22. **σιτία τε...ἐλάγχανον** 'they began both to get more food than during their march'. For λαγχάνειν 'to obtain' with accusative cp. 1, 167 ἔλαχον αὐτῶν πολλῷ πλείους. 7, 53 θεοῖσι, οἱ Περσίδα γῆν λελόγχασι. 7, 144 ἔμελλον λάξεσθαι ὀρχηδὸν ἕκαστος δέκα δραχμάς.

οὐδένα τε...ἐμπιπλάμενοι 'and because they gorged themselves unrestrainedly', 'without any care or order'. The phrase οὐδένα κόσμον is always applied by Herodotos to military matters (see 9, 59, 65, 69), here it seems to be used in opposition to the idea of an orderly distribution of rations.

23. **καὶ ὕδατα μεταβάλλοντες.** The καί connects this closely with ἐμπιμπλάμενοι, the two main clauses being connected by τε...τε, 'joined to the change in the water they had to drink'. One would have thought that the mere change of water (independently of any idea of excess) must have been for the better.

CHAPTER CXVIII.

1. **ἄλλος ὅδε λόγος.** The existence of such a widely different account among the Greeks, from whom Herodotos would get his information, may explain the story in Aeschylos quoted above in the notes to c. 115. And the fact that it professed to give intelligence of what happened on the Strymon points to some difficulty or delay which had taken place there.

6. **ἐπὶ νεὸς...ἐπιβάς** 'having gone on board'. At p. 66, l. 18 we have ἐπιβῆναι ἐπὶ τὴν νέα because there the act of embarkation is the principal one, here the fact of his being on board as opposed to being on foot.

8. **κυματίην** here 'tempestuous', 'raising billows'. In 2, 111 applied to a river. **καὶ δή** 'and so'. For γάρ see p. 76, l. 18.

9. **χειμαίνεσθαι** the infinitive in a subordinate clause of *oratio obliqua*, see p. 61, l. 6. The word is here used impersonally, 'the storm grew worse and worse'. Cp. 7, 191 ἡμέρας γὰρ δὴ ἐχείμαζε τρεῖς. But χειμαίνεσθαι is translated by others 'it (τὴν νέα) was tossed by the storm'. It is a very rare word. Pindar (P. 9, 57) uses it metaphorically φόβῳ κεχείμανται φρένες.

ὥστε explains γεμούσης 'the ship beginning to fill, as might be expected with so many of the Persians accompanying Xerxes on deck'. For ὥστε = ὡς or ἅτε cp. 9, 37 ὁ δὲ ἐν τούτῳ τῷ κακῷ ἐχόμενος ὥστε τρέχων περὶ τῆς ψυχῆς...ib. 70 πολλῷ πλέον εἶχον τῶν Λακεδαιμονίων ὥστε οὐκ ἐπισταμένων τειχομαχέειν.

11. **ἐνθαῦτα** 'thereupon', 'in these circumstances'. Cp. 9, 26 ἐνθαῦτα ἐν τῇ διατάξι ἐγένετο λόγων πολλὸς ὠθισμὸς κτλ.

16. **τις διαδεξάτω...κηδόμενος** 'let each of you show his care for the king'; τις is here equivalent to ἕκαστος, but more indefinite. διαδεξάτω is constructed like φανήτω. [For such construction by analogy cp. πείθεσθαι with gen. 6, 12.] For τις with imperative see also p. 59, l. 24. 9, 98 μνησθῆναί τινα χρὴ κτλ. 6, 9 Ἄνδρες Ἴωνες, νῦν τις ὑμέων εὖ ποιήσας φανήτω τὸν βασιλέος οἶκον.

17. **ἐν ὑμῖν** 'on you depends my safety', cp. 6, 109 ἐν σοὶ νῦν, Καλλίμαχε, **ἐστὶ ἢ** καταδουλῶσαι Ἀθήνας ἢ κτλ. See also, p. 53, l. 26.

18. **προσκυνέοντας** 'salaaming'. See 7, 136; Plutarch Them. 27 ἡμῖν πολλῶν νόμων καὶ καλῶν ὄντων κάλλιστος οὗτός ἐστι τιμᾶν βασιλέα καὶ προσκυνεῖν ὡς εἰκόνα θεοῦ τοῦ πάντα σώζοντος.

20. **οὕτω δὴ** 'when this had been done', p. 12, l. 25.

21. **ὡς δὲ ἐκβῆναι** see l. 9; p. 61, l. 6.

23. **στεφάνη** this feminine is rare for a 'crown'. In Aristoph. Eq. 968, where it is used, the words profess to be part of an oracle. The compounds στεφανηφόρος (5, 102) which are used in Attic (Andoc. 19, 11 etc.), στεφανηπλοκεῖν (Arist. Thesm. 448) and others refer rather to 'garlands'.

CHAPTER CXIX.

οὔτε ἄλλως...πάθος 'neither in other respects nor in regard to what is said to have happened to the Persians'. So 4, 147 ἄλλως 'for other reasons'.

27. **εἰ γάρ δή** 'for if really', 'for if as is alleged'.

1. **ἐκ** for ὑπό, frequent in Herodotos. See p. 62, l. 26.

ἐν μυρίῃσι...ἀντίξοον 'out of ten thousand opinions I don't think one would be for denying'; or, as we should say, 'not one man in ten thousand would deny'. **ἀντίξοος** used in Ionic for ἐναντίος. Cp. 6, 7 etc.

2. **μὴ οὐκ...τοιόνδε** 'that the king would have acted as follows'.

For μὴ οὐ after a verb expressing denial, especially when it is itself negatived, see p. 28, l. 20; 6, 88 οὐκέτι ἀνεβάλλοντο μὴ οὐ τὸ πᾶν μηχανήσασθαι. G. § 283, 6—7.

3. τοὺς ἐκ τοῦ καταστρώματος 'those *on* the deck', cp. p. 26, l. 22.

4. ἐς κοίλην νέα 'below deck', i.e. to the part of the ship occupied by the rowers. Observe the absence of the article, κοίλη ναῦς being a technical term. Cp. Xen. Hell. 1, 6, 19 ἐξ ἁπασῶν τῶν νεῶν τοὺς ἀρίστους ἐρέτας ἐκλέξας καὶ τοὺς ἐπιβάτας εἰς κοίλην ναῦν μεταβιβάσας. Thus ναῦς ἄκρα = 'a prow'.

5. ἰόντων Φοινίκων 'being mere Phoenikians', cp. p. 53, l. 28. But in this case, as Rawlinson points out, skilled Phoenikian rowers would have been more valuable to the king than Persian nobles.

6. ὅκως οὐκ ἄν...ἐξέβαλε the construction is varied, as so often in Herodotos, from the infinitive in apposition with καταβιβάσαι, to the subordinate phrase ὅκως οὐκ ἄν ἐξέβαλε dependent on μίαν γνώμην οὐκ ἔχω ἀντίξοον. In this phrase ὅκως = ὅτι, a use confined to poetry in Attic. Cp. 1, 37 ἢ λόγῳ ἀναπεῖσον ὅκως μοι ἀμείνω ἐστὶ ταῦτα οὕτω ποιεόμενα. 3, 115 οὐ δύναμαι ἀκοῦσαι τοῦτο μελετῶν ὅκως θάλασσά ἐστι τὰ ἐπέκεινα Εὐρώπης. Goodw. *M. and T.* § 78.

8. ὁδῷ...στρατῷ 'using a road along with the rest of the army' means 'by the same mode of conveyance as the rest of the army', i.e. marching on land to Sestos and thence by ship to Abydos.

CHAPTER CXX.

10. φαίνεται..."Ἄβδηρα 'for it is clear that he got as far as Abdera' i.e. and therefore could not have embarked at Eion which is much west of Abdera. ξεινίην...συνθέμενος cp. 7, 116 ξεινίην τε ὁ Πέρσης τοῖσι Ἀκανθίοισι προεῖπε καὶ ἐδωρήσατό σφεας ἐσθῆτι Μηδικῇ.

12. ἀκινάκῃ a short straight sword, see 9, 80.

13. τιήρῃ χρυσοπάστῳ 'a tiara sprinkled with gold' (πάσσω). The tiara was a stiff cap or fez. That which Xerxes gave was apparently what Plutarch calls a κίταρις (Themist. 29) which was confined to the kings,—the *tiara recta*, stiffened and variously ornamented. See Rich, *s.vv. Cidaris* and *tiara*.

17. πρὸς τοῦ Ἑλλησπόντου 'in the direction of the Hellespont', p. 44, l. 18; p. 45, l. 23.

18. **ὅθεν δή...φασι** 'the place from which the framers of this story pretend that he went on board the ship'. δή emphasises Herodotos' incredulity. **ἐπὶ τὴν νέα** '*the* ship', i.e. the ship about which this story is told. For the case see on p. 65, l. 6.

CHAPTER CXXI.

20. **οἱ δὲ Ἕλληνες** resuming the narrative from c. 112.
21. **ἐξελεῖν** see p. 60, l. 23.
22. **αὐτῶν** i.e. of the Karystians. For the plural pronoun following the name of a country cp. 5, 63 ἀπεκαλέοντο ἐκ Θεσσαλίης ἐπικουρίην· ἐπεποίητο γάρ σφι συμμαχίη πρὸς αὐτούς. For the reverse, ταύτην after the mention of the people of a country, p. 69, l. 14; Soph. O. C. 942.
24. **ἐξεῖλον** 'they set apart'. Cp. 9, 81 δεκάτην ἐξελόντες τῷ ἐν Δελφοῖσι θεῷ. ib. Παυσανίῃ δὲ πάντα δέκα ἐξαιρέθη τε καὶ ἐδόθη.
25. **Ἰσθμὸν...Σούνιον** on the former was a temple of Poseidon, on the latter of Athene. Stein quotes two instances of the dedication of a captured ship from Thucydides 2, 84; 92.
26. **Αἴαντι** see c. 63. **αὐτοῦ** 'on the spot', i.e. near the scene of the battle.
27—8. **διεδάσαντο...ἀπέπεμψαν** notice the force of the middle and active voices, 'they divided among themselves', 'they despatched'.

67 1. **ἀνδριὰς** sc. of Apollo, see Pausan. 10, 14, 3 ἀνέθεσαν δὲ καὶ Ἀπόλλωνα ἀπὸ ἔργων τῶν ἐν ταῖς ναυσὶν ἐπί τε Ἀρτεμισίῳ καὶ ἐν Σαλαμῖνι. There seems also to have been at Olympia a statue of Salamis better answering to this description. See Pausan. 5, 11, 5 Σαλαμὶς ἔχουσα ἐν τῇ χειρὶ τὸν ἐπὶ ταῖς ναυσὶν ἄκραις ποιούμενον κόσμον.
3. **Ἀλέξανδρος** see c. 34. For his wealth derived from gold mines, see 5, 17.

CHAPTER CXXII.

5. **κοινῇ** 'jointly', i.e. in the name of all the Greeks, not of any particular State.
8. **τὰ ἀριστήϊα** i.e. an offering on account of their having obtained the prize of valour, see c. 93. Plutarch Themist. 17.
9. **ἀστέρας**. These golden stars are presumed to represent the twin Dioskuri, the special patrons of sailors. Horace Od. 1, 12, 27

quorum simul alba nautis
stella refulsit,
defluit saxis agitatus humor,
concidunt venti fugiuntque nubes,
et minax, quod sic voluere, ponto
unda recumbit.

They were believed to have appeared on board the Lakedaemonian ships at Aegospotami (Plutarch Lys. 12) and the Spartans accordingly dedicated some stars at Delphi after the battle (Cic. de div. 1, 75). Some difficulty has been felt at the number of the stars (τρεῖς l. 10): but the third is generally supposed to have represented Ἀπόλλων Δελφίνιος.

10. ἐπὶ τῆς γωνίης 'in the corner of the Pronaus'. Kroisos sent two great bowls, one gold and the other silver, which were originally placed on the right and left of the entrance to the ναός, but after the fire the gold bowl was removed to the treasury, and the silver one placed ἐπὶ τοῦ προνηίου τῆς γωνίης (1, 51).

CHAPTER CXXIII.

16. ἐπὶ τοῦ Ποσειδέωνος τῷ βωμῷ 'on the altar of Poseidon', that is, outside the temple of Poseidon, which stood near the stadium and the diolcos. The voting tickets were placed on the altar and taken from it by the voters, in order to add solemnity to their decision and to lay special obligation on them to vote honestly. Thus the βουλή at Athens, when electing a commissioner to decide a case of special importance as to the custody of the shrine at Delos, did so ἀπὸ τοῦ βωμοῦ φέρουσα τὴν ψῆφον, Demosth. de Cor. § 134.

17. κρίνοντες 'intending to decide upon', 'with a view to decide upon'. The present participle is used of a purpose in the immediate future.

18. ἐνθαῦτα 'thereupon', 'on this occasion', p. 28, l. 12.

ἐτίθετο τὴν ψῆφον 'gave his vote', 'placed it in the urn'. In legal language the juror was said φέρειν ψῆφον, but we have also Lysias 24 § 23 μηδαμῶς ταύτῃ θέσθε τὴν ψῆφον. τιθέναι ψήφους is used of calculating with pebbles Demosth. de Cor. § 229.

20. οἱ πολλοί 'the majority'. Plutarch (Malig. Her. 40) says that the vote for the second place was unanimous. In the life of Themistokles c. 17 he repeats the statement, and also affirms that

they actually gave the first prize to Themistokles (καίπερ ἄκοντες ὑπὸ φθόνου). See on p. 49, l. 8.

21. ἐμουνοῦντο 'were each in a minority of one'.

CHAPTER CXXIV.

23. ταῦτα κρίνειν 'to decide this point', i.e. who was to have the first prize.

25. ἀκρίτων 'without having come to a decision', Plut. Malig. 40 τέλος τῆς κρίσεως οὐ λαβούσης. This active or rather middle sense of ἄκριτος does not appear to occur elsewhere. Stein quotes the active use of ἀπίστους 'distrustful of' in 9, 98. We may also cp. Anthol. 7, 439, 1 ἄκριτε Μοῖρα 'Oh fate that dost make no distinctions!' and ἄκριτος τόλμη (Polyb. 3, 19, 9) 'undistinguishing boldness' i.e. rashness.

1. πολλὸν Ἑλλήνων σοφώτατος 'by far the cleverest man in Greece'. Obs. the absence of the article, in speaking of the Greek world generally. The cleverness or natural ability (σοφία) of Themistokles is what especially strikes Thucydides, though he does not use that word, but οἰκεία ξύνεσις, see 1, 138.

2. νικῶν 'though successful in the ballot', 'though according to the votes he ought to have had the prize'.

6. μέν νυν a frequent collocation in Herodotos. The μέν belongs to ἀριστηΐα answered by σοφίης δέ, the νυν to the whole sentence 'then' or 'so then'.

ἀριστηΐα Stein supposes the loss of some word such as ἀνδραγαθίης to answer to σοφίης, quoting Plutarch Them. 17 Λακεδαιμόνιοι δ' εἰς τὴν Σπάρτην αὐτὸν καταγαγόντες Εὐρυβιάδῃ μὲν ἀνδρείας, ἐκείνῳ δὲ σοφίας ἀριστεῖον ἔδοσαν. But Herodotos, probably using ἀριστηΐα in the technical sense of 'first prize for valour', did not think any further definition necessary. p. 61, l. 13; p. 6, l. 23.

9. αἰνέσαντες sc. the Lakedaemonians, and as the 300 youths represent the Lakedaemonians the construction is carried on, without change. p. 23, l. 2 οἱ δὲ ἐκ τῆς ἔξω ἠπείρου, Ἀθηναῖοι μὲν πρὸς πάντας τοὺς ἄλλους παρεχόμενοι νέας κτλ.

11. οἵ περ ἱππέες καλέονται. The three hundred picked youths in Sparta, selected by the ἱππαγρέται appointed by the Ephors. Though called 'horsemen' they consisted both of cavalry and hoplites, and acted as a body guard to the kings, see Dionys. Hal.

2, 13 παρ' ἐκείνοις (Λακεδαιμονίοις) οἱ γενναιότατοι τῶν νέων τριακόσιοι φύλακες ἦσαν τῶν βασιλέων, οἷς ἐχρῶντο κατὰ τοὺς πολέμους παρασπισταῖς, ἱππεῦσί τε οὖσι καὶ πεζοῖς. Müller however seems to doubt whether they were ἱππεῖς at all, as in the case of οἱ κατεστεῶτες τριακόσιοι who were with Leonidas (7, 205); and the expression of Herodotos here οἵ περ καλέονται shows that they were not in the ordinary sense cavalry. Müller's Dorians, vol. 2 p. 252.

12. οὔρων τῶν Τεγεητικῶν i.e. to the frontier of Laconia and Arcadia; the road North leading through Tegea. μοῦνον δή 'absolutely the only man'. The Spartans were always chary of bestowing honours, and particularly averse from encouraging strangers in Sparta. See 9, 35.

CHAPTER CXXV.

16. ἄλλως δὲ 'and besides', see p. 65, l. 26. Herodotos seems to mean that, besides being personally hostile to Themistokles, he had a class prejudice against him as of a social rank above his own. ἐπιφανεῖς *nobiles*, cf. 7, 114 ἑπτὰ Περσέων παῖδας ἐόντων ἐπιφανέων ἀνδρῶν.

17. φθόνῳ καταμαργέων 'stark mad with jealousy'. μαργᾶν is fairly common in the dramatists, but this compound is apparently ἅπαξ λεγ. We have ὑπομαργότερος in 3, 29; 6, 75.

22. ἐὰν Βελβινίτης that is, 'if I were the inhabitant of the most insignificant place in Greece', Belbina being a small island 10 miles off Sunium. In Plutarch Them. 18 the retort is made more telling by the reproach being addressed to him by an inhabitant of the little island of Seriphos, and thus giving Themistokles a handle for his reply ἀληθῆ λέγεις, ἀλλ' οὔτ' ἂν ἐγὼ Σερίφιος ὢν ἐγενόμην ἔνδοξος, οὔτε σὺ 'Ἀθηναῖος. Plato Rep. 329 has Σερίφιος in his version of the story too.

CHAPTER CXXVI.

25. νῦν l. 6. ἐς τοσοῦτο ἐγένετο 'amounted to what I have said', 'this was the upshot of these proceedings', p. 57, l. 19.

27. ἐκ τῶν Πλαταιικῶν 'by his subsequent conduct at the battle of Plataea',—in which he showed great foresight, and contrived to escape with a large body of men. See 9, 66, 89.

28. **τοῦ** assimilation of relative. G. § 153.

1. **προέπεμπε** 'was engaged in escorting'.
2. Thus μέν p. 68, l. 25 and δέ l. 26 express contemporaneous action. Cp. 6, 6 Ἱστιαῖος μέν νυν...ἐποίευν ταῦτα, ἐπὶ δὲ Μίλητον... ναυτικὸς ἦν στρατὸς προσδόκιμος.
5. **καὶ οὐδέν κω κατεπείγοντος** 'and there being as yet no hurry'. The absolute participle of κατεπείγει used impersonally. Hippocr. de fract. 762 οὐδὲν κατεπείγει, and perhaps Demosth. in Timocr. § 18 περὶ ὧν οὐδὲν ἴσως ὑμᾶς κατεπείγει νῦν ἀκοῦσαι. Others make it agree with Μαρδονίου 'and as he was not yet pressing him at all to join the rest of the army'. Herodotos nowhere else uses the active ἐπείγειν, though frequently the middle.
6. **οὐκ ἐδικαίου** 'he did not think proper', 'he could not make up his mind'. Cp. 9, 19 οὐκ ἐδικαίευν λείπεσθαι τῆς ἐξόδου Λακεδαιμονίων.
7. **μὴ οὐκ ἐξανδραποδίσασθαι** cp. p. 28, l. 20; p. 66, l. 2. G. § 283, 7. ... ἐδικαίου. μὴ ... ἐξανδραποδίσασθαι,
    οὐκ   „   „   οὐκ   „   „

This usually takes place after a negatived verb containing itself some negative notion, such as forbidding or hindering, because it is after such verbs that μή with the infinitive usually occurs.
8. **παρεξεληλάκεε** 'had marched past them', i.e. on his return journey.
10. **ἐκ τοῦ φανεροῦ** 'openly'. 9, 1 καὶ τότε ἐκ τοῦ φανεροῦ παρῆκε Μαρδόνιον ἐπὶ τὴν Ἑλλάδα.
11. **ὥς** = οὕτω. Cp. 9, 18, 35.

CHAPTER CXXVII.

12. **ἐνθαῦτα δὴ** 'it was in these circumstances'. p. 65, l. 11.
13. **ἐπολιόρκεε** 'began the siege of'.
14. **ἀπίστασθαι** 'that the Olynthians were on the point of revolting', the present expresses the intention in the immediate future. See on 6, 53 τάδε δὲ κατὰ τὰ λεγόμενα ὑπ' Ἑλλήνων ἐγὼ γράφω. 6, 82 μαθεῖν δὲ αὐτὸς οὕτω τὴν ἀτρεκείην ὅτι οὐκ αἱρέει τὸ Ἄργος, 'that he is not to take', 'that he will not take'.

ταύτην sc. Ὄλυνθον understood from Ὀλυνθίους above, cp. p. 66, l. 22.

16. ἐξαναστάντες 'having been turned out', used both of the country and the people. Cp. p. 22, l. 24. 2, 171 ἐξαναστάσης πάσης Πελοποννήσου ὑπὸ Δωριέων...οὐκ ἐξαναστάντες Ἀρκάδες διέσωζον αὐτὴν μοῦνοι.

17. κατέσφαξε...ἐς λίμνην 'took them out of the town to a marsh and killed them'. Cp. the action of the Aeginetan nobles in a similar massacre, when they took their victims to a lonely spot outside the town. 6, 91.

20. ἴσχον 'got possession of', implying that they still had it when Herodotos wrote. Notice Χαλκιδέες without the definite article,—'Chalkidians', not Bottiaei who used to have it.

CHAPTER CXXVIII.

21. ἐξελών, p. 61, l. 19.

22. ἐντεταμένως...προθύμως, notice the variation of the words, in sense nearly identical, to avoid harsh repetition.

25. οὐ γὰρ ὦν λέγεται 'for in fact it is not told'.

26. ὅκως...γράψειε 'whenever he wrote a letter'. See p. 26, l. 11; p. 63, l. 17.

28. παρὰ τὰς γλυφίδας 'close to the notched end'. γλυφίδες is used for the whole butt-end of the arrow, and consequently Aeneas Tact. 31, 26 quoting this story says περὶ τὰς γλυφίδας ἑλίξαντες τὸ βιβλίον.

1. πτερώσαντες 'having covered it with feathers'. The piece of 70 biblus or bark was wound round the arrow and then covered with the feathers (probably fixed in a piece of leather), partly for concealment and partly for the ordinary purpose of steadying the arrow.

8. παρῆν δὲ...συμμαχίη parenthetical, explaining the plural στρατηγοῖς, 'now there were there allied troops from the other states in Pallene also'. For συμμαχίη=σύμμαχοι, the abstract for the concrete, cp. φυγαὶ for φυγάδες 3, 138; δουλεία for δοῦλοι Thucyd. 5, 23, 4; ἡ ἀρχὴ for οἱ ἄρχοντες Lys. IX. § 16.

10. ἐπιλεξαμένοισι, cp. p. 12, l. 2.

11. μὴ καταπλῆξαι 'not to confound him with the charge of treason'. Herodotos does not use this word elsewhere, and two MSS. (R and S) have καταπλέξαι 'to involve in'.

CHAPTER CXXIX.

17. ἐγεγόνεσαν 'had elapsed'. Cp. 1, 113 ὡς δὲ τρίτη ἡμέρη τῷ παιδίῳ ἐκκειμένῳ ἐγένετο. 9, 39 ἡμέραι δέ σφι ἀντικατημένοισι ἤδη ἐγεγόνεσαν ὀκτώ.

ἄμπωτις 'ebb', cf. 7, 198 ἐν τῷ ἄμπωτις καὶ ῥηχίη ἀνὰ πᾶσαν ἡμέρην γίνεται.

18. χρόνον ἐπὶ πολλόν 'lasting a long time'. For ἐπί see p. 26, l. 20.

19. παρηίϊσαν 'tried to pass it into Pallene'. The Persians were on the north of the town which stretched right across the neck of the Isthmus; they tried to take advantage of the unusually low tide to get past the town so as to be able to attack it on its south and less defensible side (Thucyd. 1, 64, 2). They would have to go somewhat far out to pass the end of a mole or breakwater (χηλή) which ran out into the sea (Thucyd. 1, 63, 1).

20. τὰς δύο μὲν μοίρας sc. ὁδοῦ or τοῦ τενάγεος 'two-fifths of the way across the salt marsh'.

22. ἔσω εἶναι 'so as to be on Pallene south of the town'. Herodotos speaking as a Southern Greek means 'south' by ἔσω, *cis*. So ἔξω and εἴσω Πυλῶν Demosth. de Cor. 304.

24. πολλάκις γενομένη 'though it (a πλημμυρίς of some kind) takes place frequently'. The variations of tide in the Mediterranean are as a rule slight; but at particular places, such as the Euripus, the Straits of Messina, and others, the peculiar configuration of the shore produces currents which, acted on by the tides, cause a violent ebb and flow at certain times of the year and under the influence of certain winds.

δή 'accordingly', continuing a narrative, cp. 6, 5 περὶ Σάρδις μὲν δὴ ἐγένετο ταραχή. 6, 26 ταῦτα μὲν δὴ οὕτω ἐγένετο.

71   1. ῥηχίη opp. to ἄμπωτις in 2, 11: while πλημμυρίς indicates that it was not merely an ordinary flowing tide, but a high one, a flood tide.

2. Ποσειδέωνος ἐς τὸν νηόν. A temple of Poseidon was naturally erected on a narrow isthmus between two seas, just as in the case of the Isthmus of Corinth.

3. οὗτοι...οἵ περ, it was the very men in the Persian army that committed the impiety 'who also perished in the sea'.

CHAPTER CXXX.

9. ὁ ναυτικὸς sc. στρατός, cp. 7, 100 ἐς μὲν τοσόνδε ὁ ναυτικὸς στρατὸς εἴρηται. For the omission of στρατός cp. p. 72, l. 7; 7, 97 τοῦ δὲ ναυτικοῦ ἐστρατήγεον οἵδε.

10. ὡς προσέμιξε 'when it had reached Asia'. Cp. 6, 96 ἐπεὶ δὲ...προσέμιξαν τῇ Νάξῳ. 7, 168 μόγις δὲ ἀναχθέντες προσέμιξαν τῇ Πελοποννήσῳ.

13. ἐπιλάμψαντος, p. 8, l. 2. So 1, 190 τὸ δεύτερον ἔαρ ὑπέλαμπε 'began to appear'.

πρώϊος 'early in the season', cp. Thucyd. 4, 6, 1 ἅμα δὲ πρῷ ἐσβαλόντες καὶ τοῦ σίτου ἔτι χλωροῦ ὄντος.

14. Περσέων...οἱ πλεῦνες ἐπεβάτευον 'most of the epibatae were Persians and Medes'. It is expressed very oddly: lit. 'but it was of Persians and Medes that the greater number went on board as marines'.

17. ἀδελφιδέος 'brother's son'.

20. οὐδ' ἐπηνάγκαζε 'nor did anyone try to make them do so'.

23. ἐλεύσεσθαι. This future of ἔρχομαι is Ionic. It was used in Attic poetry; but rarely if ever in Attic prose of the classical period; the only exception is Lysias 22 § 11 where Cobet reads τρέψεσθαι.

25. σταθμεύμενοι ὅτι 'judging from the fact that'. Some word like τούτῳ or τῷδε must be understood. Cp. 7, 214 τοῦτο γὰρ τῷδε χρὴ σταθμώσασθαι ὅτι οἱ τῶν Ἑλλήνων πυλαγόραι ἐπεκήρυξαν κτλ.

26. ἄσμενοι ἀπαλλάσσοντο 'were only too glad to get away from them'. Cp. 9, 52 ἔφευγον ἄσμενοι τὴν ἵππον.

27. ἐσσωμένοι ἦσαν τῷ θυμῷ 'they had been cowed in spirit', cp. 9, 122 ἐσσωθέντες τῇ γνώμῃ πρὸς Κύρου. Thucyd. 4, 37, 1 εἴ πως...ἐπικλασθεῖεν τῇ γνώμῃ...καὶ ἡσσηθεῖεν τοῦ παρόντος δεινοῦ. 7, 71, 3 τὴν γνώμην ἐδουλοῦντο.

4. ὠτακούστεον 'they were trying to hear news', 'they listened anxiously for news'. Used of troops sent to reconnoitre in Xen. Cyr. 5, 3, 56. Cp. Demosth. de fals. Leg. § 288 περιερχόμεθα... ὠτακουστοῦντες τί τὰ τῶν Ἀρκάδων, τί τὰ τῶν Ἀμφικτυόνων...So of a man sent into Syria to see whether things were favourable for the

attempt of Demetrius ὠτακουστήσοντα καὶ κατοπτεύσοντα τὰ ἐκεῖ συμβαίνοντα Polyb. 31, 21, 1. Cp. Poll. 2, 83 ἐκαλοῦντο δέ τινες ὦτα καὶ ὀφθαλμοὶ βασιλέως...ἀπό τε τῶν ὤτων τούτων τὸ ὠτακουστεῖν πεποίηται.

ὅκῃ πεσέεται...πρήγματα 'whether Mardonius would be successful or no'. Cp. 7, 163 καραδοκήσαντα τὴν μάχην ᾗ πεσέεται.

CHAPTER CXXXI.

7. οὔκω συνελέγετο 'was not beginning to muster'.
ὁ ναυτικός, p. 71, l. 9.
9. ναύαρχος, p. 22, l. 9. The title is altogether a Spartan one; but when the Spartans first instituted the office is not known. From the beginning of the Peloponnesian war there seems to have been a ναύαρχος with a second in command, called ἐπιστολεύς, appointed every year, who was independent of the king. See Underhill on Xenoph. Hellen. 1, 5, 1.

16. τῆς ἑτέρης οἰκίης, of the junior royal family, the Eurypontidae. See Hist. and Geogr. Index, *Herakleidae*.

19. ἐστρατήγεε, notice this word used of a commander of a naval force. The Athenians had no separate establishment of naval commanders.

CHAPTER CXXXII.

21. Ἰώνων ἄγγελοι 'some Ionians as envoys'. Stein remarks that Ἰώνων is a partitive genitive. These messengers were not officially sent from the Ionians, but were certain Ionians who took upon themselves the task of attempting to get help for their country. The presence of the Persian fleet would probably prevent any open or public mission.

25. οἱ στασιῶται σφίσι γενόμενοι 'who having made a conspiracy with each other'. σφίσι = ἑωυτοῖσι = ἀλλήλοις. 1, 142 αὐταὶ δὲ αἱ πόλιες...σφίσι ὁμοφωνέουσι. 6, 12 ἔλεξαν πρὸς ἑωυτοὺς τάδε. 6, 42 συνθήκας σφίσι αὐτοῖσι τοὺς Ἴωνας ἠνάγκασε ποιέεσθαι.

3. ἐξενείκαντος 'having betrayed', 'made known'. Cp. 3, 74 πίστι λαβόντες καὶ ὁρκίοισι ἢ μὲν ἕξειν παρ' ἑωυτῷ μηδ' ἐξοίσειν μηδενὶ ἀνθρώπων τὴν ἀπὸ σφέων ἀπάτην ἐς Πέρσας γεγονυῖαν.

4. οὕτω δή 'in these circumstances', or 'when this had taken

place'. See on 9, 15. ὑπεξέσχον 'removed secretly'. Cp. 6, 74 ὑπεξέσχε ἐς Θεσσαλίην.

5. καὶ δὴ καὶ τότε 'and so finally came at this time to Aegina'. p. 21, l. 22; p. 56, l. 13.

7. οἱ 'they, however'.

9. οὔτε τῶν χώρων ἐοῦσι ἐμπείροισι, στρατιῆς τε...ἐδόκεε εἶναι. For οὔτε...τε cp. 6, 16. For the change of subject (*parataxis*) cp. 6, 30, 123. Everything beyond Delos, i.e. to the north and east of Delos, was an object of terror to the Greeks; for they were unacquainted with the lie of the countries (i.e. the islands and the Asiatic coast), and they imagined every place to be full of armed men. The Greek sailors were not at this period familiar with the navigation of the Aegean, with the exception perhaps of the Aeginetans, Corinthians, Chalkidians, and possibly the Athenians, and this was a joint fleet. As far as Delos they were used to go for the yearly festival. Rawlinson thinks the idea of such ignorance on the part of the Greeks a gross exaggeration, and not accounted for by fifteen years' cessation of such voyages since the Ionian revolt. But though at this distance of time fifteen years seem insignificant, it is a considerable period in the lives of sailors, whose energies would have been engaged elsewhere; and we must remember that an appreciable part of the fleet consisted of ships sent from towns not used to such expeditions, and the movements of it were likely to be measured not by the boldness of the bravest, but by the fears of the most timid. Grote v. p. 298.

11. ἠπιστέατο 'believed', p. 3, l. 21. δόξῃ 'as a matter of conjecture'.

καὶ Ἡρακλέας στήλας 'were as far off as the Pillars of Herakles'. The Pillars of Herakles were the end of all things westward to the Greek (ἵν' ὁ ποντομέδων πορφυρέας λίμνας ναύταις οὐκέθ' ὁδὸν νέμει 'where the Sea-lord of the purple main no further grants a pathway to sailors' Eurip. Hipp. 744); and Herodotos only seems to mean here that the Peloponnesians thought Samos an immense distance off, and the voyage to it too great to be undertaken; he does *not* mean that they had any theory about the exact distances.

12. συνέπιπτε δὲ τοιοῦτο ὥστε 'and by a coincidence it so happened that', p. 8, l. 18.

15. τὸ μέσον...σφέων 'all that lay between them'.

CHAPTER CXXXIII.

17. **δή**, resuming the narrative from l. 8 μόγις μέχρι Δήλου Cp. p. 76, l. 28.

19. **ἐνθεῦτεν ὁρμεόμενος**, p. 61, l. 30. κατὰ τὰ χρηστήρια 'to the various oracles', 'from oracle to oracle'. 1, 30 περιῆγον τὸν Σόλωνα κατὰ τοὺς θησαυρούς (Ab.).

20. **Εὐρωπία**, of the town Europos in Karia.

21. **τῶν**, referring to χρηστηρίοισι understood after χρησόμενον 'to consult the oracles', though in this sense χρᾶσθαι is often used absolutely without being followed by any case. **οἷά τε**, for the suffix τε see on p. 10, l. 9.

22. **ἀποπειρήσασθαι**, p. 34, l. 27.

24. **οὐ γὰρ ὦν λέγεται**, p. 69, l. 25.

CHAPTER CXXXIV.

27. **φαίνεται ἀπικόμενος** 'notoriously arrived at Lebedaea'.

1. **καταβῆναι παρὰ Τροφώνιον** 'to descend into the cavern of Trophonius'. Cp. Arist. Nub. 507 ὡς δέδοικ' ἐγὼ | εἴσω καταβαίνων ὥσπερ εἰς Τροφωνίου. See Biographical Index.

2. **καὶ δή...ἀπίκετο** 'and above all on arriving at Thebes, which he did first'. For another similar consultation of Greek oracles, see 1, 46.

3—5. **τοῦτο μὲν...τοῦτο δὲ**, p. 40, l. 5.

4. **ἔστι δὲ...χρηστηριάζεσθαι** 'now it is allowed, as at Olympia, to consult the oracle there by means of burnt sacrifices', i.e. in contradistinction to the method at Delphi and other places, where the inquirer entered the shrine and received the answers from the προφήτης, here on the other hand the oracle was declared by inspection of the victims offered on the altar. Cp. Pind. Olymp. 13, 2 ἵνα μάντιες ἄνδρες ἐμπύροις τεκμαιρόμενοι παραπειρῶνται Διὸς ἀρχικεραύνου. To this πυρομαντεία Sophokles refers O. T. 21 ἐπ' Ἰσμηνοῦ τε μαντείᾳ σποδῷ.

6. **κατεκοίμησε ἐς Ἀμφιάρεω** 'caused him to pass the night in the temple of Amphiaraos'. Cp. 9, 93. For the practice of passing the night in a temple see 1, 31; Aristoph. Plut. 669—671. The object in this case was to obtain an oracle by a dream. Paus. 1, 3,

5 κριὸν θύσαντες καὶ τὸ δέρμα ὑποστρωσάμενοι καθεύδουσιν ἀναμένοντες δήλωσιν ὀνείρατος. The dream is given in Plut. Arist. 19. For the pregnant use of ἐς cp. id. 411 κατακλίνειν αὐτὸν εἰς Ἀσκληπίου | κράτιστόν ἐστι. This temple of Amphiaraos, according to Rawlinson, was not at Thebes but near Oropos. He quotes Pausan. 1, 34, 2. Livy 45, 27 *inde Oropum Atticae ventum est ubi pro deo vates Amphilochus colitur.* But the former only says that there was *a* temple of Amphiaraos, 1½ miles from Oropos, and that the Oropians were the first to regard Amphiaraos as a god (θεὸν δὲ Ἀμφιάραον πρῶτοις Ὠρωπίοις κατέστη νομίζειν, ὕστερον δὲ καὶ οἱ πάντες Ἕλληνες ἥγηνται). And Livy says no more, even if *Amphilochus* is altered to *Amphiaraus.*

8. διὰ χρηστηρίων ποιεύμενος 'by means of an oracle', 'speaking in an oracular response'. Cf. 6, 4 μετὰ δὲ Ἱστιαῖος δι' ἀγγέλου ποιεύμενος...ἔπεμπε βιβλία.

9. ὁκότερα, cp. δεύτερα, p. 67, l. 20. οἷά τε p. 73, l. 21.

CHAPTER CXXXV.

13. θῶμά μοι μέγιστον γενέσθαι λέγεται 'a thing is related by the Thebans to have happened which is a matter of the greatest surprise to me'. θῶμά μοι = ὃ θαυμαστόν ἐστί μοι.

14. ἐλθεῖν ἄρα 'for (they say) that Mys came'. For ἄρα introducing the words of another, cf. Aeschin. in Ctes. § 137 τολμᾷ λέγειν βλέπων εἰς πρόσωπα τὰ ὑμέτερα, ὡς ἄρα Θηβαῖοι τὴν συμμαχίαν ὑμῖν ἐποιήσαντο κτλ. Herodotos often prefaces an anecdote with this word, see p. 4, l. 27.

15. περιστρωφώμενον...χρηστήρια 'in the course of his series of visits to all the oracles'.

16. τὸ τέμενος, see p. 20, l. 17. It is here used for the temple and inclosure.

17. ἔστι Θηβαίων 'belongs to the Thebans', i.e. is in the Theban territory.

18. ὑπὲρ...οὔρεῖ 'East of the lake Copais and close to the mountain', i.e. Mt. Ptoum.

21. ἀπὸ τοῦ κοινοῦ 'representing the (Theban) State'. 5, 109 ἡμέας ἀπέπεμψε τὸ κοινὸν τῶν Ἰώνων.

22. ἀπογραψομένους 'for the purpose of taking notes of'. For ἀπογράφειν and ἀπογράφεσθαι see 7, 100. The middle is used here

because Herodotos is thinking not of their actually writing down the words, but of their purpose in coming to the temple.

ἔμελλε sc. ὁ θεός. πρόκατε 'forthwith', 1, 111.

24. ἔχεσθαι, p. 26, l. 20. οὐδὲ ἔχειν...πρήγματι 'and did not know what to do about it', i.e. they could not take down the words, as they had been sent to do, as they did not understand them. For βαρβάρῳ see p. 11, l. 3.

27. τὴν ἐφέροντο 'which they were carrying', 'which they had in their hands'.

29. φάναι δὲ Καρίῃ...γλώσσῃ χρᾶν 'that he was giving his answer in the Karian language'. The Karians were βαρβαρόφωνοι, Hom. Il. 2, 867. What Herodotos is surprised at is that the promantis should be able to speak Karian. It is possible that some Karian sentence had been prepared on purpose to prevent the Theban commissioners from knowing what the answer was, in order that the medizing Thebans might not afterwards lay the blame of their medizing on the oracle. Or, if the sentence of the oracle contained any reference to the projected alliance of Athens with the Persians (cc. 136, 141), it might be prudent that the Thebans should be kept in the dark about it. Thirlwall 2, p. 323. Grote 5, p. 4.

CHAPTER CXXXVI.

1. ἐπιλεξάμενος, p. 70, l. 10. ὅ τι δὴ λέγοντα ἦν 'what the oracles said, whatever it was'. Herodotos does not know what the oracles were, but he connects with them the step Mardonius next took of trying to win over Athens. See last note.

4. προσκηδέες 'relations by marriage'. Cp. κηδεστής, κῆδος (7, 189).

8. τῷ δή 'to whom, as is well known'. For δή referring to known facts, cp. 6, 44, 45.

9. ἅμα δὲ...πυθόμενος 'and at the same time because Mardonius was informed'. The causal participle answers to the ἅμα μὲν ὅτι ...ἦσαν in l. 4.

10. πρόξενος. Individuals were ξένοι to each other; when the connexion was between a State and an individual he was called πρόξενος, and the relationship προξενία. Cp. 9, 85. εὐεργέτης, p. 45, l. 2.

12. ἄρα, p. 74, l. 15.

15. ἐπίστατο. For the irregularity of a verb connected by τε with a participle (ἀκούων) cp. p. 45, l. 13; p. 73, l. 11. For ἐπίστατο see p. 3, l. 21; p. 13, l. 22; p. 46, l. 19.

τούτων δὲ προσγενομένων 'but if they joined him',—if he could get the Athenian fleet on his side.

κατήλπιζε 'he quite expected', κατα- intensive.

18. κατύπερθέ οἱ τὰ πρήγματα...τῶν Ἑλληνικῶν sc. πρηγμάτων 'that his power would be superior to that of the Greeks'. For πρήγματα 'power' cp. 6, 13 κατεφαίνετό σφι εἶναι ἀδύνατα τὰ βασιλέος πρήγματα ὑπερβαλέσθαι.

19. τάχα δ' ἄν...προλέγοι 'and it may perhaps be the case that the oracles also gave him a forewarning of this'. An expression used in 1, 70 of a similar tentative and doubtful explanation. Herodotos generally uses the present optative in such contingent statements, even though referring to past events. Cp. 5, 59 ταῦτα ἡλικίην ἂν εἴη κατὰ Λάϊον τὸν Λαβδάκου.

21. ποιέεσθαι, notice the middle—'to secure as his ally'. τοῖσι δὴ πειθόμενος 'in obedience to which it was that he sent him'. δή marks the clause as representing the thought of Mardonius, not the writer, see 9, 11, 59.

CHAPTER CXXXVII.

23. ἕβδομος, see Biogr. Index, s. vv. *Alexander, Perdikkas*. Thucyd. 2, 99, 100; 5, 80.

3. ἐς τὴν ἄνω Μακεδονίην, cp. 7, 128 Μακεδόνων τῶν κατύπερθε οἰκημένων, i.e. Makedonia north of Pindus.

4. ἐθήτευον 'acted as labourers'. The θῆτες are not δοῦλοι but hirelings, for originally slaves, properly so called, were said not to have existed in Greece, see 6, 137.

6. τὰ λεπτὰ τῶν προβάτων 'the smaller cattle', i.e. sheep and goats. Cp. 1, 133. For the use of πρόβατα for cattle generally cp. 2, 41 τὰς βοῦς τὰς θηλέας σέβονται προβάτων πάντων μάλιστα. 4, 61 θύουσι καὶ τἆλλα πρόβατα καὶ ἵππους μάλιστα. [πρόβατον any animal that walks—i.e. does not fly or swim.]

9. ἡ δὲ γυνὴ τοῦ βασιλέος, cp. the description of the Princess Nausikaa in the Odyss. 6, 57 sqq. going to the river to wash

the clothes: and the harvest scene in the shield of Achilles (Il. 18, 559)

αἱ δὲ γυναῖκες
δεῖπνον ἐρίθοισιν λεύκ' ἄλφιτα πολλὰ πάλυνον.

ἔπεσσε 'used to knead'.

10. ὅκως δὲ ὀπτῷτο 'and whenever the loaf was being baked': for the frequentative optative with ὅκως see p. 26, l. 11; p. 63, l. 17; p. 69, l. 26.

11. διπλήσιος...αὐτὸς ἑωυτοῦ 'twice as great'. 1, 203 τῇ εὐρυτάτῃ ἐστὶ αὐτὴ ἑωυτῆς. p. 45, l. 12.

13. ἐσῆλθε 'it occurred to'. Cp. 7, 46 ἐσῆλθέ με λογισάμενον κατοικτεῖραι. 6, 125 ἰδόντα δὲ τὸν Κροῖσον γέλως ἐσῆλθε. καὶ φέροι ἐς μέγα τι 'and had some important significance'. Cp. 4, 90 ἐς ἄκεσιν φέροντα. 6, 42 ἐς νεῖκος φέρον. 1, 120 ἐς τί ὑμῖν ταῦτα φαίνεται φέρειν;

17. οὕτω, i.e. when they had received their pay. For οὕτω expressing the completion of an action previously expressed, cp. p. 12, l. 25; p. 65, l. 20.

18. κατὰ τὴν καπνοδόκην 'by the smoke-vent'; apparently not like our chimney, but an aperture in the centre of the roof,—by which Philokleon endeavours to escape in the 'Wasps', Arist. Vesp. 139—143. See 4, 103; Becker's *Charicles*, p. 271; *Gallus*, p. 279. For γάρ anticipatory, see p. 3, l. 10.

ἦν...ἐσέχων 'was making its way in', cp. 2, 11 κόλπος θαλάσσης ἐσέχων ἐς τὴν Ἀραβίην χώρην ἐκ τῆς Ἐρυθρῆς θαλάσσης.

19. θεοβλαβής 'under an infatuation sent from heaven'. Cp. 1, 127 ὥστε θεοβλαβής. The notion contained in the sentence *quem deus vult perdere prius dementat* is often expressed by Greek writers. See Lycurg. in Leocr. 92 οἱ γὰρ θεοὶ οὐδὲν πρότερον ποιοῦσιν ἢ τῶν πονηρῶν ἀνθρώπων τὴν διάνοιαν παράγουσιν. Demosth. 3 Phil. 54; Aeschin. in Ctes. § 117; Polyb. 23, 10.

24. δεκόμεθα, cp. p. 63, l. 11.

25. τὸν ἥλιον, i.e. the circle of sunlight admitted by the round smoke-vent.

27. τοῦ ἡλίου, partitive gen. 'a draught of the sunshine'. By this Perdikkas meant first to take possession of the hearth, and secondly of the whole land, the lordship of the Sun being symbolical of his claim. The German editors compare some German customs of taking possession of property by a symbolic reception from God

and the Sun (*Sonnenlehen*). 'On entering into possession the new lord rode forth in the morning in armour and with drawn sword towards the East, and as soon as the sun rose waved his sword three times crosswise in the air'. Stein.

CHAPTER CXXXVIII.

28. **οἱ μὲν δή**, the usual formula of Herodotos in dismissing a portion of a story and continuing, p. 77, l. 20 etc.

29. **τις τῶν παρέδρων** 'one of his council'. **οἷόν τι χρῆμα** 'the significance of the action of the boy'.

30. **σὺν νόῳ** 'deliberately', *avec intention*: in p. 45, l. 9 it means *certa ratione* 'on deliberate plan'.

2. **τῷ θύουσι.** For sacrifice to rivers see 6, 76 (to the Erasinos 77 in Argos); 7, 113 (to the Strymon).

5. **οἵους τε**, p. 10, l. 9.

9. **ὑπερφέροντα τῶν ἄλλων.** The genitive follows this verb on the analogy of all verbs implying comparison of excess or defect. In p. 81, l. 14 ὑπερφέρω is used without a case.

10. **ἥλω** 'was caught by the country people sleeping in the garden'.

12. **ὑπὸ χειμῶνος** 'owing to the effects of winter', cp. p. 1, l. 3. 5, 10 ὑπὸ τούτων (μελισσῶν) οὐκ εἶναι διελθεῖν τὸ προσωτέρω.

13. **καὶ τὴν ἄλλην Μακεδονίην** 'the rest of Makedonia also', i.e. the country which, besides what he has already called 'upper Makedonia', was called generally Makedonia in the time of Herodotos, extending eastwards as far as the Strymon and south to the borders of Thessaly.

CHAPTER CXL.

25. **μετίημι** 'I remit', 'I forgive', 6, 59 τὸν προσοφειλόμενον φόρον μετίει ὁ βασιλεύς.

26. **τοῦτο μὲν...τοῦτο δέ**, p. 40, l. 5.

τὴν γῆν σφι...ἔθλωσι. This offer was long remembered. See Dem. de Cor. 202 καὶ παρὰ τοῦ Περσῶν Βασιλέως μετὰ πολλῆς χάριτος τοῦτ' ἂν ἀσμένως ἐδόθη τῇ πόλει, ὅτι βούλεται λαβούσῃ καὶ τὰ ἑαυτῆς ἐχούσῃ τὸ κελευόμενον ποιεῖν καὶ ἐὰν ἕτερον τῶν Ἑλλήνων προεστάναι.

28. **ἰόντες αὐτόνομοι**, that is, without having a tyrannus imposed upon them by Persian influence, or being included in a Satrapy under a Persian governor.

ἱρά. On the destruction of the temples at Athens, see c. 53.

1. **τούτων δὲ ἀπιγμένων** 'such being the orders received by me from the king'.

2. **τὸ ὑμέτερον** 'your action', almost = ὑμεῖς, cp. 3, 155 ἤδη ὦν ἦν μὴ τῶν σῶν δεήσῃ αἱρέομεν Βαβυλῶνα.

3. **νῦν τί μαίνεσθε;** So Stein punctuates. Other editions have λέγω τάδε νῦν· τί μαίνεσθε κτλ. Stein's arrangement seems the better. He quotes 1, 120; 5, 106.

5. **ἂν ὑπερβάλοισθε**, p. 13, l. 18.

7. **καὶ τὰ ἔργα** 'and the great things which it did'. Cp. prol. ἔργα μεγάλα τε καὶ θωυμαστὰ τὰ μὲν Ἕλλησι τὰ δὲ βαρβάροισι ἀποδεχθέντα.

11. **παρισούμενοι βασιλεῖ** 'setting up to be equal to the king'. Cp. 4, 166 ὁ δὲ Ἀρυάνδης τῆς Αἰγύπτου ὕπαρχος ὑπὸ Καμβύσεω κατεστεὼς ὑστέρῳ χρόνῳ παρισούμενος Δαρείῳ διεφθάρη.

12. **θέαν δὲ...αὐτῶν** 'and continually risking your own safety'. See p. 38, l. 26.

13. **παρέχει** = πάρεστι p. 5, l. 1.

14. **βασιλέος ταύτῃ ὡρμημένου** 'the king being inclined in this direction'. Cp. 1, 158 οἱ Κυμαῖοι ὁρμέατο ἐκδιδόναι Πακτύην Πέρσῃσι· ὁρμεομένου δὲ ταύτῃ τοῦ πλήθεος κτλ.

15. **ὁμαιχμίην** = συμμαχίην 7, 145. **συνθέμενοι** p. 66, l. 12. **ἄνευ τε δόλου καὶ ἀπάτης**, a regular treaty clause, see 1, 69; 9, 7; Thucyd. 5, 18, 4; 5, 47, 2.

19. **ἐξ ἐμεῦ.** For ἐκ with the genitive of the agent see p. 62, l. 26; 6, 13 τὰ γινόμενα ἐκ τῶν Ἰώνων. 9, 16 ὅτι δεῖ γενέσθαι ἐκ τοῦ θεοῦ.

21. **ἐνορέω...οὐκ οἴοισί τε ἐσομένοισι** 'I see in you that you will not be able'. The construction is very loose and may be explained as an instance of a participle taking the place of accusative and infinitive, or better with Stein by regarding ἐνορέω as equivalent to σύνοιδα and taking its construction as in 9, 60 συνοίδαμεν δὲ ὑμῖν ὑπὸ τὸν παρεόντα τόνδε πόλεμον ἐοῦσι πολλὸν προθυ-

μοτάτοισι. So Herod. constructs πείθεσθαι with genitive on the analogy of ὑπακούειν (6, 12), διαδεξάτω on that of φανήτω (p. 65, l. 16).

25. χεὶρ ὑπερμήκης 'a very long arm'. Cp. the English proverb 'Justice has a long arm'; and the Scriptural phrase 'with a stretched out arm'. Cp. 4, 155 τέῳ δυνάμει, κοίῃ χειρί; Abicht quotes Ovid Heroid. 17, 16 *an nescis longas regibus esse manus.*

26. μεγάλα προτεινόντων 'when they (the Persians) offer liberal terms'.

27. ἐν τρίβῳ τε μάλιστα οἰκημένων τῶν συμμάχων πάντων 'seeing that you most of all the allied states lie right in the way'. Alexander seems to mean that Athens lies directly in the path of Mardonius on his march to the Peloponnesus; which is not wholly true: though it was true that the Athenians were likely to be attacked again first, before Mardonius ventured to proceed Southward.

29. ἐξαίρετον...ἐκτημένων 'the land you possess being one specially marked out for a fighting ground' 'to be the scene of the contest between the two parties'. μεταίχμιον is properly 'a space between two armies', see 6, 77, 112. That Attica was not a good ground for actual fighting, especially for cavalry, Mardonius soon discovered, see 9, 13.

30. ἀλλὰ πείθεσθε, cp. p. 31, l. 16 ἀλλ' ἐμοὶ πείθεο.

CHAPTER CXLI.

5. τῶν λογίων. For these oracles see 5, 90 ἔτι τε πρὸς τούτοισι 79 ἐνῆγόν σφεας οἱ χρησμοὶ λέγοντες πολλά τε καὶ ἀνάρσια ἔσεσθαι αὐτοῖσι ἐξ Ἀθηναίων, τῶν πρότερον μὲν ἦσαν ἀδαέες, τότε δὲ Κλεομένεος κομίσαντος ἐς Σπάρτην ἐξέμαθον.

10. συνέπιπτε ὥστε, p. 8, l. 18; p. 73, l. 12.

11. τὴν κατάστασιν 'their audience' before the people. Cp. 9, 1. 3, 46 καταστάντες ἐπὶ τοὺς ἄρχοντας.

ἐπανέμειναν...διατρίβοντες 'for the Athenians had purposely delayed because they expected them to come'. The participle represents the main sentence. Cp. p. 57, l. 17.

14. ἐπ' ὁμολογίῃ 'with a proposal for a composition', or,

'with a view to making a composition'. Cp. Dem. 293 ἐπὶ σωτηρίᾳ πάντα πράττειν.

15. **ἐπίτηδες ὧν ἐποίευν** 'they did this (i.e. waited) therefore purposely'.

CHAPTER CXLII.

18. **διαδεξάμενοι** sc. τὸν λόγον 'taking up the discourse in their turn'.

19. **ἡμέας δέ.** Notice the emphatic position of ἡμέας 'us (as opposed to Alexander) the Spartans sent'. The speech is introduced by δέ because of this reference to the speech of Alexander. For a similar use of δέ cp. p. 35, l. 8; p. 76, l. 20; 5, 33.

20. **κατὰ τὴν Ἑλλάδα** 'in Greece'.

22. **κόσμον φέρον**, p. 29, l. 23.

23. **ὑμῖν δὲ δή** emphatic δή 'but to you especially'.

24. **καὶ διὰ πάντων** 'and above all others', p. 19, l. 25; p. 36, l. 17.

25. **ἠγείρατε...ὑμεῖς.** The Spartans mean to refer the origin of the war to the help given by Athens to the Ionians. Cp. 5, 97 αὗται δὲ αἱ νέες ἀρχὴ κακῶν ἐγένοντο Ἕλλησί τε καὶ βαρβάροισι. The Spartans had refused to help the Ionians, 5, 49.

26. **περὶ τῆς ὑμετέρης ἀρχῆς...ἐγένετο** 'and it was in behalf of your own dominion that the contest arose'. This can hardly mean to refer to any claim of Athens to supremacy in Greece; for such a notion would have been absurd at this period. Nor does it mend matters to read ἀρχήν with Schaeffer, which could hardly mean 'in defence of your territory'. We must suppose either that the Spartans mean to imply that the ships sent by Athens to Ionia were sent on the ground of some shadowy claim of the Athenians to a primacy among the Ionians; or, with Abicht, that the reference is to the attempts of the Persians to force the Athenians to recall the Peisistratids (5, 96).

1. **φέρει καὶ ἐς.** Cp. p. 76, l. 14.

2. **ἄλλως τε** 'and besides', 'on other grounds', p. 65, l. 26.

4. **καὶ τὸ πάλαι** 'from time immemorial'. The reference is to mythical or heroic times. See Isocrates Panegyr. §§ 55, 56 (the Herakleidae and Adrastos). Cp. §§ 64—67.

6. **καρπῶν...διξῶν ἤδη** 'of what was now two harvests'. The

harvest of B.C. 480 had been destroyed by the Persians (c. 50); and after Salamis probably the sowing for the next harvest had been partial and late, and was afterwards much damaged in the spring of B.C. 479 by Mardonius (9, 13).

7. οἰκοφθόρησθε 'ye have lost your property', or, 'have had your property destroyed'. 1, 196 ἐλόντες ἐκακώθησαν καὶ οἰκοφθορήθησαν. 5, 29 ὥρεόν σφεας δεινῶς οἰκοφθορημένους. οἶκος includes all a man's estate, not merely his house (οἰκίη), cp. 7, 224 τὸν οἶκον πάντα τὸν ἑωυτοῦ ἐπέδωκε.

9. τὰ...οἰκετέων ἐχόμενα 'whatever you have pertaining to your families unfit for war'. For οἰκεταί cp. p. 56, l. 26. For ἐχόμενα cp. 1, 120 τὰ τῶν ὀνειράτων ἐχόμενα 'things in the way of dreams'. 3, 25 τὰ σιτίων ἐχόμενα εἶχον 'what they had in the way of food'. 5, 49 χρυσοῦ ἐχόμενον οὐδέν.

10. ἐπιτρέψειν 'that they will provide for their support', just as the Troezenians did in the previous year, see on c. 41.

11. ἔστ' ἄν...συνεστήκῃ 'as long as the war lasts'. Cp. 7, 225 τοῦτο (this struggle) συνεστήκεε μέχρι οὗ οἱ σὺν Ἐπιάλτῃ παρεγένοντο. 1, 74 τῆς μάχης συνεστεώσης τὴν ἡμέρην ἐξαπίνης νύκτα γενέσθαι.

12. ἀναγνώσῃ, p. 28, l. 23. λεήνας 'by his softened version of the message of Mardonius'. Cp. 7, 9 ἐπιλεήνας τὴν Ξέρξεω γνώμην.

14. τύραννος γὰρ ἐών. The kings of Makedonia are not called 'tyrants', but βασιλεῖς. The term is used here *ad invidiam*.

16. βαρβάροισι. The Spartans at home called all other people whether Hellenic or barbarian ξεῖνοι (9, 11); but here, speaking to Athenians, they adopt an Hellenic attitude and employ the customary word.

CHAPTER CXLIII.

19. καὶ αὐτοί 'we as well as you'. The author of the reply was Aristeides, according to Plutarch Arist. c. 10.

22. ὀνειδίζειν 'to throw that in our teeth', 'to bring it up in a hostile spirit'. γλιχόμενος (γλίσχρος 'sticky') 'eager for', 'clinging to'. A rare word in Attic, but several times used by Herodotos in three constructions: (1) with περί, 2, 102 δεινῶς γλιχόμενοι περὶ

τῆς ἐλευθερίης—though here Van Herwerden omits περί. (2) with gen. as here, cp. 3, 72 τοῦ αὐτοῦ γλιχόμεθα. (3) with ὡς and a verb, 7, 161 ὡς στρατηγήσεις αὐτῆς γλίχεαι.

24. πειρῶ ἀναπείθειν. For the threefold construction of πειρᾶσθαι in Herodotos, see on p. 57, l. 18.

26. ἔστ' ἄν...ἔρχεται 'as long as the sun traverses the same path by which he now goes'. Cp. Soph. Phil. 1329

καὶ παῦλαν ἴσθι τῆσδε μή ποτ' ἐντυχεῖν
νόσου βαρείας, ὡς ἂν αὐτὸς ἥλιος
ταύτῃ μὲν αἴρῃ, τῇδε δ' αὖ δύνῃ πάλιν.

Plut. Arist. 10 τοῖς δὲ παρὰ Μαρδονίου τὸν ἥλιον δείξας—Ἄχρις ἂν οὗτος, ἔφη, ταύτην πορεύηται τὴν πορείαν, Ἀθηναῖοι πολεμήσουσι Πέρσαις ὑπὲρ τῆς δεδῃωμένης χώρας καὶ ἠσεβημένων καὶ κατακεκαυμένων ἱερῶν. And the Scriptural 'as long as the sun and moon endureth'.

81 1. ἀμυνόμενοι 'wreaking vengeance for'. Valknaer proposed the future participle ἀμυνεόμενοι. But the present participle is used of repeated or continuous action whatever may be the tense of the main verb. For the Persian destruction of the temples see c. 53.

2. τῶν...ὄπιν 'feeling no reverence for whom', see on 9, 57 οὔτε δαιμόνων οὔτε θεῶν ὄπιν ἔχοντας, and the note there on this poetical word.

3. τοῦ λοιποῦ 'on any future occasion', genitive of the time within which. p. 37, l. 25 and Index.

6. οὐδὲν ἄχαρι 'any severity', 6, 9; but there is also an idea conveyed in it of ingratitude or breach of former ties, cp. 1, 108; 7, 52.

7. πρόξεινον, p. 75, l. 10.

CHAPTER CXLIV.

11. αἰσχρῶς...ἀρρωδῆσαι 'but you appear to your shame, though thoroughly knowing the Athenian spirit, to entertain a fear'. Cp. 9, 7 ὑμεῖς δὲ ἐς πᾶσαν ἀρρωδίην τότε ἀπικόμενοι μὴ ὁμολογήσωμεν τῷ Πέρσῃ, ἐπείτε ἐξεμάθετε τὸ ἡμέτερον φρόνημα σαφέως, ὅτι οὐδαμὰ προδώσομεν τὴν Ἑλλάδα, κτλ.

14. τοσοῦτος...τά...'A relative in the neuter may refer to a number of inanimate antecedents, even when they are all mas-

culine or feminine': cp. Isocr. Panath. 217 ταῦτα εἶπον οὐ πρὸς τὴν εὐσέβειαν οὐδὲ πρὸς τὴν δικαιοσύνην οὐδὲ πρὸς τὴν φρόνησιν ἀποβλέψας ἃ σὺ διῆλθες. Madv. G. G. 97. μέγα = οὕτω μέγα from the influence of τοσοῦτος, which like τοιοῦτος is sometimes followed by an explanatory simple relative instead of the more precise οἷος or ὅσος. ἀρετῇ 'excellence' 'fertility', see 4, 198; 7, 5. ὑπερφέρουσα, see p. 77, l. 9.

15. τά...Ἑλλάδα 'on receiving which we shall be willing to enslave Greece by joining the Persians'.

17. διακωλύοντα μή. See on p. 66, l. 2. And cp. p. 60, l. 20 ἐπεί τέ σφι ἀπέδοξε μήτ' ἐπιδιώκειν κτλ.

18. μηδ' ἢν 'even if', the negative arises from the previous μή.

21. ἐς τὰ μέγιστα 'to the uttermost of our power', cp. πρὸς τὰ μέγιστα p. 11, l. 7.

22. τὸ Ἑλληνικόν...ὁμόγλωσσον 'another motive is GREECE, allied as she is in blood and language'. It is difficult to express in a word all that is implied in τὸ Ἑλληνικόν,—the feeling of a common tie, in spite of much difference and hostility, which after all distinguishes everything Greek from everything barbarian.

24. ἤθεά τε ὁμότροπα 'community of habits'. The best commentary perhaps to these words will be furnished by Thucydides 1, 6. The distinguishing features common to all Greeks are here mentioned,—blood, language, religious worship, customs.

25. οὐκ ἂν εὖ ἔχοι 'it cannot be right', 'it will never be right'. Ἀθηναίους, notice the absence of the definite article 'that Athenians (of all people in the world) should betray'.

28. ὑμέων ἀγάμεθα τὴν πρόνοιαν 'we thank you for your foresight on our behalf'. There is a slight irony in the words.

3. οἰκέτας, p. 80, l. 10. καὶ ὑμῖν...ἐκπεπλήρωται 'and for your part indeed you have done all that you are bound to do': i.e. 'any service you owe us has been fully paid by this generous offer'.

4. λιπαρήσομεν οὕτω ὅκως ἂν ἔχωμεν 'we will hold out as best we may'. Cp. 9, 45 λιπαρέετε μένοντες. 5, 19 μηδὲ λιπάρεε τῇ πόσι. For ὅκως = ὡς cp. 5, 89.

5. νῦν δέ 'but as to our present duty'. ὡς οὕτω ἐχόντων 'seeing that things are as we say', referring to their declared intention of maintaining their resistance.

7. οὐκ ἑκὰς χρόνου 'at no distant date'. Herodotos every-

where else uses ἑκάς of space. For its use in regard to time cp. Aesch. Ag. 1638 εἶα δὴ φίλοι λοχῖται, τοὔργον οὐχ ἑκὰς τόδε. For the genitive χρόνου cp. the analogous construction of πρόσω τῆς νυκτός 2, 121.

11. ἡμέας 'we' i.e. you and ourselves. προβωθῆσαι 'should advance to oppose him'. They afterwards found fault with the Lakedaemonians ὅτι περιεῖδον ἐμβαλόντα τὸν βάρβαρον ἐς τὴν Ἀττικὴν ἀλλ' οὐ μετὰ σφέων ἠντίασαν ἐς τὴν Βοιωτίην 'that they tamely allowed the Barbarian to invade Attica, instead of accompany them into Bōeotia to resist him there' (9, 6).

HISTORICAL AND GEOGRAPHICAL INDEX.

ABAE, cc. 27, 33, 134.

A city of Phokis on the frontier of Boeotia situated upon one of the tributaries of the Kephisos. It contained a rich temple and oracle of Apollo, and had been inhabited by a Thrakian tribe who afterwards passed over to Euboea. It appears to have recovered from the damage done by the Persians, for it is mentioned as the only town in Phokis that did not share in the Sacred War (B.C. 357—346) and offered a refuge for fugitives: for which however it suffered by the burning of its temple [Paus. 10, 35, 2].

ABDERA, c. 120.

A city on the coast of Thrakia some ten miles east of the river Nestos, colonized first from Klazomenae and afterwards by the Teians [1, 168]. It was the birthplace of several famous men, Hekataeos the historian, and Protagoras, Demokritos and Anaxarchos the philosophers.

ABRONICHOS, c. 21.

An Athenian, son of Lysikles, employed by Leonidas to watch the fleet at Artemisium, and bring news of the result of the battle.

ABYDOS, cc. 117, 130.

In Mysia, situated on the Asiatic side of the Hellespont, opposite Sestos, at the narrowest point in the strait. The head of Xerxes' bridge was at a point somewhat to the north of it, where the breadth of the strait is 7 stades (less than a mile): see 7, 34. It was founded by a colony from Miletos.

ACHAIA, c. 36.
ACHAIANS, cc. 47, 73.

The inhabitants of Achaia, the northern district of the Peloponnese. The *Achaioi* in the time of Homer inhabited Argolis, Lakonia, and Messenia, but at some period subsequent to that they were expelled by the Dorians and driven into the northern district, from which they expelled the Ionian inhabitants, and which afterwards retained their name. They were a confederacy of twelve chief cities, ten of which were on the sea coast [1, 145]. The name was also preserved in Northern Greece in the district of Achaea Phthiotis round Mt Orthrys [7, 132].

ACHERON, C. 47.

A small river in Epeiros, which falls into the Ionian Sea at a place called the Sweet Haven [γλυκὺς λιμήν], *Port Fanari*.

ADEIMANTOS, cc. 5, 59, 61, 94.

A Corinthian, son of Okytos, commanding the Corinthian contingent in the allied fleet. He is accused of having played the coward at Salamis.

AEAKIDAE, cc. 64, 83—4. AEAKOS, c. 64.

The descendants of Aeakos, son of Zeus and Aegina. Gaining great reputation for his justice as ruler of Aegina, Aeakos became one of the three judges in Hades. His descendants were the national heroes of Aegina, Thessaly and Salamis:

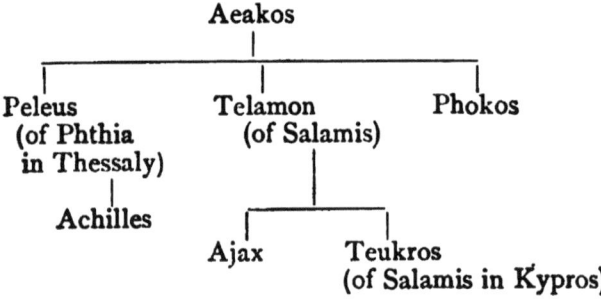

The myth was that Peleus and Telamon joined in killing Phokos, and that therefore Peleus was driven to exile in Phthia, Telamon in Salamis. See 5, 80.

AEGALEOS, C. 90.

A mountain chain in Attica extending from Parnes to the east of the bay of Eleusis. Its southern slope overlooks the gulf and island of Salamis.

AEGINA, cc. 41, 60, 63, 79, 81, 83—4, 131, 132.

AEGINETANS, the, cc. 1, 45, 74, 84, 86, 91—3, 122.

An island in the Saronic gulf, about eight miles due south of Salamis and about double that distance east of the coast of Argolis. At the time of the Persian invasion it was an independent state, though it had formerly been subject to the people of the opposite Dorian town of Epidauros, from which the island had been peopled

[5, 83; 8, 46]. The Aeginetans had however long ago thrown off the control of Epidauros, and had become possessed of a powerful navy and considerable wealth. They had from very ancient times been at enmity with Athens, which is described by Herodotos [5, 82 sq.] as beginning with an attempt on the part of the latter to carry off the olive-wood images of the national heroes of Aegina, the Aeakidae. But a more likely account is that which represents the Aeginetans as making frequent attacks upon the Attic coast, and using their power at sea, on which they were supreme before B.C. 500, to annoy and injure Athenian commerce. The quarrel was further embittered by help given to the Boeotians against Athens a few years earlier [5, 81], and when Darius about 493—2 B.C. sent round to the Greek states for earth and water, Aegina was one of the states which complied, actuated perhaps as much by jealousy of Athens as by fear of Persia. This led to a formal complaint against them by Athens to Sparta. The Spartans took hostages for their fidelity whom they entrusted to the Athenians, and whom the Athenians before and after Marathon refused to return. The war which followed continued after B.C. 489 [7, 144], to carry out which Themistokles persuaded the Athenians to build a fleet. The threatened invasion of Xerxes however forced Athens and Aegina to make peace, and thus Aeginetan ships served at Salamis, and next year their soldiers served at Plataea. Aegina finally became entirely subject to Athens during the administration of Perikles, who always regarded its independence as a standing menace to Athens and was wont to call it 'the eyesore of the Peiraeus' [Plut. Peric. 8]. And in B.C. 431 the Athenians expelled the Dorian inhabitants and placed Attic settlers in their room [Thucyd. 2, 27; 7, 57].

AEOLIDAE, the, c. 35.

The inhabitants of a town and district at the foot of Parnassos in Phokis. The exact site seems uncertain.

AEROPOS.

(1) c. 137.

An Argive, one of the brothers of Perdikkas the ancestor of the kings of Makedonia.

(2) c. 139.

A descendant of Perdikkas, and father of Alketas.

AESCHREAS, c. 11.
An Athenian, father of Lykomedes.

AETOLIANS, the, c. 73.

According to one myth Aetolos, king of Elis, son of Endymion, having slain Apis fled to the district of the Achelous which was called Aetolia after him. According to another the Aetolians helped to convey the Dorian invaders from Antirrhium to Rhium in the

Peloponnese, and received the district of Elis as their reward [Paus. 5, 3, 5]. The Aetolians living north of the Corinthian Gulf were a peculiar people little known in the rest of Hellas. They lived in open towns or hamlets and used only light armour; but were warlike and brave. In B.C. 426 the Athenian general Demosthenes invaded Aetolia, but was defeated by a combined army of all the Aetolian states [Thucyd. 3, 94—8]. The Aetolians showed the same determination in resisting the Gallic invasion B.C. 279; and the Aetolian League from about B.C. 220 was the rival of the Achaean League in Greece, until reduced by the Romans in B.C. 189.

AGLAUROS, C. 53.

Daughter of Kekrops. She had a temple, or rather sacred grotto on the north side of the Acropolis, from which tradition said that she had cast herself, as a sacrifice for her country.

AJAX, c. 63.

Son of Telamon, and one of the heroes of Salamis. See *Aeakidae*. In the Iliad he is the greatest warrior next to Achilles, but has no special authority in council.

AKERATOS, C. 37.

The prophet in the temple of Apollo at Delphi.

ALABANDA, C. 136.

A town in Karia, mod. *Arab-Hissar* on the Marsyas (*Tchinar Aksa*), about 20 miles S. of Tralles. It was afterwards in Roman times a place of great wealth, the seat of a district court, and the birthplace of many famous orators.

ALEXANDER, cc. 34, 121, 126—7, 136—7, 139—143.

Alexander, son of Amyntas I., king of Lower Makedonia, the chief cities of which were Edessa and Pella. His family claimed to be Greek as descended from an Argive named Têmenus [Her. 8, 137; Thucyd. 2, 90], whose grandson Perdikkas first established the dynasty. Alexander, though he appears as acting with Xerxes under compulsion, had thirty years before shown that he was a man of courage and address. At that time (B.C. 510) the Persian general Megabazus, who had been commissioned by Darius, after his unfortunate Scythian expedition, to obtain the submission of Makedonia, sent seven ambassadors of high rank to the court of Amyntas. They obtained the symbols of submission from the aged king and were royally entertained by him, but an insult offered by them to some ladies of the court so enraged the young Prince Alexander, that he had them assassinated, and all their rich equipments dispersed [5, 19—21]. Though when king he had been unable to resist submitting to Xerxes, he had still shown his interest in the Greek cause by taking the trouble to send envoys to the army despatched to guard the pass between Ossa and Olympus urging them not to attempt to hold so dangerous a position [Her. 7, 173]; and in the following year he showed, by coming to warn the Greeks before Plataea, on which side his wishes really lay [9, 45]. He had great wealth derived from the product of gold and silver mines [5, 17], which he commemorated by presenting a gold statue or statuette of himself to the god at Delphi. He was succeeded by his son Perdikkas II. some time before 432 B.C. [Thucyd. 1, 57] and after B.C. 463 [Plut. Cim. 14]. His Argive descent was admitted by the managers of the Olympic games, who allowed him to enter for the foot-race [5, 22].

ALKETAS, c. 139.

One of the early kings of Makedonia, father of Amyntas.

ALKIBIADES, c. 17.

The father of Kleinias, and grandfather of the great Alkibiades. He was the head of one of the richest and noblest families at Athens, which traced its descent from Eurysakes, son of Ajax.

ALYATTES, c. 35.

King of Lydia, and father of Kroisos. In his reign [B.C. 625—560] the Kimmerians, a horde of Scythian barbarians who had forced their way into Asia, were expelled from Lydia; and the encroachment upon Karia and Ephesos was begun which was consummated by his son Kroisos (q. v.).

AMBRAKIOTS, the, c. 45.

Ambrakia was a town and district on the river Arachthos, seven miles from the shore of the Ambrakian gulf. It was a colony from Korinthos [Thucyd. 2, 80], and though it only contributed the moderate contingent of 500 men to the Greek army of defence, it played an important part afterwards in the Peloponnesian war on the side of the Peloponnesians; and in the time of Pyrrhus (circ. B.C. 290) was the capital of Epeiros.

AMEINIAS, cc. 84, 93.

An Athenian, of the deme Pallene.

AMPHIARAOS, c. 134.

According to some legends a son of Apollo and Hypermnestra, according to others of Oikles and Hypermnestra, and descended from the seer Melampus. He was joint king of Argos with Adrastos, was one of the heroes engaged in the expedition of the Argo, the Kalydonian boar-hunt, and the expedition of the Seven against Thebes. In the last, as he fled from Periklymenos, the earth opened and swallowed him up, and he was made immortal by Zeus. Besides sanctuaries at Argos and Sparta, he had a temple and oracle near Oropos [1, 46].

Amphikaia, c. 33.

A town of Phokis in the valley of the Kephisos. Pausanias says [9, 33, 9] that its right name, as evidenced by the decree of the Amphiktyonic Council for its destruction, was Amphikleia. There was a story connected with it exactly like that of Bethgellert, in which the child is defended from a wolf, not by a dog, but by a serpent, which was accordingly worshipped, and the town called by some 'Οφιτεία [ὄφις].

Amphissa, c. 32.

A town in the territory of the Ozolian Lokrians, situated on the heights above the Krissean plain (mod. *Salona*). It was afterwards destroyed by order of the Amphiktyonic Council for cultivating the parts of the territory of Krissa, which had been consecrated, and for levying severe tolls upon the worshippers coming from Sicily and Italy to the shrine of Delphi, but was afterwards restored [Strab. 9, 3, 4]. The people of Amphissa reckoned themselves to be Aetolians (q. v.) not Lokrians.

Amyntas.

(1) cc. 136, 139—140.

King of Makedonia, son of Alketas and father of Alexander (q. v.). He was an aged man in B.C. 510, and much terrified by the ambition and aggressiveness of Darius, to whose envoys he gave the required symbols of submission. When his son Alexander planned his bloody revenge against these envoys the old king was first induced to retire, in spite of his alarm at his son's evident anger and dangerous temper [5, 17—20]. He was on terms of friendship with the Peisistratids, and offered Hippias the town of Anthemos when he was expelled from Athens [5, 94]. Besides his son Alexander, he had a daughter Gygaea married to a Persian named Bubares [8, 136].

(2) c. 136.

A son of the Persian Bubares and Gygaea sister of Alexander of Makedon. He is called 'Amyntas of Asia', to distinguish him from the father of Alexander.

Anagyrasios, c. 93.

Of the deme Anagyros, which was on the coast of Attica between the Piraeus and Sunium.

Anaxandridas, c. 71.

Son of Leon, king of Sparta of the elder house. He died shortly before B.C. 502. Herodotos [5, 39—41] tells us that his first wife, who was also his niece, had no children; and that therefore the Ephors urged him to put her away and marry another.

He refused to do so from love to his wife. The Ephors accordingly, as a compromise, suggested that without divorcing his first wife he should take another. He accordingly—a thing hitherto unheard of at Sparta—married a second wife, a daughter of Prinetadas, and had by her a son Kleomenes. Soon afterwards his first wife, to the surprise of all, became the mother of three sons in quick succession, Dorieus, Leonidas, Kleombrotos. Kleomenes succeeded his father and died leaving only a daughter, Gorgo, about 495 B.C. Dorieus had meanwhile, after an adventurous life, died in Sicily [7, 205], and Leonidas succeeded. Kleombrotos was the father of Pausanias (q. v.).

ANDRIANS, the, c. 66. ANDROS, cc. 108, 111, 112, 121.

Andros was the most northern and, next to Naxos, the largest of the Cyclades, being 21 m. long by 8 m. broad. It was fertile and rich in vines; but its inhabitants pleaded poverty when Themistokles demanded a contribution in B.C. 480 after the battle of Salamis [8, 111]. 'The Athenians', said Themistokles, 'have brought two strong gods, Persuasion and Necessity'. 'But we', answered the Andrians, 'have two unprofitable gods who never quit our island, Poverty and Helplessness'.

ANDROMADAS, c. 85.

A Samian, father of Theomestor (q. v.).

ANTIDORUS, c. 11.

A native of Lemnos.

ANTIKYRA, c. 21.

There were two towns of this name, one in Phokis on the gulf of Corinth; the other in Malis. The latter seems to be the one referred to here [and in 7, 198]. It was near the modern town of *Zitúni*. Both towns were noted for the cultivation of hellebore.

APHETAE, cc. 4, 7, 8, 11, 12, 14.

A town and roadstead on the coast of Magnesia in the Pagasaean gulf. Strabo says that it was so named as the place from which the Argo started, just as Pagasae was called as the place at which the Argo was built ($\pi\eta\gamma\nu\mu\iota$). He says that Aphetae was near ($\pi\lambda\eta\sigma\iota\sigma\nu$) Pagasae; but this cannot be taken very literally. Pagasae is at the very head of the gulf, and the whole story shows that the Persian fleet could not have been so far removed from Artemisium [Strab. 9, 5, 15].

APHIDNAIOS, c. 125.

Of Aphidna, a fortified town in Attica, some few miles beyond Dekeleia on the road from Athens to Oropos. It was a very ancient town, one of the original twelve which Theseus was believed to have united into one Athenian State. It was celebrated in mythology as the place in which Theseus concealed Helen, when he carried her off as a child of seven years old; and accordingly her brothers Castor and Pollux took the town when they invaded Attica in search of her. Aphidna also was the birthplace of the poet Tyrtaeos, and of the tyrannicides Harmodios and Aristogeiton. Its exact site seems uncertain, but it has been supposed that some remains of fortifications on a hill now called Kotroni mark its situation.

APOLLO, c. 134. See *Ismenios* and *Ptous*.

AREIOPAGOS, the, c. 52.

A hill at Athens, sacred to Ares, and separated from the western side of the Akropolis by a depression of some few yards breadth. It was chiefly noted for being the place at which the Council met in the open air for trials in cases of murder and sacrilege.

ARES, c. 77.

God of war, son of Zeus and Herè.

ARGAIOS, c. 139.

Son of Perdikkas the first Greek sovereign of Makedonia (q. v.).

ARGIVES, the, c. 73. ARGOS, cc. 137—8.

Argos was the chief town of Argolis, the north-eastern province of Peloponnese. The dispute of the Argives with Sparta for possession of the narrow district along the coast immediately south of Argos, called Kynuria, had kept them in constant hostility with the Spartans. And their sufferings from the invasion of the Spartan king Kleomenes in B.C. 495—3, and the consequent rebellion of their own slaves [6, 72—83], had not only crippled them, but made them more than indifferent, positively hostile to the cause of the Greeks against the Persians; they are said to have even sent to Persia inviting the invasion [7, 150—2], and certainly took no part in resisting it. In the following year they showed their friendship by warning Mardonius of the approach of the army of the Peloponnese [9, 12]. This alliance with Persia was maintained for many years afterwards [7, 151; Thucyd. 2, 67].

ARIABIGNES, c. 89.

A son of Darius, and brother of Xerxes. He was commander in chief of the Persian fleet [7, 97].

ARIARAMNES, c. 90.

A Persian. His friendship to the Ionians had probably been conceived during some official employment in Asia Minor.

ARIPHRON, c. 131. Father of Xanthippos (q.v.)

ARISTEIDES, CC. 79, 91, 95.

The son of Lysimachos, of the deme Alopekae. In his youth he had been a friend of the reformer Kleisthenes, and when in after years he came to hold various offices in the state he so distinguished himself for his strict integrity, that he received by general consent the title of the Just. He was one of the ten Strategi at Marathon, and, after the battle, was left with the men of his tribe to guard the captives and collect the spoil, while the rest of the army hurried back to Athens to confront the Persians who had sailed thither round Sunium. His great rival, Themistokles, who had also been one of the Strategi at Marathon, rose to great power and influence during the ten years from B.C. 490 to B.C. 480, owing principally to his energetic measures in inducing the Athenians to equip a powerful fleet for the prosecution of the Aeginetan war, which ships, as Herodotos says, 'saved Hellas' by crushing the invasion of Xerxes at Salamis. The political rivalry between the two statesmen had been stopped in the way peculiar to Athens by a vote of ostracism, in which the majority voted against Aristeides [B.C. 483]; but when the invasion of Xerxes was actually approaching, the Athenians recalled Aristeides, and he joined the fleet at Salamis. After Salamis, though the reputation of Themistokles was enormous, the confidence of the people seems to have rested most upon Aristeides. He was elected sole commander (στρατηγὸς αὐτοκράτωρ) of the 8000 hoplites sent to join the Greek army against Mardonius; and in the period which followed he was almost continually in command in the Aegean. It was his high character which induced the allies, irritated by the folly and arrogance of Pausanias, to transfer the command of the allied fleet to Athens; and it was he who organised the Confederacy of Delos [B.C. 477—6], and arranged the assessment of the φόρος on a footing of equity always looked back upon by the allies themselves with satisfaction. As a statesman he had been connected with the more aristocratic party in opposition to Themistokles. But after 479 B.C. their positions seem to have been reversed to some extent. It was Aristeides who carried a measure throwing open to all citizens the archonship formerly confined to the *pentacosiomedimni*, the richest class of citizens according to the assessment of Solon; while his frequent absence in command of the fleet separated him from the reactionary party at home, and kept him in sympathy with the class of citizens engaged in foreign service, who were observed to be more distinctly democratic than those who remained at home. The year of his death is variously stated as B.C. 469—8; and the place according to some was Pontus, according to others, Athens. But all agree that he retained the affection and respect of his fellow-citizens to the last; and that he showed by the smallness of the means which he left behind him, that he had made no personal gains in the public service. His tomb was long shown at Phalerum, and his daughters were portioned at the public cost, while his son Lysimachos had a grant of land and a pension.

Life by Plutarch.

ARKADIA, c. 26. ARKADIANS, the, cc. 72—3.

The central district of the Peloponnese. Its natural strength, being walled in on every side by considerable mountain ranges, preserved it from invasion, and its Pelasgan inhabitants therefore were not displaced by the Dorians who overran and settled most of the rest of the Peloponnese. This fact is to be remembered in studying Peloponnesian politics. Its mountainous scenery, and the antiquity of its inhabitants, caused it to be regarded as the natural home of primitive simplicity and pastoral life. It consisted of a number of independent townships, the most notable of which were Tegea and Mantinea, the only Arkadian towns mentioned as furnishing troops at Plataea [vid. 9, 27—8].

ARTABANOS, c. 26.

Son of Hystaspes, brother of Darius, and uncle of Xerxes. He had dissuaded Xerxes from his expedition against Greece [7, 10—17], had warned him of the insecurity of the loyalty of the Ionians [7, 46—52], and had been sent to Susa in charge of the kingdom when Xerxes was starting [7, 52—3].

ARTABAZOS, cc. 126, 128—9.

Artabazos, son of Pharnaces, commanded the Parthians and Chorasmians [Her. 7, 6], and was held in high estimation among the Persians. He escorted king Xerxes back to the Hellespont after Salamis, at the head of 60,000 picked troops, and spent the winter of 480—8 in trying to reduce the towns of Potidaea and Olynthos. He killed all the inhabitants of the latter city and handed it over to certain Chalkidian settlers in the neighbourhood. But he was not so successful with Potidaea. The citizens of this town offered a stout resistance for three months: and finally he lost a large number of his men in trying to enter the town at an ebb tide round the breakwater, or mole, which protected the harbour [χηλή Thucyd. 1, 63]. Artabazos then raised the siege, retired to join Mardonius in Makedonia, and marched with him southward in the spring. His force however was now reduced to 40,000 men, with which he escaped after Plataea, and with part of which at any rate he arrived safely in Asia; where he still retained the confidence of the king, who sent him in B.C. 478—7 as Satrap to Sardis, in place of Megabates, when Pausanias offered to negotiate with the Persian monarch [Thucyd. 1, 129]. From that time we hear no more of him.

ARTACHAEOS, c. 130.

A Persian, father of Artayntes.

ARTAYNTES, c. 130.

A Persian left by Xerxes in command of his fleet, and conquered in the following year at Mykale (9, 102, 107).

GEOGRAPHICAL INDEX.

ARTEMIS, c. 77.

The virgin Goddess, daughter of Zeus and Leto.

ARTEMISIA, cc. 66—8, 68—9, 93, 101, 107.

Queen of Halikarnassos in Karia, daughter of Lygdamis. She was married to the king of Halikarnassos, and on his death succeeded to the royal power, though she had a grown-up son, Pisindelis, who was the father of another Lygdam;s, king of Halikarnassos at the time that Herodotos left his native city. Besides Halikarnassos her dominions included Kos, Nisyros and Kalydna. She furnished five triremes to the fleet of Xerxes [7, 99]; and was so much trusted by him, that, when he retreated after Salamis to the Hellespont, he committed his children to her care to convey to Ephesos [8, 101—2]. Photios [*Biblioth.* 492] says that she committed suicide by throwing herself off the Leucadian rock ('the lover's leap') in remorse for having put out the eyes of a youth called Dardanos of Abydos, whom she had loved in vain. Her portrait was among the paintings on the 'Persian Stoa' in the agora of Sparta [Pausan. 3, 11, 3].

ARTEMISIUM, cc. 4, 6, 8, 40, 42—5, 66, 76, 81.

A name applied to the line of coast on the north of Euboea. It was so called from a temple of Artemis situated on the extreme point of the island. The name was also especially applied to the extreme northern promontory of Euboea, and probably to the town which had gathered round the haven. But of this town we know nothing. The name is common to other places, as for instance a promontory in Karia.

ASIA, cc. 109, 118—9, 130, 136.

Herodotos knew somewhat less than a third of Asia, that part, namely, which was included in the Persian Empire. Earlier still the name was sometimes used merely of the district afterwards called Lydia [Homer, Il. 2, 461].

ASINE, c. 73.

A town in Messenia on the west coast of the Koronaean gulf (*Sinus Messeniacus*), on the opposite coast of which stood Kardamyle. It is called 'near Kardamyle' to distinguish it from Asine in Argos, from which the Dryopians (q. v.) had come, when expelled by the Argives from their three towns of Hermione, Asine, and Halice.

ATARNEUS, c. 106.

A tract of Mysia opposite Lesbos [1, 160], near the river Kaikos (6, 28); it had been given up to the Chians by the Persians in return for the surrender of the Lydian tyrant Pactyas, who had taken refuge at Mytilene, after his revolt against Kyros.

ATHENÈ, cc. 55, 104. ATHENÈ PRONAIA, cc. 37—9. ATHENÈ SKIRAS, c. 94.

The goddess Athenè was fabled to have sprung fully armed from the head of Zeus. She was guardian deity of Athens, which was named after her. The most venerable temple on the Acropolis was hers; her sacred bird was stamped on the Attic coins; and in every respect she represented the Athenian nationality.

The temple of ATHENÈ PRONAIA at Delphi abutted on the road from Phokis, and was the last of four temples standing thus at the entrance of the town. *Pronaia* means 'living in front', i.e. at the entrance of the town: but Pausanias (10, 8, 6) calls it the temple Ἀθηνῆς Προνοίας 'of Athenè the goddess of forethought'.

The position of the temple of ATHENÈ SKIRAS in Salamis is doubtful. It has generally been believed to be near the northern promontory the Skiradion; but Stein places it in the South close to the old town of Salamis [quoting Plut. Solon 10]. The objection to this is that it supposes the Korinthians to be escaping round the S. of the Island, which seems unlikely. The title Skiras is connected with two temples of Athenè in Attica, and from it the month Skirophorion and the festival Skirophoria were named.

ATHENIANS, the, cc. 1, 2, 5, 10, 17—8, 21—2, 40—2, 44, 51—5, 68, 70, 74—5, 84, 86, 91, 93—4, 109—111, 136, 140—4.

ATHENS, cc. 34, 46, 48, 50, 56, 66—8, 102, 106, 118, 125, 136, 141.

During the summer of B.C. 480 Athens was in the hands of the Persians, and though the inhabitants partially returned after the battle of Salamis, they quitted the town again in the spring of 479 B.C. at the approach of Mardonios, and were for the most part housed in the island of Salamis, while Athens itself was for a time again occupied by Mardonios. The Athenians were all along the life and soul of the resistance to Persia. They, with the help of 1000 Plataeans only, had conquered at Marathon in B.C. 490; they had organized the confederacy of the southern states formed in B.C. 481—480 to repel Xerxes; at Artemisium and at Salamis their ships numbered nearly as many as those of all the other allies together; and though at Plataea it was the Spartans and Tegeans who alone were engaged with the Persians, the Athenians were meanwhile employed in what was probably a more serious encounter with the Boeotians; and in the consequent attack upon the Persian fortified camp the Spartans could not succeed without their help. It was her patriotism and valour in this war which among other causes led to the subsequent supremacy of Athens in Hellas. Until after the Persian wars Athens was practically an open town; the Acropolis had been fortified by a wall constructed by Pelasgan builders, but any other defences it may have possessed must have been of the very slightest. After the Persian wars the Acropolis was devoted to sacred buildings, while the town itself was defended by a ring wall of about 7 miles in circumference.

ATTICA, cc. 10, 40, 49, 51, 60, 65, 96, 144.

Thucydides (1, 2) observes that Attica, partly because it lay out of the road from the north to southern Greece, and partly because its soil was not very fruitful, had in former times seldom been invaded, and therefore had not undergone those frequent changes of inhabitants which had befallen the rest of Greece. The people therefore regarded themselves as Autochthonous, or native to the soil. It is a peninsula of which the greatest length is 50 miles and breadth 30 miles; its whole contents 700 square miles. Its geological formation is primitive limestone; and it is so mountainous that only half its square contents is available for cultivation. The hills are generally bare and rugged, giving a meagre sustenance to sheep and goats, and but scantily sprinkled with pines, dwarf-oaks, lentisk, arbutus and bay trees. The plains in the country, and there is none of importance except that of Athens itself, have but a light soil thinly covering the rock, not generally fitted for corn-growing, and not fruitful in anything except olives and vines. It is badly supplied with water; its streams are mountain torrents nearly dry in the summer, and there is no lake or natural reservoir. The name has been generally derived from ἀκτή, 'headland' or 'coastland', but Curtius suggests that it is rather ἀστική from ἄστυ.

AUTONOOS, c. 39.

One of the deified men or heroes worshipped at Delphi.

BAGAEOS, c. 130.

The father of Mardontes (q. v.).

BAKIS, cc. 20, 77, 96.

Nothing is known of this personage beyond the fact that a number of oracles were extant, the collection of which was attributed to him. These were consulted by individuals and states in times of danger and uncertainty: Herodotos quotes them in 9, 43: and Aristophanes parodied the style of these prophecies in the Equites and elsewhere [see Eq. 123 sq., Av. 899, Pax 1009]; which does not at all prove that he was wholly incredulous in respect to them. We are told that there were three prophets of this name (which means 'the Speaker', cp. βάζειν), one of Boeotia, who is the one quoted by Herodotos, another of Attica, and a third of Kaphyae in Arkadia.

BAKTRIANS, c. 113.

Inhabitants of Baktria (*Balk*) separated from Ariana and from the Sakae by Mt Paromisos (*Hindú-Kúsh*) on the south and east, and from Sogdiana on the north-east by the river Oxus, and from Morgiana (*Khorassán*) on the west. Their contingent in the grand army under Sisamnes carried bows of cane [7, 64—6], some on foot and some on horseback [ib. 86]. They were included in the twelfth Satrapy by Darius [3, 92].

BASILEIDES, C. 132.

The father of an Herodotos, an Ionian, who is supposed by some to have been a relation of our historian.

BELBINE, C. 125.

An island in the Saronic gulf, not far from Sunium, mod. *Island of St George*. There was however another place of the same name in Lakonia, on the borders of Arkadia, which may possibly be meant here [Steph. Byz., Pausan. 8, 35, 3].

BERMIOS, C. 138.

The range of mountains in lower Makedonia extending north to the R. Lydias and south to the R. Haliakmon, and enclosing large plains between it and the sea.

BISALTAE, C. 116.

A Thrakian people inhabiting a district west of the Strymon, in which were the Andrian colonies of Argīlus and Arethusa [7, 115]. They were a warlike race, who, though afterwards conquered by the Makedonians, long retained their name and nationality.

BOEOTIA, CC. 45, 144.

Boeotia was the district immediately to the north of Attica, bounded on the south-west by that part of the Corinthian Gulf called the *mare Alkyonium*, on the north and north-east by the territory of the Opuntian Lokrians and the Euripos, and on the west by Phokis. Between it and Attica lay the mountain range of Kithaeron and Parnes, which was crossed by two passes, one called Dryoskephalae leading from Eleusis by Eleutherae and Hysiae to Plataea, and another from Athens by Phylè (on Mt Parnes) into the valley of the Asopos and direct to Thebes. Extending from sea to sea it barred the way into Attica and the Peloponnese, and being also suited by its plains for military evolutions was often the scene of campaigns. It is divided geographically into two districts, the northern one containing two wide plains, those of Orchomenos and Thebes, but completely surrounded by mountains; the other, or southern Boeotia, containing the long and sometimes wide valley of the Asopos. Politically Boeotia was a somewhat loose confederacy of free towns, which varied in number at different times. Nine towns are known as belonging to the confederacy, viz. Thebes, Orchomenos, Lebadea, Coronea, Copae, Haliartos, Thespiae, Tanagra, Anthedon. Of these Orchomenos in Homeric times seems to have been far the most important, but for a long while before the Persian war Thebes had been the leading state. These states were free, according to the Hellenic custom, but for certain purposes they were under the control of deputies or *Boeotarchs* elected by each state, who were again controlled by consultative senates.

BOEOTIANS, the, cc. 34, 38, 50, 66, 113.

The Boeotians were a mixed race. Aeolian Hellenes had emigrated from Thessaly and settled there, partly absorbing the earlier Pelasgic inhabitants; and in Thebes there had also been a Phoenikian colony called Kadmeians, whose name still survived in the citadel of Thebes, the Kadmeia. Not only, therefore, were they divided in race from the people of Attica and the Peloponnese, but against the former they were embittered by the feuds which always sprung up between conterminous Greek states, the especial object of contest in their case being generally the possession of Oropos, which commanded the eastern and easiest road from Attica to the north, as well as Oenoe and Hysiae commanding the pass of Dryoskephalae. They and the Chalkidians of Euboea had in B.C. 506 joined Kleomenes of Sparta in ravaging Attica, in the interest of the expelled Hippias [Her. 5, 74]; and had subsequently helped to protect the Chalkidians against the consequent Athenian vengeance [ib. 77]; and this enmity to Athens in a great measure accounted for the eagerness with which they as a nation medized. Yet there seems to have been a considerable party of loyalists even at Thebes; and at Thermopylae there were 700 Thespians and 400 Thebans serving in the army of Leonidas, though the latter soon deserted [7, 202].

BOTTIAEI, c. 127.

Originally the inhabitants of the district between the rivers Haliakmon and Axius, the original seat of the Makedonian kingdom, and containing Pella, which was afterwards the capital of the kingdom [7, 123]. The Bottiaei were afterwards driven by the Makedonians eastward to the neighbourhood of Pallene [Thucyd. 2, 99].

BUBARES, c. 136.

A Persian who married Gygaea sister of Alexander of Makedon. He had been despatched to investigate the fate of the Persian ambassadors who had been assassinated at the Makedonian court in B.C. 510, but had apparently been induced by a bribe of money, and the hand of Gygaea, to hush the matter up [5, 21].

CHALKIDIANS, the, cc. 1, 44—5.

The inhabitants of Chalkis in Euboea. Chalkis (mod. *Egripo*) on the Euripos, where the channel is divided by a rock—which now forms a central pier for the bridge uniting Euboea with the continent,—was a flourishing commercial town which had sent colonies in very ancient times to Sicily and Italy and the north of Greece. The oldest Hellenic colony in Italy, Kumae, was from Chalkis (perhaps in conjunction with the Asiatic Kymaeans), and the Chalkidian colonies in Sicily, Naxos and Zancle (Messina), had in their turn been the source of four other flourishing Sicilian towns. It was early a rival and opponent of Athens: and in B.C. 506, after it had taken part in the confederacy formed by Kleomenes against Athens, the Athenians conquered it and divided part of its territory among 4000 lot-holders or kleruchs [5, 77].

CHERSIS, c. 11.

Father of Gorgos, king of Salamis in Kypros (q. v.). He was the son of Siromos s. of Euelthon, and appears to have been a Phoenikian. See 5, 104.

CHERSONESOS, c. 130.

The Thrakian Chersonese [mod. *Peninsula of Gallipoli*] forms the northern shore of the Hellespont. It was fertile, and contained eleven or twelve cities, of which the most important were Kardia, Elaeos, Sestos, Pactya, and Madytos [7, 33; Xen. Hell. 3, 2, 10]. Its length is about 50 miles, and the breadth of the Isthmus about 5. It had formerly been under the government of Miltiades, but all its cities except Kardia were taken at the end of the Ionian revolt, by the Phoenikians in the interest of Persia [6, 33].

CHIOS, cc. 105—6, 132.

The island of Chios [mod. *Scio*] lies about 5 miles from the coast of Lydia, its length being about 32 miles, and its width varying from 8 to 18 miles. It is a rocky ($παιπαλοέσσα$) island, and chiefly productive of wine and gum-mastic from the *lentiscus* growing in it. Settlers from Krete, Euboea, and Karia had replaced or amalgamated with its ancient inhabitants who were Leleges with a mixture of Pelasgians from Thessaly. Its inhabitants were very wealthy [Thucyd. 8, 24, 3—4].

DAMASITHYMOS, c. 87.

Son of Candaules, and king of the Kalyndians (q. v.) in Karia.

DARIUS, c. 89.

Darius of the clan of the Achaemenidae, the son of Hystaspes. He served under Kambyses in Egypt in B.C. 525 [3, 39]; after whose death he joined the other nobles in a plot to kill the Magus who pretended to be Smerdis son of Kyros [3, 70], and when this man was killed he secured the throne for himself [3, 84—7]: the other Persians submitting on condition that he should marry Atossa the daughter of Kyros. He was the organiser of the huge dominions thus acquired; dividing them into twenty satrapies, and appointing to each the amount of tribute to be paid by it to the royal exchequer. In his reign (from B.C. 521 to 485) occurred the Ionian revolt, and, arising from the help rendered by Athens to the rebels, the expedition led by Dates and Artaphernes which failed at Marathon.

GEOGRAPHICAL INDEX. 215

He was making preparations for a renewal of the struggle when he died.

DAULII, the, c. 35.

The inhabitants of Daulis a town of Phokis. The town was destroyed during the Sacred War [B.C. 357—346], but seems to have revived, and was remarkable for the size and courage of its inhabitants, as well as for the abundance and density of its forests [Paus. 10, 41]. See *Drymos*.

DELOS, cc. 132—3.

The Cyclades were so called because they were regarded as being in a circle (κύκλος) round Delos, which was familiar to all Greeks from the fame and sanctity of its temple of Apollo, for a long time the meeting-place of the Ionian Congress. This had been removed since about B.C. 530—20 by Polykrates of Samos to Ephesos; but its yearly festival was still largely attended, and the Ionian cities sent splendid θεωρίαι to do honour to the god. Hence the voyage as far as Delos was, as we learn here, familiar to the Greek sailors, though all beyond was strange and alarming. It is the smallest of the Cyclades, lying close to the larger island Rheneia, which was properly the place of residence of the Delians, Delos itself being reserved for sacred purposes.

DELPHI, cc. 27, 35, 81, 114, 121—2.

DELPHIANS, the, cc. 37—9.

Delphi, the seat of the famous oracle of Apollo, was in a religious sense the centre of Greece. To it men from all parts of Greece, and indeed of the known world, came to consult the Oracle on every imaginable difficulty, great or small. The answers of the Pythian priestess were regarded with the greatest respect, and often decided the policy of a state, and the question of peace or war. The care of the temple was the joint business of the Phokian league, and the claim of the Delphians to the exclusive custody of it, supported as they were in that claim by Sparta, led to a war in which the Athenians finally restored the privilege to the Phokian league [Thucyd. 1, 112]. This was about B.C. 449: but more than a hundred years before (B.C. 595—585) there had been a more serious 'Sacred War' brought on by the greed of the people of Kirrha, the port of Delphi, in levying heavy exactions on visitors to the shrine, and which ended in the destruction of Kirrha [Plut. Sol. XI.]. So important did the Greeks consider free access to this sacred place. Its freedom and inviolability was the special business of the Amphiktyonic League which met there and at Thermopylae alternately. The splendid temple standing at the time of the Persian invasion was a comparatively recent erection; the more ancient building, which yet was the fourth that had been built, was burnt in B.C. 548, and the new one was built by the Alkmaeonidae, who went beyond their contract in facing the pronaos with Parian marble. The town of Delphi stood in a kind of natural amphitheatre to the S. of the sloping foot of a precipitous two-headed cliff which terminates the range of Parnassos. The valley is watered by the river Pleistos flowing to the S.W. into the Krissaean gulf. The name of the town in the Homeric poem is Pytho (Πυθώ), hence the 'Pythian games', and the 'Pythia', i.e. the priestess who delivered the oracles.

DEMARATOS, c. 65.

Son of Ariston, whom he succeeded as king of Sparta. He incurred the enmity of the other king Kleomenes by thwarting him in his attack upon Athens [5, 75]; and in Aegina [6, 59 sq.]. Accordingly Kleomenes resolved to get rid of him, and the Delphian oracle was induced to declare that he was not the true son of Ariston. After a while he was deposed and went into exile. He lived in various places in Greece, finally crossing over to Persia where Darius received him with honour. He accompanied Xerxes in his expedition into Greece; though he had evinced the remains of patriotic feelings by previously warning his countrymen of the coming danger [7, 239]. For his conversations with Xerxes see 7, 101—4, 109. His family long occupied the places in Asia which were given him as a reward [Xen. Hell. 3, 1, 6].

DEMOKRITOS, c. 65.

A commander of a trireme of Naxos, who according to Plutarch (de malig. Her. 36) greatly distinguished himself in the battle of Salamis, taking five of the enemy's ships, and rescuing a Greek vessel that had been captured.

DIKAEUS, c. 65. An Athenian exile in the Persian army.

DORIANS, the, cc. 31, 43, 45, 66, 73, 141.

The Dorians, according to the myth, were descended from Doros the eldest son of Hellen, and gradually migrated step by step southward, under different appellations, until they finally settled in the Peloponnesos [1, 56]. The main fact, that the Dorians were a migration from the North, pushed away by the encroachments of northern barbarians, may be regarded as historical. They occupied Korinthos, Lakonia, Argos and Messenia; and presently sent out a considerable number of colonies; the principal of which were in Korkyra and Sicily to the west, and in Karia in the east.

DORIS, cc. 31—2, 43.

A small district between the Mounts Oeta and Parnassos, consisting of the valley of the Pindos. The Lakedaemonians regarded this place as their metropolis, and in B.C. 456 sent an expedition to assist the inhabitants against an attack of the Phokians [Thucyd. 1, 107, 2].

DRYMOS, c. 32.

A town of Phokis in the valley of the Kephisos. There was a town of the same name, which means an 'Oak forest', in Euboea. For the woody nature of the district, see under *Daulii*. Pausanias calls it Δρυμαία [10, 3, 2], and tells us of an ancient temple of Demeter Thesmophoros existing there [10, 39, 12].

DRYOPIANS, cc. 46, 73.

DRYOPIS, cc. 31, 43.

Dryopis bordered on Malis, extending from the Sperkheios to some way beyond Mt Oeta. The Dryopes were probably a Pelasgic race, and when expelled from their native country scattered in various directions; into Argolis, where they built the towns of Hermione, Asine and Eion; into Euboea, where they had Styra and Karystos; and into the islands of Kythnos, Mykonos, and Kypros. See under *Asine*. Müller's *Dorians*, vol. i. p. 45—7. Her. 1, 56, 146.

EGYPTIANS, the, cc. 17, 68.

The Egyptians, whose civil, religious, and military organisation was the most ancient of any known to the Greeks, and from whom many of the institutions of Greece were traced, had been conquered by the Persians under Kambyses B.C. 525 [3, 10 sq.]; had rebelled against the Persians in the reign of Darius B.C. 486 [7, 1—19], and had thus prevented him from renewing his attack upon Greece. Being again subdued by Xerxes they, like the rest of the subject states, furnished a contingent to the Grand Army [7, 25, 89], and their 200 ships did conspicuous service at Artemisium.

EÏON, cc. 118, 120.

A Thrakian town on the mouth of the Strymon, serving as the harbour town of Amphipolis, from which it was about 3 miles distant. It was at this time under the command of a Persian named Boges [7, 113], and remained in Persian hands till B.C. 476 when it was captured by Kimon son of Miltiades [Thucyd. 1, 98].

ELATEIA, c. 33.

The largest and, next to Delphi, most important city of Phokis. It stood on a gentle elevation in the midst of a large plain in the valley of the Kephisos. The Elateians professed to be of Arkadian [i.e. Pelasgic] origin; and long remained a powerful state, holding out successfully against Kassander the Makedonian, and later on against Mithridates. For this latter exploit they were made a free city by the Romans [Paus. 10, 34, 1—6].

ELEANS, the, c. 72. ELIS, cc. 27, 73.

Elis was the north-western province of the Peloponnesos. The

Eleans, who were of kin to the Aetolians, are chiefly prominent in Greek history from the fact of their having the management of the Olympic games, held within their borders in the valley of the Alpheios.

ELEUSIS, cc. 65, 85.

Eleusis, situated on a bay called by the same name, was about 11 miles from Athens, from which it was approached by the Sacred Way. It is opposite Salamis and at the mouth of the western branch of the Attic Kephisos. It was famous throughout Greece, and a place of especial sanctity in the eyes of the Athenians, from the celebration of the mysteries in its great temple of Demeter, to which the citizens of Athens yearly went in solemn procession, and which were attended by the pious from all parts of Greece.

ELLOPIA, c. 23.

A district in the N.-West angle of Euboea lying round Mt Telethinos. It formed a part of a district called Oria ('Ωρία or 'Ωρεία) belonging to the town of Histiaea. Some time after the battle of Leuktra (B.C. 371) the Ellopians were removed to Histiaea, which by that time had come to be called Oreos. The mythological derivation of Ellopia was from Ellops son of Ion; which means that the Ellopians were Ionians. Herodotos calls it μοῖρα 'an allotment', Strabo χωρίον 'a small district' [Strab. 10, 1, 3].

EPHESOS, cc. 103, 105, 107.

A town on the coast of Asia at the mouth of the Kayster, with a harbour called Panormos which is now silted up. It was one of the twelve Ionian towns [1, 142, 148], and in the time of Polykrates was regarded as religiously the centre of the Ionians, their yearly festival being called the Ephesia [Thucyd. 3, 104]. It was now in the hands of the Persians, who apparently guarded it carefully, so that it had taken no part in the Ionian revolt. The reason of this was that it was the starting-point of the great road through Sardis into central Asia. Hence we find in this book that Xerxes sends his children to Ephesos, that they may go safely up the country. And hence it is that Panionios sends the unfortunate boys for sale to Ephesos and to Sardis [c. 105]. It was said to have been founded by Androklos, son of the Athenian Kodros.

EPIDAURIANS, the, cc. 1, 43, 72.

EPIDAUROS, c. 46.

Epidauros was a town on the coast of Argolis, opposite the island of Aegina, which it had originally colonised and retained more closely under its power than was usually the case with colonies [Her. 5, 83]. The inhabitants were Dorians, and it was noted for its temple and worship of Aesculapios, and for the celebration of certain orgies or mysteries of which Herodotos says 'it is not lawful to speak'.

ERECHTHEUS, cc. 44, 55.

A mythical king of Athens, son of Hephaestos and Atthis d. of Kranaos. To him were attributed the establishment at Athens (1) of the worship of Athenè, (2) the Panathenaea, (3) the building of the temple of Athenè Polias, which in historical times formed part of the Erechtheum. Herodotos calls him earth-born [γηγενής] as his mother 'Ατθίs is an earth-nymph, 'Ατθίs Γῆ. Cp. Hom. Il. 2, 546,

οἱ δ' ἄρ' 'Αθήνας εἶχον, ἐϋκτίμενον πτολίεθρον,
δῆμον 'Ερεχθῆος μεγαλήτορος, ὅν ποτ' 'Αθήνη
θρέψε Διὸς θυγάτηρ—τέκε δὲ ζείδωρος ἄρουρα—
κὰδ δ' ἐν 'Αθήνῃς εἷσεν, ἑῷ ἐνὶ πίονι νηῷ.

ERETRIANS, the, cc. 1, 46.

The inhabitants of Eretria in Euboea. They had assisted Miletos in the Ionic revolt [B.C. 501] with 5 triremes, in return for assistance received from Miletos in some quarrel with Chalkis [Her. 5, 99]: for this they were made a special object of attack by Dates and Artaphernes in B.C. 490. They took the town and carried off all the inhabitants they could catch to Susa; where they were received kindly by Darius and settled in a district called Ardericca, about 35 miles from Susa, where they remained for some generations. But though the town was thus depopulated, a considerable number of the inhabitants escaped falling into the hands of the Persians by taking refuge in the mountains in the centre of Euboea [id. 6, 100—120]. These people must have returned after the defeat of the Persians at Marathon, and have restored the prosperity of their town; for they supplied 600 hoplites at Plataea, besides sending these seven triremes to Artemisium and Salamis [id. 9, 21].

ERINEOS, c. 43.

A town of Doris on the R. Pindos, a tributary of the Kephisos. It was one of the four cities—the Tetrapolis—which were regarded as the original home of the Dorians. [Strab. 914, 10.]

ETROCHUS, c. 33.

A town in Phokis. It appears not to have been an important place, and remained a mere open village after the destructive attack of the Persians [Paus. 10, 3, 2].

EUBOEA, cc. 8, 13, 20, 68—9, 86.
EUBOEANS, the, cc. 5, 6, 7, 13, 19, 20.

Euboea is a long narrow island extending from the Malian gulf as far south as about half the length of Attica. Where it approaches nearest the coast of the mainland it was believed to have been separated by an earthquake. The channel (the Euripos) is narrow enough to admit of a bridge, which was first made by the Boeotians in B.C. 410. Its natural formation divides it in three; each part being marked by a range of mountains, Mt Telethios in the north, Mt Dorphys in the centre, Mt Ocha in the south. The chief towns in these divisions were, Histiaea (Oreos) in the north, Chalkis and Eretria in the centre, Styra and Karystos in the south; and these three divisions were also mainly inhabited by three different races respectively, Ellopians (Ionians), Abantes (see *Abae*), Dryopians (q. v.). For the interference of Athens in Euboea see *Chalkidians*.

EUMENES, C. 93.

An Athenian of the deme Anagyros, who distinguished himself at Salamis.

EURĪPOS, C. 15.

The channel between Euboea and the mainland—whence the modern name of Negropont [i.e. Egripo (Euripos) Ponte=bridge]. It was the natural course for ships to take coming from the north, and has been called by some historians the sea-Thermopylae, being the key to the south of Greece by sea, as Thermopylae by land: at its narrowest point opposite Chalkis it is only 40 yards across.

EUROPE, cc. 51, 97, 108, 109.

Herodotos conceived of Europe as a large continent of unknown extent towards the west and north, no man being able to say whether the sea bounded it in those two directions. The whole world was divided into Asia and Europe; in Asia was included Libya as far as the valley of the Nile, which bounded Europe in one direction while the Kolchian Phasis bounded it on the other [4, 45].

EUROPIAN, cc. 133, 135.

An inhabitant of the Karian town Europus, or as some write it Euromus [see Steph. Byz. s. vv. Εὔρωμος, Εὐρωπός]. There were other towns of the same name in Makedonia and Syria. That the Karian one is meant here is shown by the story in c. 135, and by Pausanias 9, 23, 6, who recounts this same anecdote. Its site seems uncertain; Colonel Leake placed it near the modern *Iakli*.

EURYBIADES, cc. 2, 42, 48, 57, 59, 60, 62—3, 74, 79, 108, 124.

Son of Eurykleides, the commander of the Spartan ships, and therefore of the combined fleet. Though the account of his proceedings does not give a very lively idea of firmness or capacity, his countrymen honoured him with the prize for valour after Salamis, while they gave the prize for wisdom to Themistokles [8, 124].

GEOGRAPHICAL INDEX. 221

EURYKLEIDES, CC. 2, 42, 62.

A Spartan, father of Eurybiades.

GAUANES, C. 137.

One of the Argive youths, descendants of Temenos, who fled from Argos to Illyria and thence to upper Makedonia; the younger of the three, Perdikkas, founding the dynasty of Makedonia. He appears not to be mentioned elsewhere.

GERAISTOS, C. 7.

A town and promontory (*Cape Mandili*) at the extreme south of Euboea. It possessed a great temple of Poseidon. The town does not seem to have been important except as a place of call for ships sailing from Attica to the Islands or Asia Minor. See Hom. Odyss. 3, 177 ἔς τε Γεραιστὸν ἐννύχιαι κατάγοντο (in Nestor's account of the Greek return from Troy).

GORDIAS, C. 138.

Father of Midas (q. v.). He is called Gordi*os* by Aelian, V. H. 4, 17, and by Strabo (12, 5, 3), who places his home in Phrygia on the river Sangarios.

GORGOS, C. 11.

King of Salamis in Kypros. He had been shut out of his own town by a trick of his brother Onesilos, because he refused to join the Ionian revolt from Persia: but flying for safety to the Persians he had been reinstated [5, 104, 115].

GYGAEA, C. 136.

A sister of Alexander of Makedonia (q. v.) married, as a peace-offering, to a Persian named Bubares [5, 21].

HALIKARNASSOS, C. 104.

Though his own birthplace, Herodotos says very little of Halikarnassos. He tells us that it was one of the Dorian Hexapolis in Asia Minor, of which the other members were Lindos, Telysos and Kamisos in Rhodes, and Kos and Knidos on the mainland, but was expelled from the Union, which thus became a Pentapolis [1, 144]. Halikarnassos, thus separated from the other Dorian states, appears to have become very rapidly Ionicised. It was the largest and strongest city in Karia, a colony from Troezen in Argolis, standing on the slope of a precipitous rock and an isthmus called Zephyrium. It shared the fate of the other Asiatic Greek cities in becoming subject to Persia; and, like the others, fell under the rule of a dynasty of tyrants founded by Lygdamis, who remaining loyal to the Persians gradually became lords of all Karia. It continued to be important until its destruction by Alexander the Great, from which it never entirely recovered [Diod. XVII. 23. Curtius 2, 9].

HELLAS, cc. 3, 4, 18, 22, 44, 57, 60 § 1, 62, 66, 68 § 1, 76, 100—1, 108—9, 114—5, 142, 144.

HELLENES, cc. 4—11, 14—18, 23, 30, 44, 46, 56, 65, 68 § 2, 70, 72, 75—6, 80, 82—4, 87, 89, 94, 96—8, 102, 107—8, 110—2, 121—2, 124, 130—3, 142.

HELLENIC, cc. 6, 17, 81, 85, 87, 144.

Hellas and *Hellenes* are in the widest sense; the latter including all united by a common descent from Hellen, common language, and, in the main, common religion; and the former indicating all lands inhabited by them. It is also used in the more restricted sense of continental and island Greece.

HELLESPONTOS, cc. 51, 87, 97, 107—110, 115, 117—8, 120.

The narrow strait (varying from 1 to 3 miles in breadth) between the Thrakian Chersonese and Asia. There were numerous Greek colonies on its shores attracted there by the trade, especially in corn, with the peoples round the Black Sea [6, 26, 33].

HEPHAESTOS, c. 98.

The god of fire, and of the metallic arts which required fire. In the Iliad he is represented as lame [κυλλοποδίων 18, 37], but as a skilful artificer [Il. 1, 571 κλυτοτέχνης, 15, 311 χαλκεύς], and the maker of the brazen starry palace in which he lived [Il. 18, 370]. Herodotos found his worship well known in Egypt [2, 2, 3, 99, 101]. At Athens the Lampadephoriae were held in his honour, but also in honour of Pan [6, 105].

HERAKLEIDAE, cc. 114, 131.

The 'Herakleidae of Sparta' are the two royal families of Sparta, the representatives of which both claimed descent from Herakles. They were not Dorians [5, 72], but were supposed to have returned under Hyllos son of Herakles to the Peloponnese with the Dorian invaders, from which they had been expelled by Eurystheus. The two families branched off from Aristodemos fourth in descent from Herakles [see c. 131].

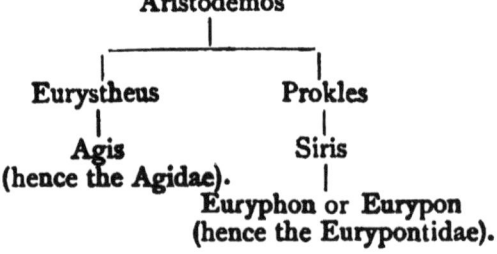

HERAKLES, cc. 43, 131.

The worship of Herakles, according to the common legend son

of Zeus and Alkmena, was the most widely spread in Greece of any god. Herodotos found a deity worshipped in Egypt under the same name [2, 43, 145], at Tyre [2, 44], and in Skythia [4, 59]; though the Greek legends concerning him were unknown to the Egyptians [2, 43]. The peculiarity of the worship of Herakles was that it combined the two kinds, that paid to a hero and that to a God [2, 44]. He is the mythical ancestor of the royal families of Sparta and of Lydia [1, 7; 7, 204], and his temples were found in innumerable places. He represented to the Greek mind the highest idea of human strength and triumphant manhood, to which heaven itself was open.

HERMIONE, c. 73. HERMONIANS, the, cc. 43, 72.

A town on the S.E. coast of Argolis, on a gulf to which it gives a name. It was one of the three Argive towns (the others being Halice and Asine) inhabited by Dryopians (q. v.).

HERMOTIMOS, cc. 104, 106.

One of the eunuchs in the service of Xerxes, a native of Pedasus (q. v.).

HERODOTOS, c. 132.

A son of Basileides (q. v.) and perhaps a relation of the historian; he appears to have been a native of Chios.

HISTIAEA, cc. 23, 25, 66, 85.

A town on the north of Euboea. It was afterwards called Oreos, from the general name of the district in which it stood. After the Persian war it was subject to Athens and revolting in B.C. 445 was taken by Perikles, its inhabitants removed, and Athenian citizens put in [Thuc. 1, 114]. See *Ellopia*.

HOLLOWS OF EUBOEA, the, c. 13.

By τὰ κοῖλα τῆς Εὐβοίης was meant, says Strabo, all the part between Aulis and the district of Geraestos; for the shore there bends into a deep bay, but towards Chalkis approaches the mainland again [Strab. 10, 1, 15]. The Persian ships therefore had rounded Geraestos when they were caught by the storm. This was a dangerous coast from its broken and abrupt nature and its variety of currents. Cp. Livy 31, 47 est sinus Euboicus, quem *Coela* vocant, suspectus nautis. And Eurip. Troad. 84 πλῆσον δὲ νεκρῶν κοῖλον Εὐβοίας μυχόν. This last quotation is in favour of the geographical description given above; for it refers to the return of the Greeks from Troy, the natural course being that which they took when going out, viz. by Aulis and the Euripos, in which case they would necessarily pass through the *sinus Euboicus*, but not past Cape Kaphareos, between which and Geraestos some would place 'the Hollows'.

HYAMPEIA, c. 39.

One of the two peaks of Parnassos immediately above the fountain of Kastalia at Delphi.

HYAMPOLIS, c. 34.

A city in Phokis on the Kephisos and a short distance north of Abae (q. v.), on the road leading from the latter town to Opos. The town was said to have been colonised by natives of Thebes driven out by Kadmos. It was again destroyed by Philip of Makedon; but many of its ancient buildings were standing in the time of Pausanias (2nd cent. A.D.) and Hadrian built a covered walk (στοά) there [Paus. 10, 35, 4].

HYDARNES, cc. 113, 118.

Son of the Hydarnes who was one of the assassins of the false Smerdis [3, 70]. He was the leader of the Immortals, the 10,000 picked men of the Persian army [7, 83, 211]. His descendants became kings in Armenia [Strabo 11, 14, 15].

ILLYRIANS, c. 137.

The inhabitants of the country including the modern Dalmatia, Herzegovina, Montenegro, with parts of Croatia, Bosnia, and Albania. Herodotos appears to have known little about them; and only mentions one tribe by name, the Eneti, who are probably the ancestors of the Veneti of Italy [1, 196].

INDI, c. 113.

For the Indians serving in the army of Xerxes see 7, 65; 9, 31. They were the inhabitants of Punjaub and the valley of the Indus, beyond which Herodotos' knowledge of India did not go [3, 98; 4, 40]. They had been partially subdued by Darius [4, 44].

ION, c. 44.

Ion, son of Xuthos, son of Hellen, the mythical ancestor of the Ionians.

IONIA, cc. 109, 132.

IONIANS, the, cc. 10, 19, 22, 46, 48, 85, 90 [f. Jas, 130], 132.

Those of the Hellenic settlers in Greece who according to the myth were descended from Ion, son of Xuthos, the third son of Hellen. They appear first to have settled in the northern district of the Peloponnese, afterwards called Achaia [Her. 7, 94] and in Attica and Euboea. Athens was regarded (though without any certain historical basis) as the μητρόπολις of the Ionian states established in various parts of Greece. The most numerous and flourishing were those in Asia Minor, such as Ephesos and Miletos, and when Herodotos speaks of 'the Ionians' he usually means these Asiatic states between the river Hermos on the north and the district of Miletos on the south. They consisted of twelve states, viz. Miletos, Myos, Priene, *in Caria;* Ephesos, Kolophon, Lebedos, Teos, Klazomenae, Phokaea, Erythra, *in Lydia;* and two islands, Samos and Chios. These states signalised their connexion by a yearly meeting at the Pan-Ionium, near the temple of Poseidon on the promontory of Mykalè, or at a later period at Ephesos [see Her. 1, 142; Thucyd. 3, 104].

ISCHENEOS, c. 92.

A man of Aegina, father of Pytheas (q. v.).

ISMENIOS, c. 134.

Ismenian Apollo means the temple of Apollo at Thebes, built on a hill, at the foot of which flowed the river Ismenos [1, 52, 92; 5, 60—1; Pausanias 9, 10, 2].

ISTHMUS, the, cc. 40, 49, 56—7, 60, 71—4, 79, 121, 123.

The Isthmus of Corinth is called *the* Isthmus by Herodotos and Thucydides; when any other is meant it is distinguished by some explanatory word as Παλλήνης, Χερσονήσου, or the like. At the time of the Persian war the Greeks of the Peloponnese looked to the Isthmus as their chief protection, because it could be passed only by two difficult roads, and admitted of being effectually blocked by artificial means.

ITALIA, c. 62.

By Italy Herodotos seems to mean what was afterwards Lucania, and especially the Greek colonies planted on its coast [see note ad loc.]. Calabria he calls Iapygia [3, 138; 4, 99], and it does not seem clear whether Tarentum is conceived as being in Italy proper [1, 24; 3, 138; 7, 170]. The most northerly Greek towns on the W. coast mentioned by him are Velia and Posidonium, the former of which is said to be in Oenotria [1, 167]. He seems to have known nothing of central Italy; but the Tyrrhenians on the N. of the Tiber are mentioned several times [1, 163, 166—7; 6, 17, 22]; and he seems to have some confused notion of the Kelts living north of Umbria: though he appears to place both further west than Italy, while he thinks that 'Alpis' is the name of a river [4, 49].

ITHAMITROS, c. 130.

A Persian commander, nephew of Artayntes. Both shared in the defeat at Mykalè, but escaped with their lives [9, 102].

KALLIADES, c. 51.

Archon Eponymos at Athens for the year B.C. 480—479.

KALYNDIANS, the, c. 87—8.

The inhabitants of Kalynda a town in Karia on the borders of Lykia.

KAPHAREOS, c. 7.

The northern of the promontories at the southern extremity of Euboea (mod. *Xylohpago*).

KARDAMYLE, c. 73.

A town of Messenia on the eastern shore of the *Sinus Messeniacus*, subject from ancient times to the Lakedaemonians; though in Homer (Il. 9, 150) it is spoken of as belonging to Agamemnon.

KARIANS, the, cc. 19, 22. KARIA, c. 135.

The inhabitants of Karia, a district to the S.-West of Asia Minor. Herodotos, who was born in Halikarnassos an Hellenic town in Karia, asserts that the Karians came thither from the Islands, and that, while in the Islands, they were called Leleges, a sister people of the Pelasgians. Thucydides also says that the occupation of the islands by Karians was proved by the tombs opened by the Athenians in B.C. 425, in order to purify the island by removing the corpses. His theory is that, being great smugglers, they were driven from the Islands by Minos of Crete [Thucyd. 1, 8; 3, 104]. Their language though not Hellenic had a large admixture of Hellenic words (Her. 1, 171], and when Homer (Il. 2, 867) calls them βαρβαρόφωνοι he may be indicating (as Rawlinson remarks) not so much their separation from the Greeks, as the fact that they attempted an intercourse from which others shrank.

KARNEIA, the, c. 72.

A national festival held at Sparta (as also in other cities of the Peloponnese, as well as Dorian cities elsewhere) in honour of Apollo Karneios. It lasted nine days, beginning on the 7th day of the Spartan month Karneios [August].

KARYSTIANS, the, c. 66. KARYSTOS, 112, 121.

The inhabitants of Karystos in the S. of Euboea near Mt Ocha. The neighbourhood was celebrated for its marble quarries. The people were Dryopes (q. v.).

KASTALIA, c. 39.

A fountain at Delphi at the foot of Parnassos, at the entrance of the ravine which separates the two peaks. It is identified with a spring of remarkably pure water now called *Aio Jánni*.

KEIANS, cc. 1, 46.

The inhabitants of Keos, an island lying off the promontory of Sunium, 12 m. long by 8 broad. They were a colony from Athens.

GEOGRAPHICAL INDEX.

KEKROPIDAE, the, c. 44.

KEKROPS, cc. 44, 53.

Kekrops, father of Erechtheus (q. v.), the mythical first king of Athens: hence the Athenians are called in poetry Kekropidae [compare *Romulidae, Aeneadae* as the name for Romans]. Herodotos seems to assert that it was once a real national appellation.

KEOS, c. 76.

Some have thought that the Island of Keos opposite the promontory of Sunium is meant: but the distance is too great from Phalerum to allow us to suppose that the Persian left would rest on the Island of Keos. It appears possible that both Keos and Kynosoura are places (though unknown) on the coast of Attica between Phalerum and Sunium. This is the view of Grote: but Col. Leake places them in Salamis, and with him other commentators agree—Rawlinson, Abicht; while Stein seems to think that both names Keos and Kynosoura belong to the narrow tongue of land in Salamis opposite Psyttaleia, and that Keos was the ordinary name of it, Kynosoura a less known one.

KEPHISOS, c. 33.

The only considerable river in Central Greece. It rises in the range of Oeta, and flows through Doris, Phokis, and Boeotia into the Kopaic lake, a reservoir which is relieved by subterranean channels. It receives a considerable number of affluents on both sides in its course. There is another river of the same name in Attica.

KILIKIA, cc. 14, 100.

KILIKIANS, the, c. 68.

Kilikia is the south-eastern district of Asia Minor bordering on the Mare Internum opposite Kypros. On the east it is bounded by Mt Amanos, though Herodotos extends it to the Euphrates [50, 52]; and on the north it is separated from Kappadokia and Lykaonia by the range of Taurus. It was an important province, because of the length of its seaboard, the fertility of its soil, and its position in regard to Syria.

KLEINIAS, c, 17.

The father of the great Alkibiades, and a son of a man also named Alkibiades (q. v.). He was killed at the battle of Koroneia, in the war between Athens and the Boeotians B.C. 447 [Plutarch, Alkibiad. 1].

KLEOMBROTOS, c. 71.

Kleombrotos, the father of Pausanias, was son of Anaxandridas and twin brother of Leonidas. When Leonidas fell at Thermopylae leaving one son Pleistarchos, a minor, Kleombrotos became regent, but died in the autumn of 479 or spring of 478, and was succeeded in the regency by his son Pausanias.

KOLIAS, c. 96 [Κωλιὰς ἄκρα].

The name of a promontory in Attica about 2½ miles from Phalerum [Pausan. 1, 1, 5], modern *Cape St Kosmas*. There was a temple of Aphrodite in it [Arist. Nub. 52].

KOPAIS, c. 134.

A lake in Boeotia surrounded by mountains, from which it received abundant drainage. The water thus collected found its way out by hidden passages in the limestone rock called now *Katavóthrae*, principally at the east end (Mt Ptoum); besides some artificial tunnels constructed to prevent the waters flooding the district. Though large it is shallow, except at the east end. In summer it nearly dries up, in the winter it covers an area of about 90 miles. Attempts are now being made to drain it off altogether. In the Iliad (5, 709) it is called Κηφισίς.

KORINTHOS, cc. 45, 94.

KORINTHIANS, the, cc. 1, 5, 21, 43, 59, 61, 72, 79.

The territory of Korinthos was separated from the Megarid on the north by the range of Geraneia, and from Argolis on the south by that of *Oneum*, 'the Ass's back'. The isthmus averages about 3½ miles in breadth, and very little of it is fertile. Korinthos itself consisted of an acropolis, the Acrokorinthos (1900 ft), with a town round it enclosed with walls, and joined to its harbour on the western coast, Lechaeum, by long walls, like those of Athens, extending a little more than a mile. Its port on the east coast, Kenchreae, was more than eight miles distant. The position of Korinthos made it naturally the seat of commerce from early times, and in it the art of building ships of war or triremes was first practised. Holding also the pass between northern Greece and the Peloponnese, it had a greater influence in Hellenic politics than the character of its rich and luxuriant citizens seems to warrant. The prevailing element in its population was Dorian, and its inclination was therefore generally to side with Sparta rather than Athens. In the Persian war it did not play a very dignified or conspicuous part. At Salamis its ships were said, perhaps untruly (see *Introduction*), to have been turned to flight (8, 94), and at Plataea its soldiers were among those who retreated to the Heraeum and returned too late for the battle (9, 69). Its ships and men however did some good service at Mykalè (9, 102). The wall which the Peloponnesians built across the isthmus, about eight miles east of the town, was often reconstructed afterwards, and remains of one of uncertain date can still be traced. Korinthos was the mother city of many flourishing colonies, Syracuse, Korkyra, Potidaea and others.

KORYKIAN CAVE, the, c. 36.

This cave is at a considerable elevation in Mt Parnassos, above the broad upland plain lying high above the modern village of Delphi. It is a wide chamber 300 feet long by 200 feet broad, with fine stalactites hanging from the top: from this a narrow passage leads into another chamber 100 feet long. It is an excellent place of refuge, and was used for that purpose in the last Greek revolutionary war. It was dedicated to Pan and the Nymphs.

Κούρη, ἡ, c. 65.

'The daughter', that is Persephone, daughter of Demeter. It was a name under which she was specially worshipped in Attica. See *Eleusis*.

KRANAOI, the, c. 44.

An ancient Pelasgic name for the inhabitants of Attica, which seems to mean the 'craggy', i.e. the inhabitants of the craggy land. As usual however it was derived from Kranaos a king of Attica.

KRESTONIKE, c. 116.

The country of *Krestonia*, a district in Makedonia (originally Thrakia) with a town called *Kreston*, north of Mygdonia, inhabited for the most part by Pelasgi [1, 57; 7, 127. Thucyd. 4, 109].

KRIOS, c. 92.

An Aeginetan, father of Polykrites. He was a man of influence at Aegina, and resisted the action of the Spartan king there in demanding hostages from the Aeginetans [6, 50, 73]. He was known as an athlete [Arist. Nubes 1356].

KRITOBULOS, c. 127.

A man of Torone appointed governor of Olynthos by Artabazos.

KROISOS, cc. 35, 122.

King of Lydia from B.C. 560 to B.C. 546. He completed the conquest of the Asiatic Greeks begun by his father Alyattes (q. v.). When the Persians under Kyros were threatening to subdue all Asia he tried to strengthen himself by alliances with the Babylonian Belshazzar, with Amasis of Egypt, and with Sparta (1, 69). He consulted also all the Greek oracles he could hear of and made magnificent offerings to Delphi [1, 51—3]; and thus strengthened he advanced to meet Kyros near Sinope. The battle was not decisive, but Kroisos returning home with a view of renewing the war in the following year, and disbanding his army, was surprised by a rapid movement of Kyros, his capital Sardis taken, and himself made prisoner [1, 76 sq.]. The romantic story of his preservation when on the point of being burnt will be found in 1, 86 sq.

KRONIDES, c. 77.

Son of Kronos, i.e. Zeus.

KROTONIANS, the, c. 47.

The inhabitants of a Greek town—Krotona—in Bruttium in the south of Italy. It was a colony of Achaians established in B.C. 710, and at this time was very powerful. The chief events in its history up to this time had been the establishment of Pythagoras and his School there about B.C. 540, and its destruction of Sybaris B.C. 510.

KYME, c. 130.

A town in Aeolis, sometimes called Kyme Phrikonis [1, 149], and Amazonia, from a supposed foundress Kyme, an Amazon, was situated N. of the River Hermos near a place now called *Sanderli*. In conjunction with the Chalkidians of Euboea it is said by some to have founded the colony of Cumae in Italy [Strabo 5, 4, 4].

KYNOSOURA, cc. 76—7.

'The dog's tail' was the name of a long strip of land near Marathon, but this cannot be the place meant here. In all probability it means a long tongue of land in Salamis. See *Keos*.

KYNURII, the, c. 73.

The inhabitants of a district to south-east of Argolis. It was the possession of this strip of territory lying between Lakonia and the *Mare Myrtoum* that was the cause of the constant enmity between the Argives and Spartans. See *Argos*. The same (prae-Hellenic) people are also found in the west of Arkadia, where their principal city is Gortys.

KYPRIANS, the, cc. 68, 100.

The inhabitants of Kypros, an island opposite the coast of Kilikia. It was especially valuable as connecting Asia Minor with Syria, and especially with the Phoenikian navy. It had been under the power of Amasis of Egypt (2, 182), but had been with the rest of Asia and Egypt made tributary to Persia (3, 91): and though it had joined in the Ionic revolt it was reduced by the Persian arms (5, 116). The island was inhabited by a mixed race; some cities having been colonised from Salamis and Athens, some from Arkadia and Kynthos, and others by Phoenikians and Aethiopians [7, 90], the earliest settlers being Phoenikians. The island is 150 miles long, and its greatest breadth is about 40 miles.

KYTHNOS, c. 67. KYTHNIANS, the, c. 46.

One of the Cyclades, between Keos and Seriphos, mod. *Thermia*. Its inhabitants were Dryopian (q. v.) and the island was at one time called Dryopis.

GEOGRAPHICAL INDEX. 231

LAKEDAEMON, cc. 48, 124, 125.

LAKEDAEMONIANS, the, cc. 1, 2, 25, 43, 72, 85, 114, 124—5, 141, 144.

The inhabitants of the whole district, Lakedaemon or Lakonia, over which the city of Sparta (which contained 8000 men, Her. 7, 234) was supreme. Sometimes the word is used as equivalent to 'Spartans'; sometimes the two are distinguished; and sometimes it is applied to other than the full Spartan citizens, as to the Perioekoi in 9, 11; sometimes to all the inhabitants or soldiers of Lakonia. The Lakedaemonians exercised supreme influence in the Peloponnese, though not actual government except in Lakonia and Messenia; and though they were not as yet powerful at sea, the habit of regarding them as the natural leaders of a joint expedition prevailed even against the claims of Athens, which were founded on her superior fleet.

LEBADEIA, c. 134.

A town on the western frontier of Boeotia, between Mt Helicon and Chaeroneia, the seat of the oracle of Trophonios [1, 46]. Mod. *Livadhia*.

LEBAIA, c. 137.

This town in Upper Makedonia is not mentioned by any other writer. It appears to have been the seat of the old kingdom of Makedonia.

LEMNOS, cc. 11, 81. LEMNIANS, the, c. 73.

Lemnos (mod. *Stalimene* = εἰς τὰν Λῆμνον) is off the coast of Thrakia about half way between Athos and the Hellespont. It is a rocky island with many signs of volcanic action and possessing two towns Hephaestia and Murina. Its inhabitants were said to have been first a Thrakian tribe, the Sinties, who were expelled by the Minyae, the descendants of the Argonauts; these were succeeded by Pelasgians, who in their turn became Atticised, and the island was in the power of Athens from about B.C. 500. For the stories connected with this event, see 6, 137—140.

LEONIDAS, cc. 15, 21, 71.

King of Sparta from B.C. 491 to B.C. 480. He was a younger son of Anaxandridas and succeeded to the kingdom on the death of his brother Kleomenes, whose daughter Gorgo he married, and by whom when he fell at Thermopylae he left a young son, Pleistarchos, under the guardianship of his brother Kleombrotos. Kleombrotos died in the same year and was succeeded in the regency and guardianship of Pleistarchos by his son Pausanias (q. v.). Leonidas seems to have been fully aware of the hopelessness of his position at Thermopylae, and to have done his best to prevent more Greeks being involved in his disaster than could be helped; this unselfishness, joined to his singular gallantry, has secured him the first rank among the patriots of Greece [Her. 7. 204—222].

LEUKADIANS, the, cc. 45, 47.

The inhabitants of Leukadia (*Santa Maura*), a considerable island off the coast of Akarnania, about 20 miles long. Its chief town was Leukas, a colony from Corinth, at the extreme north of the island, separated from the mainland by a narrow strait.

LEUTYCHIDES, c. 131.

A king of Sparta and commander of the joint fleet in B.C. 479.

LOKRIANS, the.

There were two districts called Lokris, (1) that of the Opuntian Lokrians, (2) that of the Ozolian Lokrians.

(1) OPUNTIAN LOKRIANS, cc. 1, 66.

They inhabited the eastern half of a district lying on the coast of the Malian Gulf separated from Thessaly by the range of Mt Oeta. Their principal town was Opus. They had given earth and water to the Persian emissaries [7, 132] but were now serving the Persians unwillingly, having taken the Greek side at Thermopylae [7, 23].

(2) OZOLIAN LOKRIANS, the, c. 32.

They inhabited a narrow district on the coast of the Gulf of Korinth, bounded on the north by Aetolia and on the east by Phokis. It was a mountainous and unproductive country and never played a great part in Hellenic history. The only towns of importance in it were Amphissa (*Salina*) and Naupaktos (*Lepanto*).

LYKOMEDES, c. 11.

A brave Athenian, son of Aeschreas, who gained the prize of valour at Artemisium.

LYSIMACHOS, cc. 79, 95.

An Athenian, father of Aristeides (q. v.), of the deme Alopekè. He seems to have been a man of small fortune, although Plutarch (Arist. 1) says that there was some doubt as to his having had absolutely nothing to leave his son.

Μακεδνὸν ἔθνος, c. 43.

The 'Makedni' was the name which according to Herodotos (1, 56) was borne by the Dorians (q. v.) when settled in Pindos, i.e. Doris. According to the myth Makednos is a grandson of Pelasgos, and son of Lykaon of Arkadia. Thus by this term Herodotos seems to trace a connexion between the old Makedonians and the prae-Hellenic inhabitants of the Peloponnese.

Μακηδονία, ἡ ἄνω, c. 137.

MAKEDONIANS, the, cc. 34, 126—7, 138, 142.

Makedonia, the most northern district of Greece, was separated

GEOGRAPHICAL INDEX.

from Thessaly by the Cambunian range of mountains, and was divided from Illyricum and Epirus on the west by Mts Scardus and Lingon. Though it afterwards, under Philip and his son Alexander, became supreme over Greece, it possessed no influence there at present, and was scarcely regarded as Hellenic at all. It was in a semi-barbaric state, and was being slowly organised by its kings, who were, or claimed to be, of Argive descent (see *Alexander*). They had been reduced to subjection to Persia in B.C. 493—2 [Her. 6, 44].

MARDONIOS, cc. 26, 67—8, 97, 99—102, 107, 113—5, 126, 129, 136, 140—2.

Son of Gobryas by a sister of Darius, whose daughter Artazostra he married. He first appears in Greek history as the agent of Darius in B.C. 493 in carrying out a new policy in regard to the Ionian states. The Persian government had insisted on the maintenance of the Tyrants in these cities, but Mardonios now established democracies in them, apparently with the idea of conciliating Greek feeling in favour of the Persian supremacy,—a policy so unlike that which had generally been pursued by Persia, that Herodotos seems to expect that his assertion will be disbelieved [6, 43]. Mardonios, however, while pushing on his conquests into Europe, sustained reverses at the hands of the Thrakians and was removed from his command [6, 45, 94]. We next hear of him as urging the reluctant Xerxes to his great expedition against Greece [7, 5, 9], in which he was one of two commanders-in-chief of the land forces [7, 82]. After Salamis he persuaded Xerxes to return home, and was left behind with 300,000 men to complete the subjugation of Greece. He fell next year at Plataea.

MARDONTES, c. 130.

Son of Bagaeos, leader of the contingents in the Persian army that came from the islands in the Erythraean Sea [7, 80]. He fell at Mycale in B.C. 479 [9, 102].

MEDES, the, cc. 31, 40, 43—4, 67, 87, 113—4, 141—3.

The Medes were an Aryan people [Her. 7, 62], who when first heard of inhabited a district south of the Caspian, now called Khorassan. Thence they emigrated, and by the middle of the 7th century B.C. were settled in the country known as Media Magna. For a while they were partially or wholly subject to the Assyrian monarchy, but after a time they shook off this subjection and became the dominant power in Asia, a Median monarchy being probably first established about B.C. 635—630 by Kyaxares. This monarch, about B.C. 624, attacked and took Nineveh. From this period the great Assyrian monarchy is divided into two independent kingdoms—Medes and Babylonians. The Medes, under Kyaxares, subdued the part of Asia 'beyond the river Halys' [Her. 1, 103], and even threatened Asia Minor. The successor of Kyaxares, Astyages, was conquered by Kyros at the head of the mountain tribe of the Persians. The result was a new combination, and a new monarchy overrunning the whole of Asia, conquering Babylon and Lydia. This is sometimes called the Persian empire, sometimes the Medo-Persian. We read in Daniel of the 'laws of the Medes and Persians', as though that were the official designation; and the Greeks spoke of their great enemies as 'Medes' or 'Persians' indifferently, and of those Greeks who joined them as 'medizing'; but Herodotos clearly distinguished the two peoples, giving the palm of valour to the Persians.

MEGARA, c. 60. The MEGARIANS, cc. 43, 46, 48, 66.

Megara stood on the Saronic Gulf, a mile inland, with a harbour town of Nisaea, to which it was joined by long walls. It was on the road from Athens and Eleusis to the Peloponnese through the isthmus, and its friendship or neutrality was therefore of great importance to Athens and to the Peloponnesians. The district belonging to it—the Megarid—extended right across the N. of the isthmus and contained a port on the Corinthian Gulf called Pagae. The Megarians were Ionians, but had been at one time under the dominion of the Dorians of Korinthos. At this time however Megara was independent. Geographically it belongs rather to Attica, for the range of Gereneia shuts it off from Korinthos and was crossed by three difficult passes, whereas it was open towards Attica; and indeed the greater part of it seems once to have been united with Attica politically [Her. 5, 76].

MELIANS, the [Μηλιεῖς], cc. 43, 66. MELIS, c. 31 [Malis].

The inhabitants of Malis [Mēlis], a district of Thessaly between the R. Spercheios and Mt Oeta. They had given earth and water to the Persian king [Her. 7, 132], and were now serving in the army of Mardonios. Malis was surrounded by mountains, but contained wide plains, in which the Persian cavalry had been matched successfully with the Thessalian [id. 7, 196—8].

MELIANS, the [Μήλιοι], cc. 46, 48.

The inhabitants of the island of Melos, one of the Cyclades, south of Siphnos. It is about 15 miles by 8. It was inhabited by Dorians from Sparta, who displaced the earlier Phoenikian settlers: these in their turn were displaced by Athenians in B.C. 416.

Μήτηρ, ἡ, c. 65.

'The Mother', that is, Demeter, the most venerable of the goddesses; daughter of Kronos. She represented mystically the secret powers of nature, and it was in her name that the most solemn mysteries were celebrated, especially at Eleusis. See *Eleusis*, and Κόρη.

MIDAS, c. 138.

King of Phrygia [1, 14], notorious for his wealth and effeminacy. According to one legend he was originally king of the Briges in Makedonia, whence he migrated to Phrygia. It was in this Makedonian kingdom that the 'gardens' here mentioned were supposed to be, near Mt Bromion.

MNESIPHILOS, cc. 57—8.

A philosophic statesman of the same deme (Phrearroi) as Themistokles, and one whom Themistokles is said by some to have especially imitated [Plut. *Themist.* 2], as Mnesiphilos himself imitated Solon.

MOUSAIOS, c. 96.

A number of oracular poems were current under the name of Mousaios, who is often coupled with Orpheus, as early as B.C. 520. Both his country and age were uncertain, but he seems to have written in connexion with the Mysteries. His poems were said to have been edited by Onomakritos of Athens, who foisted in various verses. These poems were also said to contain a clear prophecy of the battle of Salamis [8, 96; 9, 43].

MUNYCHIA, c. 76.

A lofty elevation on the east of the peninsula of the Peiraeus. It had on the summit a sacred enclosure called Bendideion round a temple of the Thrakian Artemis.

MYS, cc. 133—5.

A Karian of Europus serving in the army of Mardonios.

MYSIA, c. 106.

A district in Asia Minor extending from the shores of the Propontis to Lydia. At this time it included part of the country afterwards reckoned in Bithynia, see 6, 122. It had formerly been conquered by Kroisos [1, 28], and was afterwards included in the Persian empire, being ranked in the 2nd Satrapy by Darius [3, 90].

NAXIANS, the, c. 46.

The inhabitants of the island of Naxos one of the Cyclades; of which it was the largest and most wealthy [5, 28]. They had resisted the attempt of Aristagoras to force back the exiled oligarchs, which gave rise to the Ionian revolt [5, 30 sq.]; and were afterwards subdued by the Persians and treated with great cruelty [6, 96]. The inhabitants were Ionians, and in B.C. 466 were made subject to Athens [Thucyd. 1, 98].

NEOKLES, c. 110.

The father of Themistokles [q. v.].

NEŌN, cc. 32—3.

A town in Phokis at the foot of a peak of Parnassos called Tithorea. Pausanias says that in the verses of Bakis the inhabitants are called Tithoreis, and he supposes that the latter name supplanted the former in course of time [Paus. 10, 32, 9].

OENONE, c. 46.

An ancient name of the island Aegina (q. v.).

OKYTOS, cc. 5, 59.

A Corinthian, father of Adeimantos (q. v.).

OLYMPIA, the, cc. 26, 72.

The Olympic festival held every fifth year at Olympia in Elis. At this festival every Hellene had a right to take part in the sacrifice to Zeus Olympios, and to compete in the various contests. While they were going on, the Eleans as managers sent notice to the various Greeks that a truce was to be observed, and a state violating this truce would be excluded from the sacrifice and the games [see Thucyd. 5, 49].

OLYNTHUS, OLYNTHIANS, c. 127.

A town at the head of the Toronaic Gulf, between the two peninsulas of Pallene and Sithonia, which afterwards became the chief town of the Chalkidic Greeks [Thucyd. 458], and was very prominent in the controversies of the Athenians and Makedonians. It had been visited by the Persian fleet on its way down south, and like other towns had been forced to supply a quota of men and ships [7, 122]: at this time it was inhabited by Bottiaei (q. v.).

ORCHOMENIANS, the, c. 34.

The inhabitants at Orchomenos in Boeotia. Orchomenos was once the largest and most important town in Boeotia. In the catalogue of ships in the 2nd Iliad 29 towns of Boeotia are mentioned as supplying 50 ships in all, of which Orchomenos sends 30. But in historical times it was surpassed and supplanted by Thebes. It was twice destroyed by Thebes, in B.C. 368 and 346, and though restored by the Makedonians never recovered its former importance. It stands in a rich and fertile plain, and was inhabited by the Minyae, whence it is often called the 'Minyan Orchomenos' to distinguish it from the towns of the same name in Arkadia, Euboea, and Thessaly. Its modern name is *Skripa*.

ORNEATES, the, c. 73.

A general name for the *perioekoi*—unenfranchised farmers—of Argos. The name arose from the inhabitants of Orneae, probably Achaeans, who about B.C. 580 were conquered by Argos and reduced to this position, just as were the perioekoi of Sparta. Compare for the title given to a class from a particular town the Italian *Caerites*, and perhaps the Spartan *Helots* (q. v.) from Helos, which was the derivation accepted by some. In B.C. 418 we find the Orneatae serving in the Argive army (Thucyd. 5, 72), but in B.C. 416 the Spartans seem to have established at Orneae a settlement of men hostile to the Argive government, and in retaliation the Argives utterly destroyed the town (Thucyd. 6, 7).

Orneae was north-west of Argos on the frontier of Mantineia.

PAEONIA, c. 115.

A district in the centre of upper and lower Makedonia. Its inhabitants were of different blood from the surrounding Makedonians, and claimed to be descended from the Teukri [5, 13, 24, 98].

PALLENE, cc. 126—9.

The westernmost of three projecting headlands of the Chalkidic peninsula, mod. *Kassándhra*. On the narrowest part of it stood the town of Potidaea.

PALLENEUS, c. 84.

A man of the deme Pallene in Attica, of the tribe Antiochis.

PAMPHYLIANS, the, c. 68.

Pamphylia was a narrow tract of country bordering on the Mare Lykium, immediately west of Kilikia, and bounded on the north by Pisidia. Its chief towns were Attalia, and Perga.

PANAETIOS, c. 82.

A man of the island of Tenos (q. v.).

PANIONIOS, cc. 105—6.

A slave-dealer of Chios.

PANOPEIS or PANOPE, cc. 34—5.

This town, which was afterwards called Phanoteus, was on the frontier between Boeotia and Phokis in the valley of the Kephisos, on the right bank of the river, about two miles from Chaeroneia. It was a mere collection of mountain huts without agora or public buildings. [Paus. 10, 4, 1.]

PARAPOTAMII, or PARAPOTAMIA (Steph. Byz.), cc. 33—4.

A town in the fertile part of the valley of the Kephisos. Pausanias seems to think that the name belonged rather to a district than a πόλις; and at any rate the town was not restored after the destruction by the Persians.

PARIANS, the, c. 67. PAROS, c. 112.

The inhabitants of the island of Paros, the third largest of the Cyclades. The Parians seem to have been a people much respected by other Greek communities [5, 28], and to have been of a peculiarly cautious nature, as evinced in their conduct here recorded, and in their readiness (to avoid farther committing themselves) to pay a sum of money on the demand of Themistokles (8, 112). The only remarkable event in their history up to this time had been the unprovoked and unsuccessful attack upon them by Miltiades [6, 132—8] in the year after the battle of Marathon. The island was celebrated for its marble, and for its figs.

PARNASSOS, cc. 27, 32, 35, 37.

A range of mountains in Phokis, rising at its highest point (Lykorea) 8000 feet. The range terminates in a double peak above Delphi.

PAROREATAE, c. 73.

'Dwellers by the mountains', a term applied by Herodotos to the inhabitants of a district of Elis south of the Alphaeos. They were according to him descendants of the Minyae who were expelled from Lemnos by the Spartans [4, 101].

PAUSANIAS, c. 3.

Pausanias, the Spartan commander in the campaign of 479 B.C. and commander-in-chief of the Greek forces at Plataea, was of the elder royal family—that is of the branch which was descended from the elder son of Aristodemos, who was fourth in descent from Herakles [see *Herakles*]—and was a cousin of Leonidas, as will be seen from the accompanying pedigree [Her. 5, 39—41; 7, 204; 9, 64]:—

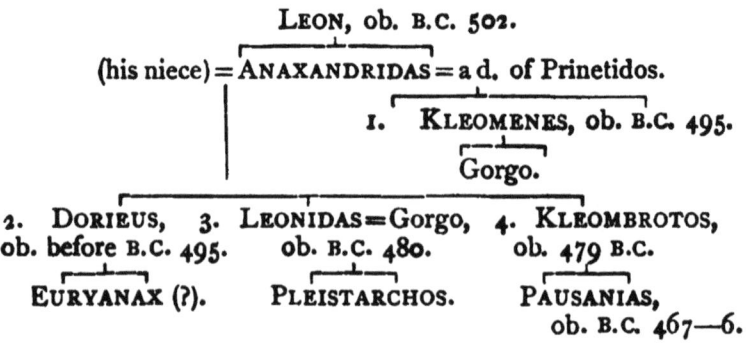

Upon his death at Thermopylae Leonidas was succeeded by his son Pleistarchos, a minor, and his brother Kleombrotos became guardian of the young king and regent. Kleombrotos died early in the year 479 B.C., and his son Pausanias then became regent in his place and guardian of Pleistarchos. This was his position when the Peloponnesian army collected to oppose Mardonios. We have no particulars of the life of Pausanias before this date, and his subsequent history is only casually alluded to by Herodotos [5, 32; 8, 3]. But fuller details are given by Thucydides [1, 94, sq.] and by Diodorus Siculus [11, 44—6], and Cornelius Nepos has written a life of him founded on what he found in Thucydides.

The event in his life referred to in the text was his conduct in B.C. 478 when in command of the allied fleet at Byzantium. His haughty and violent conduct caused many complaints to be sent home to Sparta, and he was recalled, and superseded by Dorkis. He was subsequently convicted of treasonable correspondence with Persia and starved to death in the temple of Athenè, in which he had taken sanctuary.

PEDIEIS, the, cc. 35, 102.

A town in Phokis, in the valley of the Kephisos.

PEISISTRATIDAE, c. 52.

The descendants of Peisistratos, who was tyrannus in Athens from B.C. 560 to 527 with intervals of banishment. His son Hippias was expelled in B.C. 510: and after living for a time in the Troad, had been received at the Persian court (5, 96), and had accompanied the Persian forces at Marathon (6, 107). At the time of the battle of Salamis Hippias was dead, but his descendants and their partizans still seem to have been with the Persian king.

PELASGI, the, c. 44.

The ancient inhabitants of Greece, who, like the Hellenic immigrations which superseded or absorbed them, were an Aryan race. Herodotos imagines that they spoke a barbarous (non-Hellenic) language, but we have no certain means of deciding whether this be so. They were great builders and reclaimers of land, and settled especially in the rich plains of Thessaly and Argos [1, 57; 2, 51; 6, 137—140]. A reminiscence of their building at Athens was the 'Pelasgic wall' of the Akropolis, and the place called τὸ Πελασγικὸν beneath it [5, 64; Thucyd. 2, 16; Paus. 1, 28, 2. C.I.G. 2374].

PELION, c. 12.

A long ridge of mountains in Thessaly, extending from Ossa to the promontory of Sepias. For a considerable distance it descends precipitously to the sea, and prevents any inlet or harbours for ships.

PELOPONNESE, the, cc. 40, 43, 49, 50, 57, 60, 65, 68, 70—2, 100—1, 141.

PELOPONNESIANS, the, PELOPONNESIA, c. 70.

The Peloponnese ('Island of Pelops') is not a name known in

Homeric times. In the Iliad the only name given to the whole seems to be Argos, for Ephyra in Elis is spoken of as being in μυχῷ Ἄργεος ἱπποβότοιο Il. 6, 152; cf. Odyss. 4, 173 where 'Argos' refers to Laconia, and 3, 251 where the Peloponnese is called Ἄργος Ἀχαιϊκόν. And, finally, some have regarded ἀπίη in *Il.* 1, 269, 'the distant land', as a territorial name for the Peloponnese. The name Peloponnese was certainly subsequent to the settlement of the Dorians and was referred by the Greeks to the wealth and power of Pelops, son of Tantalos. It contains about 1780 square miles, and at the time of the Persian war was divided into six provinces, Elis, Messenia, Lakonia, Argolis, Achaia, Arkadia—of which the two last were much less Hellenised than the others. Achaia, as its name imports, having served as a place of retreat for the ancient Achaean inhabitants before the invading Dorians, and Arkadia from its strong mountain barriers having been able almost entirely to resist their attack, retained its Pelasgic inhabitants.

PERDIKKAS, cc. 137—8.

Founder of the Makedonian dynasty, which lasted until the death of Alexander III., son of Alexander the Great [B.C. 311]. The descent of Perdikkas from Temenos of Argos [whence the family was called Temenidae, q. v.] is given also by Thucydides [2, 99; 5, 80]. But the legend varied, some writers counting two kings of Makedonia before Perdikkas, Karanos and Kaenos; and although the Hellenic descent of these kings was admitted by the managers of the Olympic games, Demosthenes [3 Phil. § 40] denied it.

PERSIANS, the, cc. 10, 15—6, 24, 27, 31, 33, 38—42, 45, 51, 58—61, 68, 70—1, 82, 95—8, 100—1, 106—8, 113, 116—9, 126, 129, 141.

The Persians, an Aryan race like the Medes, were a mountain tribe led down about B.C. 550 by Kyros against the Median king Astyages in his capital Ecbatana. The overthrow of Astyages was followed in B.C. 546 by the conquest of Lydia, and by that of Babylon in B.C. 538. From the overthrow of Astyages the Median Empire became the Empire of the Medes and Persians; but the royal family were Persian, and the Persians still were a distinct race, and in the opinion of Herodotos [9, 68] the best soldiers, and indeed the centre and mainstay of the royal army. A very distinct character of the Persians may be traced in Herodotos; he represents them as 'brave, lively, spirited, capable of witty and keen repartees' [1, 127, 141; 6, 1; 8, 81], 'but vain, weak, impulsive, and hopelessly servile to their lords' [3, 25; 7, 56, 223; 9, 113]. Rawl.

PHALERUM, cc. 66—7, 92—3, 108.

A town on the eastern point of the Bay of Phalerum, of which the Peiraeus forms the western point. Before, and at the time of, the Persian war it was the principal harbour of Athens. After that time though joined by a wall to Athens it was superseded by the much safer harbour on the west of the Peiraeus.

PHARNACES, c. 126.

A Persian, father of Artabazos [7, 66].

PHAYLLOS, c. 47.

A famous athlete of Krotona, who won the Pentathlum twice and the long race once at the Pythian games [Paus. 10, 9, 2]. He is referred to in Aristophanes [Acharn. 215; Vesp. 1206] as a kind of type of speed. The Scholiast on the former passage seems to confound him with another Phayllos who won a victory at Olympia (in leaping and running in armour), which Pausanias says expressly this Phayllos did not do.

PHILAON, c. 11.

A brother of Gorgos, king of Salamis, in Kypros (q. v.).

PHLIASIANS, the, c. 72.

The inhabitants of Phlios, a town and small territory to the N. of Argolis and S. of Sikyonia. The people were Dorians and generally in close alliance with Sparta. The territory consisted of a high valley surrounded by mountains. Phlios sent 200 men to Thermopylae [7, 202].

PHILIPPOS, c. 139.

A Makedonian king, son of Argaeos, and grandson of Perdikkas [q. v.].

PHOENIKIANS, the, cc. 85, 90, 97, 100, 118—9, 121.

The Phoenikians inhabited the north of Palestine, from which they had sent out numerous colonies to Kypros, Africa, and Europe. Herodotos says that they came to Palestine from the borders of the Red Sea (1, 1). They had been from very ancient times a great seafaring people, and had had the great bulk of the mercantile business of the Mediterranean. It was they who supplied the greater and most powerful part of the fleet of Xerxes (7, 89), it was they who constructed the bridge of ships across the Hellespont (7, 34), and were the most skilful engineers of the canal across Athos (7, 23). See *Tyre* and *Sidon*.

PHOKIS, cc. 31—2, 35.

PHOKIANS, the, cc. 27—33, 134.

Phokis was a considerable district bounded on the S. by the Gulf of Corinth, and by Doris and eastern Lokris on the N. It contained the range of Parnassos and the sacred city of Delphi, which however was inhabited by a different race,—probably Dorians.

Phokis politically was a confederacy of towns mostly situated in the valley of the Kephisos, and the Phokians were looked upon as a people of Aeolian or Achaean race. They were almost perpetually at enmity with the Thessalians and indeed had built a wall across the pass of Thermopylae to check their raids [7, 176]; and, according to Herodotos, their chief motive for not joining the Persians earlier was hatred of the Thessalians. Even when some of them did in the following year join Mardonios, a large number refused, and mustering round Parnassos assisted the Greeks [9, 31].

PHRYGIA, c. 136.

PHYLAKOS,

(1) c. 39.

One of the national heroes of Delphi. His phantom is said to have again appeared to protect the Delphians when in B.C. 280 the Gauls under Brennus were attacking Delphi [Paus. 10, 23, 3].

(2) c. 85.

A man of Samos, son of Histiaeos.

PINDOS, c. 43.

A town in Doris, on a river of the same name running into the Kephisos. It was one of the Doric tetrapolis, see *Erineos*.

PLATAEA, c. 50.

PLATAEANS, the, cc. 1, 44, 50, 66; τὰ Πλαταιικά, c. 126.

The territory of Plataea was separated from Attica on the S. by Kithaeron,—Eleutherae which came between having voluntarily enrolled itself with Attica [Paus. 1, 38, 8],—and from the territory of Thebes on the N. by the river Asopos. Toward the east, along the valley of the Asopos, it was limited by the village of Hysiae. The town stood 'on the steep and rugged slopes which fall from the heights of Kithaeron into the valley on the north. In this lower ground, and near the walls of the city, two small rivers take their rise, and flow in opposite directions'—Oëroe flowing west to the Corinthian Gulf, Asopos to the east into the Euboic Gulf. Plataea is 7 miles from Thespiae, 6½ miles from Thebes. The Plataeans had long been disinclined to share the policy of the Boeotian league, and having been accordingly persecuted by the Thebans they had put themselves under the protection of Athens about B.C. 501 [3, 108. Thucyd. 3, 68]. This union had been cemented by the fact of the 1000 men sent by Plataea alone of the Greek states to help the Athenians at Marathon. The subsequent history of the town includes its siege and destruction by the Thebans in B.C. 429—7, its partial restoration in B.C. 387, a second destruction by the Thebans in B.C. 374, and its final restoration in B.C. 338. At its destruction in B.C. 427 the bulk of its inhabitants were admitted to Athenian citizenship.

GEOGRAPHICAL INDEX. 243

POGON, c. 42.

The harbour of Troezen, in Argolis; so named from the shape of the bay, 'the Beard'.

POLYAS, c. 21.

A man of Antikyra (q. v.) employed as an outlook man on the coast of Trachis.

POLYKRITOS, cc. 92—3.

Son of Krios, one of the chief men of Aegina [6, 73].

POSEIDON, cc. 55, 123, 129.

Son of Kronos, brother of Zeus, and God of the Sea.

POTIDAEA, cc. 127—9.

A city placed in the isthmus which joined Pallene to the mainland. It was a colony from Korinthos [Thucyd. 1, 56], and had already submitted to the Persians [7, 123]. After the repulse of Artabazos narrated in this book it sent a contingent to the Greek army which fought at Plataea [9, 28, 31]. In B.C. 432 Potidaea broke off from the Athenian alliance formed after the Persian wars, and was consequently besieged and after a long resistance taken by the Athenians [Thucyd. 2, 70]. After various vicissitudes it was taken and its inhabitants destroyed and removed by Philip of Makedon [B.C. 341—340]; and it was afterwards refounded by Cassander, after whom it was called *Cassandreia*, and having passed from the Makedonian to the Roman Empire, in the time of Augustus it received a Roman colony. It was finally destroyed by the Huns.

PSYTTALEIA, cc. 76, 95.

A small island lying between Salamis and the Peiraeus, now called *Lipsokutali*. Aeschylos describes it as 'small and offering ill harbourage for ships' [*Pers.* 450]. It is about a mile long, 300 yards broad, and very rocky and low.

PTOUM. APOLLO PTOUS, c. 135.

Mt Ptoum was on the S. E. of the Lake Kopais extending to the Euboean Sea [Mod. *Paled* and *Strutzina*]. The temple and oracle of Apollo Ptous was in the slope of the mountain about 2 miles from the town of Akraiphia.

PYTHEAS, c. 92.

An Aeginetan, who was captured by the Persians when serving in B.C. 480 as a soldier on board an Aeginetan vessel, which was one of three vessels keeping watch at Skiathos. He fought with such gallantry that his captors in admiration gave him his life, and took pains to cure his numerous wounds [7, 181].

RHODOPE, c. 116.

A range of mountains in Thrakia separating the valley of the Nestos from that of the Hebros, mod. *Despoto Dagh* (with a part of the *Balkan*).

SAKAE, c. 113.

A powerful Asiatic tribe [whose name by some has been connected with that of the Saxons, by others with that of the Skyths] which was conquered by Kyros [1, 153], and seems to have furnished one of the most trustworthy contingents to the Persian army [6, 113]. They appear to have inhabited the steppes of what is now called Kirghiz Khosacks in Tibet.

SALAMIS,

(1) c. 11.

A town in Kypros, supposed to be a colony from the island of Salamis led out by Teukros. It was destroyed in Trajan's reign by an earthquake, and restored subsequently under the name of Constantia.

(2) 11, 40—2, 44—5, 49, 51, 56, 60, 65, 70, 74, 76, 81, 86, 89, 90—6, 121—2, 124, 126, 130.

An island about 10 miles long off the coast of Attica, between which and the mainland the channel at its narrowest is about 1 mile across. It had belonged to Athens since about B.C. 600, when according to the common statement the claim of the Athenians as against the Megarians was confirmed by five Spartan arbitrators owing to the skilful pleading of Solon [Plutarch, Solon, c. 10].

SAMOS, cc. 85, 130, 132. SAMIANS, c. 85.

A considerable island off the coast of Karia, rich from its great pottery manufactories. From about B.C. 535 to B.C. 522 it was under the rule of Polykrates, who acquired a powerful navy, extended his dominion over several of the neighbouring islands, warred against Miletos, and wished to form a great confederacy of Ionian states with Samos as the central power. After the fall of Polykrates, in the course of the disputes as to his successor, the Persian force in the island inflicted a cruel massacre on the inhabitants; and then handed the island over to a brother of Polykrates, Sylosôn, whose son Aeakes continued to hold the tyranny, although tributary to Persia, until the deposition of the Ionian tyrants by Aristagoras in B.C. 500. When the Persians subsequently restored Aeakes, a number of the Samians accepted the invitation of the people of Zankle (Messene) to go to Sicily and occupy Calacta. Aeakes however appears to have died or been deposed about the time of the battle of Salamis, and Theomestor (q. v.) put in his place [3, 39—47, 54—6, 120—5; 6, 13, 22, 25].

SAMOTHRAKE, c. 90.

A small island opposite the coast of Thrakia consisting of a huge volcanic crater Mt Saŏke [5,500 feet]. The inhabitants were originally Pelasgi, and practised a mystic worship called τὰ Καβείρων (=Corybantes, Strab.) ὄργια [2, 51]. The islanders possessed a tract of land on the continent, from Doriskos to Lissos, which was protected by a line of fortresses [7, 59, 108]. It was called 'Thrakian Samos' to distinguish it from the larger island near Karia. See Il. 13, 12 ἐπ' ἀκροτάτης κορυφῆς Σάμου ὑληέσσης Θρηικίης. It was said in still earlier times to have been called Δαρδανία [Steph. Byz.], and still earlier Μελίτη [Strabo].

SARDIS, cc. 105, 117.

The capital of Lydia, situated on the slope of Mt Tmolos, and on either bank of the Paktolos. It seems to have been but slenderly furnished with defences, but its citadel was all but impregnable [see Polyb. 7, 15—17; 8, 17—18]. After its capture by Kyros [1, 84] it became the chief seat of the Persian government in Asia Minor, and the residence of the satrap and sometimes of the king.

SEILENOS, c. 138.

A satyr, always represented as the attendant of Dionysos. He invented a flute, which he is constantly depicted as playing. It was a tradition that he could be captured and bound with flowers, and could then be compelled to prophesy: it is some capture of this sort to which Herodotos refers. For the moral Apologue which went by the name of the discourse of Seilenos to Midas, see Aelian V. H. 3, 18.

SEPIAS, c. 66.

A promontory in Magnesia opposite the island of Skiathos.

SERIPHIANS, the, cc. 46, 48.

The inhabitants of Seriphos, one of the Cyclades immediately south of Kythnos. It possessed iron and copper mines, but was poor and insignificant, and used in later times by the Romans as a place of exile.

SICILY, c. 3.

At the time of the Persian war the coasts of Sicily were studd with Hellenic colonies. The earliest was Naxos (Taurom   ) settled in B.C. 735 by the Ionians from Chalkis. Naxos in ˙ s turn had settled Catana and Leontini. Besides this Chalkis ad also settled Zankle (Messene); and Megara had sent a colony   Thapsos (circ. B.C. 700). But the most famous and powerful   all was the Corinthian colony of Syracuse [B.C. 734], which h   its turn sent out at least five other colonies in Sicily, and   s possessed of a decisive hegemony among the other states   hese colonies were naturally for the most part on the eastern and south-eastern coast: on the western the Carthaginians were making settlements, and the Hellenic colonies in Sicily were engaged in a contest with them at the same time as the eastern Greeks were fighting for life with the Persians.

SIDON, c. 67. SIDONIANS, the, cc. 78, 92.

An ancient city of Phoenikia, celebrated as a great mercantile and naval centre, and for its manufactures in embroidery, dyes, and glass. The skill of Sidonian women in embroidery is alluded to in the Iliad [6, 292; see Her. 2, 116], as also of its workers in metal [Il. 23, 741]; it was however outstripped in prosperity by Tyre.

SIKINNOS, cc. 75, 110.

A Persian by birth, who having been captured and enslaved became the paidagogos of the children of Themistokles, and was employed by him to take his message to Xerxes. Plutarch, Themist. 12, 82.

SIKYONIANS, the, cc. 1, 43, 72.

The inhabitants of Sikyon, a town and district usually classed as part of Korinthia, though it was independent of Korinthos. It lay in the valley of the Peloponnesian river Asopos. It had formerly been governed by tyranni, of whom we hear of Kleisthenes, the maternal grandfather of the Athenian reformer [5, 67]. The inhabitants were Dorians and were accustomed to act in war under the direction of Sparta [6, 92]; they appear from the same passage to have been wealthy, for they submitted to pay Argos a war indemnity of 500 talents (about £24,000) for joining Kleomenes in his invasion of Argos about B.C. 510.

SIPHNIANS, the, cc. 46, 48.

The inhabitants of Siphnos, one of the Cyclades immediately south of Seriphos. The island once possessed gold and silver mines, but when these were worked out it became exceedingly poor and unimportant.

SIRIS, cc. 62, 115.

A town in Italy, in the district of Lucania, on the shore of the Gulf of Tarentum and at the mouth of a river of the same name. It was a very ancient town, believed to have been colonised by Trojans,—but between 700 and 600 B.C. Ionians from Kolophon had settled in it. About 430 B.C. it seems to have fallen under the power of Tarentum, and its inhabitants afterwards were transferred to Herakleia. The Ionian colonisation seems the only conceivable ground for the claim of Themistokles for the Athenians of having any rights there.

GEOGRAPHICAL INDEX. 247

SKIATHOS, cc. 7, 92.

A small island opposite the promontory of Sepias. A colony of Chalkidians has displaced the former Pelasgic inhabitants.

SKIONE, cc. 8, 128.

A city on the peninsula of Pallene. The inhabitants considered themselves to be Achaeans from the Peloponnese [Thucyd. 4, 120, 1]. The town revolted from Athens to the Spartans under Brasidas in B.C. 423, was besieged by the Athenians, and very cruelly treated when taken [id. 5, 32].

SKIRAS, c. 94.

An epithet of Athenè (q. v.) of uncertain meaning. There was a temple of Athenè Skiras at Phalerum [Paus. 1, 1, 4; 36, 3]: there was also a festival called Skirophoria or Skira [Arist. Eccl. 16]; and one of the Attic months was called Skirophorion.

SKIRONIAN WAY, the, c. 71.

The coast road,—the most easterly of the three which passed the Isthmus of Corinth. It owes its name to the fact that for several miles it is carried along a cornice cut in the face of the rocks called the Skironian Rocks, from the name of a mythical robber who haunted the place and was slain by Theseus.

SKYLLIAS, c. 8.

A man of Skione, a famous diver. He taught his daughter Hydna the same art. And for their good services on this occasion,— in the course of which they lost their lives,—the Amphictyonic Council honoured them by dedicating statues of both father and daughter at Delphi [Paus. 10, 19, 1—2].

SOSIMENES, c. 81.

A man of Tenos, father of Panaetios.

SPARTANS, the, cc. 2, 42, 125. SPARTA, cc. 114, 124, 132, 142—4.

The Spartans, properly so called, were only those who possessed full citizenship. They were the descendants of the conquering Dorians who had seized the land and reduced the population either to the state of unenfranchised farmers (perioekoi) or praedial slaves (Helots). They were comparatively few in number [about 8000 at this period, 7, 234], and their peculiar institutions tended to check any increase. They were looked upon as the head of the Dorians, and the natural leaders of all Greece in the field; they actually ruled two-thirds of the Peloponnese, and exercised an informal hegemony in the rest, except in Argos. We must distinguish between 'Lakedaemonians' and 'Spartans', the former Her. generally uses as including all the inhabitants of Lakonia; the latter refers simply to the ruling class as full citizens. See for instance 9, 28, 'Ten thousand Lakedaemonian troops were on the right wing, five thousand of whom were Spartans.'

STRATTIS, c. 132.

A tyrant of Chios, who had accompanied Darius on the Skythian expedition, as far as the Danube [4, 138], and was probably a nominee or partisan of the Persian supremacy, which would help to account for this plot against his life.

STRYMON, cc. 115, 118. STRYMONIAN WIND, c. 118.

The modern *Struma* (or in Turkish *Karasu*) a river which forms the boundary between Makedonia and Thrakia. The sources of it mentioned in c. 115 are in Mt Skemios, from whence it flows into the Strymonic Gulf, being navigable a few miles above Amphipolis. The 'Strymonian wind' seems to mean a wind blowing from its mouth.

STYREANS, the, cc. 1, 46.

The inhabitants of Styra, a town in Euboea, near Karystos, inhabited originally by Dryopians (q. v.).

SUSA, cc. 54, 99.

Susa on the Choaspes (*Kerkhah*) was the capital of the province of Susiana, which lies at the head of the Persian Gulf, and is bounded on the east by Persis, and the west by Assyria, and on the north by Media. From the time of Kyros it was one of the chief royal residences [1, 188; 4, 83].

TEGEAN FRONTIERS, c. 124.

Tegea was a town in the south-east of Arkadia about 10 miles S. of Mantineia. It was on the road from Sparta to Attica and North Greece. It had been in close alliance with Sparta since about B.C. 500.

TELAMON, c. 63.

King of Salamis, father of Ajax and Teukros. See *Aeakidae*.

TELLIAS, c. 27.

A mantis or seer of Elis. Another member of the mantic family of Telliadae is mentioned in 9, 37 as serving Mardonios as seer.

TEMENOS, c. 137. TEMENIDAE, c. 138.

Temenos, of Argos, was the reputed ancestor of the Makedonian kings, hence called Temenidae. Temenos was an Herakleid, son of Aristomachos, and returned to the Peloponnesos with the other Herakleidae [Apoll. 2, 8, 5; Paus. 2, 18, 7].

TENIANS, the, cc. 66, 82, 83.

Inhabitants of Tenos, one of the Cyclades, separated by a very narrow channel from the southern point of Andros. It was also called 'Ὑδροῦσσα (well-watered), and 'Οφιοῦσσα (isle of snakes), whence the word Tenos is derived from the Phoenikian *Tanoth* = a snake; and a snake often appears on its coins. The island is about 60 miles in circumference and is famous for its vines.

TETHRONIUM, C. 33.

A city of Phokis, built on a plain in the valley of the Kephisos.

THEBANS, the, cc. 50, 134—5. THEBES, C. 134.

Thebes subsequent to the Homeric age became the most powerful city in Boeotia, that position being occupied in the Homeric times by Orchomenos. The district of Thebes, the Thebais, a rich corn land, was divided from that of Plataea by the river Asopos. The city was built on an elevation of 150 feet above the plain on a spur of Mount Teumēsos, and the citadel or Kadmeia probably stood at the southern end of the town. The Thebans were believed to be a colony from Phoenikia led by Kadmos. Perhaps this difference of blood may partly account for their zealous medizing; but a long-standing enmity to Athens was the immediate motive. They sent 400 men indeed to support Leonidas at Thermopylae, but these men took the earliest opportunity of deserting to the Persian side [7, 203, 233].

THEMISTOKLES, cc. 4, 5, 19, 22—3, 57—8, 59, 61—3, 75, 79, 92, 108—112, 123—5.

Themistokles was the son of Neokles, an Athenian of moderate position. His mother according to some was Abrotonon, a Thracian woman, according to others Euterpe of Karia. He was therefore only a half-blood Athenian. But before the age of Perikles the father's citizenship was sufficient to give a man his full rights. His abilities shewed themselves early, and he came forward in public life as an opponent of Aristeides, and an advocate of a forward and ambitious policy for Athens. He commanded the levy of his tribe at Marathon; but it was between that event and B.C. 480 that he began to exercise a decisive influence in the state. It was on his advice that the profits of the mines at Laurium were devoted to the building a fleet, which, as Herodotos says, proved the salvation of Hellas, though their primary object was the prosecution of the Aeginetan war. We see in this book how powerfully he contributed to the successful resistance to Persia in B.C. 480. In the next year the command of the troops at Plataea was committed to Aristeides [9, 28], and that of the fleet to Xanthippos, Diodorus says, from the prejudice excited against Them. by the honours given him at Sparta [11, 27]. In fact although the reputation acquired by Themistokles in 480 made him the most famous man in Greece, the

Athenians seem to have preferred to entrust their most important interests abroad to others, especially to Aristeides. Meanwhile Themistokles at home was busied in carrying out the great works of the town walls, and the fortification of the Peiraeus, which he saw offered a harbour far superior to the old one at Phalerum. This latter work was probably not finished at the time of his ostracism. But these things were not done without opposition and the loss of popularity. The Athenians liked being told that the Peiraeus would enable them if their town were taken 'to fight the world at sea'; but the expenses and self-sacrifice required brought odium on the author of the plans. And his opponents Kimon and Alkmaeon managed about 471 B.C. to secure his ostracism. He retired to Argos, and in B.C. 467 was accused of having been in correspondence with Pausanias, who had been condemned and starved to death at Sparta for treasonable dealings with the Persian court. Orders were given to arrest him; but getting warning he fled to Korkyra, thence to Admetos king of the Molossians, thence to Ephesos. From that town he opened communication with Artaxerxes, was received honourably at the Persian court, and provided with handsome pensions and a residence at Magnesia. There he died, some say by his own hand, because he despaired of giving the king the help he had promised against Athens, or, as the story which Thucydides believed asserted, by a natural death, B.C. 460. Mr Grote seems to assume the guilt of Themistokles in regard to the correspondence with Persia; but not so the authorities used by Plutarch, or Thucydides, who speaks of him with the warmest admiration.

Life by Plutarch. Thucyd. 1, 74—138.

THEOKYDES, c. 65.

An Athenian, father of Dikaeos (q. v.).

THEOMESTOR, c. 85.

Son of Androdamas, made Tyrant of Samos in succession to Aeakes, who had been restored after the suppression of the Ionic revolt [9, 90]. See *Samos*.

THERMAIC GULF, the, c. 127.

That portion of the Aegean Sea which is enclosed by the coasts of Thessaly and Makedonia on the W. and N., and by the Chalkidic peninsula on the E. It takes its name from the city of Thessalonika, anciently called Therma, situated at its head.

THERMOPYLAE, cc. 15, 24, 27, 66, 71.

The scene of the famous resistance to the Persian invasion, and of the death of Leonidas, was a narrow pass between the extremity of Mt Oeta and the sea. The range of Oeta stretches right across Greece, and the passes were few and difficult. It was necessary that so large an army as that of Xerxes should go by this as the shortest and easiest. The narrowest point was that between two mountain streams, the Asopos and Phoenix, which now fall into the Spercheios, but then into the sea: 'there there was only a narrow causeway sufficient for a single carriage' [7, 199]. Its name was given it on account of some hot sulphur springs. The nature of the pass is now quite altered, the sea has receded, the Spercheios has brought down so much alluvial deposit that its course is changed, and there is now a broad marshy plain covered by rice-fields between the mountain and the sea.

THESPIANS, the, cc. 50, 66, 75. THESPIAE, cc. 25, 50.

The inhabitants of Thespiae, a town of Boeotia about six miles W. of Thebes, which possessed a harbour at Kreusis in the Korinthian Gulf. The Thespians had been as loyal as Plataea to the Greek side, partly no doubt from enmity with Thebes. At Thermopylae they were the only men who refused to quit Leonidas in his extremity, and all their 700 perished with him [id. 7, 222, 226]; the rest of the citizens took refuge in the Peloponnese; and 800 of them were with the army at Plataea [9, 30].

THESPROTIANS, the, c. 47.

The inhabitants of a district in the south-west portion of Epiros opposite the islands of Korkyra and Paxos. Their chief town was Ephyra (Kichyros) on the Kokytos. At one time they had the control of the oracle of Dodona, which was at Dramisos.

THESSALIANS, the, cc. 27—32, 113—5, 126, 129, 131—3, 135.

Thessaly is the province between Makedonia on the N., Epeiros on the W., and Phthiotis on the S. It is a great alluvial plain surrounded by mountains and drained by one river system, that of the Peneus and its tributaries. The plain was exceedingly rich and fertile, and particularly famous for its breed of horses, and accordingly Thessalian cavalry were the most renowned in all Greece. There were several leagues or combinations of towns in Thessaly, the most powerful being that of which the centre was Larissa, but there was no one central government. The Thessalians had joined Xerxes under compulsion [7, 172—4], except in the case of the Aleuadae [7, 6], and were ready to turn against him at the first sign of failure [9, 89].

THRAKIA, c. 117. THE THRAKIANS, c. 116.

The district N. of Makedonia bounded on the E. by the Euxine. Towards the N.W. the frontier between it and the Keltic tribes was undetermined; but Herodotos regards the Danube as separating it from Skythia [4, 99]. For the number and warlike nature of the tribes, see 5, 3. The Persians had extended their power along its coast, but had not penetrated far inland [4, 93; 5, 2].

THRIASIAN PLAIN, the, c. 65.

The Thriasian Plain, skirting the Bay of Eleusis, was divided from Athens by the hills of Aegaleos, and was bounded on the north by Mt Parnes. Through it, close to the coast, went the Sacred Way to Eleusis. The greatest length of the plain is nine miles. It was in parts so low and marshy that the Sacred Way had to be raised like a causeway, while the northern and western part of the plain is stony and barren. Its name was derived from a hamlet close to Eleusis, of which the exact position is not known.

TIGRANES, c. 26.

A Persian, one of the family or clan of the Achaemenidae, to which the royal family of the Persians belonged [1, 125; 3, 65].

TIMODEMOS, c. 128.

A man of the Attic deme of Aphidnae, who was a political opponent of Themistokles.

TIMOXENOS, c. 128.

A man of Skione (q. v.) who commanded a contingent of his countrymen in Potidaea

TITHOREA, c. 32.

One of the peaks of Parnassos. The name seems to have also been applied to the district at the foot of the mountain, and to the town of Neon (q. v.). The natives supposed it to have been derived from a mountain nymph, Tithorea. [Paus. 10, 32, 9.]

TORONAEANS, c. 127.

An inhabitant of Torone, a town situated on the S.W. of the peninsula of Sithonia, the central one of the three Chalkidic peninsulas. It was a colony from Chalkis in Euboea, and was originally the chief Greek city in those parts. Like the other Chalkidic towns it had been forced to supply a contingent to the Persian army and navy [7, 122]. From it the gulf between Pallene and Sithonia was called the Toronaic Gulf.

TRACHINIA, c. 31.
TRACHIS, cc. 21, 66.

A town and district at the foot of Mt Oeta in Thessaly. The name (=rugged) is derived from the nature of the rocks surrounding the plain. In B.C. 426 the Lakedaemonians built Herakleia in its territory as a centre of Lakedaemonian influence.

TRITEEIS, c. 33.

Triteeis or Tritea was a town in Phokis in the valley of the Kephisos.

TROEZENIANS, the, cc. 1, 43, 72.

The inhabitants of Troezen, a town in the S.E. corner of Argolis. It was a very ancient town and had long been in alliance with Athens ; and when the Athenians quitted their town before the battle of Salamis, a large number of their women, children, and old men were received at Troezen and honourably entertained, a daily allowance being voted from the treasury, and free leave being given to the children to pluck fruit [Plut. Them. 10]. The reason of this was that Troezen, though occupied by the Dorians, retained a large admixture of its original Ionic inhabitants who came from Karia; and there had been from old times a religious connexion between it and Athens as belonging to the same Amphiktyony, the centre of which had been the temple of Poseidon at Kaluria (Poros) in the Troezenian domain. Troezen was the mother-town of Herodotos' native place, Halikarnassos.

TROPHONIOS, C. 134.

According to one story Trophonios was the son of Erginos, according to another of Apollo. He and his brother Agamedes built the temple of Apollo at Delphi, as well as a treasure-house for king Hyrieus [Paus. 9, 37, 5]. After his death he was worshipped as a hero, and his cavern near Lebadeia (q. v.) was visited as an oracle. An elaborate account of the mode of descending into this cavern, apparently artificially constructed, is given by Pausanias, 39, 5—12. Cp. Aristoph. Nub. 597. The oracle of Trophonios was one of those consulted by Kroisos before the invasion of Kyros [1, 46].

TYRE, C. 67.

An ancient city of the Phoenikians in the north of Palestine. The priests of the great temple of Herakles told Herodotos that the city had been founded 2300 years before his visit, i.e. circ. B.C. 2755 [2, 44]. It consisted of two towns, one on the mainland, the other on two islands half a mile from the coast. Alexander the Great when besieging it made a causeway across this strait, round which sand has accumulated; and the islands are thus connected with the mainland by a sandy neck half a mile broad. At the time of the Persian wars it was still rich and prosperous, with a great mercantile navy, though it was with the rest of Phoenikia subject to Persia. Alexander the Great entirely destroyed its inhabitants, and put in some Karian colonists; and after being a subject of contest between the Egyptian and Syrian kings, who attained those dominions after Alexander's death, it finally became part of the Roman province of Syria. For an account of its former glories, and its 13 years' siege by Nebuchadnezzar, see Ezekiel cc. 26, 27. How completely Tyre fell from its old position may be gathered from the fact that the geographer Stephanos [circ. A.D. 500] under the head of Τύρος merely says νῆσος ἐν Φοινίκῃ, not noticing a town at all.

XANTHIPPOS, C. 131.

Father of Pericles, Strategus at Athens B.C. 479 and commander of the Athenian contingent at Mycale.

XERXES, cc. 10, 15, 16, 22, 24—5, 34—5, 52, 54, 64—7, 69, 81, 86, 88—90, 97, 99, 100—1, 103, 105, 107—8, 110, 113—5, 118—20, 129, 140, 143—4.

Though a younger son of Darius he succeeded to the crown because his mother Atossa was a daughter of the great Kyros, and the Persians had only submitted to have Darius as king on the condition that by marrying a daughter of Kyros the royal line should be traced to the great Persian conqueror [7, 3—4]. Xerxes had been very doubtful as to the policy of invading Greece, but had been persuaded to do so principally by Mardonios. Though he was the handsomest and most stately man in his whole great army [7, 187], he presents all the worst features of an Eastern monarch, without the personal courage that did something to excuse them in the eyes of his people. If now and then (see 7, 146; 8, 69) some traits of more liberal sentiment or greater insight into justice are related of him, they can do little to relieve the dark colours in which Herodotos portrays this man, whose character may be said to point the moral of the whole of his history. He is the embodiment of swollen pride and unchecked tyranny and luxury, against which the $\phi\theta\acute{o}\nu os$ of the gods is inevitably wakened.

XUTHOS, c. 44.

Son of Hellen, and father of Ion and Achaeos, and therefore the mythical ancestor of the Ionians and Achaeans [7, 93].

ZEUS, c. 116.

Herodotos represents here by the name of the supreme deity of the Greeks the Persian supreme god Ormuzd, as in 1, 131; 2, 55; 5, 105.

ZOSTER, c. 107.

A promontory in Attica formed by the termination of Mount Hymettos, mod. Cape *Lumbardhas*. Opposite to it is the island Phaura, mod. *Fleva*.

APPENDIX.

The Ionic Dialect.

The dialect in which Herodotos wrote is called the New Ionic, that is, the language of the Ionic cities of Asia Minor in the fifth century B.C., and those islands of the Aegean colonised by Ionians. By the 'Old Ionic' is meant the language of the *Iliad* and *Odyssey* (though it seems probable that the foundation of the language of these poems was Achaean or Aeolic, and that they were Ionicised subsequently), the Homeric Hymns and Hesiod. The oldest Greek literature therefore known to us was written in various developments of the Ionic dialect. The Attic, such as we find it in Thucydides and the Tragedians, is a still later development; but as the Athenian literature (from about B.C. 450 onwards) is best known to us, and has survived in much larger quantity than any other, we for convenience compare the forms of the Ionic dialect with those of the Attic as a standard, although in most cases the Ionic forms are the older. Herodotos [b. B.C. 484], a contemporary of Sophocles, lived just at the parting of the ways when the Attic literature was beginning to supplant all others, yet he deliberately adopted the Ionic dialect as still the best for prose composition, though he was by birth a Dorian. He was, then, writing in an acquired dialect, and was moreover a wanderer and scholar who had conversed with men of all dialects, and studied their writings; it was likely therefore that his style should show signs of modification in word-forms, as well as in idiom, from the standard Ionic; but still the Ionic as we find it in his writings shows decisively how it had developed, sometimes less, and sometimes in a different way, than the other dialects.

Many words are used by him in a sense different from that in which Attic writers of his own time would have used them, but yet in the same sense in which they are used in Homer; or again, words which had become obsolete, or used only by poets in Athens, are still employed by him in their primitive sense as the natural and prosaic terms. The same phenomenon may be seen in our own and other languages. A Yorkshireman, or an Eastern Counties man, may often be heard using words that are almost or entirely unknown to the Londoner, but which were the ordinary terms in use in the days of Chaucer or even of Shakespear. Even with a printed literature men of the same stock, if divided by place and circumstance, will develope the same language in widely different ways. Take for example the many idioms used by Americans differing from our usage in England, yet of which we may often find the counterpart in our older writers. What was likely then to be the case between two and three thousand years ago, with means of intercourse infinitely less efficacious, and a literature often not written at all, and of course when written infinitely confined in circulation? They did what was natural: each community gradually adopted peculiar terms and idioms; sometimes one retained a more archaic form than another, sometimes the same community would diverge much more than the other from the primitive form. They did not always alter in the same way, and no one division of the Hellenic race could claim a monopoly of archaic forms or a distinct supremacy in primitive correctness. The laws which such phonetic changes follow help us to track the original form through the maze of divergent modification, but they cannot always tell us why one set of people modified less or more than another, or in this way or that. The most marked features of the Ionic as compared with the Attic dialect are (1) that the contraction of two vowels is generally resolved into its component vowels, (2) that the η sound (Etacism) is generally preferred to the a, though the reverse change is not infrequent.

The following is a conspectus of the variations of the Ionic dialect of Herodotos from that of the Attic[1].

[1] Taken with modifications and additions from that of Dr K. Abicht, *Uebersicht über den Herodotischen Dialect.* Leipzig, 1869.

A. Letters.

I. Consonants.

(1) In three words the tenuis takes the place of the aspirated consonant, δέκομαι, αὖτις, οὐκί (Att. δέχομαι, αὖθις, οὐχί).

(2) In three words the positions of the aspirate and tenuis are reversed, ἐνθαῦτα, ἐνθεῦτεν, κιθών (Att. ἐνταῦθα, ἐντεῦθεν, χιτών).

(3) κ is found in the place of π in the interrogative pronouns and adverbs, κοῖος, κόσος, κότερος, κῇ, κοῖ, κοῦ, κῶς, κίθεν, κότε [Att. ποῖος, πόσος etc.]; in the relatives, ὁκοῖος, ὁκόσος, ὁκότερος [Att. ὁποῖος etc.]; and in the adverbs οὔκοτε, οὐδέκοτε, οὔκω [Att. οὔποτε etc.].

(4) The prepositions ἀντί, ἀπό, ἐπί, κατά, μετά, ὑπό, neither in elision nor composition, take the aspirated consonant before an aspirate, e.g. ἀπ' οὗ, μετ' ἅ, κατά [= καθ' ἅ], κατ' ἕνα, ὑπιστάναι, ἀπικνέομαι, ὑπίημι, μετέντες. In the same way οὐκ does not become οὐχ before an aspirate.

(5) σσ is not changed into ττ, e.g. θάλασσα, γλῶσσα, τάσσω, ἐλάσσων, are the invariable forms in Ionic.

(6) σσ becomes ξ, e.g. διξύς, τριξύς.

II. Vowels.

(1) α (Attic) into ε, as ἔρσην 'male', τέσσερες, ὀπέων (ὀπάων).

(2) ᾰ (Attic) into η, as διπλήσιος, πολλαπλήσιος.

(3) ᾱ (Attic) into η,

(*a*) In root syllables, as ῥηϊδίως, ἠήρ, κρήτηρ, νηός, τριήκοντα, πρῆγμα, πέπρηγμαι.

(*b*) In derivatives, as θέ-ητρον, νε-ηνίης, ἴρ-ηξ, Αἰγινῆται, ἰ-ητρός, ἀνι-ηρός.

(*c*) In compounds, as γενεη-λογέω, διή-κονος.

(*d*) In the adverbs λάθρη, λίην, πέρην.

(4) ᾱ (Attic) into ω, as παιωνίζω, θῶκος.

(5) ε (Attic) into ᾰ, as τάμνω, τράπω [but we find τρέψω, ἔτρεψα], μέγαθος.

(6) ε (Attic) into ι, as ἱστίη (ἑστία), ἐπίστιος = ἐφέστιος.

(7) η (Attic) into ᾰ, as μεσαμβρίη, ἀμφισβατέω, πεντακόσιοι.

(8) η (Attic) into ω, as πτώσσω.

(9) ω (Attic) into η, as Φθιῆτις, Θεσσαλιῆτις, Ἰστιαιῆτις, and the derivatives Φθιήτης, Ἀμπρακιήτης etc.

(10) ο into α as ἀρρωδέω [Att. ὀρρωδέω].

III. Diphthongs.

(1) α into αι, as αἰετός, αἰεί.

(2) αῦ into ω, as θῶμα [but θῶυμα, θωυμάζω, also see I. 11], τρῶμα.

(3) ε into ει, as εἴρομαι, εἰρωτέω, εἰρύω, εἰλίσσω, εἴνατος, εἰνακόσιοι, εἵνεκεν, κεινός, ξεῖνος, στεινός.

(4) ει into ε, as ἐς, ἔσω, μέζων, κρέσσων, πλέων, fem. of adj. in -υς as βαθέα, ὀξέα, and in the tenses of δείκνυμι, as δέξω, ἔδεξα, δέξαι, ἐδέχθη, ἐδέδεκτο, also ἔργω, ἔωθα, and in all proparoxytons in -ειος, -εια, -ειον, as ἐπιτήδεος[2], ἐπέτεος.

(5) ει into ι, as ἴκελος, προσίκελος, ἴλη.

(6) ευ into ι, as ἰθύς, ἰθέα, ἰθύ, ἰθύνω [Att. εὐθύς].

(7) ο into ου, as μοῦνος, νοῦσος, νουσέω, Οὔλυμπος, οὔνομα, οὐνομάζω, ὁ οὖρος (ὄρος a boundary), τὸ οὖρος (τὸ ὄρος), ὁ οὐδός (threshold), but ἡ ὁδός (way): in trisyllable forms γούνατα, δούρατα, from γόνυ, δόρυ.

(8) οὐ into ω, as ὦν (οὖν), τοιγαρῶν, οὔκων, γῶν (γοῦν).

---

[2] Still the comp. and superl. of ἐπιτήδεος seem to be in -ότερος, -ότατος as though the word were ἐπιτήδειος.

THE IONIC DIALECT.

B. Syllables.

(1) Solution and Contraction.

(*a*) ου into οε, as ἀγαθοέργος, δημιοέργος.

(*b*) οη into ω, as ὀγδώκοντα, and in the following forms of βοᾶν and νοεῖν,—βῶσαι, βώσασθαι, ἔβωσε, ἐβώσθην, ἐννώσας, ἐννενώκασι, ἐννένωντο, νενωμένος, ἐπενώθη, also βωθέω (βοηθέω)*.

(2) Diaeresis.

(*a*) ει into ηϊ, (1) in substantives in -ειᾱ as βασιληίη = regnum [but βασίλεια = regina], ἐπιστρατηίη; (2) in subst. in -ειον, as χαλκήϊον, ἀριστήϊον [the forms προάστειον and προαστήϊον are both found, see 1, 78; 3, 142]; (3) adject. in -ειος, as οἰκήϊον, βασιλήϊος³.

(*b*) η into ηϊ, as δηϊόω, κληίς, χρηΐζω, Θρηϊκίη.

(*c*) ῳ into ωϊ, as πατρώϊος, πρωΐ [except ζῷον, ᾠόν, Τρῳάς, Κῷος, Ἀχελῷος].

(3) Elision.

(*a*) ν ἐφελκυστικόν is not used in the Ionic of Herodotos⁴. οὕτω does not become οὕτως before a vowel (9, 82).

(*b*) Elision (comparatively rare) takes place in (1) the prepositions ἀμφί, ἀνά, ἀντί, ἀπό, διά, κατά, μετά, παρά, ὑπό; (2) in most cases where ἅμα stands before a vowel; (3) most frequently in ἀλλά, δέ; (4) often in μηδέ, οὐδέ, τε, γε.

(4) Crasis.

(*a*) Like Attic, τἆλλα, ταὐτά, τἀγάλματα, τἀνθρώπου, τἀληθέος.

---

[3] Exceptions are the proper names Δαρεῖος, Ἀργεῖος, Ἠλεῖος, Καδμεῖος. * In 7, 144 most MSS. have προβοηθῆσαι, but not R or S.

[4] In some MSS. however, the ν ἐφελκυστικόν is used throughout. It appears also in the oldest MS. of the treatise written by Lucian in imitation of the dialect and style of Herodotos. In the oldest Ionic we possess, that of the Iliad, it of course frequently occurs.

(b) ο, οι, and ω with α, ὡνήρ, ὥνθρωπος, ὥνθρωποι, οὕτερος, τοὔτερον, τἄτερα, ὧλλοι, τὠρχαῖον, τὠληθές, τὠπό, ὤνθρωπε, ὧναξ. [The MSS. mostly have οἱ ἄλλοι.]

(c) In the reflexive pronouns ἑαυτοῦ, ἐμαυτοῦ, σεαυτοῦ, which in Ionic would be ἕο αὐτοῦ, ἐμέο αὐτοῦ, σέο αὐτοῦ, we have ἑωυτοῦ, ἐμεωυτοῦ, σεωυτοῦ. From ὁ αὐτός, ὡυτός, ὡυτοί, τὠυτό.

(d) Four with καί, καλὸς κἀγαθός, κἀκεῖθε, κἀκεῖνος, κἀμοί (as in Attic).

C. Declension.

[The dual forms are not used in Herodotos.]

I. Substantives and Adjectives.

First Declension.

(1) The gen. plur. ends in -εων, as γνωμέων, τιμέων, γενεέων (γενεή), πασέων, μελαινέων, αὐτέων (f.) [but we must except from this rule adjectives, pronouns and participles in -ος, -η, -ον which have their gen. plur. fem. paroxyton, as ἄλλων, φίλων, ἐκείνων, ἁλισκομένων, τούτων*].

(2) Dat. pl., universally in -ῃσι or ῇσι, as γνώμῃσι, αὐτῇσι.

(3) α in all cases of the sing. becomes -η as χώρη, -ης, -ῃ: ἰσχυρή, -ῆς, -ῇ. The ᾰ is retained in nom. and acc. but becomes η in gen. and dat. as

ἀλήθεια, -ᾰν, -ης, -ῃ
μοῖρα, -ᾰν, -ης, -ῃ
μία, -ᾰν, -ης, -ῃ.

(4) -ης makes the gen. sing. in -εω, proparoxyton,

πολιήτης
— ήτην
— ήτεω   } sing.
— ήτῃ

— ήτας
— ητέων } plur.
— ήτῃσι

* Stein gives τουτέων f. 5, 31 ; 9, 115 and elsewhere; also ἀλλέων 9, 115.

THE IONIC DIALECT.

Like this are declined proper names Μίδης, Λεωνίδης, Πέρσης, Ξέρξης[5]: also δεσπότης, except that the acc. δεσπότεα occurs 1, 11; 91.

(5) Words that in Attic are contracted are written in the uncontracted form in Herodotos, as μνᾶ, συκῆ, in Herodotos

[μνέα]   συκέη
μνέαι   -έης
μνέων   -έην
μνέας   συκέαι
            συκέων

χρυσέος, -έη, -έον
— -έον, -έην, -έον
— -έου, -έης, -έου
— -έῳ, -έῃ, -έῳ

Second Declension.

(1) The only peculiarity in case-ending is the dat. plur., which always ends in -οισι or -οῖσι, as λόγοισι, θεοῖσι, καλοῖσι.

(2) Words in -οος, -οη, -οον or -εος, -εη, -εον are not contracted, as πλόος, ἁπλόος, -όη, -όον, ὀστέον, χρύσεος, -έη, -εον.

(3) The so-called 'Attic Declension' in -ως is confined to proper names in Herodotos, as Ἀρκεσίλεως, Μενέλεως (from λεώς), as also Μίνως, Ἄθως, Ἀμφιάρεως. Instead of λεώς, νεώς, κάλως, λαγώς Herod. uses ληός[*], νηός, κάλος, λαγός. So also instead of πλέως, ἴλεως, ἀξιόχρεως Herod. uses πλέος, -η, -ον, ἴλεος, -ον, ἀξιόχρεος, -ον. Thus too the words compounded of γῆ, as βαθύγεως, μελάγγεως, μεσόγεως, ὑπόγεως, are represented in Herod. by βαθύγαιος, μελάγγαιος, μεσόγαιος, ὑπόγαιος.

(4) Herod. generally uses πολλός, -ή, -όν, though he also uses the commoner πολύς, πολλή, πολύ.

---

[5] But the accusative Ξέρξεα in 8, 22, 69; 9, 1 is supported by some good MSS., as also Λυκίδεα in 9, 5.   [*] But see Bähr on 5, 42.

THE IONIC DIALECT.

Third Declension.

(1) In the uncontracted and imparisyllabic words the forms used by Herod. are the same as those used by Attic writers.

(2) The contracted declensions are declined as follows:

βασιλεύς	πόλις	νηῦς
-λέος	πόλιος	νεός
-λεῖ	πόλι	νηΐ
-λέα	πόλιν	νέα
-λεῦ		
-λέες	πόλιες	νέες
-λέων	πολίων	νέων
-λεῦσι	πόλισι	νηυσί
-λέας	πόλις	νέας

Like πόλις are declined ὕβρις, ὄψις, φύσις, κρίσις, πίστις, παίδευσις, κατάστασις, χῆτις, etc., and the proper names Τόμυρις, Μυῖρις, Σμέρδις, Σᾶϊς, Ἆπις, Ἄμασις, Δᾶτις, Μέμφις, Θέτις, Πάρις, Ἶσις and the plural Σάρδιες, -ιων, -ισι, -ιας.

But
  Ἄρτεμις, -ιδος, -ιδα
  ἔρις,   -ιδος, -ιν
  χάρις,   -ιτος, -ιν

(3) Neuters in -ος, substantives and adjectives in ης, substs. in -υς and -υ, and adjects. in -υς resolve all contractions:

γένος	Ἀστυάγης	ἀληθής -ές
γένεος	-γεος	ἀληθέος
γένεϊ	-γεϊ	ἀληθέϊ
γένεα	-γεα	ἀληθέα -ές
γενέων		ἀληθέες -έα
γένεσι		ἀληθέων
		ἀληθέσι
		ἀληθέας -έα

THE IONIC DIALECT.

Proper names contracted to -κλῆς are thus declined :

Θεμιστοκλέης voc. -κλες
-κλέος
-κλεῖ
-κλέα

Thus Περικλέης and Ἡρακλέης.

(4) Substantives in -ως and -ω, such as αἰδώς, ἠώς, εὐεστώ, πειθώ, are declined as in Attic, except that some proper names as Ἰώ, Λητώ make the accus. sing. in -οῦν.

(5) Neuters in -ας, as γέρας, κέρας, τέρας, have their genitives and datives sing. and plur., and acc. plur., in -εος, -εῖ, -εων, -εσι, -εα [not -αος, etc.] with the single exception of γῆρας, -αος, -αϊ.

II. PRONOUNS.

(1) Personal Pronouns [ἐγώ, σύ, ἕ].

(a) Herod. uses the uncontracted forms of the gen. sing. ἐμέο, σέο, ἕυ, and rarely ἐμεῦ, σεῦ, εὗ.

(b) Dat. σοί, but in enclisis τοι.

(c) For the dat. m. and f. αὐτῷ and αὐτῇ Herod. uses οἱ. Acc. μιν = αὐτὸν -ήν and ἑαυτὸν -ήν, and also for αὐτό.

(d) The nom. and dat. plur. of the three personal pronouns are the same as in Attic. The third person plural is

N. σφεῖς, A. σφέας, G. σφέων, D. σφίσι, σφι,

but σφίσι and σφι differ in usage ; σφι (enclitic) = αὐτοῖς or αὐταῖς, σφέας = αὐτούς, -άς, but σφίσι = ἑαυτοῖς or ἑαυταῖς. [There is frequent confusion in the MSS. between σφίσι and σφι.]

The gen. and acc. plur. are not contracted

ἡμέων   ὑμέων   σφέων (σφεων)
ἡμέας   ὑμέας   σφέας (σφεας)

Herodotos also uses σφε as acc. 3rd per. of all genders and numbers, and σφέα = αὐτά (n. pl.).

THE IONIC DIALECT.

(2) Relative Pronouns.

(a) ὅς, ὅσπερ, in nom. sing. and plur.

ὅς, ἥ, τό
οἵ, αἵ, τά

but in oblique cases the consonantal form is used, as

G. τοῦ, τῆς, τοῦ
τῶν, τῶν, τῶν, etc.

Note 1. Of the prepositions not admitting of elision ἐν, ἐκ, ἐς, περί, πρό, πρός, σύν, ὑπέρ,

πρό and ὑπέρ seldom occur with simple relative.

περί usually follows its case, as τῆς πέρι.

ἐν, ἐκ, ἐς, πρός, σύν, take the consonantal form, as ἐν τῷ, σύν τοῖσι etc. Except where ἐν, ἐξ, ἐς form with the relative an expression of time, as

ἐν ᾧ = *quo tempore*
ἐς ὅ = *usque ad id tempus*
ἐξ οὗ = *ex quo tempore.*

So also ἄχρι οὗ, μέχρι οὗ.

Note 2. On the other hand the prepositions which admit of elision—ἀντί, ἀπό, διά, ἐπί, κατά, μετά, παρά, ὑπό—take only the aspirated form of the relative, δι' ἧς, ἐπ' ᾧ etc., except when they follow their case, as, τῷ πάρα [but παρ' ᾧ].

(b) ὅστις, ὅ τι do not take the consonantal form. In place of the Attic ὅτου, ὅτῳ, ὅτοισι Herod. uses ὅτευ, ὅτεῳ, ὀτέοισι, and for ἅτινα he has ἅσσα (not ἅττα).

(c) Interrogative and indefinite Pronoun τις

τίς   τίνες
τέο (τεῦ)   τέων
τέῳ   τέοισι
τίνα   τίνας

D. Conjugation.

I. The Augment.

The usage of Herodotos with regard to the temporal and syllabic augments is the same as in Attic[6] with the following exceptions:

(*a*) The temporal augment is omitted in purely Ionic forms, such as, ἀγινέω (ἄγω), ἀμείβομαι, ἀναισιμόω, ἀρρωδέω, ἀρτέομαι (ἀρτάω), ἑσσόω (ἡσσάω), ὀρτάζω (ἑορτάζω), οὐρίζω [but ὠνόμασται 9, 32, though the Ionic form οὐνομάζω is given in some MSS.; in 9, 44 however they all have ὀνομάζω], ἔργω (εἴργω)[7].

(*b*) Also in the poetical verbs, ἀεθλέω, ἀλυκτάζω, ἐλινύω.

(*c*) Also in all verbs beginning with the diphthongs αι, αυ, ει, ευ, οι, as, αἰδέομαι, αἰνέω, αἱρέω, αἰτέω, αὔξω, εἰρωτέω, εὕδω, εὐτυχέω, εὑρίσκω, οἰκέω, ἀνοίγω, οἴχομαι.

(*d*) Also in the verbs ἐάω, ἐργάζομαι, ἔωθα [pluperf. ἐώθεα], while on the other hand the augmented forms ἦσαν, εἶχον, ἦλθον, ἤλασα are always found.

(*e*) In cases of double augment the syllabic is omitted as ὤρεον [Att. ἑώρων].

(*f*) Neither temporal nor syllabic augment occurs in verbs with frequentative termination, as ἄγεσκον, ποιέεσκον, βαλεσκόμην, ἴσχον, ἔχεσκον.

II. Change of ν into α, when -ται or -το comes immediately after the stem.

(*a*) In the 3rd pers. plur. of perf. and pluperf. pass.: First in impure forms, as ἀπίκατο, ἐτετάχατο, τετάφαται, ἀγωνίδαται, ἐσκευάδαται, δεδέχαται, ἀπίκαται, διεφθάρατο; in these

---

[6] The augment, as in Attic, is often omitted in the pluperf., as τετελυτήκεε, δέδοκτο, ἐνδεδύκεε, etc. And when πρό is compounded with an augmented word there is no contraction, as προέβαινε, προέβαλε (not προὔβαινε etc.).

[7] Under this head may come the fact that the MSS. seem to favour ὤρμηται (see 4, 16), but ὁρμέατο (1, 158; 9, 61).

forms the Root consonant is aspirated except when it is δ, and in the word ἀπίκαται -ο; SECOND in pure Roots, the preceding vowel being shortened, as ἠπιστέατο, ἡγέαται, ἠρτέαται, οἰκέαται, κέαται, ὡρμέαται, βεβλέαται, ἀναπεπτέαται, ἀποκεκλέατο, ἐνεπιδεικνύατο, ἐκεκοσμέατο.

(*b*) In the 3rd pers. plur. pres. and imperf. pass. of verbs in -μι, as τιθέαται, ἐτιθέατο, ἱστέαται, δυνέαται, ἔαται, κατέατο, ἐνεπιδεικνύατο, ἐκεκοσμέατο, ἐπεκέατα.

(*c*) in optative endings pres. or aor., as ἀγοίατο, βουλοίατο, γευσαίατο, τισαίατο, ἀνελοίατο.

III. Resolution of Contractions:

(*a*) pluperf. -εα, -εας, -εε, -εσαν, as ἐώθεα, ἐώθεας, ἐώθεε, ἐώθεσαν, ἐληλύθεε, ἐόργεε.

(*b*) 2nd pers. indic. midd. and pass.
primary tenses -εαι, as οἴχεαι, ἔσεαι.
historic „ -εο, as ἐγένεο, ἐπίκεο.

So also the present imperat. midd., as ἔπεο, πείθεο, ἀπαλλάσσεο. But the 2nd pers. sing. of the subj. midd. is always contracted, as οἴχῃ, γένῃ, δέξῃ, ὑποθήκῃ. Also 2nd aor. infin. act., as μαθεῖν, ἐλθεῖν, σχεῖν.

(*c*) ῶ resolved into -έω in the Aorist subj. pass. of all verbs, in the 2 aor. subj. of verbs in -μι or verbs formed on the analogy of verbs in -μι, as αἱρεθέω, ἐσσωθέωμεν, ἐξαναστέωμεν, προσθέω, θέωσι (ἔθην), βέω (ἔβην), but the 2nd and 3rd persons are contracted, as νικηθῆς, φανῇ, ἐκβῇ, θῆται.

(*d*) In Verbs in -εω, -αω, -οω, the uncontracted forms are used:

(1) -εω, as
pr. καλέω -έομαι   subj. καλέω -έωμαι   opt. καλέοιμι -εοίμην
    καλέεις -έῃ   καλέῃς -έῃ   καλέοις -έοιο
    καλέει -έεται   καλέῃ -έηται   καλέοι -έοιτο
imperat. κάλεε
        imperf. ἐκάλεον -εόμην   infin.   καλέειν
                ἐκάλεες -εο   part.   καλέων
                ἐκάλεε -έετο   part. mid. ap. καλεόμενος

THE IONIC DIALECT.

Note 1. The only exception is δεῖ, δεῖν, the imperfect of which however is ἔδεε. In five verbs ἀγνοέω, διανοέομαι, θηέομαι, νοέω, ποιέω, in which the termination -εω or -εομαι is preceded by a vowel, εο or εου becomes ευ, as ἀγνοεῦντες, ἐθηεῦντο (ἐθηέοντο), θηεύμενοι.

The imperfect of θηέομαι has the Attic contraction, as ἐθηεῖτο (1, 10).

ποιέω has ευ throughout, ποιεῦσι, ποιεῦντες, ἐποίευν[8], ποιεῦμαι, ποιεύμενος, ἐποιεύμην, ἐποιεῦντο.

εω remains uncontracted, as νοέων, but οη becomes ω, as νενωμένον.

Note 2. This rule of resolving contractions applies also to liquid futures, as ἐρέω, κερδανέεις, ὑπομενέουσι, κατακοντιέει, κομιέει, ἀτρεμέειν, κομιέαι (mid.), χαριέεσθαι, ἀπολέοντες, but when a vowel precedes εο or εου they become ευ, as ἀνταγωνιεύμενος, κομιεύμεθα, ὀπωριεῦνται, ἐπιστιεύμενοι[9].

(2) verbs in -αω

(a) With exception of the dissyllable verbs κλάω, ψάω, σμάω [also ἐῶ, βιῶμαι, ἰῶμαι] all contractions are resolved not into -αω -αο -αου, but into -εω -εο -εου, as ὁρέω, ὁρέουσι, ὁρέων, ὁρέομαι, ὁρεόμενος. On the other hand -αει, -αε become -ᾷ and -ᾳ as
                ὁρέω, ὁρᾷς, ὁρᾷ
                ὤρεον, ὤρᾳς, ὤρᾳ
[though in 8, 36 the best MSS. have ἀπώρων].

(b) And as in verbs in -εω, when a vowel precedes -εο or -εου they become ευ, as ἀνιεῦνται, βοεῦντες.

(c) The future of ἐλαύνω is ἐλέω, ἐλέων.

(d) χράω, χράομαι, contract in α [Attic η], as χρέομαι, χρᾶται, χρᾶσθαι, χρεώμενος[10].

---

[8] ἐποίευν 8, 64; 9, 25 etc., but also ἐποίεον 9, 8 and 11; ποιέεο 8, 68.

[9] In 9, 6 we have ἀμυνεῦσι for ἀμυνέουσι although -εου is not preceded by a vowel; cp. βάλευ for βάλου [εο] 8, 68; δοκεῦντα 9, 77.

[10] In 9, 24 as in 4, 151; 7, 34; 9, 41, etc. one MS. (P) gives χρεόμενοι, but the greater authority in all cases seems to be for χρεώμενος, while the best MSS. give χρεόν (not χρεών) as the neut. part.; see 9, 46 etc.

(e) But in tenses of verbs in -αω where the Attic has ᾱ, the Ionic has η, as βιηθῆναι, βιήσασθαι, πειρηθῆναι, πειρήσασθαι.

(3) Verbs in -όω.

The verbs in -όω are contracted as in Attic, except that when -οο or -οου are preceded by a vowel they become ευ, as ἀντιεύμενος, δικαιεῦσθαι, οἰκηιεῦνται, ἀξιεύμεθα, ἐξομοιεῦντες, δικαιεῦσι. Thus ἀξιόω is conjugated in Herodotos

<table>
<tr><td colspan="2">Pres.</td><td colspan="2">Imperf.</td></tr>
<tr><td>ἀξιῶ</td><td>ἀξιεύμεν</td><td>ἠξίευν</td><td>ἠξιεῦμεν</td></tr>
<tr><td>ἀξιοῖς</td><td>ἀξιοῦτε</td><td>ἠξίους</td><td>ἠξιοῦτε</td></tr>
<tr><td>ἀξιοῖ</td><td>ἀξιεῦσι</td><td>ἠξίου</td><td>ἠξίευν</td></tr>
</table>

Mid. Inf. ἀξιοῦσθαι   Part. Mid. ἀξιεύμενος

Imperf. M.
ἠξιεύμην
ἠξιεῖ
ἠξιοῦτο
ἠξιεύμεθα
ἠξιοῦσθε
ἠξιεῦντο

Thus also, ἀντιεῦνται, ἑτεροιεῦντο, ἐδικαιεῦντο.

IV. Verbs in -μι.

(a) τίθημι, τιθεῖς τιθεῖ...τιθεῖσι
ἵημι, ἱεῖς ἱεῖ... ἱεῖσι
like a verb in -εω.
ἵστημι, ἱστᾷς ἱστᾷ...ἱστᾶσι
like a verb in -αω.
δίδωμι, διδοῖς διδοῖ...διδοῦσι
like a verb in -οω.

Note 1. Perf. pass. part. of μετίημι, μεμετιμένος (Attic μεθειμένος).

Note 2. Imperf. ind. act. of τίθημι,
ἐτίθεα, ἐτίθεες, ἐτίθεε
ἐτίθημεν, ἐτίθετε, ἐτίθεσαν.

(b) ἵστημι.

The 2nd and 3rd pers. plur. perf. are ἕστατε and ἑστᾶσι.
Partic. perf. ἑστεώς·

(c) δείκνυμι.
The 3rd pers. plur. pres. indic. is δεικνῦσι (Attic δεικνύᾱσι).
Pres. partic. δεικνύων. Imperf. indic. ἐδείκνυον -ες -ε.

(d) εἰμί *sum.*
2nd pers. sing. εἶς [Attic εἶ]. 1st pers. plur. εἰμέν [Attic ἐσμέν]. 3rd p. plur. εἰσί [but ἔασι in an oracle 1, 66].
Subjunct. ἔω. 3rd p. plur. ἔωσι.
Opt. εἴην. 3rd p. plur. εἴησαν (εἶεν)[11].
Part. ἐών ἐοῦσα ἐόν.
Imperf. ἦν, ἦσθα, ἦ [ἔσκε 1, 196: 6, 133, and ἦε 1, 181, and ἔην 7, 143]. ἦσαν [ἔσκον 4, 129; 1, 196. ἔσαν MSS. 6, 5].
Another form less frequent is
ἔα (2, 19), ἔας (1, 187),...ἔατε (5, 92).

(e) εἶμι *ibo.*
Imperf. indic. ἤια, ἤιε, ἤισαν [Att. ᾖα, ᾖε, ᾖεσαν].

(f) οἶδα, οἶδας, οἶδε, ἴδμεν, ἴστε, οἴδασι.
For ἴδμεν is found οἴδαμεν [2, 17; 4, 46; 7, 214], συνοίδαμεν [9, 60].
Subj. εἰδέω. Opt. εἰδείην.
Pluperf. (=imperf.) ᾔδεα, ᾔδεε, ᾐδέατε, ᾔδεσαν.

E.

(1) ὧς is often used for οὕτω.
(2) The following Ionic Verb forms also are to be noted:
 (a) 1st aor. for εἶπον
   εἶπας, 9, 45,
   εἶπαν, 9, 11,
   ἀπειπάμεθα, 9, 7,
   εἶπαι, 8, 68.
 (b) From λαμβάνω
   λάμψομαι, 9, 31, καταλαμψόμενος, 6, 39.

[11] In 7, 6 we have ἐνέοι as though from ἐνέοιμι.

καταλαμφθέντες, 9, 58,
καταλελάβηκε, 9, 60,
ἀπολελαμμένοι, 9, 51.

(c) From φέρω

ἐσενηνεῖχθαι (ἐνηνεῖγμαι), 9, 41,
ἐξενηνειγμένος, 9, 72,
ἐπενείκας, 8, 10,
ἀνηνείκαντο, 8, 32.

(d) αἴρειν (ἀείρειν)

ἀερθέντες, 9, 52.

(e) δείκνυμι

fut. δέξω,
1st aor. ἔδεξα, δέξαι,
ἐδεξάμην, ἐδέχθην,
perf. pass. δέδεγμαι,
plup. pass. ἐδέδεκτο,
imper. pass. δεδέχθω, 8, 8.

(f) εἴκω

perf. οἶκα, 4, 82; part. οἰκώς, -ός, 8, 9.

(g) πλώειν and πλέειν are both found in good MSS.

(h) ἀξάμην, ἄξαντο [ἄγω], 8, 20.

(i) ἀναγνῶσαι, 8, 57—8.

(j) Variations in accent ἐρῆμος 9, 3; ὁμοῖος 5, 58; ἑτοῖμος 5, 31, 91.

INDEX.

[*References are by page and line of the text.*]

Accusative, extension of time 57, 19; *with infinitive for dative* 60, 23
ἀγάλματα *burnt by Persians* 59, 18
ἄγαμαι 81, 28
ἀγγαρήϊον 52, 13
ἄγειν ἡσυχίην 58, 16
ἀγῶνας δραμεῖν περί 55, 10; ἀγὼν ἐγένετο περί 79, 26
ἀθάνατοι, οἱ 62, 19
αἴνη 61, 22
αἰωρεῖσθαι ὑπὲρ μεγάλων 53, 7
ἀκινάκης 66, 12
ἀκούειν ἄριστα 49, 4
ἄκριτος 67, 25
ἀκροβολίσασθαι 32, 3
ἀλαλαγμός 20, 6
ἀλλ' οὐ γάρ 4, 28
ἀλογεῖν 64, 10
ἅμα...καί 51, 26
ἀμείνονες ἑαυτῶν ἤ 45, 12
ἀμηχανίη 62, 8
ἄμπωτις 70, 17
ἀμφὶ κόλεως 55, 27; οἱ ἀμφί 62, 1
ἄν *omitted in apodosis* 31, 27; *emphatic position of* 58, 13
ἀναβολάς, ἐς 11, 19
Ἀναγκαίη 61, 2
ἀναγνῶσαι 28, 23; 29, 9; 53, 4; 80, 12
ἀναγράφειν 48, 4
ἀναζεύγνυμι 29, 27
ἀναισιμόω 21, 25
ἀνακινδυνεύειν 35, 14; 53, 5
ἀνακρούεσθαι 44, 5
ἀνακῶς 59, 25
ἀναλαμβάνειν 59, 12
ἀναμάχεσθαι 59, 11
ἀναπλάσασθω 59, 24
ἀναρπασθμενοι 15, 29
ἀνέχειν 5, 5
ἄνομαι 37, 22
ἀντίξοος 66, 1
ἀντιπόλεμοι 35, 19
ἄνω 64, 4; 76, 3
ἀνωρίην 62, 4
ἀπαλλάσσειν 35, 17; -εσθαι 40, 4
ἀπέδοξε 60, 20
ἀπειληθέντες ἐς ἀναγκαίην 59, 9
ἀπηγορεύειν μή 64, 10
ἀπό *in direction of* 40, 10; *at* 49, 24; 50, 3
ἀποδοκεῖ μήτε 60, 20
ἀποθήκη χάριτος 59, 27
ἀποκοιμᾶσθαι 40, 23
ἀπολαβεῖν 64, 2
ἀπολύεσθαι 29, 17
ἀπομαστιγόω 59, 21
ἀπότειρα 6, 21; ἀποπειρᾶσθαι 34, 27; 73, 22
ἀποράω 19, 15
ἀπορρίπτω 49, 1
aposiopesis 31, 14
ἄρα 53, 22; 59, 28; 74, 14
ἀρετή 14, 22
ἀριθμὸν ποιεῖσθαι 4, 20
ἀριστήϊον 4, 22: τὰ ἀριστήϊα 67, 8
ἀρρωδέειν 81, 11
ἄσμενοι 10, 1; 71, 26
ἀσπίδες 15, 16
ἀτάσθαλος 59, 18
ἅτε 36, 16; 38, 26; 45, 7
αὐτοὶ *ultro* 5, 20
αὐτοῖσι ἀνδράσι 9, 18
αὐτόνομοι 77, 28

INDEX.

αὐτὸς ἑωυτοῦ διπλήσιος 76, 11
αὐτόχθων 38, 9
ἄχαρι 81, 6
ἄχρηστος 62, 7

βάλλεσθαι ἐπὶ σφέων αὐτῶν 59, 7
βάρβαροι 8, 17
βαρβαρόφωνος 11, 3
βάσανος 60, 7
βιβλίον 11, 4
βίος 'means' 14, 8
βουλόμενος, ὁ, 25, 2; 33, 10;
  βουλομένοις γενέσθαι 54, 15

captured city, the Gods desert a 22, 1
γάρ anticipatory 56, 13; 57, 24; 59, 22
γαυλός 51, 20
γεωπείνης 62, 6
γλιχόμενος 80, 22
γλυφίδες 70, 1
γνώμην τίθεσθαι 58, 12
γνωσιμαχέειν 16, 13
γραμματισταί 48, 4

δαιμόνιοι 44, 15
dat. of accompanying circumstances 9, 21, 25; of agent 62, 16
δέ in apodosi 62, 18; at beginning of a speech 79, 19
δεικνύναι ἐς 63, 8
δείλη πρωΐη 3, 26; ὀψία 5, 19
δέχεσθαι (of omens) 63, 11; 76, 24
δῆθεν 3, 9
διά exceeding 19, 25; 36, 17; 79, 23; διὰ χρηστηρίων 74, 9
διαβάλλειν 12, 17; 60, 1
διαδέχεσθαι 79, 17
διακελεύεσθαι 44, 13
διακωλύειν μή 81, 17
διαλέγειν 57, 17; 62, 16
διαναυμαχέειν 32, 1
διαχοῦν 51, 19
διέκπλοος 4, 22
διεστᾶσι 52, 5
δικαιοῦν 69, 6

διπλήσιος ἑωυτοῦ 76, 11
δοκέειν ἐμοί 12, 14; 31, 24, ὡς ἐμοὶ δοκέειν 33, 28
δραμεῖν ἀγῶνας περί 55, 10
δρόμον θέειν 38, 26, cp. 78, 12

ἐᾶν, οὐκ, 'to dissuade' 31, 3; 36, 15; 54, 23
earth and water given to the king 24, 13
earthquakes 20, 3
ἐγκατακοιμηθῆναι 74, 13
ἕζεσθαι ἐκ τοῦ μέσου 12, 7
εἶναι, πρότερον 53, 21; ἑκὼν εἶναι 64, 8
ἐκ in 26, 22; τοὺς ἐκ καταστρώματος 66, 3; ἐκ τῶν 53, 24; ὡς ἐκ κακῶν 54, 5; =ὑπό 62, 26; 65, 1; ἐκ τῶν Πλαταιικῶν 68, 27; ἐκ τοῦ φανεροῦ 69, 10; with gen. of agent 77, 25
ἑκὰς χρόνου 82, 7
ἐκδωρίζειν 38, 20
ἐκεχάριστο 3, 20
ἐκλείπειν ἐς 25, 16
ἑκόντες εἶναι 16; 20
ἐκφέρεσθαι γνώμην 35, 2; ἐξενείκαντες 73, 3
ἐλεύσεσθαι 71, 22
Eleusinian mysteries, the 32, 19 and 23
ἐν σοὶ ἐστί 29, 25; 53, 26; 65, 17
ἐνθύμιον 27, 18
ἐντεταμένος 64, 20
ἐντὸς χρόνου 55, 28
ἐξαιρεῖν 60, 23; 61, 19; 66, 24; 69, 21
ἐπάϊστος 70, 15
ἐπαμμένος 56, 8
ἐπεάν 55, 26
ἐπ' ἐξεργασμένοις 50, 11; ἐπὶ τοῖς κατήκουσι πρήγμασι 54, 27; ἐπ' ὁμολογίῃ 79, 14
ἐπεξελθεῖν 52, 19
ἐπεστραμμένα [ἔπη], 31
ἔπεσχον 17, 21
ἐπήβολος 61, 9
ἐπί adverbial 34, 25; 62, 18;

INDEX.

(1) acc. 'with a view to' 2, 5;
extension of time 26, 20; 71,
18; of space 57, 25; 'so as to be
upon' 33, 20; 'up to' 58, 11;
64, 18; ἐπὶ τὴν νέα 66, 18; (2)
gen. 'in direction of' 33, 19;
limitation ἐπ' ἑωυτῆς 17, 15;
ἐπὶ νεός 49, 18; 65, 6; ἐπὶ τῆς
γωνίης 67, 10; (3) dat. 'depending on' ἐπ' ἡμῖν 16, 7; (4)
'in circumstances of' 50, 11;
54, 27; 79, 14; ἐπὶ μισθῷ
76, 5
ἐπιλάμπειν 61, 13
ἐπιλέγειν 25, 7; -εσθαι 11, 23;
12, 1; 25, 12; 70, 10; 75, 1
ἐπίσταμαι 3, 21; 13, 22; 46, 19;
51, 23; 73, 11
ἐπιτυχεῖν 54, 24; 55, 16
ἐπιφέρεσθαι 31, 2; 47, 19
ἔργον 55, 4; 77, 7
ἐς, σωθῆναι, 48, 23; ἐς τοσοῦτο
68, 25; ἐς τὰ μέγιστα 81, 21
ἐσσωμένοι τῷ θυμῷ 71, 27
ἔστ' ἄν 3, 2; 80, 11, 26
ἔσω 2, 23; 70, 22; ἐσωτέρω 34,
13
εὖ ἔχειν 81, 25
εὐεργέτης 45, 2
εὕρημα εὑρηκέναι 59, 13
εὐφρόνη nox 7, 2
ἔχειν ἀνακῶς 59, 24; ἀναγκαίως
ἔχει 78, 2; ἔσχε 60, 16
ἔχεσθαι pass. 26, 28; 74, 25;
with gen. 6, 17; 58, 20, 28;
80, 10
ἐών 'real' 35, 8

ζώνην λύεσθαι 66, 15

ἤ following παρὰ δόξαν 2, 21
ἤδη 53, 30; 58, 27; with superlative 56, 4; 57, 1
ἤθεα 54, 1; 81, 24
ἥκειν εὖ 61, 5
ἦμαρ, ἐλεύθερον 41, 9
ἦν ἄρα 59, 28
genitive, partitive 7, 1; 41, 12;
72, 21; 76, 27; topographical

7, 18; 30, 23; of time within
which 37, 25; 40, 23; 57, 19

θέειν περί 78, 12
θεοβλαβής 76, 19 .
θητεύειν 76, 4
θνητόν 52, 2
θυμιᾶν θυμήματα 52, 17
θυμός 64, 12
θῶμα 74, 13
θωρηκοφόροι 62, 11
heroes, worship of 20, 16

ἵζεσθαι ἐπί 26, 9; ἐς 37, 16
ἰθύ straight towards 20, 10
indicative future in oratio obliqua 54, 6
infinitive for imperative 35, 5;
in subordinate sentences 49, 22;
50, 2; for indicative 61, 6
Ionian revolt, the 12, 15
ἵππος, ἡ, 15, 23; 62, 12
ἱστία 49, 19

καθύπερθε 75, 17
καί = or 38, 21; 'simultaneously'
43, 25; τώυτὸ καί 23, 16;
τοῖσι καί 61, 16; καί with alternative clause 49, 10; 53, 17
καὶ γὰρ δὴ καί 13, 24; καὶ δὴ καί
21, 22; 12, 5; 72, 5; following ἄλλα τε 25, 17
καπνοδόκη 76, 18
καραδοκέω 34, 17; 36, 22
κατά with acc. 'opposite' 19, 21;
44, 16; cp. 27, 1; 'in regard
to' 43, 25; 44, 15; 'on account
of' 56, 20; with gen. 27, 5
καταδύεσθαι 47, 18
κατακοιμᾶν 74, 6
κατακοπείς 48, 21
καταλαμβάνειν 'to overtake' 4, 5;
27, 26; 63, 1
καταμαργέων 68, 17
καταπλέκω 43, 23
καταπλήσσω 70, 11
καταρρήγνυσθαι τοὺς κιθῶνας 52,
19
καταφρονεῖν construction of 6, 4

κατεπείγειν 69, 5
κατεχόμενος 64, 22
κατῆρες 11, 11
κατορύσσειν 19, 4
κείρειν 17, 21; 32, 15
κεῖσθαι 49, 12
κεραΐζω 45, 6
κινδυνεύειν, construction of 30, 9; 33, 7; 39, 9
kings of Sparta 22, 11
κοίλη ναῦς 66, 4
κοινῇ 67, 5; τὸ κοινόν 74, 21
κομίζεσθαι 11, 19; 57, 27; 60, 18
κόρος 41, 6
κόσμον οὐδένα 64, 22; κόσμον φέρειν 29, 23; 79, 22
κρησφύγετον 26, 7
κρίσις 36, 17
κυματίης 65, 8

λαγχάνειν 64, 22
λαμπαδηφορίη 52, 11
λεαίνω 80, 12
λείπεσθαι 62, 10
λιπαρέειν 82, 4
λιπαρός 41, 5
λόγον διδόναι 4, 14; λόγος 'account' 55, 11; 'reputation' 6, 13; κατὰ λόγον 62, 4

μάλιστα μέν—εἰ δὲ μή 12, 5
μελεδαίνειν 63, 26
μελιτόεσσα 21, 24
μέλλω construction of 2, 2; 4, 5, 17; 45, 10; 51, 12
μέμφομαι 57, 7
μέν...δέ of simultaneous action 69, 2
μέσαι νύκτες 40, 7
μέσον, τό 73, 15; μέσου, ἐκ τοῦ 12, 7; 38, 23
μεταβάλλων 59, 5
μεταστησάμενοι 54, 11
μετεξέτεροι 5, 8; 45, 16
μέχρι 2, 13; 44, 16
μὴ οὐ 28, 20; 52, 7; 53, 20; 66, 2; 69, 7
μηνοειδές 9, 6

mood, change of 53, 3; 56, 24; 66, 3
μυρσίνῃσι στορέσαι 52, 16

νέμεσθαι 64, 3
νέφος 59, 13
νεώτερόν τι 11, 15; ποιέειν 79, 20
νησίς 40, 5; 50, 23
νησιῶται 60, 24; 61, 24
νήσων, διά 58, 10
νικᾶν, ἐνίκα placuit 4, 15; opp to ἑσσοῦσθαι τῇ γνώμῃ 39, 13
νόθος 55, 20
νόμῳ χειρῶν, ἐν 47, 2
νόου, ἐκ παντός 51, 24
numbers, mistake in 24, 25

οἰκέται 3, 22; 23, 9; 56, 26; 59, 24; 80, 10
οἷοί τε 10, 9
ὅκου 63, 17; 53, 27
ὅκως iterative 26, 11; 48, 14; 56, 7; 69, 26; 76, 10; 56, 7;= ὅτι 66, 5
ὅκως ἄν 7, 21; ὅκως μή with fut. 9, 2
olive, the sacred 27, 23—28
Olympic festival, the 7, 1; 14, 12; prize at 14, 15
ὁμαιχμίη 78, 15
ὁμόγλωσσον 81, 21
ὁμότροπος 81, 24
ὅπις 81, 2
optative and subjunctive in coordinate sentences 4, 4 and 10; 40, 13; also opt. and fut. 37, 5
optative, iterative 26, 10; 63, 17, 26; after ἐλπίζειν μή 26, 27: see under ὅκως
oracles 21, 19; 26, 5; 31, 20
ὁρμεόμενος 61, 30; 73, 19
ὁροσάγγαι 45, 3
ostracism 41, 20
οὐ with infin. 58, 25
οὐκ ἐᾶν 31, 3; 36, 15
οὔτε...τε joining participle and verb 73, 9
οὕτω 12, 25; 65, 20; 76, 17

INDEX.

οὕτω δή 50, 9; 12, 25; 65, 20; 73, 4
ὄφις 21, 21

πάθῃ, ἤν τι, 55, 11
πάθος 53, 28; 65, 26
πανδημεί 21, 6; 37, 26; πανστρατιῇ 15, 2; 34, 8
πανοικίῃ 56, 28
παρ' ἑωυτοῦ *de suo* 3, 9
παρακρίνεσθαι 36, 26
παρεξελαύνειν 69, 8
παρέχει *impersonal* 5, 1; 16, 18; 39, 27; 53, 18; 78, 13
participle and indicative coordinate 45, 13; 60, 11; 73, 10; 75, 15
πατρόθεν 48, 4
πείθεσθαι *construction of* 43, 5
Πειθώ 61, 2
πειρᾶσθαι *with infin.* 53, 15; 58, 16; 80, 24; ποιεῖν πειρώμενον 57, 17; *with gen.* 54, 14; 62, 6
πεντηκόντεροι 1, 11; 24, 8
πεποιημένος *mid.* 2, 7
πέρην 19, 8; περαίη 23, 8
περί *with acc.* 15, 19; 20, 17; *with gen.* 38, 26; 39, 9; 55, 10; 78, 13
περιβάλλεσθαι 4, 26
περιεῖναι 2, 8; περιγίγνεσθαι 30, 15
περιπετής 10, 26
περιπίπτειν 9, 11
περιστρωφώμενος 74, 15
πίπτειν '*happen*' ὅκῃ πεσέεται τὰ πρήγματα 72, 4
phantoms, appearance of 20, 7
plural (poetical) 28, 21
πλοῖον 60, 6
πλώω = πλέω 3, 11
ποιεῖσθαι, ἅμιλλαν 6, 11; ἀριθμόν 4, 20; βουλήν 21, 5; δεινόν 8, 14; δεινὸν χρῆμα 9, 14; 49, 13; ἑωυτοῦ 29, 7; ἐς ἀναβολὰς τὴν ἀποχώρησιν 11, 19; θῶυμα 39, 5; μηνοειδές 9, 6; ναυμαχίην 25, 2; λήθην 41, 25; λόγον 39, 5; περὶ πλείστου 21, 9;
συμφορήν 53, 1; σύμμαχον 75, 21
πόλεμος *personified* 2, 11
πολλὸς ἦν 29, 13
present for immediate future 67, 17
πρήγματα 55, 8; 75, 17
πρό 3, 6; 39, 9
προβωθέειν 82, 11
προθεῖναι 25, 1; 29, 12
πρόκατε 74, 23
προκατῆσθαι 19, 16
προνοίης, ἐκ, 46, 1
πρόξεινος 75, 10; 81, 7
πρός *adverbial* 16, 8; 21, 3; 36, 5; 48, 5; 49, 11
πρός *on the side of,* ἑωυτῶν 12, 16; ἡμῶν 30, 14; '*in the direction of*' 44, 18; 45, 23; 66, 17; *acc.* '*in comparison with*' 23, 2
προσκηδέες 75, 4
προσκυνέειν 65, 19
προσχωρεῖν *adjungere se ad* 30, 28
προφήτης 19, 13
πρώιος 71, 13
πρώτοισι, ἐν 36, 16
πτερόω 70, 1
πυρφόρος 4, 6
Pythian games, the 24, 20
πώγων 56, 1

ῥαπίζεσθαι 29, 17
relative, attraction of 53, 20
ῥηχίη 71, 1
rivers, sacrifice to 77, 2

Schiste Hodos, the 20, 28
σημήιον 48, 25
σιγῇ 39, 5
σοί, *emphatic position of* 36, 8
σοφός 60, 3; σοφώτατος 68, 1
σταθμεύμενοι 71, 25
στασιῶται 72, 19
στόμα, κατά 6, 18
στρατόπεδον *fleet* 22, 2; 43, 1
στρεπτόφοροι 62, 18
subject, change of 51, 17; 73, 7

INDEX.

subjunctive after historic tense (dramatic) 4, 10; 40, 17; in orat. obl. 50, 9; with conditional relative without ἄν 12, 16; 58, 26
συγχέειν 52, 19
συμμαχίη 70, 8
συμμῖξαι 29, 4; 34, 20; 42, 1
συμπίπτειν ὥστε 8, 18; 73, 12; 79, 11
συμφέρω 45, 25; 46, 9
συμφορῇ χρᾶσθαι 11, 18
συνέστασάν τινι 38, 25
σύνθημα 4, 17
σφίσι = ἀλλήλοις 72, 25
σχεῖν, πρός 21, 1; ἐς 20, 27; 21, 13

ταμίας τοῦ ἱροῦ 26, 1
τάπερ καὶ ἐγένετο 59, 30
ταξίαρχοι 34, 23
τάχος, ὡς τάχεος εἶχε 57, 22
τε...καί denoting simultaneity 21, 3; 43, 18
τε suffix 3, 5; 10, 9
τέμενος, 20, 17
τιήρης χρυσόπαστος 66, 13
τιμωρίη 25, 9
τις = ἕκαστος 59, 24; 65, 16
τίσιν δοῦναι 44, 13
tmesis of preposition 17, 24; 34, 23; 46, 26
τό = τί relat. 21, 3
τοῦτο μέν...τοῦτο δέ 40, 6; 46, 9; 55, 2; 74, 3; 77, 26; the first τοῦτο omitted 30, 5
τράπεσθαι, ἐς φυγήν 9, 15; πρὸς τὰ πρόβατα 10, 21; πρὸς τὰς πύλας 27, 7; πρὸς ἄλλας [τριήρεις] 46, 9
trierarchies 9, 24
τριηκόντεροs 11, 15
tripod at Delphi, the memorial 43, 10
τύραννος (Makedonian) 80, 14

ὕβρις 41, 6

ὑπεραρρωδέω with dat. 38, 4
ὑπερβολή 61, 26
ὑπερφυής 64, 7
ὑπερφέρειν 77, 9; 81, 14
ὑπὸ τὸν πεζόν 49, 3; ὑπὸ χειμῶνος 77, 12
ὑποστάντες 48, 10
verbal substantive governing a case 41, 11

φαίνεσθαι ἐών 68, 3; νικῶντες 599; ἀπικόμενος 73, 27
φάναι 46, 17
φάτις ἔχει 50, 11
φερόμενοι 48, 15; φέρουσα 45, 26; πλέον ἔφερε ἡ γνώμη 53, 7; τὸ πᾶν φέρων 53, 12; φερόμενος οὐ τὰ δεύτερα 55, 23; φέρειν ἐς 76, 14; 80, 1
φθόνος of the gods 59, 16
φορμοί 37, 23
φρονεῖν τὰ τινος 18, 12; 39, 24; 40, 2
φύλακος 21, 21
φύσις 20, 13

χειμαίνεσθαι 65, 9
χεὶρ ὑπερμήκης 78, 25
χειρῶν νόμῳ, ἐν 47, 2
χρᾶν 74, 29
χρηστηριάζεσθαι 74, 4
χοῦς 15, 26
χώρην, κατά 41, 18; 58, 2

ψελιόφοροι 62, 18
ψῆφον τίθεσθαι 67, 18

ὠθισμὸς λόγων 41, 15
ὥρη 7, 1; 8, 9
ὡς with gen. absol. 40, 16; 42, 21; 47, 14
ὡς ἄν 4, 10
ὡς εἰπεῖν 63, 16
ὡς τότε 5, 1
ὥστε = ἅτε 65, 9
ὠτακουστεῖν 72, 4
ὦφλε δειλίην 14, 17

CAMBRIDGE: PRINTED BY J. & C. F. CLAY, AT THE UNIVERSITY PRESS.

THE PITT PRESS SERIES

AND THE

CAMBRIDGE SERIES FOR SCHOOLS AND TRAINING COLLEGES.

Volumes of the latter series are marked by a dagger †.

COMPLETE LIST.

GREEK.

Author	Work	Editor	Price
Aeschylus	Prometheus Vinctus	Rackham	2/6
Aristophanes	Aves—Plutus—Ranae	Green	3/6 each
,,	Vespae	Graves	3/6
,,	Nubes	,,	3/6
Demosthenes	Olynthiacs	Glover	2/6
Euripides	Heracleidae	Beck & Headlam	3/6
,,	Hercules Furens	Gray & Hutchinson	2/-
	Hippolytus	Hadley	2/-
	Iphigeneia in Aulis	Headlam	2/6
	Medea	,,	2/6
	Hecuba	Hadley	2/6
	Helena	Pearson	3/6
,,	Alcestis	Hadley	2/6
,,	Orestes	Wedd	4/6
Herodotus	Book IV	Shuckburgh	*In the Press*
,,	,, V	,,	3/-
,,	,, VI, VIII, IX	,,	4/- each
,,	,, VIII 1—90, IX 1—89	,,	2/6 each
Homer	Odyssey IX, X	Edwards	2/6 each
,,	,, XXI	,,	2/-
,,	,, XI	Nairn	2/
,,	Iliad VI, XXII, XXIII, XXIV	Edwards	2/- each
,,	Iliad IX, X	Lawson	2/6
Lucian	Somnium, Charon, etc.	Heitland	3/6
,,	Menippus and Timon	Mackie	3/6
Plato	Apologia Socratis	Adam	3/6
,,	Crito	,,	2/6
	Euthyphro	,,	2/6
	Protagoras	J. & A. M. Adam	4/6

THE PITT PRESS SERIES, ETC.

GREEK continued.

Author	Work	Editor	Price
Plutarch	Demosthenes	Holden	4/6
,,	Gracchi	,,	6/-
	Nicias		5/-
,,	Sulla	,,	6/-
,,	Timoleon	,,	6/-
Sophocles	Oedipus Tyrannus	Jebb	4/-
Thucydides	Book III	Spratt	5/-
,,	Book VI	,,	In the Press
,,	Book VII	Holden	5/-
Xenophon	Agesilaus	Hailstone	2/6
,,	Anabasis Vol. I. Text	Pretor	3/-
	,, Vol. II. Notes	,,	4/6
	,, I, II	,,	4/-
	,, I, III, IV, V	,,	2/- each
	,, II, VI, VII	,,	2/6 each
	,, I, II, III, IV, V, VI	Edwards	1/6 each
	(With complete Vocabularies)		
	Hellenics I, II	,,	3/6
	Cyropaedeia I	Shuckburgh	2/6
,,	,, II	,,	2/-
,,	,, III, IV, V	Holden	5/-
	,, VI, VII, VIII	,,	5/-
	Memorabilia I	Edwards	2/6
	,, II	,,	2/6

LATIN.

Author	Work	Editor	Price
Bede	Eccl. History III, IV	Lumby	7/6
Caesar	De Bello Gallico		
	Com. I, III, VI, VIII	Peskett	1/6 each
	,, II–III, and VII	,,	2/- each
,,	, I–III	,,	3/-
,,	,, IV–V	,,	1/6
† ,,	,, I, II, III, IV, V, VI, VII	Shuckburgh	1/6 each
	(With complete Vocabularies)		
,,	De Bello Civili. Com. I	Peskett	3/-
,,	,, ,, Com. III	,,	2/6
Cicero	Actio Prima in C. Verrem	Cowie	1/6
,,	De Amicitia	Reid	3/6
	De Senectute	,,	3/6
	De Officiis. Bk III	Holden	2/-
	Pro Lege Manilia	Nicol	1/6
	Div. in Q. Caec. et Actio		
	Prima in C. Verrem	Heitland & Cowie	3/-
,,	Ep. ad Atticum. Lib. II	Pretor	3/-
,,	Orations against Catiline	Nicol	2/6
† ,,	In Catilinam I	Flather	1/6
	(With Vocabulary)		
	Philippica Secunda	Peskett	3/6

THE PITT PRESS SERIES, ETC.

LATIN *continued*.

Author	Work	Editor	Price
Cicero	Pro Archia Poeta	Reid	2/-
,,	,, Balbo	,,	1/6
	,, Milone		2/6
	,, Murena	Heitland	3/-
	,, Plancio	Holden	4/6
,,	,, Sulla	Reid	3/6
	Somnium Scipionis	Pearman	2/-
Cornelius Nepos	Four parts	Shuckburgh	1/6 *each*
Horace	Epistles. Bk I	,,	2/6
,,	Odes and Epodes	Gow	5/-
	Odes. Books I, III	,,	2/- *each*
,,	,, Books II, IV; Epodes	,,	1/6 *each*
,,	Satires. Book I	,,	2/-
Juvenal	Satires	Duff	5/-
Livy	Book I	H. J. Edwards	*In the Press*
,,	,, II	Conway	2/6
	,, IV, IX, XXVII	Stephenson	2/6 *each*
	,, VI	Marshall	2/6
,,	,, V	Whibley	2/6
,,	,, XXI, XXII	Dimsdale	2/6 *each*
,, (adapted from)	Story of the Kings of Rome	G. M. Edwards	1/6
Lucan	Pharsalia. Bk I	Heitland & Haskins	1/6
,,	De Bello Civili. Bk VII	Postgate	2/-
Lucretius	Book III	Duff	2/-
,,	,, V	,,	2/-
Ovid	Fasti. Book VI	Sidgwick	1/6
,,	Metamorphoses, Bk I	Dowdall	1/6
,,	,, Bk VIII	Summers	1/6
†,,	Selections from the Tristia (*With Vocabulary*)	Simpson	1/6
†Phaedrus	Fables. Bks I and II (*With Vocabulary*)	Flather	1/6
Plautus	Epidicus	Gray	3/-
,,	Stichus	Fennell	2/6
,,	Trinummus	Gray	3/6
Quintus Curtius	Alexander in India	Heitland & Raven	3/6
Sallust	Catiline	Summers	2/-
,,	Jugurtha	,,	2/6
Tacitus	Agricola and Germania	Stephenson	3/-
,,	Hist. Bk I	Davies	2/6
,,	,, Bk III	Summers	2/6
Terence	Hautontimorumenos	Gray	3/-
Vergil	Aeneid I to XII	Sidgwick	1/6 *each*
† ,,	,, I, II, V, VI, IX, X, XI, XII (*With complete Vocabularies*)	,,	1/6 *each*
	Bucolics		1/6
	Georgics I, II, and III, IV	,,	2/- *each*
,,	Complete Works, Vol. I, Text	,,	3/6
,,	,, ,, Vol. II, Notes	,,	4/6

FRENCH.

*The Volumes marked * contain Vocabulary.*

Author	Work	Editor	Price
About	Le Roi des Montagnes	Ropes	2/-
*Biart	Quand j'étais petit, Pts I, II	Boïelle	2/- each
Boileau	L'Art Poétique	Nichol Smith	2/6
Corneille	La Suite du Menteur	Masson	2/-
,,	Polyeucte	Braunholtz	2/-
De Bonnechose	Lazare Hoche	Colbeck	2/-
,,	Bertrand du Guesclin	Leathes	2/-
* ,,	,, Part II	,,	1/6
Delavigne	Louis XI	Eve	2/-
,,	Les Enfants d'Edouard	,,	2/-
De Lamartine	Jeanne d'Arc	Clapin & Ropes	1/6
De Vigny	La Canne de Jonc	Eve	1/6
*Dumas	La Fortune de D'Artagnan	Ropes	2/-
*Enault	Le Chien du Capitaine	Verrall	2/-
Erckmann-Chatrian	La Guerre	Clapin	3/-
,,	Waterloo	Ropes	3/-
,,	Le Blocus	,,	3/-
,,	Madame Thérèse	,,	3/-
,,	Histoire d'un Conscrit	,,	3/-
Gautier	Voyage en Italie (Selections)	Payen Payne	3/-
Guizot	Discours sur l'Histoire de la Révolution d'Angleterre	Eve	2/6
Hugo	Les Burgraves	,,	2/6
*Malot	Remi et ses Amis	Verrall	2/-
* ,,	Remi en Angleterre	,,	2/-
Merimée	Colomba (*Abridged*)	Ropes	2/-
Michelet	Louis XI & Charles the Bold	,,	2/6
Molière	Le Bourgeois Gentilhomme	Clapin	1/6
,,	L'École des Femmes	Saintsbury	2/6
,,	Les Précieuses ridicules	Braunholtz	2/-
,,	,, (*Abridged Edition*)	,,	1/-
,,	Le Misanthrope	,,	2/6
,,	L'Avare	,,	2/6
*Perrault	Fairy Tales	Rippmann	1/6
Piron	La Métromanie	Masson	2/-
Ponsard	Charlotte Corday	Ropes	2/-
Racine	Les Plaideurs	Braunholtz	2/-
,,	,, (*Abridged Edition*)	,,	1/-
,,	Athalie	Eve	2/-
Saintine	Picciola	Ropes	2/-
Sandeau	Mdlle de la Seiglière	,,	2/-
Scribe & Legouvé	Bataille de Dames	Bull	2/-
Scribe	Le Verre d'Eau	Colbeck	2/-
Sédaine	Le Philosophe sans le savoir	Bull	2/-
Souvestre	Un Philosophe sous les Toits	Eve	2/-
,,	Le Serf & Le Chevrier de Lorraine	Ropes	2/-

THE PITT PRESS SERIES, ETC.

FRENCH continued.

Author	Work	Editor	Price
*Souvestre	Le Serf	Ropes	1/6
Spencer	A Primer of French Verse		3/-
Staël, Mme de	Le Directoire	Masson & Prothero	2/-
,,	Dix Années d'Exil (Book II chapters 1—8)		2/-
Thierry	Lettres sur l'histoire de France (XIII—XXIV)	,,	2/6
,,	Récits des Temps Mérovingiens, I—III	Masson & Ropes	3/-
Villemain	Lascaris ou les Grecs du XVe Siècle	Masson	2/-
Voltaire	Histoire du Siècle de Louis XIV, in three parts	Masson & Prothero	2/6 each
Xavier de Maistre	La Jeune Sibérienne. Le Lépreux de la Cité d'Aoste	Masson	1/6

GERMAN.

The Volumes marked * *contain Vocabulary.*

Author	Work	Editor	Price
*Andersen	Eight Fairy Tales	Rippmann	2/6
Benedix	Dr Wespe	Breul	3/-
Freytag	Der Staat Friedrichs des Grossen	Wagner	2/-
,,	Die Journalisten	Eve	2/6
Goethe	Knabenjahre (1749—1761)	Wagner & Cartmell	2/-
,,	Hermann und Dorothea	,, ,,	3/6
,,	Iphigenie	Breul	3/6
*Grimm	Selected Tales	Rippmann	3/-
Gutzkow	Zopf und Schwert	Wolstenholme	3/6
Hackländer	Der geheime Agent	E. L. Milner Barry	3/-
Hauff	Das Bild des Kaisers	Breul	3/-
,,	Das Wirthshaus im Spessart	Schlottmann & Cartmell	3/-
,,	Die Karavane	Schlottmann	3/-
*,,	Der Scheik von Alessandria	Rippmann	2/6
Immermann	Der Oberhof	Wagner	3/-
*Klee	Die deutschen Heldensagen	Wolstenholme	3/-
Kohlrausch	Das Jahr 1813	Cartmell	2/-
Lessing	Minna von Barnhelm	Wolstenholme	3/-
Lessing & Gellert	Selected Fables	Breul	3/-
Mendelssohn	Selected Letters	Sime	3/-
Raumer	Der erste Kreuzzug	Wagner	2/-
Riehl	Culturgeschichtliche Novellen	Wolstenholme	3/-
,,	Die Ganerben & Die Gerechtigkeit Gottes	,,	3/-
Schiller	Wilhelm Tell	Breul	2/6
,,	,, (*Abridged Edition*)	,,	1/6

THE PITT PRESS SERIES, ETC.

GERMAN *continued.*

Author	Work	Editor	Price
Schiller	Geschichte des dreissigjährigen Kriegs. Book III.	Breul	3/-
	Maria Stuart	,,	3/6
	Wallenstein I. (Lager and Piccolomini)	,,	3/6
	Wallenstein II. (Tod)	,,	3/6
Sybel	Prinz Eugen von Savoyen	Quiggin	2/6
Uhland	Ernst, Herzog von Schwaben	Wolstenholme	3/6
	Ballads on German History	Wagner	2/-
	German Dactylic Poetry	,,	3/-

SPANISH.

Le Sage & Isla	Los Ladrones de Asturias	Kirkpatrick	3/-

ENGLISH.

Author	Work	Editor	Price
Bacon	History of the Reign of King Henry VII	Lumby	3/-
,,	Essays	West	3/6 & 5/-
,,	New Atlantis	G. C. M. Smith	1/6
Cowley	Essays	Lumby	4/-
Defoe	Robinson Crusoe, Part I	Masterman	2/-
Earle	Microcosmography	West	3/- & 4/-
Gray	Poems	Tovey	4/- & 5/-
† ,,	Ode on the Spring and The Bard	,,	8d.
† ,,	Ode on the Spring and The Elegy	,,	8d.
Kingsley	The Heroes	E. A. Gardner	2/-
Lamb	Tales from Shakespeare	Flather	1/6
Macaulay	Lord Clive	Innes	1/6
,,	Warren Hastings	,,	1/6
,,	William Pitt and Earl of Chatham	,,	2/6
† ,,	John Bunyan	,,	1/-
† ,,	John Milton	Flather	1/6
,,	Lays and other Poems	,,	1/6
Mayor	A Sketch of Ancient Philosophy from Thales to Cicero		3/6
,,	Handbook of English Metre		2/-
More	History of King Richard III	Lumby	3/6
,,	Utopia	,,	3/6
Milton	Arcades and Comus	Verity	3/-
,,	Ode on the Nativity, L'Allegro, Il Penseroso & Lycidas	,,	2/6
† ,,	Comus & Lycidas		2/-
,,	Samson Agonistes		2/6
,,	Sonnets	,,	1/6
,,	Paradise Lost, six parts	,,	2/- *each*
Pope	Essay on Criticism	West	2/-

THE PITT PRESS SERIES, ETC.

ENGLISH *continued*.

Author	Work	Editor	Price
Scott	Marmion	Masterman	2/6
,,	Lady of the Lake	,,	2/6
,,	Lay of the last Minstrel	Flather	2/-
,,	Legend of Montrose	Simpson	2/6
,,	Lord of the Isles	Flather	2/-
,,	Old Mortality	Nicklin	2/6
,,	Kenilworth	Flather	2/6
Shakespeare	A Midsummer-Night's Dream	Verity	1/6
,,	Twelfth Night	,,	1/6
,,	Julius Caesar		1/6
,,	The Tempest		1/6
	King Lear		1/6
	Merchant of Venice		1/6
	King Richard II	,,	1/6
	As You Like It	,,	1/6
,,	King Henry V	,,	1/6
,,	Macbeth	,,	1/6
Shakespeare & Fletcher	Two Noble Kinsmen	Skeat	3/6
Sidney	An Apologie for Poetrie	Shuckburgh	3/-
Wallace	Outlines of the Philosophy of Aristotle		4/6

West	Elements of English Grammar		2/6
,,	English Grammar for Beginners		1/-
,,	Key to English Grammars		3/6 *net*
Carlos	Short History of British India		1/-
Mill	Elementary Commercial Geography		1/6
Bartholomew	Atlas of Commercial Geography		3/-

Robinson	Church Catechism Explained		2/-
Jackson	The Prayer Book Explained. Part I		2/6
,,	,, Part II *In preparation*		

MATHEMATICS.

Author	Work	Editor	Price
Ball	Elementary Algebra		4/6
†Blythe	Geometrical Drawing		
	Part I		2/6
	Part II		2/-
Euclid	Books I—VI, XI, XII	Taylor	5/-
,,	Books I—VI	,,	4/-
,,	Books I—IV	,,	3/-
	Also separately		
,,	Books I, & II; III, & IV; V, & VI; XI, & XII		1/6 *each*
,,	Solutions to Exercises in Taylor's Euclid	W. W. Taylor	10/6
	And separately		
,,	Solutions to Bks I—IV		6/-
,,	Solutions to Books VI. XI		6/-

7

THE PITT PRESS SERIES, ETC.

MATHEMATICS continued.

Author	Work	Editor	Price
Hobson & Jessop	Elementary Plane Trigonometry		4/6
Loney	Elements of Statics and Dynamics		7/6
	Part I. Elements of Statics		4/6
	,, II. Elements of Dynamics		3/6
	Elements of Hydrostatics		4/6
	Solutions to Examples, Hydrostatics		5/-
,,	Solutions of Examples, Statics and Dynamics		7/6
,,	Mechanics and Hydrostatics		4/6
†Sanderson	Geometry for Young Beginners		1/4
Smith, C.	Arithmetic for Schools, with or without answers		3/6
,,	Part I. Chapters I—VIII. Elementary,. with or without answers		2/-
,,	Part II. Chapters IX—XX, with or without answers		2/-
Hale, G.	Key to Smith's Arithmetic		7/6

EDUCATIONAL SCIENCE.

†Bidder & Baddeley	Domestic Economy		4/6
†Bosanquet	The Education of the Young from the *Republic* of Plato		2/6
†Burnet	Aristotle on Education		2/6
Comenius	Life and Educational Works	S. S. Laurie	3/6
	Three Lectures on the Practice of Education:		
Eve	I. On Marking		
Sidgwick	II. On Stimulus	1 vol.	2/-
Abbott	III. On the Teaching of Latin Verse Composition		
Farrar	General Aims of the Teacher	1 vol.	1/6
Poole	Form Management		
†Hope & Browne	A Manual of School Hygiene		3/6
Locke	Thoughts on Education	R. H. Quick	3/6
†MacCunn	The making of Character		2/6
Milton	Tractate on Education	O. Browning	2/-
Sidgwick	On Stimulus		1/-
Thring	Theory and Practice of Teaching		4/6
†Shuckburgh	A Short History of the Greeks		4/6
†Woodward	A Short History of the Expansion of the British Empire (1500—1902)		4/-
†	An Outline History of the British Empire (1500—1902)		1/6 net

LONDON: C. J. CLAY AND SONS,
CAMBRIDGE UNIVERSITY PRESS WAREHOUSE,
AVE MARIA LANE.
GLASGOW: 50, WELLINGTON STREET.

Lightning Source UK Ltd.
Milton Keynes UK
UKHW02f0604200918
329215UK00010B/474/P